AN INTRODUCTION TO COMPUTERS AND INFORMATION SYSTEMS

DR. ROBERT A. RADEMACHER, CDP

Chairman and Professor
Computer Information Systems Department
Colorado State University

and

DR. HARRY L. GIBSON

Professor
Computer Information Systems Department
Colorado State University

Published by

J25   **SOUTH-WESTERN PUBLISHING CO.**

CINCINNATI   WEST CHICAGO, ILL.   DALLAS   PELHAM MANOR, N.Y.   PALO ALTO, CALIF.

ISBN: 0-538-10250-0

Library of Congress Catalog Card Number: 82-60845

2 3 4 5 6 7 8 K 0 9 8 7 6 5 4 3

Printed in the United States of America

Cover photograph by © Joel Gordon 1982

Part 1 opener photo: Ramtek
Part 5 opener photo: Courtesy of Bell Laboratories

CONTENTS

PREFACE

Instructors in introductory computer courses face a changing technology, large classes, and students with varied interests and abilities. This comprehensive, introductory textbook is appropriate for persons affected by, or intending to enter, the computer field. Topics have been selected on the basis of currency and relevancy, and the text is written at a non-technical level to effect widespread applicability. Our guess is that the study of computers and information systems will probably join mathematics and English as graduation requirements within the next decade. Even today, some institutions require students to buy personal computers to promote their computer literacy.

This new book is designed specifically to meet the text requirements of the basic computing course for two-year and four-year colleges. Our central theme is the application of computers and information systems to business functions. To the greatest extent possible, each of the five parts is independent of the others. Thus the major topics can be taught in any desired order to meet the needs of a variety of classes. The textbook is designed to support a one-term course with or without language instruction.

Parts 1 and 2 trace the development of computer technology and its impact on organizations. The computer industry is probably the most dynamic of all disciplines and fields. It has directly changed the production, marketing, and financial aspects of business as well as the art and science of management. While computers have done much to improve the quality of life, people still represent the most important component in the creation, transmission, and management of information. Part 3 explores this human interface and the increasingly important role of software.

Part 4 discusses the application of the systems development cycle to business-oriented, computer-based systems. Because we are aware of the increasing importance of information systems topics in business and applied computer science departments, our treatment of these topics is more comprehensive than that found in most introductory textbooks. Part 5 concludes with a discussion of the most current technology affecting today's "information industries."

Why publish another introductory computer textbook? Because too many basic texts gather dust on the student's bookshelf. Most introductory texts are "loaded" with facts — generally adequate and up to date, but often too technical and unexciting. *An Introduction to Computers and Information Systems* is written in a way that involves the student personally in the learning process. We agree with Confucius when he said, "I hear and I forget; I see and I remember; I do and I understand."

Our comprehensive teaching package involves and enlightens the student in the latest topics relating to computers and information systems. Chapter instructional material includes

— objectives listed prior to each chapter,
— end-of-chapter summaries,
— lists of key terms,
— supporting newspaper/magazine articles,
— real-world applications, and
— relevant pictures and illustrative material.

The teacher's manual provides

— teaching suggestions,
— answers to end-of-chapter questions,
— transparency masters of key illustrations, and
— a comprehensive test bank.

A student study guide reinforces conceptual development using

— completion items and crossword puzzles for terminology review,
— true-false, multiple-choice, and matching questions,
— exercises and problems with varied levels of cognition, and
— an answer key for selected material.

In the future, computer literacy will be a requirement for all citizens. A knowledge of the components and criteria for developing information systems will also be required of all business employees. In the development of this textbook we have blended modern computer technology, current applications, and state-of-the-art systems topics with effective instructional pedagogy. We are confident that instructors and students will find these materials a useful and effective aid in studying computers and information systems.

ROBERT A. RADEMACHER
HARRY L. GIBSON

AN INTRODUCTION
TO COMPUTERS
AND
INFORMATION SYSTEMS

PART 1 INTRODUCTION TO ELECTRONIC DATA PROCESSING

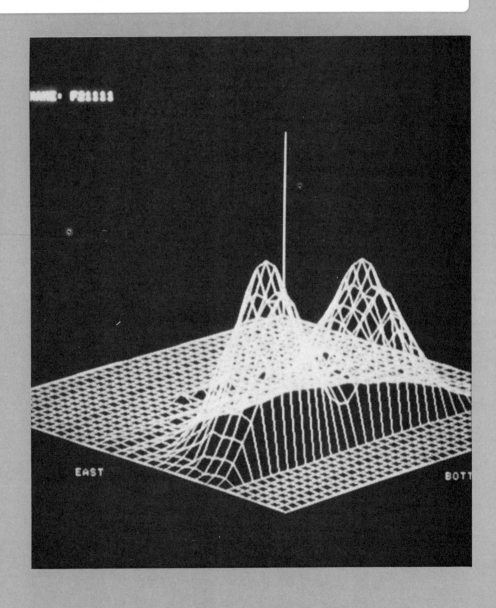

This section provides a foundation for studying the role of computers and information systems in organizations. You are presently a participant in the computer explosion; in this section you will study how computer use developed and the present state-of-the-art.

Chapter 1 - introduces EDP terminology.

Chapter 2 - traces the impact of the computer revolution.

1 ORIENTATION TO COMPUTERS AND SYSTEMS IN BUSINESS

CHAPTER OBJECTIVES

In this chapter you will learn:

1. The new relationship which is emerging between people and computers.
2. Key definitions, as a first step toward becoming computer literate.
3. The impact and capabilities of computers.
4. The benefits of computers to the business user.
5. The classes of business applications.
6. The definition of a system and how systems relate to business.
7. The systems life cycle and its various elements.

Computers are just systems with a great amount of unconsciousness: everything held in immediate memory and subject to programs which the operator initiates. The operator therefore is the consciousness of the computer.

—Author Unknown

The above quote illustrates an important consideration which is essential for you to think about and understand before beginning your study of computers. You should appreciate the notion that a computer is a machine or, if you will, a tool. While that tool has enormous potential, the real power of the computer comes from people. That is, people are the means by which the computer's potential is developed to its fullest.

It is also important to understand that the computer is perhaps the most important and powerful tool ever put to use in the world of business. In that world, where every competitive edge may spell the difference between profits and losses, success and failure, the use of computers by the modern organization has become essential.

Today's manager must be well versed in the computer, what it can do, and how best to make use of its capabilities. The impact of the computer on our lives and on the modern business organization will be discussed throughout this book. Note this increasing impact of business computers in the academic community as reflected in current headlines (Figure 1-1).

The U.S. Labor Department estimates that nearly two out of three workers today depend on the computer. The International Data Corporation estimates that by 1985 users will spend over $100 billion annually on computer operations. Is it possible that computers will take over the office and robots will replace factory workers? No, computer development hasn't reached this stage yet, but with the seemingly limitless potential of computer technology, it's almost possible to imagine this scenario one day becoming fact. One thing of which we can be certain, however, is that our interaction with computers *is* constantly increasing, as is the impact computers have on our lives. A new relationship between humans and machines is being forged—a relationship whose boundaries are as yet unknown.

In his book *The Third Wave*, Alvin Toffler considers this growing relationship with computers. Toffler suggests that the key to today's "intelligent environment" is the computer, and he contends that, in the future, "we will begin to use computers with a grace and naturalness that is hard for us to

Figure 1-1

'Computer Literacy' Gaining Place in Undergraduate Curriculum

By JACK MAGARRELL

Computers rapidly are becoming an essential part of the general college curriculum. At several institutions, "computer literacy" is now required for graduation. At many others, computers are being used heavily by students and faculty members in every field of study.

The idea that all students "should be acquainted with the computer in some reasonably respectable fashion is surely no more radical a thought than the proposition that they should be able to read and "write," says Stephen Whit— special projects f— Found—

bers, including a requirement that any student receiving a degree, regardless of field of study, must demonstrate "fundamen— computer literacy." To help i— the policy, R.I.T. plans to — new computing e— Compu— rea—

Market for Pocket Computers Is Expected to Take Off Soon

Adapting to Computer Age Sends Executives to School

Business, Not Scientific DPers Needed

SAN FRANCISCO—While the shortage of trained data processing professionals multiplies, universities continue to give students the wrong kind

By WILLIAM M. BULKELEY
Staff Reporter of The Wall Street Journa

It's galling to an executive wh the computer wizards who work him rattle off their jargon—"inpu "byte," "software" and so on— — the faintest no

Jobs Abound For DP Grads

By Bob Johnson
CW New York Bureau

NEW YORK—Metropolitan area computer science majors in the graduating class of 1982 will not be adversely affected by the depressed economy. In fact, major corporations are as eager as ever to hire students with computer savvy.

That was the general consensus of college placement ffices contacted by *Comput-world* in a recent telephone survey to gauge what the job arket has in store for the ring crop of would-be DPers. Yvette Negron, a recruitnt coordinator at Pace Data-

(Continued on Page 6)

Use of Computers Predicted to Improve Life

By Phil Hirsch
CW Washington Bureau

DALLAS — Increasing computer us a significan in the qualit Charles P. L

also reduce the need for travel, he added. "And if the need for travel is greatly re- ner-

SYSTEMS ANALYSTS

We need highly motivated individuals, preferably with a BS degree and with a minimum 2 years experience in the business community. If you communicate well, have DBMS education and have on-line or distributive processing experience, you may be the person ence in any of the following imagine today."[1] Toffler and other prognosticators also predict that a substantial amount of white-collar work will be done in the "electronic cottage" — in other words, on home computer terminals, eliminating the time and cost of commuting for employees trained to handle such tasks as computer programming. Since the impact of computers is expected to continue to increase, it is important that we increase our knowledge of the computer as well. The more knowledge we have about the impact of computers and their applications, the greater our understanding of this new relationship will be, particularly as it relates to modern business organizations and their management.

Cheaper computers and communications breakthroughs now allow data processing to be widely dispersed throughout organizations. Newly automated offices are increasing white-collar productivity while robots are invading the factory. This new technology (Figure 1-2) requires new techniques, new management expertise, and new systems organization. In today's computer environment, business students who graduate without computer knowledge are obsolete before they have their first job interview.

KEY DEFINITIONS

As shown in Figure 1-3, computer terms are fast becoming part of our vocabulary at an early age. In order to get the most out of this and succeeding chapters, there are several terms we must define now.

Let us begin with the *computer*. A computer is best described as a general-purpose, electronic, stored-program device. It is designed to handle program instructions as well as the data to be processed by the instructions.

Computers can be either *digital* or *analog*. A digital computer board is shown in Figure 1-4. While analog and digital boards cost about the same, their functions are very different. Digital computers operate by counting, while analog computers operate by measuring. Analog data include physical variables such as voltage, resistance, and rotation. Digital data are represented by means of coded characters such as numbers, letters, and symbols. Our study will be confined to the digital computer.

---

[1]Alvin Toffler, *The Third Wave* (New York: William Morrow and Co., 1980), p. 189.

Figure 1-2

Computer technology affects the way organizations handle information.

Photo bottom right, National Semiconductor Corporation

"'A' is for Analyst; 'B' is for Byte; 'C' is for Computer . . ."   Figure 1-3

R.E.M.

The terms data and information are often used interchangeably. However, *data* usually refers to unorganized facts, while *information* is the knowledge derived from manipulation of data—in other words, useful data.

Data processing (DP) involves transforming data by classifying, sorting, merging, recording, retrieving, transmitting, or reporting it. In other words, data processing is any operation or combination of operations which transforms data into useful information. This information can then be applied to the specific purpose for which it was intended.

Data processing does not occur in a haphazard, random fashion but rather in a highly structured *data processing cycle*. This cycle, illustrated in Figure 1-5, is a sequence of operations composed of input, processing, and output.

There is some controversy over which is more important, input or output. Naturally, the user of the output wants to be sure that the output is both accurate and reliable. On the other hand, the accuracy and reliability of output are dependent on the input which is processed to create that output. The concept of GIGO (garbage-in-garbage-out) applies here. Since the primary

Figure 1-4

An assembly worker completes assembly of a computer circuit board.

Photo courtesy of Western Electric

Figure 1-5

Input data on terminals are *processed* to provide printed *output*.

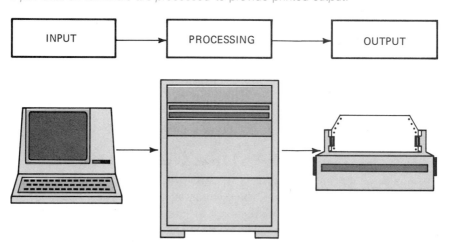

purpose of computerized systems is to provide useful information to users of those systems, we believe the output component should be given the greater emphasis.

Hardware represents the electrical and mechanical devices that make up a computer system (Figure 1-6). These include the computer and peripheral equipment such as printers, card readers, tape and disk drives, and other

Figure 1-6

Hardware includes small microcomputers for individual use as well as room-size computers.

Photos top right and bottom, NCR Corporation

input-output devices. *Software* (Figure 1-7) is a collection of programs and routines that support the operations of a computer. Software also includes documentation, rules, and operational procedures. *Programming* is the task of writing a set of instructions to direct the operations of a computer. All three of these concepts—hardware, software, and programming—will be discussed in greater detail later in the text.

Figure 1-7

Software is created and tested by programmers.

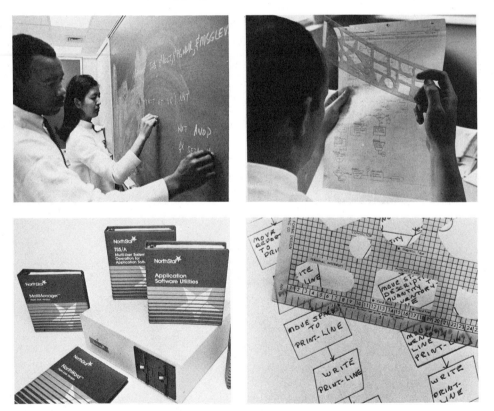

Top photos courtesy of IBM Corporation; photo bottom left, NorthStar Computers, Inc.

These few terms are only an introduction. In studying computers and their systems, a new language must be learned so that one may become computer literate. For terminology review, study the terms listed at the end of each chapter. The glossary at the end of the text will also help in building your computer vocabulary. By careful study of terms used in this book, you will be able to avoid that awful computer-related disease known as "buzzword shock syndrome."

In any case, in a pinch you can always use the "systematic buzz phrase projector" developed several years ago by Philip Broughton, a U.S. Public Health official, to help computer users talk to (and about) computer programmers and analysts. When you master this technique, you will sound intelligent, technical, and sophisticated — even if you don't have a clue as to what you're saying.

The technique is easy to use. Merely select at random a digit from each of the three columns below and combine the words opposite each number into your own technical jargon. For example, select "5," "9," and "8" and you generate "sequential mnemonic throughput," an expression bound to command instant respect!

0 automatic	0 management	0 options
1 total	1 organizational	1 flexibility
2 systematized	2 integrated	2 parameter
3 parallel	3 reciprocal	3 computer
4 functional	4 proprietary	4 programming
5 sequential	5 pseudo	5 concept
6 virtual	6 transitional	6 time-phase
7 synchronized	7 incremental	7 projection
8 compatible	8 third generation	8 throughput
9 balanced	9 mnemonic	9 contingency

Soon you may be sending memos like the one below.

To: Whom It May Concern
From: Your Name
Subject: Computer System Capabilities

In order to obtain optimal management flexibility of integrated organizational capabilities inherent in programming concepts that have been synchronized with compatible hardware, it must be emphasized that functional third-generation time-phase contingencies must be instituted with parallel responsiveness. Additionally, the monitored logistical projections representing synchronized digital options must be systematized with existing transitional policies. It is, therefore, incumbent upon analysts to use mnemonic parameters when validating pseudo inquiries in sequential operations.

IMPACT OF COMPUTERS

As we've already stated, there is no question that the computer has permanently altered our way of life. In a period of only 30 years, computers have vastly increased in capabilities and have declined dramatically in price. If the auto industry had done what the computer industry has done in the last 30 years, a Rolls-Royce would cost $2.50 and get some 2,000,000 miles per gallon! A comparable analogy in the aerospace industry would find you flying from coast to coast in one minute at a cost of 10 cents!

Electronic data processing is a fast-changing, dynamic field, the results of which can be seen almost everywhere. Computers make our modern phone service possible, entertain us at home, control our traffic signals, cook our food, serve us at the bank, control our air traffic, check us out at the supermarket, keep track of our library books, process governmental paperwork, and on and on. The list is expanding constantly with no end in sight. Not only have computers altered our life styles, but the use of computers has become very prevalent in the world of business as well. Throughout this text, our focus will be primarily on the impact that computers have had on the modern business organization.

COMPUTER APPLICATIONS IN BUSINESS

Computer Capabilities

The computer as an invention is probably not much older than your teacher or you. In the business community, it was first utilized in the 1950s. The success of the computer is based on its ability to store and process vast amounts of information quickly and accurately. It can add to, update, and retrieve information, as well as transmit information across continents via communication satellites and telephone lines. The computer can calculate, make comparisons, simulate events, and monitor ongoing industrial operations. It can do all these things (and more) reliably and with great ease and speed. As a result of technological innovations in these last two decades, the cost of computing 100,000 multiplications has decreased from $1.26 in 1952 to less than one cent today. Figure 1-8 compares costs and processing time for a mix of about 1,700 computer operations. These operations include typical business processing for data storage and retrieval, payroll, discount computation, and report preparation.

Figure 1-8

A computer mix of about 1,700 standard operations has decreased greatly in cost and processing time.

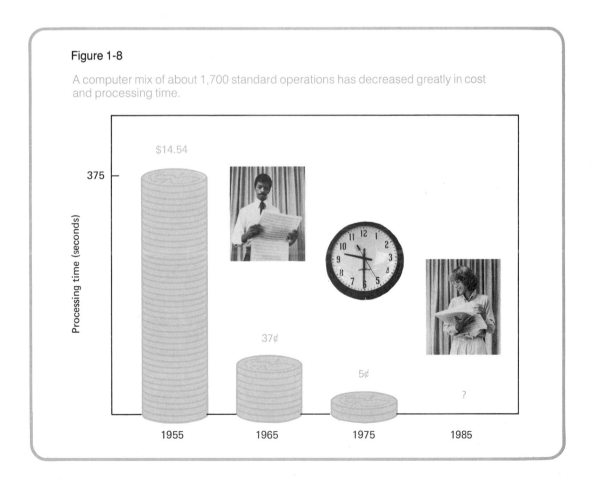

Computer Benefits

As a potential business user, you might consider the following possible benefits of using a computer. Poorly designed or improperly used systems can negate or wipe out these benefits.

Increasing Productivity. One way to improve profit margins is to cut costs. This can occur by reducing expenses for labor, equipment, overhead, supplies, or the cost of carrying inventory. A new computerized order system at Hills Bros. Coffee cut the time between receipt of order and mailing the invoice by 14 days, reduced inventory supply from five weeks to four weeks and, in addition, raised the customer service level from 96 to 99 percent.

The time for processing many tasks may be shortened. For instance, a computer may automatically complete an invoice after a clerk has typed in an account number. Increases in office productivity are discussed in Chapter 15. The computer may also increase income by getting bills out faster with better control over receivables.

Making Better Decisions. Analysis of customers, territories, products, or salespeople allows the manager to take advantage of profitable marketing actions. The computer also makes managers more efficient by freeing them from day-to-day matters that often bog them down. Thus managers can spend their time more effectively, dealing with situations that do not meet specified guidelines. (This is called management by exception.) Quantitative techniques allow managers to ask "What if?" questions for solutions to planning problems.

Classes of Business Applications

There are three main classes of computer business applications: transaction processing, functional applications, and decision support (Figure 1-9).

Transaction processing includes those business applications that are most widely used. These are clerical and bookkeeping functions that are typically first to be put on a computer. Some examples are:

Payroll	Credit card accounting
Accounts payable	Mailing lists
Billing	Tax accounting
General ledger	Utility billing
Label generation	

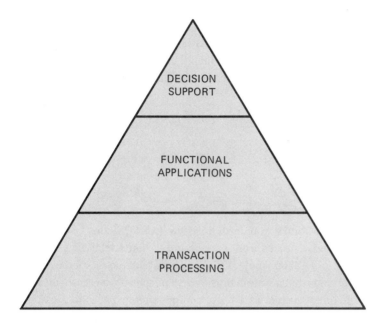

Figure 1-9

Three classes of computer business applications are used in the modern business organization.

Functional applications are usually more complex than transaction processing and are unique to each organization and its dealings. These functional applications are concerned with the control of company resources and are currently the focus of much systems design effort. Examples of functional applications are:

Order processing   Production scheduling
Inventory control   Asset depreciation
Labor distribution   Sales analysis
Warehouse control

Decision support applications are the most sophisticated applications and are being developed primarily in large organizations with highly trained systems personnel. These applications encompass large amounts of data that are often shared by two or more departments and which take considerable time and effort to develop. Several of these decision support areas are:

Simulation models   Material requirements planning
Forecasting   Machine scheduling
Financial planning models Central information file
Cash flow analysis   Statistical analysis

It is important to understand that computers, in and of themselves, would have limited value to an organization. Rather, the real value of computers is their integration into a larger system which then serves the entire organization by providing *information*. An introduction to the information systems concept follows.

ORIENTATION TO INFORMATION SYSTEMS

System Definition

The American National Standards Institute (ANSI) defines a *system* as an assembly of methods, procedures, or techniques united by regulated inter-action to form an organized whole. One significant characteristic missing from the ANSI definition is that a system must have a purpose — a reason for existing. We prefer to define a system as a set of components or parts interacting with each other to accomplish an objective (Figure 1-10). The largest system known to mankind is the universe. What would be the smallest system? Perhaps the atom, with its protons, neutrons, and electrons.

Any system that is a part of a larger system is referred to as a *subsystem*. For example, the accounting system for an organization is composed of several

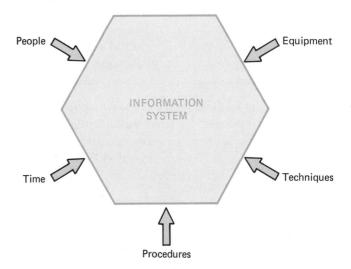

Figure 1-10

An information system
has varied components.

subsystems such as accounts payable, accounts receivable, and general ledger. Generally, what is defined as the system is the largest configuration that is under consideration at a particular time. For example, accounts payable is listed above as a subsystem of the accounting system, but accounts payable can also be considered a system in and of itself. Its subsystems might be the purchasing subsystem, the voucher subsystem, the invoice subsystem, and the receiving subsystem. Note that a system can be whatever you define it to be as long as it has three essential characteristics: unity; interacting parts or components; purpose.

System Hierarchy

This introduction to systems suggests that we exist in a hierarchy of systems. You, yourself, are a system; yet you are made up of many smaller systems such as the circulatory, respiratory, and nervous systems. A business is also a system. It is composed of many smaller subsystems that include production, marketing, personnel, accounting, and data processing.

During the 1960s, a popular concept used to describe an organization's information structure was the "total system" concept. Experts soon realized that a total system could not be precisely defined in an organization because of the interaction of its many parts. A special type of business information system that evolved from the total system concept is the *management information system* (MIS). An MIS is a business system which is designed to provide past, present, and future information appropriate for planning, organizing, and controlling the operations of the organization (Figure 1-11). Today, most information systems are not thought of as management information systems, even though their purpose is to provide information to managers. Current practice finds information systems commonly classified simply by functions such as inventory systems, personnel systems, and accounting systems.

Systems Life Cycle

Information systems in a business organization must serve the needs of managers and other users of information. These needs change constantly and sometimes very quickly. Maintaining systems to meet these new needs requires personnel to design new systems, to modify old systems, or to consolidate systems. Users and data processing personnel must work closely together to ensure that there is agreement on what these systems will provide.

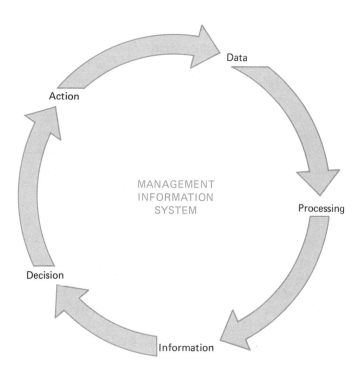

Figure 1-11

A management informa-
tion system is an ongoing
activity.

In order to bring about the desired changes, several system design tasks or activities must be accomplished. These tasks are combined into groups or phases that follow a logical sequence and are referred to as the *systems development cycle* (or systems life cycle). We have grouped these activities into seven phases—problem recognition, feasibility study or preliminary study, detail system analysis, system design, programming activities, implementation of the system, and evaluation and follow-up (Figure 1-12). Do not worry if the concepts behind these phases are not entirely clear at this point. A comprehensive discussion of the systems development cycle is introduced in Chapter 10.

SUMMARY

As our society increasingly adapts to changing technologies, new techniques, and new management expertise, new systems organization will be required. A new relationship between humans and computers is being forged, and the more knowledge we have about the impact of computers and their applications, the greater our understanding of this new relationship will be.

Computer terms are fast becoming part of our vocabulary. In a sense, a new language must be learned if one is to become computer literate.

The computer is well suited for use in business and can lead to increased productivity as well as better decision making. There are three classes of computer business applications—transaction processing, functional (operational) applications, and decision support.

Systems exist in the business world and, like all systems, go through a systems life cycle. This life cycle, as well as other information on systems, is discussed in more detail throughout the text.

Figure 1-12

Systems development involves seven specific phases.

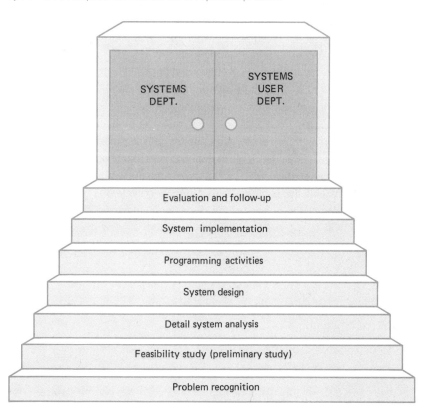

TERMS

Computer	Programming
Digital	Transaction processing
Analog	Functional applications
Data	Decision support
Information	System
Data processing	Subsystem
Data processing cycle	Management information system
Hardware	Systems development cycle
Software	

QUESTIONS

1. What is the difference between a digital computer and an analog computer?
2. What is the difference between data and information?
3. What does data processing include?
4. How do hardware and software differ?
5. How have computers altered our way of life?
6. What are some computer capabilities?
7. How can a computer increase business productivity?
8. How can a computer aid in better decision making?
9. Describe the three classes of computer business applications.
10. What is a system? How is a business system unique?
11. What is the purpose of an information system?
12. Identify the phases of the systems development cycle.

ARTICLE

"Computer Literacy" Gaining Place in Undergraduate Curriculum

Computers rapidly are becoming an essential part of the general college curriculum. At several institutions, "computer literacy" is now required for graduation. At many others, computers are being used heavily by students and faculty members in every field of study.

The idea that all students "should be acquainted with the computer in some reasonably respectable fashion is surely no more radical a thought than the proposition that they should be able to read and write," says Stephen White, director of special projects for the Alfred P. Sloan Foundation.

Among the signs of the computer's growing role in the curriculum:

- The Rochester Institute of Technology has adopted a set of goals for computer literacy for both students and faculty members, including a requirement that any student receiving a degree, regardless of field of study, must demonstrate "fundamental computer literacy." To help implement the policy, R.I.T. plans to invest $4.2-million in new computing equipment.
- Computer literacy will be a graduation requirement for all students at Hamline University, starting with freshmen entering next fall and transfer students entering in the fall of 1983.
- Dartmouth College, where 93 per cent of the students already have used computers without being required to do so, plans to start selling and renting computers to students next fall.
- Wells College, after offering a two-week-long course to faculty members with no previous computer experience, finds instructors in French and philosophy writing their own computer programs for use by students in their classes.
- A freshman English seminar at Cornell University on "mastering the essay" has students writing their essays on a computer. The essays are better, their instructor says, because students are less reluctant to make revisions when it can be done electronically without retyping the whole paper.
- Allegheny College, in establishing a major in computer science, adopted a faculty proposal that concluded that a liberal-arts college nowadays has a responsibility to offer a good program in computer science.

continued

One of the most dramatic plans for expanding computer literacy is a proposal at Carnegie-Mellon University to require each student to have a personal computer within the next three or four years.

Carnegie-Mellon's president, Richard M. Cyert, said last week that computer literacy—the ability to use a computer in their studies—already was nearly universal among students in the university's colleges of science, engineering, and humanities and social sciences. In the college of fine arts, he said, student and faculty use of computers is increasing.

Faculty members in the humanities have become avid users of computers, Mr. Cyert said, and use the university's computer system for word processing more extensively than faculty members in Carnegie-Mellon's other colleges.

Allegheny College's proposal for a new degree program said the rationale for considering computer science a liberal-arts discipline "lies in the nature of computer science as an intellectual discipline itself, in the potential for the cross-fertilization of important ideas between computer science and other disciplines, and in the contributions that such a course can make toward the intellectual development of our students."

At Hamline, computer literacy has been defined as follows:

"A theoretical understanding of the computer, its auxiliary procedures, and its systems as intellectual tools; an understanding of the significance and breadth of computer applications in American society; and a demonstration of the ability to use the computer in the solution of a significant intellectual problem."

In a paper on the role of quantitative study in liberal education, published last year by the Alfred P. Sloan Foundation, Mr. White, the foundation's director of special projects, called the computer "one of the most powerful tools that has ever been brought into being for the service of the individual who seeks to understand his world and the way it wags."

"Like writing," he said, "it is a technology of thought."

Mr. White said that in recommending that all students should have a reasonable acquaintance with computers he did not mean "that all students should be converted to master computer operators, any more than one would propose that all students be converted to expert calligraphers or masters of English prose style."

Jack Magarrell, in The Chronicle of Higher Education, *April 21, 1982, p. 1.*

DISCUSSION QUESTIONS

1. Should computer classes be required of all college students? Why or why not?

2. To what extent do different academic disciplines need computer literacy?

APPLICATION

Fastest Bookkeeper Is Replaced With Small Business Computer

What does an office products dealership do when it loses one of the world's fastest bookkeepers? Simply replace her with a small business computer. That's what happened at All Types Office Supply Co., in Chicago.

"She was the fastest typist and calculator operator I had ever seen," says Larry Weniger, president and partner. "That's why we delayed getting into computers."

About 20 percent of the business is walk in, 15 percent wholesale and 65 percent commercial accounts which are comprised of small and medium size businesses. Annual sales are in excess of $1 million. Products include office and art supplies, machines, furniture and repairs.

Weniger figures the system will pay for itself in two years. Besides replacing one full-time employee and improving cash flow, it allows the firm to conduct twice as much business without adding personnel.

Since the system was installed in 1979, a faster return on invoices has helped the company's cash flow. "The invoices go out the same time as with the manual system, but the money comes in faster — I really don't know why." It may be because of one of the things he likes best about the system — its professionalism. Invoices are neatly printed in a crisp, concise, accurate and businesslike format.

"We shopped around quite awhile because even a small system is a big investment. We shopped at NOPA conventions, checked the big mainframe manufacturers and finally settled on a systems house called Applied Information Management (AIM) in Roselle, Illinois.

"AIM consulted with us, determined our requirements and recommended that we include order processing. They provided the equipment, programming, installation, training and ongoing support services.

"My first thought was that I didn't want to change my procedures to fit a new system," he continued. "We didn't have to change our paper flow with AIM, but we eliminated steps."

Since the firm has only 14 employees, payroll was the easiest function to automate, taking only two days — while receivables took two weeks. All procedures — order processing, invoicing, accounts receivable and payable, general

continued

ledger and product pricing—were completely operational within six months.

Under the manual invoicing system, staffers typed every invoice. An order coming in over the telephone went to the pricer for a price, then to the order filler and back to the pricer to be extended and totalled. Then, if there was a backorder, one copy went to the purchasing agent for ordering. A new invoice was made for backorder items.

Now, a telephone order is recorded on an inhouse form. The pricing is already in the computer. The order is entered and a three-part picking ticket is automatically printed. One copy goes to the order filler and if a backorder, on to the purchasing agent. The second is a packing list and the third goes back to the system to be confirmed.

The AIM system automatically puts it in an invoice file and creates a new picking ticket for backorder items. At day's end, it prints invoices and posts to accounts receivable. It also updates sales statistics. Although it follows the old paper flow, four steps are eliminated: pricing out, extending and totalling, backorder typing, and posting of books.

"It is easier to stay on top of receivables now. I'm able to pinpoint in seconds how much and how long customers owe us. We used to flip through 1,000 pages of accounts to pull out past due customers and write down their names and telephone numbers. The computer lists names, telephone numbers and whether they're 30, 60, 90 or 120 days overdue," Weniger noted.

The main system benefits are
- accuracy in pricing sales.
- reduction in cost.
- professionalism.
- improved control over open orders.
- improved cash flow.
- new management reports.

Reprinted from Small Systems World, *February, 1982.*

DISCUSSION QUESTIONS

1. If you were the bookkeeper, how would you react to "being replaced by a computer"?
2. Should new computer systems conform to current business procedures or vice versa? Justify your answer.

2

THE DYNAMIC COMPUTER INDUSTRY

CHAPTER OBJECTIVES

In this chapter you will learn:

1. About individuals who pioneered the development of computer hardware.
2. About the different generations of computer development.
3. Which companies are the leading manufacturers in various EDP markets.
4. The role of IBM.
5. The impact of software development on the computer industry.
6. About the foreign marketplace for EDP.

WHO'S WHO—COMPUTER PIONEERS

The history of computers is, in itself, an interesting and important topic. A review of the history of computers puts the computer field in proper perspective and is a help in remembering computer terms. As you read the following material, try to determine who should be credited with inventing the computer.

Historians have noted the use of data processing throughout recorded history and even in hieroglyphic symbols on the walls of early cave dwellings. Counting devices and means for retaining information have been used throughout the ages. While any new technology has numerous contributors, the following individuals are often cited in current history books on data processing.

Pascal

The French mathematician, physicist, and religious philosopher Blaise Pascal developed the first adding machine between 1642 and 1644 to help his father, a civil servant, in tax calculations. This early device (Figure 2-1) replaced hand calculations with a series of wheels and levers that overlapped such that, when a sum exceeded ten, the next wheel advanced one position. It should be easy to understand the operation of this early adding machine, since automobile odometers store data in much the same way.

Jacquard

In 1804 Joseph Marie Jacquard developed an innovative weaving loom that was controlled by punched cards (Figure 2-2). The unemployment this automatic device created led to one of history's first union actions, when workers united, destroyed the looms, and attacked Jacquard as well. But the French government under Napoleon stepped in to nationalize the textile industry and, by 1812, there were thousands of Jacquard looms in France. This type of automated loom is still used today in the textile industry to produce the intricately patterned brocade and tapestry known as Jacquard weave.

Babbage

While Jacquard was changing work habits in the French weaving industry, a brilliant and eccentric English mathematician, Charles Babbage, was attempting to develop an automatic computing device for calculations. Babbage

Figure 2-1

Blaise Pascal's adding machine, the world's first digital calculator.

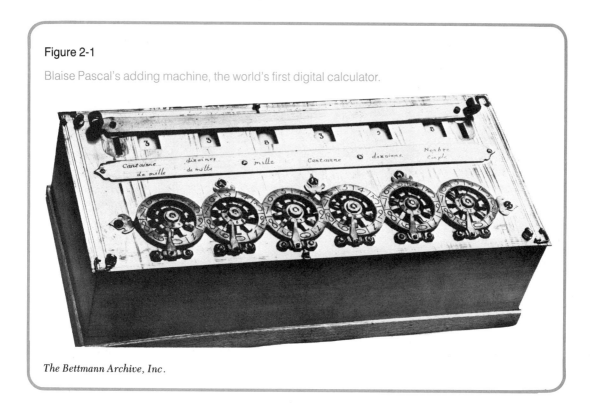

The Bettmann Archive, Inc.

was already well known for such varied inventions as the speedometer, the skeleton key, and the railroad cowcatcher. Limited by the inadequate machine tooling of the day and the withdrawal of financial support by the British government, his computational "difference" machine was never finished. With the aid of Lady Augusta Ada Lovelace, daughter of the famous poet Lord Byron, Babbage turned his talents to the development of an *analytical machine* (Figure 2-3) to compute astronomical tables for the Navy. The analytical machine was to be a digital machine capable of one addition per second with data entered from punched cards and a built-in storage unit. Though this project suffered from financial and tooling limitations (and from lack of public interest), Babbage and Lovelace left 500 pages of special schematic symbols, five volumes of sketches, and 400 detailed drawings. One hundred years later *Howard Aiken*, a Harvard physicist, built a machine called Mark 1 that was the culmination of Babbage's dream.

Figure 2-2

Jacquard loom and close-up of card-holding apparatus.

The Bettmann Archive, Inc.

Figure 2-3

A section of the analytical machine conceived by Charles Babbage in 1834.

The Bettmann Archive, Inc.

Hollerith

Imagine the dilemma facing the U.S. government as it began the 1890 census. The 1880 census had taken over seven years to complete by manual methods, and by then the young country's population had increased nearly 24 percent. Herman Hollerith, a government statistician, provided the solution with a punched-card system of collecting and tabulating the data. His keypunch, sorting, and *tabulating equipment* (Figure 2-4) was extremely successful and allowed the 1890 census to be completed in less than two years. Hollerith continued to develop his card methods for railroad accounting and founded the Tabulating Machine Company at the turn of the century. Upon Hollerith's retirement in 1904, Thomas Watson, Sr., became president and later changed the name of the company to International Business Machines Corporation (IBM).

Figure 2-4

Herman Hollerith's electrical tabulating equipment.

The Bettmann Archive, Inc.

Atanasoff

In a 1973 dispute between Honeywell and Sperry Rand over early computer patent rights, a U.S. District Court gave credit for developing the first electronic computer device to John V. Atanasoff, a physics professor at Iowa State University. Completed in 1942, his *ABC computer* was unique because it utilized digital instead of the analog concepts previously used in computer design. The two leading equipment manufacturers of the day, IBM and Remington Rand, reportedly saw little commercial value in this computer. If Atanasoff had patented his machine, perhaps his impact on computer history would be more widely acknowledged.

Mauchly and Eckert

In 1945, two University of Pennsylvania scientists, John Mauchly and Presper Eckert, designed and developed the Electronic Numerical Integrator and Computer (*ENIAC*), an electronic device often acknowledged to be the first modern electronic computer (Figure 2-5). Based on Atanasoff's design ideas, the machine had 19,000 vacuum tubes (12 were needed to represent each decimal digit) and 500,000 soldered joints, and it weighed more than 30 tons. This early computer required enormous amounts of power to operate and was a tube-replacement nightmare.

The ENIAC project was funded by government grants for the development of ballistics calculations for artillery firing tables. These calculations were no easy task; an operator with a desk calculator typically spent a day or more to compute a single trajectory. ENIAC could add 5,000 numbers per second or multiply 300 numbers per second. Students in computer classes often complain about the hours it takes to write programs; however, it took several days to program instructions for ENIAC since each instruction had to be internally wired. ENIAC was finally completed two months after Japan surrendered. Newer computers forced ENIAC into an early retirement (1955) at the Smithsonian Institution.

Eckert and Mauchly subsequently developed the UNIVAC-1, the first electronic computer offered as a commercial product (Figure 2-6). The *UNIVAC* became famous when it correctly predicted Dwight Eisenhower's victory in the 1952 presidential election. General Electric, in 1954, was the first private American company to purchase one of these computers.

Figure 2-5

The Electronic Numerical Integrator and Computer (ENIAC) developed by John Mauchly and Presper Eckert.

Sperry Univac

von Neumann

John von Neumann, a mathematics genius at Princeton, is sometimes called the intellectual father of computers (Figure 2-7). He has been credited with developing highly significant stored-program theory, and his 1946 paper entitled "A Preliminary Discussion of the Logical Design of an Electronic Computing Instrument" is the authoritative statement on storing data and instructions in computers. He was first to point out the advantages of binary-based circuitry over its decimal counterpart. Von Neumann's IAS computer, developed in 1952 for the Institute for Advanced Study at Princeton, was the

Figure 2-6

UNIVAC-1.

Sperry Univac

prototype for later large-scale computers. Von Neumann also defined and promoted flowcharts as logic aids and, in a separate field of endeavor, was involved with the development of the atomic bomb.

Now, who do you think deserves credit for inventing the computer? Do Pascal and Jacquard deserve credit for their ability to automate computational procedures that were previously manual? Was the analytical machine designed by Babbage and Lovelace the first computer even though it existed only on paper? Should Hollerith's successful punched-card system be credited with beginning the "Computer Revolution"? There is no doubt that most modern computing devices are direct descendants of early machines built by Atanasoff, Mauchly and Eckert, and von Neumann. Only time will tell whether von Neumann's recognition in the academic community, Atanasoff's acknowledgment by the courts, or Mauchly and Eckert's development of a marketable

Figure 2-7

John von Neumann, standing beside equipment based on his stored-program theory.

Courtesy of Princeton University

product will guarantee any of these pioneers historical claim to the title "father" of the computer.

Honorable Mention

While those individuals cited above played key roles in the evolution of the computer, many others contributed important innovations and technological discoveries. Jay W. Forrester, an M.I.T. researcher, invented magnetic core storage in 1951. In a major software development, Grace M. Hopper, a U.S. Naval officer, developed the first compiler (translator of computer languages) in 1952. She was also instrumental in the development of the popular computer language called COBOL. John Kemeny, president of Dartmouth College, pioneered computer timesharing and promoted the development of the computer language called BASIC. H. Ross Perot, a Texas tycoon, founded Electronic Data Systems (EDS), a firm that specializes in facilities management and software development for other firms. In 1970, Gene Amdahl, a former IBM engineer, formed the Amdahl Corporation, a leading manufacturer of large computers.

These are only some of the notable contributors to the development of the computer industry. In a field which is exciting, fast-changing, and always developing, major contributions are still ahead.

COMPUTER GENERATIONS

Although computer professionals do not agree on exact dates or specifics, computer developments are often categorized by *generations*. Computer generations are usually characterized by dramatic improvements in the hardware — typically tenfold or better increases in speed and reliability (Figure 2-8).

The first generation of computers (1950s) used vacuum tubes as components for the electronic circuitry. Punched cards were the main source of input, and magnetic drums were used for internal storage. First-generation computers operated in speeds of *milliseconds* (thousandths of a second) and could handle more than 10,000 additions each second. Most applications were scientific calculations.

During the second generation (early 1960s), transistors and diodes were the main circuit components. Invented by Bell Labs, the transistor was smaller, faster, and more reliable than the vacuum tube. Magnetic cores, used for main storage, could be accessed in *microseconds* (millionths of a second) with more than 200,000 additions possible each second. Business applications became more commonplace, with large data files stored on magnetic tape and disk.

The third generation of computers (late 1960s, early 1970s) was characterized by solid-state logic and *integrated circuits* (IC). Computer storage switched from magnetic cores to integrated circuit boards that provided modularity (expandable storage) and compatibility (interchangeable equipment). Software became more important, with sophisticated operating systems, improved programming languages, and new input/output methods such as optical scanning and plotters.

The current generation of computers (late 1970s, early 1980s), sometimes labeled the fourth generation, has greatly expanded storage capabilities and

Figure 2-8

Three generations of computer components, represented by vacuum tubes, transistors, and integrated-circuit silicon chips.

Photo courtesy of IBM Corporation

improved circuitry. Today's large-scale integrated circuits (LSI) have several hundred thousand transistors placed on one tiny silicon chip. Computer memories operate at speeds of *nanoseconds* (billionths of a second) with large computers capable of adding 15 million numbers per second. Multinational corporations with large databases and communications networks are providing new opportunities and challenges for these modern computers. Computer generations are summarized in Figure 2-9.

INDUSTRY DEVELOPMENT

Individuals noted above deserve much of the credit for computer development throughout the various generations. However, organizations also have had

Figure 2-9

Computer generations.

	First	Second	Third	Fourth
Time frame	1951–58	1959–64	1965–74	1975–present
Circuit component	Vacuum tube	Transistor	Silicon chip [integrated circuit (IC)]	Silicon chip [large-scale integrated circuit (LSI)]
Elements per component	1	1	1–1000	100–500,000
Internal storage	Magnetic drum	Magnetic cores	Cores, IC	Integrated circuits
Memory capacity (characters)	4,000	32,000	128,000	100 million
Popular computers	IBM 650 Univac I Burroughs 220	IBM 1401 CDC 3600 GE 635	IBM/360 Honeywell 200 NCR Century	IBM 303X Univac/6000

a role in the technological growth of electronic data processing. The chart in Figure 2-10 shows that the total U.S. computer capacity is doubling every two to four years. During the 1950s, new computers were the rule, and cost effectiveness was not emphasized. In the 1960s, emphasis in the computer industry switched to marketing. Led by IBM (International Business Machines), large, well-financed companies such as General Electric, RCA, Honeywell, Univac, Burroughs, and NCR (National Cash Register) sold tens of thousands of computers to various businesses and industries. However, despite this new marketing emphasis, computer scientists controlled machine operations and maintained an aura of computer mystique during this decade.

In the 1970s, the emphasis changed again. This was a decade marked by tremendous growth in electronic data processing (EDP). While technological developments were numerous and competition for qualified technical personnel was keen, emphasis shifted from computer technology to the actual use

Figure 2-10

The explosive growth of U. S. computer capacity.

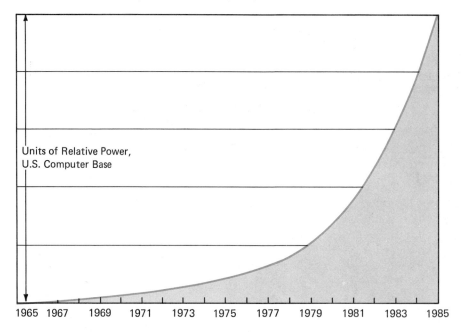

Units of Relative Power,
U.S. Computer Base

1965 1967 1969 1971 1973 1975 1977 1979 1981 1983 1985

International Data Corporation

of computers in the business community. Today, increased emphasis is being placed on the information needed by the decision maker (Figure 2-11). Consequently, software development is becoming a very important computer component.

The computer industry today is far from homogeneous. Rather, many firms specialize in one segment of this burgeoning, multibillion dollar enterprise (Figure 2-12). *Mainframe* companies manufacture medium- to large-scale computers along with the necessary systems software. IBM is the acknowledged giant in this field, with revenues almost twice that of the next eight largest companies combined. Other large mainframe companies include Burroughs Corporation, National Cash Register (NCR), Sperry Univac, Honeywell Inc.,

Figure 2-11

Changing EDP emphasis.

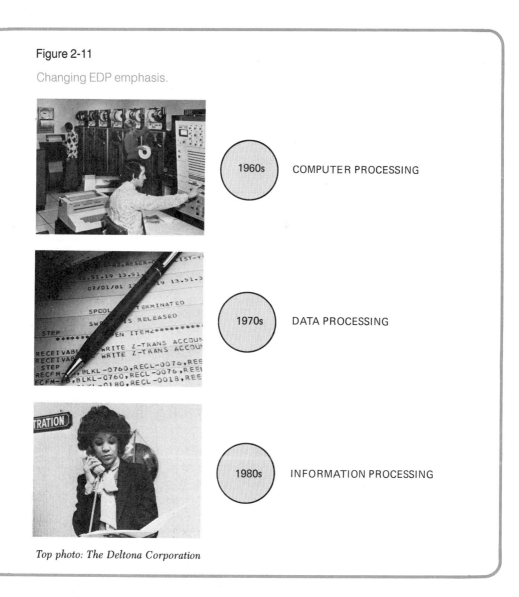

1960s	COMPUTER PROCESSING
1970s	DATA PROCESSING
1980s	INFORMATION PROCESSING

Top photo: The Deltona Corporation

and Control Data Corporation (CDC). These computer manufacturers also specialize in supplying *peripherals* (input/output devices, auxiliary computer equipment) as well as software. A listing of the major computer companies is given in Figure 2-13.

Figure 2-12

Changing market shares of computer hardware, 1975-1985.

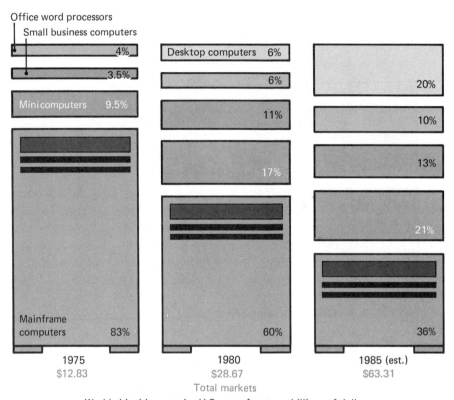

Office word processors
Small business computers

4%	Desktop computers 6%	20%
3.5%	6%	10%
Minicomputers 9.5%	11%	13%
	17%	21%
Mainframe computers 83%	60%	36%
1975 $12.83	**1980** $28.67	**1985 (est.)** $63.31

Total markets
Worldwide shipments by U.S. manufacturers, billions of dollars

International Data Corporation

THE ROLE OF IBM

Why has IBM achieved such a dominant position in the computer industry? While some have alleged that IBM uses questionable marketing strategies which may even be illegal, most industry observers would concede that superior business practices and extensive field support are largely responsible for its success. At any rate, IBM is an industry leader for computer mainframes, input devices, communications equipment, and programming languages.

Figure 2-13

Top 25 U. S. companies in the DP industry.

Rank	Company	1981 DP Revenue ($ millions)
1	International Business Machines	$26,340.0
2	Digital Equipment Corporation	3,586.6
3	Control Data Corporation	3,103.3
4	NCR Corporation	3,071.8
5	Burroughs Corporation	2,934.0
6	Sperry Corporation	2,781.0
7	Hewlett-Packard Company	1,875.0
8	Honeywell, Inc.	1,773.7
9	Xerox Corporation	1,100.0
10	Wang Laboratories, Inc.	1,008.5
11	Storage Technology	922.0
12	TRW, Inc.	855.0
13	Data General Corporation	764.4
14	General Electric Company	750.0
15	Texas Instruments, Inc.	666.7
16	Computer Sciences Corporation	624.7
17	Automatic Data Processing	613.0
18	ITT Corporation	540.0
19	Electronic Data Systems	480.6
20	Datapoint Corporation	474.1
21	Tandy Corporation	460.0
22	Amdahl Corporation	442.7
23	Apple Computer, Inc.	401.1
24	McDonnell Douglas Corporation	376.7
25	Prime Computer, Inc.	365.0

Background

The IBM 650, developed in 1954, was the computer version of the Model T. While only 1,800 of these computers were sold, IBM was able to capture roughly two-thirds of the general-purpose computer market.

In 1960, sales of the small, business-oriented 1401 and scientific 1620 allowed IBM to maintain the lead in business and education markets. In 1964,

IBM made a major breakthrough when it introduced the System/360 with its innovative integrated circuits. Shocked competitors struggled to keep pace!

In 1970, IBM took another major step, one that greatly affected the software industry. It reversed its policy of selling only complete packages of hardware, software, training, and maintenance and instead provided *unbundled* products. That is, EDP sales were broken down into separate components. This led to the rapid growth of competitors in the applications software industry, which has grown into a multibillion-dollar industry. However, the practice of unbundling has proved to be unsuited to the needs of an increasing number of microcomputer users. These small computer users often lack the expertise necessary to pick and choose between available software packages. Thus "rebundling" is becoming more and more common in catering to the very small computer user.

In 1971, IBM introduced the System/370 and continued its pattern of cost-performance gains in equipment utilization. The company has continued to expand its product line with the System 138 and 4300 series of small- and medium-sized computers, as well as its new low-cost Personal Computer. Still another development of IBM is its "H" series of supercomputers, which some industry observers label the fourth generation of computers because of greatly improved performance.

Challenges Already Met

The competitive position of IBM has led to many antitrust actions against the computer giant. Some small companies entered the computer market after financing their companies through out-of-court settlements from IBM. Litigation in the 1970s was also brought by large competitors such as Control Data, Applied Data Research, Greyhound, Memorex, and Telex. The federal government's decade-long antitrust action against IBM was dropped in early 1982 after the government decided its case was too weak.

Large, established firms have also unsuccessfully challenged IBM in the marketplace. General Electric merged its computer hardware operation into Honeywell's, while RCA sold its computer customer base to Univac, sustaining a loss of nearly $500 million.

There is no guarantee that IBM can continue its dominance in the marketplace indefinitely. Competition is growing in all segments of the computer industry, both in this country and throughout the world. This competition ranges from manufacturers of the smallest microcomputer to the largest supercomputer.

SUPERCOMPUTERS

In the 1960s, Control Data Corporation (CDC) captured the title of "supercomputer builder" by incorporating several computers into one mainframe. Burroughs expanded on this concept by combining 1,000 small computer processors into one large $10-million computer called Illiac IV. CDC countered with its Cyber 2000 series and, in 1972, Seymour Cray, formerly an engineer at CDC, began to manufacture and market giant scientific computers. The total customer base of these supercomputers is considered to be no more than several hundred organizations.

Some *supercomputers* use a form of data manipulation called vector processing, where whole series of numbers are operated on at one time. Problems that were previously unsolvable can be handled by these huge machines. For example, the largest prime number — 13,395 digits long — was found in 20 minutes on a Cray-1 (Figure 2-14).

SMALL COMPUTER SYSTEMS

Small computer systems range in value from minicomputers costing several hundred thousand dollars to microcomputers costing less than $10,000. *Minicomputers* have the same components as larger mainframes but have reduced memory and slower processing speeds. Before the advent of the minicomputer industry in the early 1960s, companies wishing to automate were forced to use a large mainframe. With the evolution of minicomputers, managers could choose computers with substantially lower costs. The minicomputer industry actually began with the production of small industrial process computers. A small business computer is shown in Figure 2-15.

The entry of the microcomputer as a viable business tool changed the data processing world even more. *Microcomputers* are very small computers powered by a *microprocessor*. The microprocessor is at the heart of the microelectronics revolution. It is a general, all-purpose circuit, placed on a silicon chip. This chip is used in calculators, watches, video games, microwave ovens, and of course, computers. While a microprocessor may cost less than $10, its power is equivalent to that of computers which cost several hundred thousand dollars in 1960.

Figure 2-14

The Cray-1 supercomputer, one of the largest computers in the world.

Cray Research, Inc.

Widely used in business today, microcomputers reputedly originated in 1974 when a company in Albuquerque, New Mexico, called Micro Instrumentation and Telemetry Systems (MITS) manufactured computer kits for the hobby market. After experiencing great success in marketing their kits through *Popular Electronics* magazine, the company was acquired by Pertec, a large manufacturer of computer-related products. A new computer company named Radio Shack joined in the microcomputer boom and sold $100 million worth of their TRS80 computers in their first 18 months. Apple, Commodore, IBM, and the other manufacturers are today competing for a market which is expected to grow tremendously in the next decade.

Figure 2-15

A small computer with disk drive, printer, and data entry stations.

Courtesy of Digital Equipment Corporation

MICROPROCESSORS

Indeed, the introduction of the microprocessor revolutionized electronic data processing. Remember, early computers required several thousand vacuum tubes, filled huge rooms, and required vast air-conditioning and power supplies. Today's microprocessors (computers-on-a-chip) are less than ¼ inch square and use less energy than a 100-watt light bulb (Figure 2-16).

Figure 2-16

(Left) A one-chip computer developed for a variety of telecommunications applications, photographed with a standard-size paper clip to dramatize its small size. (Right) A random access memory containing about 152,000 components and capable of storing more than 64,000 bits of data. The "creature" is a South American fire ant.

Left photo courtesy of Bell Laboratories; right photo courtesy of Western Electric

Chip designs are imprinted on a silicon wafer by a chemical etching process, exposure to ultraviolet light, and an acid bath that washes away unexposed areas. This process can be repeated over and over, creating successive layers of electrical circuitry on the chip. Methods and manufacturing time vary depending on the complexity of design. A chip used in a microwave oven may have only a few layers of circuitry. Microprocessor chips for the computer are the most complex chips manufactured today. Most of the steps involved in this process take place in "clean rooms" with air filters to remove the smallest particles of dust and dirt that might contaminate the chips. Usually, less than half the chips from a wafer survive the manufacturing process and are usable. Once the chips have passed testing, they are packaged with protective casings of ceramic, plastic, or metal with gold or aluminum soldering. The packaging protects the chips and also provides electrodes for hooking up their circuits to the outside world.

The first microprocessor was introduced in the 1970s by Intel Corporation. (It was this microprocessor that MITS used in its computer kits.) In the past most chips were manufactured in a 250-square-mile area south of San Francisco which has been nicknamed *"Silicon Valley"* after the silicon base on which the circuits are etched. In 1981 there were nearly 1,000 electronic firms in this fertile valley in Santa Clara County, but today electronic companies are spreading to other parts of the United States.

SOFTWARE DEVELOPMENT

While computers were first introduced in large organizations during the 1960s, smaller companies jumped on the bandwagon in the 1970s. In the 1980s, software is the new focus of attention (Figure 2-17). As the prices for software continue to increase because of the many highly skilled people required to

Figure 2-17

©Jim Orton

produce it, and as hardware prices decline, vendors are now designing hardware to match software rather than the other way around. There is a new emphasis on producing software products which are "user friendly" with functional "menus" of applications and English-like languages available for workers who are not trained in data processing (see Figure 2-18).

The development of usable software has always been a problem for computer manufacturers and business users. Most dissatisfaction with computer systems can be traced to software problems. Even today, there are still many computer users who do not realize how difficult it is to build complex commercial software. To provide for successful systems development in the future, cooperation between systems professionals and user managers is absolutely necessary. New business applications in database processing and manufacturing control need to be designed that can be used for more than a few years. While

Figure 2-18

A "menu."

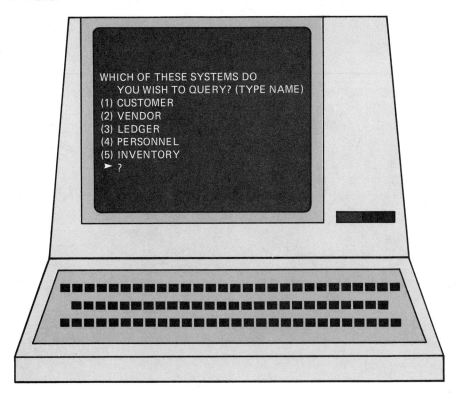

past applications have typically remained useful for ten years or so, new systems will be used for several decades. Business applications must be continuously modified to reflect new computer technology, company growth, and government regulations.

THE INTERNATIONAL SCENE

Problems of computer productivity and software development are much the same all over the world. Computer professionals do the same type of work in North America, Asia, and Europe, and foreign businesses use the same applications as firms in this country. For example, West Germany is increasing its use of point-of-sale terminals (where sales data are relayed to a central computer), while France is actively using computer terminals in its banking industry. Minicomputers in Mexico are popular for industrial process control, while the Soviet Union is increasing the billions of rubles spent annually on computer products.

West Germany, France, Italy, and the United Kingdom are the major EDP markets in Western Europe. Leading European computer manufacturers competing with IBM for this market are identified in Figure 2-19. While Western

Figure 2-19

Ranking of top European computer manufacturers by EDP revenues.

Rank	Company	Dollar Revenues ($ millions)
1	IBM (U.S.)	$9,902
2	Siemens (West Germany)	1,505
3	CII-Honeywell Bull (France)	1,444
4	ICL (U.K.)	1,300
5	Olivetti (Italy)	876
6	Sperry Univac (U.S.)	825
7	NCR (U.S.)	810
8	Digital Equipment (U.S.)	786
9	Control Data (U.S.)	764
10	Burroughs (U.S.)	734
11	Nixdorf (West Germany)	707
12	Hewlett-Packard (U.S.)	593

Reprinted with permission of DATAMATION® magazine, ©copyright by TECHNICAL PUBLISHING COMPANY, A DUN & BRADSTREET COMPANY, 1981 – all rights reserved.

Europe is the largest region for computer imports, the Middle East is using its "petrodollars" to buy computer technology. Among Communist countries, China is openly developing trade agreements with the United States, but the Soviet Union bloc is focusing on internal EDP growth through its own Riad series of computers.

When all is said and done, U.S. companies lead the computer field. While only 45 percent of the worldwide mainframe base resides in this country, U.S. firms are responsible for 80 percent of all the computers installed in the world (Figure 2-20). IBM, with over half of its profits from overseas business, has amassed a significant market share in most major countries. An exception to IBM's dominance is Japan, which is providing U.S. companies with stiff com-

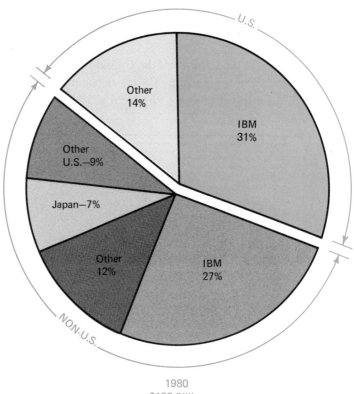

Figure 2-20

1980 worldwide installed
base of mainframes.

1980
$133 Billion

International Data Corporation

petition. Japanese companies such as Fujitsu, Hitachi, and Nippon Electric are pursuing dominance in the world market for small computers. Toward that end, Japanese industry, academia, and government have joined forces to support computer and microelectronic research. Japan's leading computer companies are identified in Figure 2-21.

Figure 2-21

Leading Japanese computer companies.

Company	Comment
Canon	Sells computers through established U.S. business equipment outlets
Epson	World leader in printer sales
Fujitsu	Number 1 computer company in Japan, strongest competition for IBM in that country
Hitachi	Another large corporation with full line of computers
Matushita	Parent company for Panasonic and Quasar electronic products
Mitsubishi	Diversified company with line of small business computers
Nippon Electric (NEC)	Large computer company in Japan, aggressive in United States
Sharp Electronics	Joint agreement with Radio Shack for pocket computers
Oki Electric	Promising line of personal computers

SUMMARY

Although only thirty years old, the computer has had a major impact on the business community. Early forerunners of the computer were Pascal's adding machine, Jacquard's automated looms, and Babbage's analytical machine. Hollerith developed a punched-card system for the U.S. census that inaugurated modern data-handling methods. World War II provided a framework for scientists Atanasoff, Mauchly, Eckert, and von Neumann to develop a series of first-generation computers.

In the EDP marketplace, IBM soon became the leading computer company in the world. While there are increasing sales for mainframe computers, peripherals, and supplies, the development of the microprocessor and package software have expanded the market potential to even the smallest business. The development of usable software is replacing hardware as the critical component in business information systems.

With increasing competition throughout the world, the leading foreign markets are Japan and Europe. The 1980s promise to be another growth decade for the computer industry.

NAMES AND TERMS

Blaise Pascal	Generation
Joseph Marie Jacquard	Millisecond
Charles Babbage	Microsecond
Howard Aiken	Integrated circuit
Herman Hollerith	Nanosecond
John V. Atanasoff	Mainframe
John Mauchly	Peripherals
Presper Eckert	Unbundling
John von Neumann	Supercomputer
	Minicomputer
Analytical machine	Microcomputer
Tabulating equipment	Microprocessor
ABC computer	Silicon Valley
ENIAC	
UNIVAC	

QUESTIONS

1. Choose several of the individuals listed under "Names and Terms" and briefly describe their contributions to computer development.
2. What were the characteristics of computer development in the various computer generations?
3. Identify three major mainframe companies.

4. Who are the top five computer companies overall?
5. How do you account for the success of IBM?
6. Why is rebundling becoming more popular?
7. Why is there no guarantee that IBM can continue its dominance in the marketplace?
8. How did CDC capture the title of "supercomputer builder"?
9. How do minicomputers and microcomputers differ from supercomputers?
10. What technology is considered to be at the heart of the microelectronics revolution?
11. Why will software be emphasized as one of the major areas of development in the computer industry in the 1980s?
12. Why do we say that computing is becoming an international language?
13. Which nation is providing U.S. computer manufacturers with their stiffest competition?

ARTICLE

Can Japan Beat Software Woes?

TOKYO—Despite recent warnings that a concentrated push by Japan to increase its software expertise might bring it to a par with the U.S., few persons here—or in the U.S.—seem convinced it can happen.

Hitachi, Ltd., now has 15 software subsidiaries with 7,000 employees. Fujitsu, Ltd., next May plans to open a $26 million software development factory where 1,300 engineers will develop commercial operating systems. But ambitious strategies such as these notwithstanding, software is more of a bane in Japan than in the U.S.

One reason Okadata feels it will be hard for the Japanese to catch up is that Japan has almost singlemindedly devoted itself to hardware expertise, so that many of its best technical people are deficient in understanding software. "The hardware manufacturer and the software designer are almost opposites," Okadata said.

Okadata is not alone in his pessimism. Yuji Ogino, manager of marketing for IDC Japan, a marketing research organization, marks Japan three years behind the U.S. in system and application software, and wonders if software troubles won't further retard her advance.

Vendors find software very hard to sell in Japan, Ogino said, because "users expect software free of charge." Such conditioning stands in direct conflict to the vendor's need to generate more revenue from software as hardware prices go down. Ogino singled out Fujitsu as one company trying to make software pay for itself by spreading software operations across the organization. But as yet, Fujitsu's first step—convincing customers to pay for software—has not really been successful, he said.

Software houses in Japan also face bigger financial headaches than their U.S. counterparts. In Japan, venture capital avenues are not open to them. Moreover, "banks are not willing to risk money on software companies," Ogino said, especially small start-ups. As a result, many software houses can survive only through large orders given to them by giants such as Nippon Co. or Fujitsu. But dependence on such orders deprives them of their independence and makes them little more than subsidiaries.

The "Japanese software is and will be inferior" theory has its dissidents, of course. Masa Tasaki, managing director

continued

of Lifeboat, Inc., of Japan, plans to export Rgy Forth, a native CP/M-based compiler, worldwide. He feels that, eventually, "Japanese software will progress to the U.S. level," and envisions Japanese and U.S. software companies cooperating in terms of sharing software engineers and marketing expertise.

Still, one wonders if it will be that easy. The difficulty of the three Japanese alphabets, especially Kanji, has proven a major stumbling block for Japanese companies. On the other hand, the Japanese language has provided the country with a natural trade barrier against U.S. companies trying to crack the small-business market.

Perhaps the best chance for Japanese and American cooperation in terms of software will be at the industrial/scientific end, where the language of mathematics is nearly universal.

DISCUSSION QUESTIONS

1. How can software expertise impede Japanese entry into United States EDP markets?
2. Why have the Japanese been so successful in marketing automobiles, television sets, watches, and other such products?

APPLICATION

Extra Programs and Services From Your Microcomputer

Stay on Top of the Business News

Too busy to keep up with the latest trends, news, and commentary reported in the business press? Turn to THE SOURCE and let *Management Contents Ltd.* provide concise abstracts from many of the leading financial publications.

Smart Money

On-line data of professional quality is at your fingertips to support your investment decisions. *UNISTOX* gives you regularly updated reports on stocks, bonds, commodities, futures, options, gold and other precious metals, money markets, mutual funds, foreign exchange and Treasury rates. *Media General Financial Services, Inc.*, provides reports and analyses of over 3,100 stocks in 58 performance categories. Complete news and price wires from all major commodity markets too, via *Commodity News Services, Inc.* And THE SOURCE continually updates in-depth economic business and financial forecasts and reports from leading economists and investment analysts.

Window on Washington

THE SOURCE gives you an electronic window on Washington that lets you monitor the schedule of Congressional committees, regulatory agencies and the President. You can extract articles on government topics of special interest, learn the latest from various commentators, and review in advance each day's scheduled activities in the nation's capital.

Computer Conferences

No need for all conferees to be in the same place at the same time — or even in different places at the same time as required for a telephone conference. In a computer conference, made possible by *Participation Systems, Inc.* via THE SOURCE — for professional seminars, business discussions, committee meetings — each participant chooses when and where to come on-line. You eliminate all the time, trouble, and expense of travel and long distance telephone tag.

Electronic Mail

Messages or reports can be transmitted and delivered within minutes by SOURCE subscribers the world over — usually at a lower cost than long-distance telephone, Telex, facsimile transmission or express mail!

continued

For messages with extra impact, you can use THE SOURCE to send an actual Mailgram Message. Compose it right on your terminal and speed it to one or many addresses simultaneously.

Chat

You can "converse" electronically with any other user who is on-line when you are, by typing and receiving messages. Schedule the time you want to be on-line together and you can interact one-on-one — and have a clearly understood meeting of minds, with *immediate written confirmation* of business decisions, price changes, purchases, and sales.

Electronic Bulletin Board and Public Forum

Post your own, and read others' "classified ads," share ideas, sell or swap merchandise.

You may even be able to use THE SOURCE to "publish" your own money-making database service, information bank, or electronic newsletter. THE SOURCE will announce it to other subscribers and pay you a royalty when others read what you've created.

Electronic Travel Service

THE SOURCE gives you complete, current domestic and international air-line schedules through *Dittler Brothers, Inc*. Through *First World Travel,* an independent travel agency, you can shop for the best rates, then, over your terminal, place ticket orders. You can rent a car and make hotel reservations electronically too.

U.P.I. News Service

Get the latest news within minutes after the stories are filed by U.P.I. correspondents around the world — well in advance of scheduled TV and radio newscasts. You can "follow the wire" as the news develops or extract full details on just those stories of specific interest to you.

When Dig You Must

Research experts around the world can provide fast information on virtually any subject. *INFORMATION ON DEMAND* via THE SOURCE will send you electronic or hard copy of any document or article you want, and IOD is available to produce research papers on any topic in every major language.

Purchasing and Bartering

Save time and money with computerized discount shopping on over 50,000

continued

name-brand items through *Compu-U-Store* via THE SOURCE. The best price is calculated for you automatically, including delivery charges. Comp-U-Store will accept your order and delivery will be made to your address within days. Through THE SOURCE and *Barter Worldwide, Inc.*, you can trade goods and services with other businesses or individuals.

Personal Tips and Features

THE SOURCE is a veritable encyclopedia of consumer information that can give you helpful advice on a long list of subjects, including recipes; food and nutrition; choosing the right wines; home repair and decorating; health care and medicine; the latest movie reviews from *Cineman*. The list is virtually endless.

Hobbies, Games—and a Touch of Classroom

THE SOURCE has puzzles, riddles, card tricks, and humor. There are programs covering television, collectibles, and hobbies. Dozens of electronic games for all ages range from Adventure to word games like Hangman. Instructional programs include foreign languages, poetry, spelling, mathematics, and geometry.

Creating and Computing

You can access the powerful mainframe computers of THE SOURCE to write and store your own programs, using BASIC, FORTRAN, INFOX, and PASCAL. You can file and store important lists and information, program financial routines and use our Model 1 service for financial planning, simulation, and analysis.

It's Touch and Go

THE SOURCE is accessible with virtually any microcomputer, terminal or communicating word processor. All you need is your telephone, a modem, and, with some equipment, communications software.

To come on-line, you simply dial an assigned local telephone number and place your telephone in the modem. Just follow the illustrated guide and you can access any of over 750 information and communications services by typing your commands in plain English. A "menu" for beginners takes you through simple steps to the specific information, program or service you wish. Your account number and password provide security for your files and transactions.

THE SOURCE can tell you what you need to know on a vast range of subjects, help you make timely decisions with confidence, communicate instantaneously and inexpensively across great distances *in writing,* improve your efficiency and productivity as well as reduce expenses.

continued

Cost? From as little as ten cents a minute. Although THE SOURCE is an important business management tool, it isn't limited to the office. You can access it from home, or on the road, around the clock. Use it to catch up with office work, or for self-improvement, family fun, and education.

Reprinted with permission of THE SOURCE, AMERICA'S INFORMATION UTILITY™

DISCUSSION QUESTIONS

THE SOURCE is one of the nationwide information services that may be accessed by a microcomputer or computer terminal in most large American cities.

1. Which of THE SOURCE offerings are most useful for a business manager?
2. Which are most useful for a college student?

PART

2 HARDWARE

The dynamic hardware component of computer systems provides opportunities and challenges for business organizations. You will see in this section how computer capacities for storing data have increased phenomenally, yet the physical size of the equipment has been reduced drastically. Careful study of this section will lessen your vulnerability to "computer mystique."

Chapter 3 - explores the function and performance of computer memory.

Chapter 4 - identifies the myriad of available peripheral devices.

COMPUTER SYSTEMS AND DATA STORAGE

CHAPTER OBJECTIVES

In this chapter you will learn:

1. What a computer system is and how it works to process data.
2. The meaning of the stored program concept.
3. The meaning of data hierarchy.
4. The various methods of on-line data storage.
5. How secondary storage types compare.
6. The role of an operating system.
7. Several categories of computer languages.
8. How virtual storage increases usable computer memory.
9. The characteristics of multiprocessing and multiprogramming.

To many people, the workings of the computers they rely on are a total mystery. They only know that the machines work. In some cases, this is certainly enough. However, it is also true that the more knowledge one has of *how* a machine works, the more one can utilize that machine to its fullest potential.

In the computer world, the term *user friendly* is often heard. This refers to the ease with which an individual can interact with the computer and understand what the computer has done for the user. The greater the user's understanding of and familiarity with the computer, the friendlier the computer gets.

We have taken the position that today's managers, and even more so those of tomorrow, will be using the computer as a powerful aid in making critical organizational decisions. As such, the computer will serve as a major component of the information system. To help you conceptualize what an information system is, a hospital patient billing information system is illustrated in Figure 3-1. While the computer, as we have said, is a major component of such a system, the computer is also a system by itself. It, too, has interrelated parts which work together to perform a task or goal.

A TYPICAL COMPUTER SYSTEM

A typical *computer system* is represented schematically in Figure 3-2. The components of a typical computer system include input, output, storage, and the central processing unit (CPU). Each of these components is vitally important to the functioning of the entire computer system. Because there are so many different types of input and output units, the entire topic of input and output will be discussed separately in Chapter 4.

Probably the most costly component of the computer system is the *central processing unit*. The CPU consists of the control unit, the arithmetic-logic unit, and main memory, all of which work together to electronically control the functions of the computer system. Because of the CPU's central authority in running the computer system, it is sometimes referred to as the *mainframe* unit. The components of the mainframe computer system illustrated in Figure 3-3 are connected by wires running under the floor.

The Control Unit

The *control unit* does precisely what its name implies. It performs all the control functions for the computer. More precisely, it retrieves instructions

Figure 3-1

Overview of patient billing information system.

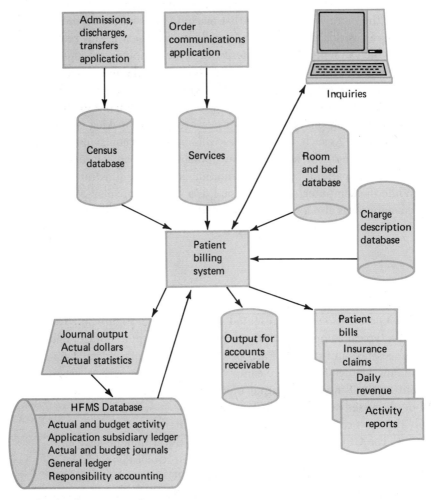

Reproduced with permission of IBM Corporation

from memory, translates those instructions into computer functions, and sends signals to the other computer hardware units to carry out those functions. It is also responsible for determining the next instruction to be executed by the computer. The control unit may be thought of as the computer's traffic cop.

Figure 3-2

Computer system components.

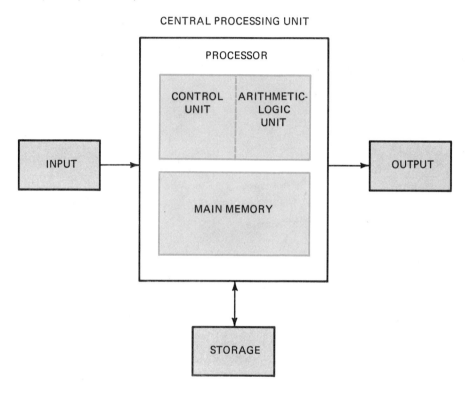

The Arithmetic-Logic Unit

The *arithmetic-logic unit* (ALU) is the computer's "number cruncher." It is the part of the CPU which performs the arithmetic calculations of addition, subtraction, multiplication, and division, and it is used to keep track of and execute instructions. The way that a computer handles data is conceptually simple: it can only calculate or compare digits. When it comes to calculation, all a modern digital computer can do is add. It is fortunate that the four arithmetic functions can all be expressed in terms of addition. Multiplication is merely continuous addition. Subtraction is the addition of the complement of the number to be subtracted. Division is the addition of complements. *Registers* are paths or conduits that connect the arithmetic-logic unit to the

Figure 3-3

Components of the Burroughs 5900 computer system.

Tape Drive Controller

Tape Drives

Central Processing Unit

Printer

Input Consoles

Printer

Disk Drive

Disk Drive

Disk Controller

Burroughs Corporation

main memory. When an instruction is fetched from main memory, it is placed in a register to await instructions from the control unit. Data are also stored in registers prior to execution in the arithmetic-logic unit (Figure 3-4).

Main Memory

Main memory, also called *primary storage,* is that memory which is directly accessible by the control unit and arithmetic-logic unit. Main memory holds instructions and data elements which are currently being used by the computer.

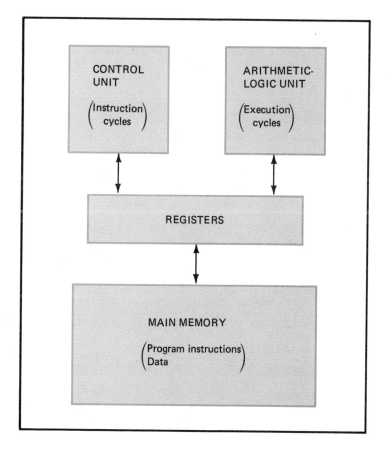

Figure 3-4

The CPU uses registers to manipulate mainframe components.

THE STORED PROGRAM CONCEPT

It is important to note here an essential point in understanding computers and how they work. Put simply, computers DO NOT POSSESS INDEPENDENT THOUGHT! Rather, a computer executes or runs *stored programs*. A computer program is a detailed set of instructions which the computer follows in order to perform data processing tasks.

All the instructions of a given program, as well as the corresponding data, are stored in main memory prior to the execution of the program. For example, a *programmer* (author of computer programs) might write a payroll program using the data in Figure 3-5 to print the report contained in Figure 3-6. The computer, by exactly following the instructions contained in the program, can print periodic payroll reports—despite the fact that the data to be processed may change. This allows one program to be used over and over again by the same business organization, or even by other organizations, to perform common business data processing tasks such as payroll, accounts payable, and inventory control.

Figure 3-5

Data for payroll program example in Figure 3-6.

Employee Name	Social Security Number	Number of Hours Worked	Pay Rate
KEYPUNCHER KATHY	732-41-9806	40	$4.50
EMM I B	083-47-8655	35	10.23
SEA C D	145-83-2259	39	7.42
WELL HONEY	334-52-1018	40	3.75
NICE I M	759-56-4273	40	8.60
YOU R	626-40-4019	42	6.70

Figure 3-6

Payroll output report.

```
    82/07/17. 12.38.45.
    PROGRAM   AIRLINE


                              TOP-FLIGHT AIRLINES


                            PAYROLL REPORT



        KATHY KEYPUNCHER        732-41-9806
            HOURS WORKED = 40       PAY RATE = $4.50      PAY = $180.00


        I B EMM                 083-47-8655
            HOURS WORKED = 35       PAY RATE =$10.23      PAY = $358.05


        C D SEA                 145-83-2259
            HOURS WORKED = 39       PAY RATE = $7.42      PAY = $289.38


        HONEY WELL              334-52-1018
            HOURS WORKED = 40       PAY RATE = $3.75      PAY = $150.00


        I M NICE                759-56-4273
            HOURS WORKED = 40       PAY RATE = $8.60      PAY = $344.00


        R YOU                   626-40-4019
            HOURS WORKED = 42       PAY RATE = $6.70      PAY = $281.40

    SRU     0.366 UNTS.

    RUN COMPLETE.




    BYE

    LROA005    LOG OFF    12.39.38.
    LROA005    SRU        0.375 UNTS.
```

DATA HIERARCHY

The most elementary way to organize data within a memory location is in the form of a code which utilizes a "1" or a "0." These 1's and 0's are called *binary digits*, or *bits*. The reason for storing elementary pieces of data in bits is that computer circuitry is electronic in nature, and electronic devices can be turned either "on" or "off." As such, the computer is a *bistable* memory device. Bistable means that it has two stable memory states: "on" or "off" — "1" or "0."

Combinations of bits are put together to form a *byte*, which represents a *character* (a letter, number, or special symbol) in a computer. Often six or eight bits are combined into a byte where the combination of 1's and 0's represents different characters. For example, in one commonly used code, 10100001 represents the letter A, and 01011001 represents the number 1. A humorous interpretation of the terms bit and byte is shown in Figure 3-7.

The way in which bits are combined to form bytes depends on which one of several standard internal character codes is used to represent each byte or

Figure 3-7

©Craig Peasley

character of information. These internal computer codes are based on the 4-bit numeric, binary-coded decimal system illustrated in Figure 3-8. Since alphabetic characters cannot be represented by just four bits (only 2^4, or 16, possible characters can be represented with four bits), extra "zone" bits are needed to allow extra capability. An 8-bit code provides storage capability for 2^8, or 256, characters.

Two 8-bit codes are commonly used in modern computers (Figure 3-9). The Extended Binary Coded Decimal Interchange Code (EBCDIC)—pronounced

Decimal Number	Binary Equivalent
0	0
1	1
2	10
3	11
4	100
5	101
6	110
7	111
8	1000
9	1001

Figure 3-8

A minimum of four bits are needed to represent decimal numbers.

"ebseedick"—is used by IBM and other mainframe manufacturers. Another code, the American Standard Code for Information Interchange (ASCII)—pronounced "askee"—is popular for data communications applications.

The letters or digits represented by each byte or character can be joined together to form one item of data such as a name or an address. This is called a *field*. Fields in turn are generally part of larger records. A *record* is a collection of fields on a related subject which are treated as a unit. Similarly, a *file* is a group of records on a related subject. Finally, the organization of files

Character	EBCDIC*	ASCII†
0	1111 0000	0101 0000
1	1111 0001	0101 0001
2	1111 0010	0101 0010
3	1111 0011	0101 0011
4	1111 0100	0101 0100
5	1111 0101	0101 0101
6	1111 0110	0101 0110
7	1111 0111	0101 0111
8	1111 1000	0101 1000
9	1111 1001	0101 1001
A	1100 0001	1010 0001
B	1100 0010	1010 0010
C	1100 0011	1010 0011
D	1100 0100	1010 0100
E	1100 0101	1010 0101
F	1100 0110	1010 0110
G	1100 0111	1010 0111
H	1100 1000	1010 1000
I	1100 1001	1010 1001
J	1101 0001	1010 1010
K	1101 0010	1010 1011
L	1101 0011	1010 1100
M	1101 0100	1010 1101
N	1101 0101	1010 1110
O	1101 0110	1010 1111
P	1101 0111	1011 0000
Q	1101 1000	1011 0001
R	1101 1001	1011 0010
S	1110 0010	1011 0011
T	1110 0011	1011 0100
U	1110 0100	1011 0101
V	1110 0101	1011 0110
W	1110 0110	1011 0111
X	1110 0111	1011 1000
Y	1110 1000	1011 1001
Z	1110 1001	1011 1010

Figure 3-9

Internal character codes for a computer.

*EBCDIC = Extended Binary Coded Decimal Interchange Code.

†ASCII = American Standard Code for Information Interchange.

into a related unit is called a *database*. The payroll file, accounts receivable file, accounts payable file, and product inventory file together might constitute a corporate accounting database. A data hierarchy from bits to database is shown in Figure 3-10.

Figure 3-10

A data hierarchy.

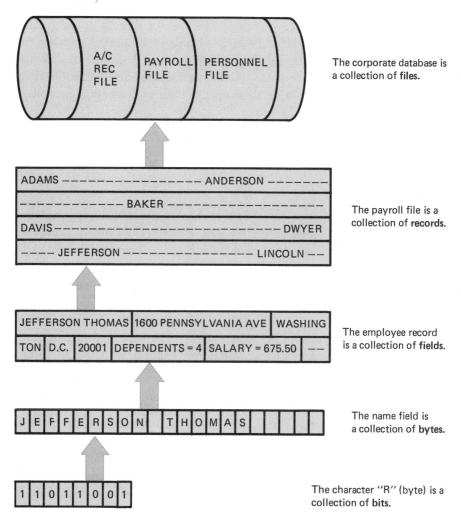

The corporate database is a collection of **files.**

The payroll file is a collection of **records.**

The employee record is a collection of **fields.**

The name field is a collection of **bytes.**

The character "R" (byte) is a collection of **bits.**

DATA STORAGE

In discussing data storage, it is important to differentiate between on-line and off-line storage *On-line* storage is that which is directly connected to the

CPU. Examples of this kind of storage include magnetic tapes and magnetic disks which are mounted on tape and disk drives and are in turn directly connected to the CPU.

Off-line storage is storage which is *not* directly connected to the CPU. Examples of this kind of storage include such items as punched cards as well as magnetic tapes and disks which are stored in tape or disk libraries. For example, large computer systems such as the Social Security Administration's database store data on thousands of reels of magnetic tape housed in large, protected off-line facilities.

PRIMARY STORAGE

As mentioned earlier in this chapter, primary storage or main memory is part of the central processing unit. Examples of primary storage methods are core memory, semiconductor storage, charged-coupled device (CCD) memory, and bubble memory.

Core memory utilizes a core which is a tiny, ring-shaped piece of magnetic material in which one bit of information is stored by magnetizing the core in a particular direction (Figure 3-11). Many thousands or millions of these magnetic cores are strung on fine wires to form *core planes*, which are then combined to represent an alphabetic or numeric character. Although cores have been extensively used in large computers in the past, other technologies are now replacing core memory.

Semiconductor storage (Figure 3-12) combines thousands of miniature components on a tiny silicon chip. Metal oxide semiconductor (MOS) is the major technology used in semiconductor memories. Semiconductor storage devices are called integrated circuits (IC), since all the necessary storage components are integrated on a single chip. When integrated circuits were developed in the 1960s, they had only a few electronic circuits on each chip. In the 1970s large-scale-integration (LSI) technology allowed several hundred circuits to be placed on a tiny chip. Today's chip densities are increasing even more with very-large-scale-integration (VLSI), where several hundred thousand electronic circuits are located on each chip.

Charged-coupled device (CCD) memory is a type of semiconductor storage that also uses silicon chips. The chips have electrical charges on small metal squares etched at each storage location. Small electrical charges are moved

Figure 3-11

In core memory, magnetic cores are organized in planes to represent characters.

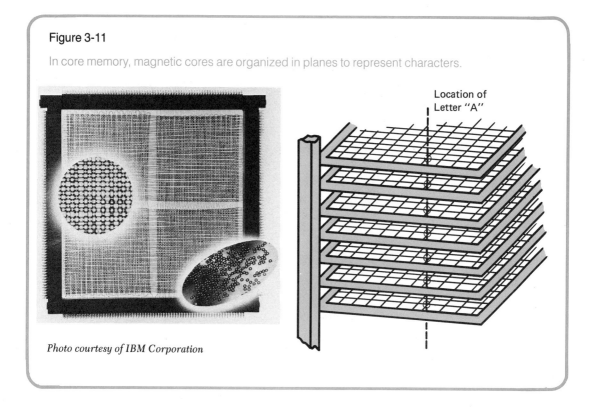

Photo courtesy of IBM Corporation

along lines of storage cells, much like the clothing on the automatic racks in a dry-cleaning establishment. As the charges pass by a station, they can be read. While CCD memory has a relatively fast transfer speed, its main disadvantage is that it is *volatile*. This means that if the electrical current is shut off, the data are lost and must be restored each time the computer device is used.

Another type of computer memory device is the magnetic bubble, or *bubble memory*. Magnetic bubbles are very small (about a micron wide, less than one-sixteenth the diameter of a human hair). Unlike data stored on CCD memory, the data are not lost if power is removed. Therefore, bubble memory is *non-volatile*, as is core memory. Basically, a bubble is a magnetic domain that exists within a thin magnetic film. Bubbles are moved around between small magnetic bars in a magnetic field (Figure 3-13). Depending on the position of the bubble, it represents either a binary "1" or a "0." Since bubbles are much

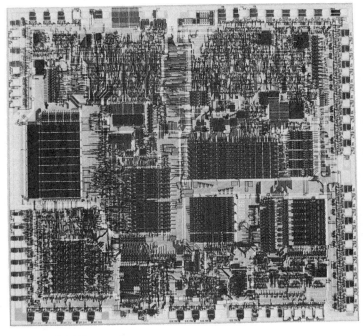

Figure 3-12

This single chip contains a
16-bit CPU and all the
other functions of a
computer.

Courtesy Intel Corporation

smaller than magnetic cores, data can be stored in a smaller area. Bell Labs has
developed a bubble chip that can store more than eight million bits of information on a one-inch square. In the future, it will be possible to store the contents
of an entire encyclopedia on a single chip. However, because of their relatively
high cost, bubble memories are not widely used for computer memory. Instead
they are used in special-application devices such as telephone circuits that store
data for voice-synthesized "operators."

By the late 1980s, computer scientists envision tiny computers refrigerated
inside tanks of liquid helium. These computers will operate a hundred times
faster than today's machines. This new technology is known as the superconducting computer or *Josephson junction* computer, based on an electronic
junction invented by Brian Josephson. Josephson shared a Nobel prize as a
graduate student at Cambridge University in England for his definition of a

Figure 3-13

A magnetic bubble memory board with up to 512 kilobytes of non-volatile storage on a 6¾-by 12-inch board.

Courtesy Intel Corporation

physical phenomenon called electron tunneling at cryogenic operating temperatures (close to absolute zero, approximately −460 °F). Research shows that, at this temperature, certain metals lose their electrical resistance and allow electrons to travel faster in a smaller space with little heat dissipation. Perhaps fast Josephson logic circuits will be the technology used in future business computers. A comparison of the different types of memory technology for on-line storage is made in Figure 3-14.

An additional point concerning access to primary storage should be noted here. Primary storage is *random access memory* (RAM) storage. That is, any one

Figure 3-14

Computer memory technology.

	Storage Method	Advantage	Disadvantage
Core	Arrays of magnetized cores, strung on fine wires	Non-volatile	Expensive (per bit)
Semiconductor	Circuitry "printed" on silicon chip	Smaller, faster than core Cost effective	Volatile (vulnerable to power failure)
Charged-coupled	Electrical charges on semiconductor chip	Transfer speed	Volatile Slower access
Bubble	Tiny cylindrical domains in a thin film	Density Easy to manufacture Non-volatile	Slower access
Josephson junction	Electronic switches using superconductivity at very low temperatures	Capacity Speed	Lack of experience with actual usage

location in main memory can be accessed without having to work sequentially through hundreds or even thousands of memory locations called *addresses*. Each address has its own identification number differentiating each memory location (Figure 3-15). Each memory location contains either an element of data or an instruction and can be referenced by the computer using its specific address. Note the memory locations in Figure 3-15 that contain data and those that contain instructions.

Part of the CPU may also contain *read-only memory* (ROM). This type of memory is integrated into the circuitry of the computer and cannot be altered without altering the computer circuitry. For example, it is possible with ROM to program specific instructions into the computer for applications such as calculating square roots or trigonometric functions. Such functions are automatically available for use by the programmer and do not need to be rewritten each time they are used. *Programmable read-only memory* (PROM) is a form of ROM where the manufacturer of the computer builds entire programs into the computer circuitry. These programs can be altered, either by the manufacturer or the user, as requirements dictate.

Figure 3-15

Memory addresses and the contents of memory. Program instructions are stored in addresses 101 to 104, and data are stored in addresses 111 to 113.

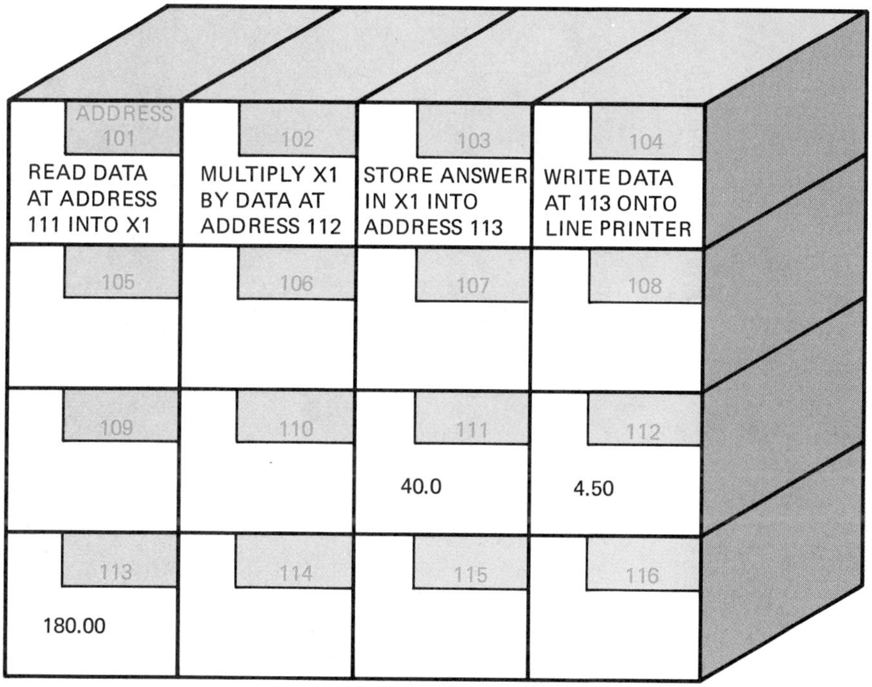

All the forms of memory discussed in this section offer a great deal of versatility to the user of a computer system. However, primary storage memory (Figure 3-16) is an expensive component of computer systems. Thus, it is necessary for computer users to employ other types of storage to hold large amounts of data in a less expensive and yet accessible manner. Secondary storage devices were created with this need in mind.

Figure 3-16

Today's memory systems are found on boards that can be "plugged in" on various computer systems.

Control Data

SECONDARY STORAGE

Secondary storage, or auxiliary storage, can take many forms, which have traditionally included punched cards, paper tape, magnetic tape, magnetic disk, and magnetic drum. Punched cards and paper tape were used for auxiliary storage in early computers. In recent times, the use of magnetic tape and disk has proliferated (Figure 3-17). Newer forms of secondary storage include floppy disks, Winchester disks, videodiscs, and mass storage devices.

Figure 3-17

Popular secondary storage media are magnetic tape and magnetic disk.

Photo top left, Wabash Tape Corporation; top right and bottom left, BASF Systems Corporation; bottom right, Verbatim Corporation

Punched Cards

Punched cards are one of the oldest and most familiar forms of data storage. Referred to as IBM cards, 80-column cards, or data cards, they were the symbol of EDP for much of the populace with the famous (or infamous) slogan "Do not fold, spindle, or mutilate." The standard punched card is illustrated in Figure 3-18. Note that there is room on a card for 80 characters (80 vertical columns). A *card field* is a group of consecutive columns reserved for a specific unit of information. Thus a 9-digit social security number would require a 9-column field.

The code used to represent characters is called the Hollerith code (remember Herman Hollerith and the 1890 U.S. census?). There are 12 rows on the standard punched card and a unique combination of 1, 2, or 3 punches represents a letter, number, or symbol. A 96-column card, introduced by IBM for its System/3 computer in 1969, utilizes the binary coded decimal (BCD) code instead of the Hollerith code. While more compact and efficient than the standard 80-column card, the 96-column card has not been adopted by other computer equipment manufacturers.

Figure 3-18

The Hollerith code uses one, two, or three punches to represent a character.

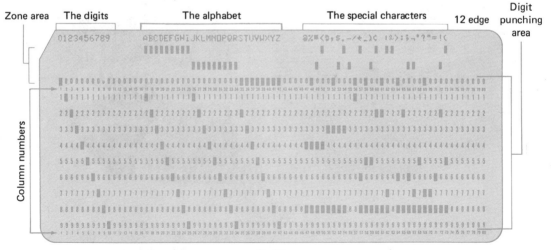

9 edge

Punched-card storage has the following advantages (compared to electronic media):

— Punched cards can be read by people as well as by machines.
— Physical rearrangement of cards is easily accomplished.
— Each card can represent a *unit record* (complete record of an event or transaction).
— Cards are inexpensive for low volumes of data storage.
— Punched cards can be used as the original document, such as a time card or invoice.

Disadvantages of punched cards include the following:

— Reading speeds are slow.
— Most business records are longer than 80 characters.
— Once punched, cards cannot be changed.
— Punched-card storage is bulky for large volumes of data.
— Damaged cards cannot be used ("Do not fold, spindle, or mutilate").

Punched Paper Tape

Punched paper tape is a continuous strip of paper used to store data in much the same manner as punched cards. The paper tape is approximately one inch wide and can have either six or eight channels. Eight-channel paper tape is based on the ASCII code (Figure 3-19). Paper tape is often punched as a by-product of other business machines such as cash registers and typewriters. This storage medium is less expensive and more compact than punched cards. Since it is a continuous medium, however, it is difficult to reinsert omitted data or to make corrections.

Magnetic Tapes

Magnetic tapes are a particularly popular form of secondary storage because of their high *data density* (the number of bytes of information per inch of tape) and their convenience in handling. Although tape densities can exceed 5,000 bytes of information per inch of magnetic tape, in most computer installations 800 or 1,600 bytes per inch (BPI) are standard. Magnetic tapes are approximately one-half inch wide and are made of Mylar-based plastic film which can be magnetized. Data are stored on a magnetic tape by running the tape over an

Figure 3-19

Eight-channel punched paper tape code.

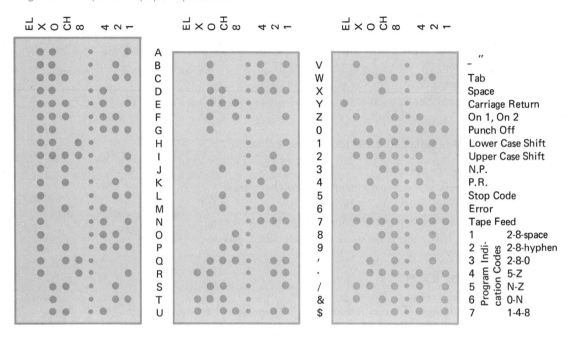

electromagnet called a *read/write head* (Figure 3-20) which magnetizes small spots on the tape. "Reading" means sensing what is already there; "writing" means creating new data on the tape.

Magnetic tapes typically have seven or nine tracks. Each track is a parallel row of magnetized spots on the tape (Figure 3-21). Seven-track tapes store information as bytes of information, where each byte consists of a six-bit code and a one-bit parity bit. Nine-track tapes use an eight-bit code and a parity bit.

The *parity bit* is a useful, automatic device to guarantee data accuracy in a computer system. Put simply, a parity bit works to ensure that errors in reading, writing, and transmission of data are detected. In an odd-parity tape unit, an odd number of 1's must be present in any byte; an even-parity tape unit must have an even number of 1's in any byte. Thus, if a speck of dust has scratched off a magnetic spot or the read/write head has made an error in printing the original byte of information, odd or even parity would not be

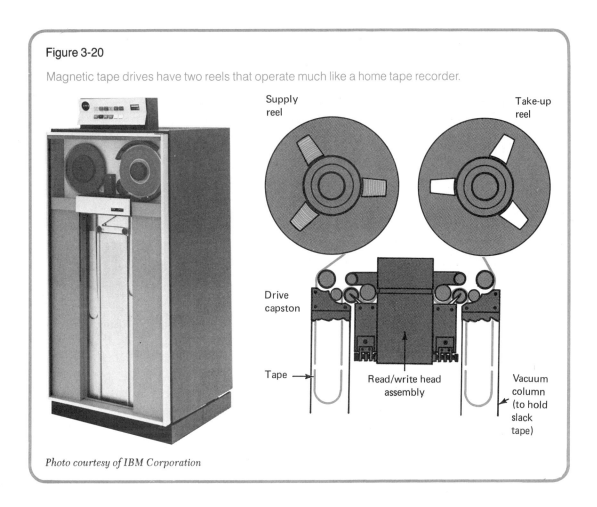

Figure 3-20

Magnetic tape drives have two reels that operate much like a home tape recorder.

Supply reel

Take-up reel

Drive capston

Tape →

Read/write head assembly

Vacuum column (to hold slack tape)

Photo courtesy of IBM Corporation

maintained. Upon reading the information from the magnetic tape, the computer would detect the incorrect parity. An error message would be written and the computer operator or a systems engineer would locate the error and rebuild the data file stored on the magnetic tape.

When reading and writing records of short length, a frequently employed technique is to group or *block* the records. Without blocking, the tape drive must constantly stop and start, stop and start, as each separate record is processed. Blocking, on the other hand, enables a large number of records to

Figure 3-21

Seven-track magnetic tape uses binary-coded data representation.

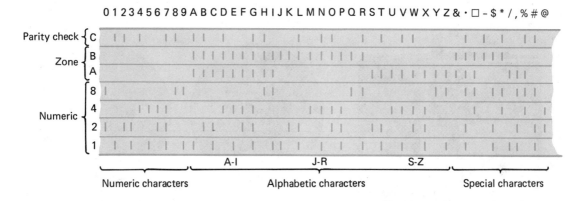

be read or written in one operation, thereby reducing processing time. Likewise, blocking can reduce wasted space on the tape. Note that when the blocking technique is not used, each record is separated by an *interrecord gap* (IRG) (Figure 3-22a). When reading data from a tape, the tape stops whenever an IRG is detected. No data can be stored on an IRG, so the space taken up by an IRG is essentially wasted space. When blocking is used, fewer gaps are required and the interrecord gap becomes an *interblock gap* (IBG) (Figure 3-22b).

Magnetic tape has several advantages:

— Magnetic tape provides relatively low-cost storage, as well as backup for disks.
— Magnetic tape provides for high-speed transfer of data to and from the CPU.
— Magnetic tapes can be erased and thus reused.
— Magnetic tapes provide high-density storage.

There are, however, some disadvantages:

— When retrieving information from or updating a tape, the entire tape must be read sequentially, which results in slow access time.
— Magnetic tape is particularly sensitive to distortion by environmental influences such as dust, humidity, and temperature variations.

Figure 3-22

"Blocking" records together allows more records to be stored on magnetic tape.

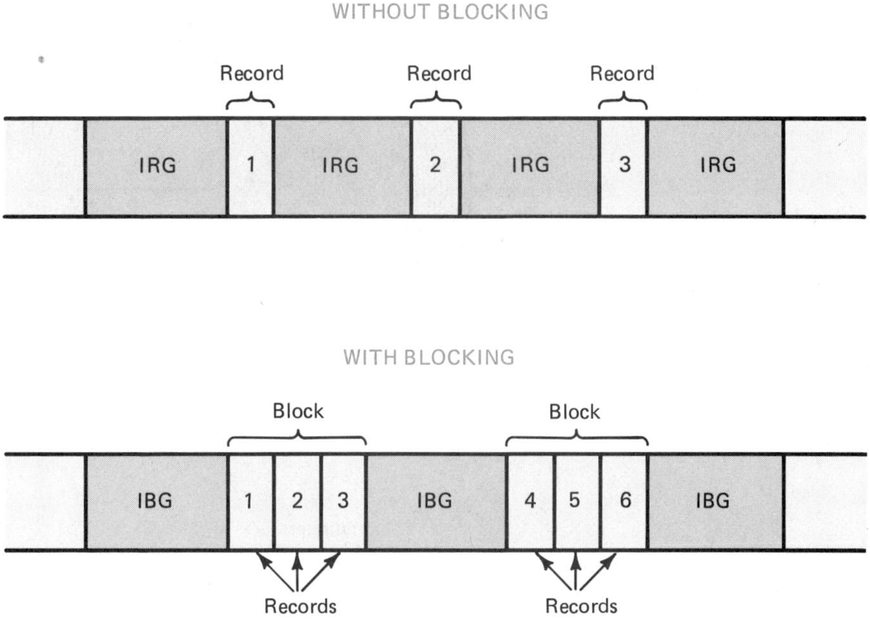

WITHOUT BLOCKING

	Record		Record		Record	
IRG	1	IRG	2	IRG	3	IRG

WITH BLOCKING

	Block				Block			
IBG	1	2	3	IBG	4	5	6	IBG

Records   Records

Magnetic Disks

Magnetic disks are metal disks coated with ferrous oxide, an easily magnetizable material. Magnetic disks allow for random access of information and overcome the slow access time commonly found in tape files.

The disks, which are usually grouped together into a *disk pack*, are separated by small air spaces to allow access for read/write heads. Each disk has approximately 200 *tracks* on which information is stored. These tracks are numbered from 0 to 199 starting with the outside perimeter of the disk. Tracks of the same number on all adjacent disks are referred to as a *cylinder* of that disk (Figure 3-23).

The disk pack is mounted on a magnetic disk drive which rotates the disk at speeds up to 1,000 revolutions per second. There are some disk drives in which the disks are permanently mounted. Many disk drives, however, allow disk packs to be removed, facilitating the storage of infrequently used data.

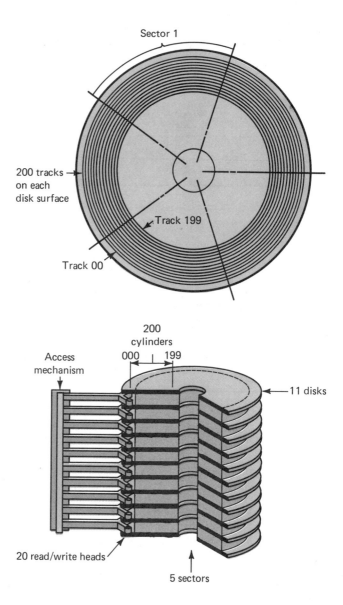

Figure 3-23

Magnetic disks store data on cylinders that have sectors and tracks.

Because of the more sophisticated hardware and software required to access information directly, the absolute cost of magnetic disk hardware is greater than that of magnetic tape hardware. However, for those applications requiring direct access to information, disk storage is likely to be more cost effective than magnetic tape, which must be accessed sequentially.

Floppy Disks

The *floppy disk*, also called a *flexible disk* or *diskette*, is also used to store programs and data (Figure 3-24). Made of plastic, the floppy disk is most often used with minicomputers and microcomputers. As with magnetic disks, data on

Figure 3-24

Typical floppy disk.

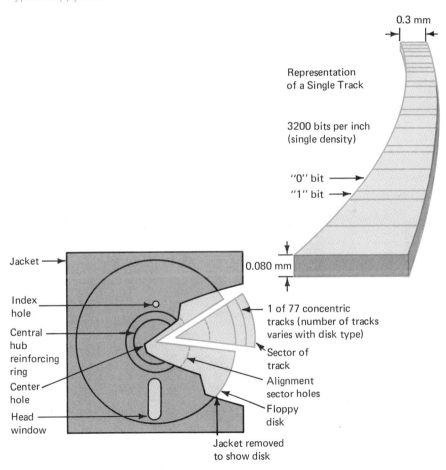

Jacket removed
to show disk

Reprinted from the December 1981 issue of MODERN OFFICE PROCEDURES and copyrighted 1981 by Penton/IPC subsidiary of Pittway Corporation

a floppy disk are stored in concentric circles called tracks. Each track is further divided into sectors. A *sector* is the amount of information that can be read or written in a single operation.

Winchester Disks and Videodiscs

Two newer types of secondary storage are increasingly used. These technologies are Winchester disks and videodiscs.

Winchester disks are sealed modules that contain both the disk and a read/write head mechanism (Figure 3-25). Since the package is sealed, little maintenance is required. In addition, they eliminate some technical problems that have been encountered with magnetic disks when read/write heads stopped and interfered with recording ability.

Winchester disk drive heads routinely "fly" above the spinning disks at speeds of 112 miles per hour, only 0.36 micron away from the disk surface. Figure 3-26 illustrates why the Winchester disk drive must be sealed. Winchester drives are available for small office computers and can even be hooked up to personal computers.

Figure 3-25

Winchester disk drive.

Photo courtesy of Hewlett-Packard Company

Figure 3-26

This drawing shows why Winchester disk assemblies must operate under sealed, clean-room conditions: even a particle of smoke dwarfs the height at which the read/write head "flies" over the spinning disks.

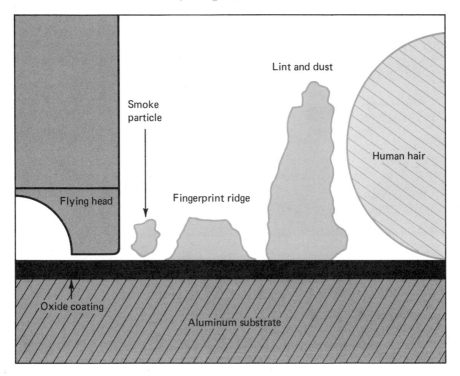

A problem that Winchester technology shares with all other forms of on-line memory is the lack of a secure backup system. How can a user protect against loss of data from disk malfunction (called "head crashes"), human error, or physical catastrophes such as fire? Today, backup systems for Winchester disk storage use floppy disks to copy needed data.

Videodiscs are a technology that may be the future revolution in information storage. A videodisc system is like a visual record player; when attached to a TV set, it can play back video and audio output ranging from movies to technical data (Figure 3-27). The principal EDP drawback of videodiscs is that they have playback capability only and cannot have new data written on them.

Figure 3-27

Videodisc and professional video recorder with playback system.

Photo at left, 3M; right, Ampex

Major computer manufacturers in the U.S. and Japan are experimenting with videodisc systems for data storage in the business office. Relatively high costs and difficulty in copying discs are causing business users to take a "wait and see" attitude regarding videodisc technology.

Mass Storage

Another type of storage generally used in very large organizations is called *mass storage*. Mass storage is an auxiliary type of storage that typically uses cartridges with data stored on short strips of magnetic tape. Control Data Corporation's mass storage system provides up to 16 billion bytes of on-line storage, while IBM's 3850 can provide up to 472 billion bytes of storage in its honeycomb arrangement of data cartridges (Figure 3-28). While access times are much slower than those of primary storage or magnetic disk storage, mass storage may be more cost effective for storing large volumes of data.

Figure 3-28

A mass storage device. Each cartridge in the honeycomb holds up to 50 million characters.

Photo courtesy of IBM Corporation

OPERATING SYSTEM SOFTWARE

Our discussion thus far has centered on the hardware components of the computer system. Major software components are needed to integrate and facilitate the processing of data.

A major integrating factor is the *operating system*. An operating system is a *software package* (group of related programs) that oversees and manages the resources of a computer system. The operating system indicates to the CPU how programs are to be read in, how they are to be processed, and what kind of output is required once processing is complete. A malfunction in the operating system software is sufficient to cause the system to crash (become inoperable).

The operating system consists of three types of programs: control programs, utility programs, and processing programs (Figure 3-29).

Control programs control the execution and flow of jobs throughout the computer system. The control programs handle all types of scheduling and

Figure 3-29

Operating systems are important software in a computer system.

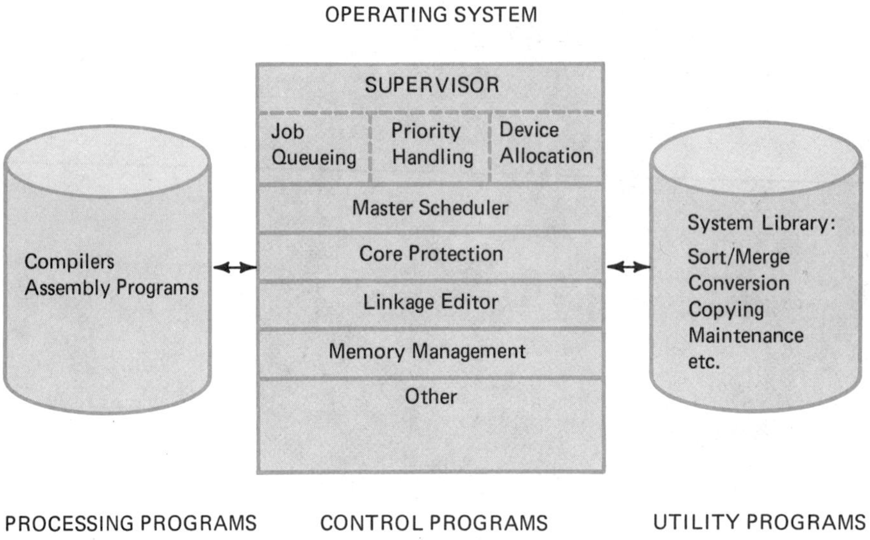

OPERATING SYSTEM

	SUPERVISOR	
Job Queueing	Priority Handling	Device Allocation
Master Scheduler		
Core Protection		
Linkage Editor		
Memory Management		
Other		

Compilers
Assembly Programs

System Library:
Sort/Merge
Conversion
Copying
Maintenance
etc.

PROCESSING PROGRAMS   CONTROL PROGRAMS   UTILITY PROGRAMS

accounting such as charging the appropriate users for the amount of computer resources they have used. The most important control program is called the *supervisor,* or the executive routine. This particular program controls the order in which programs are loaded and executed. Other control programs carry out the scheduling activities, protect the core memory, and provide the link for utility programs.

Utility programs perform frequently done tasks, thus relieving the programmer of the necessity of writing a new program each time such a task is performed. One example of a utility program would be a program which copies the contents of one magnetic tape onto another magnetic tape. This type of copy program fulfills a very important role. If the first tape were somehow damaged or destroyed, the second tape would act as a backup to ensure that vital information for the company would not be lost. This copying function is only one example of the operating system's utility programs.

Processing programs also perform commonly required functions. Examples include compilers, which are programs that translate high-level languages into machine language, and assembly programs, which translate assembly-language programs into machine language.

High-level languages are languages such as FORTRAN, COBOL, PL/1, BASIC, and PASCAL. These languages are easier to use than assembly or machine languages because of their similarity either to English or to the problem for which they are generally applied. *Assembly languages* are intermediate-level languages. They are not nearly as close to English as the high-level languages, yet they are less complex and difficult to use than machine languages are. Assembly languages use mnemonics, recognizable abbreviations of instructions. For example, "MOV A, B" instructs the control unit to move the contents of Register B to Register A. *Machine languages* consist of the zeros and ones that are directly amenable to the circuitry of the computer system. The machine-language instruction 11000000 00000001 would also move the contents of Register B to Register A.

VIRTUAL STORAGE

Virtual storage is a storage method which greatly expands the amount of computer memory available to a programmer. Normally, a professional programmer would be limited to about one million bytes (one megabyte) of memory. While this may seem like a large amount, it is actually quite small in the computer realm.

To overcome this problem, those parts of a program which are not needed immediately for processing are kept in secondary storage until they are needed. In other words, the virtual storage system automatically assigns any memory that would overflow main memory to an associated disk storage area. An on-line (directly connected to the CPU) disk system is automatically read, and the needed portion of the overflowed data is brought into main memory to be processed. This gives the illusion that main memory is unlimited.

Virtual storage uses a fixed-size portion of memory called a *page* to shuffle between primary and secondary storage. Figure 3-30 illustrates how one megabyte of real memory can be expanded to five megabytes of usable memory by paging. Another type of virtual storage utilizes a variable-size portion of memory called a *segment*. Virtual storage is found on many large-scale computer systems and even some minicomputers.

Figure 3-30

Virtual storage transfers pages from secondary storage to main memory for execution.

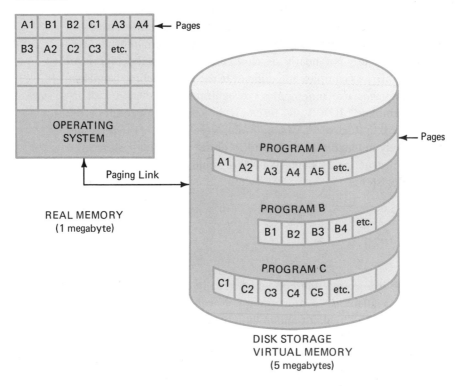

REAL MEMORY
(1 megabyte)

DISK STORAGE
VIRTUAL MEMORY
(5 megabytes)

MULTIPROGRAMMING AND MULTIPROCESSING

Both multiprogramming and multiprocessing attempt to use the resources of the computer system more efficiently. While these concepts are different, the distinction between them is often confused.

With *multiprogramming,* the CPU takes one instruction at a time from one of the many programs in main memory or from the operating system and executes that particular instruction (Figure 3-31). For example, assume a "READ" instruction is executed by the CPU. While this operation is being performed, the CPU can go on to another instruction from another program. The operating system keeps track of which instructions are being executed and

MULTIPROGRAMMING

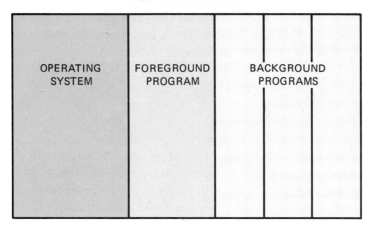

Figure 3-31

Under multiprogramming, main memory contains several programs with the CPU switching from one program to another.

from which programs. Note that while the programs are seemingly run simultaneously, in reality only one instruction is being performed at any one time by the CPU. Therefore, execution is not simultaneous.

Multiprocessing, on the other hand, is a technique which employs several processors to execute instructions simultaneously from the various programs residing in main memory (Figure 3-32). Linking several small computers to a

MULTIPROCESSING

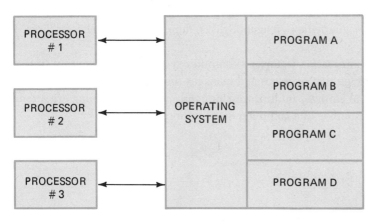

Figure 3-32

Under multiprocessing, several processors are capable of program execution.

larger mainframe is also referred to as multiprocessing. The important distinction to note is that multiprogramming uses only one processor, while multiprocessing uses more than one processor. Both techniques have substantially increased the operating capability of computer systems.

SUMMARY

The computer is a system which works to process data and provide information. A typical computer system includes input, output, storage, and the central processing unit (CPU). The CPU is an important component of the computer system that contains the control unit, the arithmetic-logic unit, and main memory.

Computers do not possess independent thought but instead execute stored programs written by computer professionals. These programs provide detailed instructions which the computer follows in order to perform data processing tasks.

Data are organized within a computer in the form of a code which utilizes 1's and 0's. These 1's and 0's are called binary digits or bits. Data are further organized into bytes, fields, records, files, and databases.

Data storage is accomplished in a variety of ways, both as part of the CPU (primary storage), and also as secondary (auxiliary) storage. Primary storage may include core memory, semiconductor memory, charged-coupled device memory, and bubble memory. Primary storage can also be random access memory (RAM), read-only memory (ROM), and programmable read-only memory (PROM). Forms of secondary storage include punched cards, paper tape, magnetic tape, magnetic disks, floppy disks, Winchester disks, and videodiscs.

A major integrating factor of a computer system is the operating system, a software package that oversees and manages the computer system's resources. Finally, virtual storage, multiprocessing, and multiprogramming are attempts to use the resources of a computer system more efficiently.

TERMS

User friendly

Computer system

Central processing unit

Mainframe

Control unit

Arithmetic-logic unit

Registers

Main memory

Primary storage

Stored program

Programmer

Binary digit

Bit

Bistable

Byte

Character

Field

Record

File

Database

On-line

Off-line

Core memory

Core plane

Semiconductor

Charged-coupled device

Volatile

Bubble memory

Non-volatile

Josephson junction

Random access memory

Address

Read-only memory

Programmable read-only memory

Secondary storage

Punched cards

Card field

Unit record

Punched paper tape

Magnetic tape

Data density

Read/write head

Parity bit

Block

Interrecord gap

Interblock gap

Magnetic disk

Disk pack

Track

Cylinder

Floppy disk

Flexible disk

Diskette

Sector

Winchester disk

Videodisc

Mass storage

Operating system

Software package

Control program

Supervisor

Utility program

Processing program

High-level languages

Assembly languages

Machine languages

Virtual storage

Page

Segment

Multiprogramming

Multiprocessing

QUESTIONS

1. Why is the CPU considered to be the most important component of the computer system?
2. What is main memory?
3. What are the main features of the stored program concept?
4. Explain the difference between bits, bytes, fields, records, files, and databases.
5. What is bubble memory?
6. What is random access memory?
7. What is the difference between read-only memory and programmable read-only memory?
8. Explain the difference between primary and secondary stoarge.
9. What are the advantages and disadvantages of punched cards? magnetic tapes?
10. Which two newer types of secondary storage may dominate in the future? Why?
11. What are the functions of control programs? utility programs? processing programs?
12. Explain the characteristics of high-level languages, assembly languages, and machine languages.
13. How does virtual storage expand the amount of memory available to a programmer?
14. How do multiprogramming and multiprocessing make more efficient use of the computer system?

ARTICLE

Tinier Than a Nerve Fiber, Faster Than a Silicon Chip

In 1962, Brian Josephson, a brilliant British graduate student, discovered a principle of super-conductivity that could be used to build an ultra-fast, ultra-powerful computer, far beyond the reach of existing semiconductor technology. Now, 18 years later, an American corporation may become the first manufacturer to put the "Josephson junction" into a real computer.

Using an electron beam like an etching tool to deposit the metal lines that form a microscopic electric circuit, technologists at the International Business Machines Corporation have assembled a Josephson-effect computer switch whose wires, the company says, are the thinnest ever devised by man. The wires, made of niobium metal, are said to be only one-500,000th of an inch wide—the equivalent of 100-200 atomic diameters, thinner than a human nerve fiber.

Dr. Josephson's discovery at Cambridge University, for which he shared the 1973 Nobel Prize in Physics, was probably the most important theoretical breakthrough for computer technology since the discovery of semiconductors. It will permit computer switching speeds between 10 and 100 times faster than those now possible with silicon-based chips. This means that vastly more data can be handled faster in smaller spaces.

Quantum Mechanics Applied

But the construction of computers based on Josephson junctions will require new manufacturing techniques as well as built-in refrigerators to chill computer components to about minus 455° Fahrenheit, only some 4° above absolute zero. The large development investment required has delayed commercial application of the Josephson junction for nearly two decades.

The strange substances that intrigued Dr. Josephson are called superconductors. They are metal-like materials that normally conduct electricity poorly, but which can be made into superconductors by chilling with liquid helium to a temperature near the absolute zero. In a superconducting state, a material offers practically no resistance to electricity and loses practically no energy through heat or other types of radiation.

Applying principles of quantum mechanics to analyze the equations of superconductivity, Dr. Josephson predicted

continued

that if superconductors were sandwiched between two electrodes and chilled with liquid helium, the entire sandwich would be superconducting. The prediction also said that if a magnetic field were applied, the superconductivity of the sandwich would instantly disappear, but that removal of the magnetic field would instantly restore it. In other words, the Josephson superconducting sandwich (junction) could be switched on or off by a magnetic field.

The prediction by the young theorist was soon confirmed by experiments.

Since the basic element in all computers is an on-off switch, the faster such a switch can operate, the better the computer will be. The great speed with which superconductivity in a Josephson chip could be switched on or off clearly recommended it as a replacement for existing silicon-based chips.

The speed of computer circuits has been hitherto limited not only by the speed of their switches but also by the lengths of their wiring. If conventional computer components are assembled too close together, heat builds up faster than it can be removed, and the computer quickly breaks down. Components therefore are kept far enough apart to allow efficient cooling, but the disadvantage is that their connecting wires must be lengthened. Although electronic signals travel along these wires at nearly the speed of light, the time needed to make the trip slows down computation drastically.

In a superconducting Josephson computer chilled with liquid helium, the heat problem is largely eliminated, and components can be moved very close together, shortening connections and speeding up electronic signals.

I.B.M. predicts that its first superconducting, Josephson-effect computer will be ready in 1984.

The discoverer himself, Brian Josephson, left the field of physics to study parapsychology.

DISCUSSION QUESTIONS

1. In what way are Josephson junctions superior to silicon chips?
2. What economic forces counter the use of this new technology?

APPLICATION

Disk Switch May Save Hospital Megabucks

MEMPHIS, Tenn. — Baptist Memorial Hospital here, the largest private hospital in the U.S., estimates it will save at least $1 million in computer room relocation costs by replacing removable disk drives with Winchesters.

Ron Scoggins, the hospital's director of data processing, was faced with the choice of relocating the computer room or finding more compact disk space than was required for its 60 assorted Digital Equipment Corp. removable pack disk drives and 22 controllers.

"Even though our data processing is distributed and runs on different machines, it is physically located in the same computer room," Scoggins explained. "This gives us environmental and operational control, but space is at a premium and we have outgrown it," he continued. The computer room has about 1,750 square feet of space.

The hospital is the city's largest employer and admits 65,000 patients annually.

Winchesters appeared to be the perfect answer, Scoggins said, because they doubled the amount of usable computer room space, were more reliable than the installed disk systems and decreased maintenance costs. The Winchester units are used in a four-per-cabinet "rack and stack" arrangement. About 40 Winchester units were installed.

The hospital chose 160M-byte Winchester disk systems made by System Industries, Inc., of Sunnyvale, California. System Industries gave the hospital a trade-in allowance on the old drives. Since the hospital's system is completely on-line, there was no need for removable media.

Energy savings were an added benefit of converting to Winchesters because they give off less heat. When the current equipment is replaced, Scoggins predicted he would be able to take an air conditioner off-line.

Handled In-House

The hospital's DP needs are handled totally in-house. The system handles every facet of the hospital's operation, including admissions, laboratory tests, pharmacy, radiology and financial operations. To do this, Baptist Memorial uses six DEC PDP-11/70s, two PDP-11/60s and four PDP-11/44s.

Scoggins estimated uptime for these systems, which run 24 hours per day, seven days per week, at 98.9 percent.

continued

The hospital's DP operation also supports a combination of 400 terminals and printers placed throughout the facility, and peripherals are constantly being added.

In analyzing the downtime, Scoggins said he found the bulk of it resulted from electromechanical devices, the disks in particular.

"We figured some form of Winchester technology could cut downtime and eliminate the need for a hardware back-up facility," Scoggins said. With the Winchesters, Scoggins expects a total system uptime of about 99.6 percent.

DISCUSSION QUESTIONS

1. What benefits other than cost savings were achieved by using Winchester disks?
2. How significant is it that the system uptime was increased from 98.9% to 99.6%?

CHAPTER 4

INPUT/OUTPUT

CHAPTER OBJECTIVES

In this chapter you will learn:

1. The different types of input/output hardware—their uses, advantages, and disadvantages.
2. The difference between visual display terminals and hard copy.
3. Why terminals are dumb or smart.
4. About the growth of graphics and POS terminals.
5. About the I/O capability of punched cards and paper tape.
6. How key-station input is used for magnetic media.
7. The types and capabilities of impact and nonimpact printers.
8. About the special, growing importance of new I/O technology.

DEFINING INPUT AND OUTPUT

A computer without input/output is like a person without senses. Through use of our senses, we receive input from our environment, process that input, and output some response. The computer functions in a similar manner. In order for a computer to be useful, there must be some way to put programs and data into the computer for processing and to get results out. In other words, there must be some way to communicate with the computer. Input/output (I/O) hardware devices have been developed for that purpose. *Input* devices feed information or data into the computer; *output* devices are used to retrieve information from computer memory for human use. The devices used to achieve computer input/output are varied. In this chapter, we will identify current I/O devices and examine their functions within the computer system.

TERMINAL INPUT/OUTPUT

Visual Display Terminal

One of the most widely used forms of input/output hardware is the *visual* (or video) *display terminal* (VDT). A visual display terminal is a device which has a keyboard for input and some type of visual display unit or screen for output. Perhaps the most popular visual display terminal used to enter data for processing is a *CRT* (cathode ray tube) *screen terminal*. A CRT displays output on a screen similar to that of a television set (see Figure 4-1). With a CRT it is possible to have *interactive processing*. This means that the user of the terminal communicates with the computer by typing commands, instructions, or data on a keyboard while the computer's responses are displayed on the CRT screen. The user who is developing a new program or who wishes to test a program is likely to use this type of terminal. Visual display terminals are most often used for the following applications:

— Interactive data entry and inquiry
— Program development
— As a system console device
— Word processing
— Intercompany communications
— Business graphics

Figure 4-1

A user at a video display terminal (VDT) enters questions by keyboard and receives responses on the cathode ray tube (CRT) screen.

Burroughs Corporation

There is controversy regarding the health hazards of using video display terminals, especially relating to low-level radiation, eyestrain, and muscular discomfort. Government and industry officials generally agree that VDT's are indeed safe and have no significant radiation hazard. However, the problems of eyestrain from VDT glare and muscular discomfort can be alleviated by using adjustable viewing screens and detachable keyboards (Figure 4-2).

Figure 4-2

A VDT designed for user comfort. The screen can be raised, tilted, and turned in all directions to improve the contrast between characters and background. The low profile of the keyboard minimizes muscular strain.

Tandberg Data

Hard-Copy Terminal

Another major type of computer terminal is the *hard-copy terminal*. Hard copy simply means that input and output are printed directly onto paper (Figure 4-3). As with the CRT screen terminal, the user of a hard-copy terminal types commands, instructions, or data on a keyboard. The computer's responses, as well as the information entered, are printed on paper, which gives

Figure 4-3

Printouts on computer paper are considered to be hard copy.

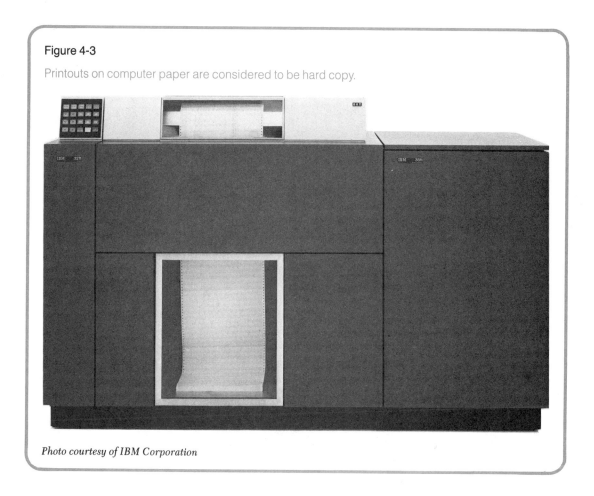

Photo courtesy of IBM Corporation

the user a permanent copy of both input and output. Permanent copies of computer output can also be acquired through the use of a printer. The various types of printers will be discussed later in this chapter.

Dumb, Smart, and Intelligent Terminals

Terminals may be grouped into three categories — dumb or conversational, smart or editing, and intelligent. A *dumb terminal* is one that is totally dependent, a slave to the computer. Dumb terminals do not process data or instructions. Instead, they act strictly as a means of communication between the user and the computer. The *smart terminal* has benefited from microprocessor technology and has an editing capability. This editing capability usually enables the users of smart terminals to:

— View two files at the same time on a split screen.
— Visually highlight text through such means as blinking or text underlining.
— Store several screens of data in a buffer.
— Transmit data in blocks rather than one character at a time.

Intelligent terminals are, in effect, small-capacity, stand-alone computers that may function independently or be incorporated into the main computer system (Figure 4-4). The term *stand-alone* is derived from the intelligent terminal's ability to function independently from the main computer.

Graphics Terminals

An exciting, relatively recent development has been the use of computer terminals that have a *graphics* capability. Increasingly, these terminals are capable of printing graphics in multiple colors, which adds an extra dimension

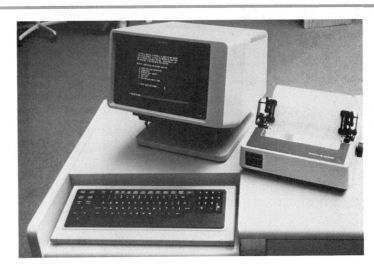

Figure 4-4

An intelligent terminal.

Sperry Univac

to their use (see Figure 4-5). Graphics means that patterns and shapes are used to display information, in contrast to the more traditional use of numbers and words. Scientists point out that pictures are processed by the right hemisphere of the brain and are then passed to the left hemisphere for further analysis. This increased involvement of the brain is why pictorial representation leads to greater understanding and retention of information.

One problem with the increased use of computers in business is data overload. For example, with data overload the manager is presented with so much written data that it often is difficult, if not impossible, to sort out the pertinent information in a short amount of time. Graphics addresses this problem through the presentation of information in the form of graphs, charts, or

Figure 4-5

A graphics terminal.

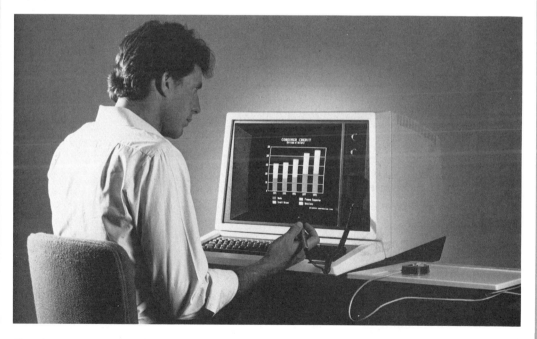

Ramtek

sales maps, making it quick and easy for the manager to note trends, exceptions, and other desired information (Figure 4-6). Increasingly, managers will also be able to run through a series of "What if?" scenarios (consideration of what might happen) which will change the graphical display instantaneously. This quick

Figure 4-6

Graphs provide pertinent information at a glance.

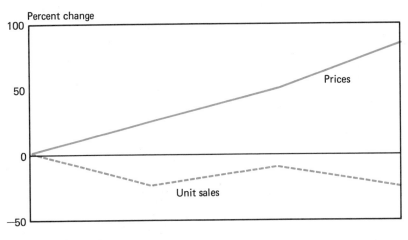

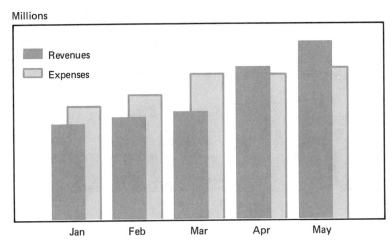

assimilation of information is a major advantage of graphics, and the resultant increase in productivity is justifying the cost of using graphics.

The use of graphics, however, is not limited to the office or board room. Another application of graphics is in the area of *computer-aided design/computer-aided manufacturing* (CAD/CAM). CAD/CAM utilizes computer systems with graphics capability for mechanical design and drafting, integrated circuit design, and other specific applications. A *digitizer* is often used to input data for graphical use (Figure 4-7).

Figure 4-7

A digitizer uses X-Y coordinates to input photographs, x-rays, maps, and engineering drawings.

 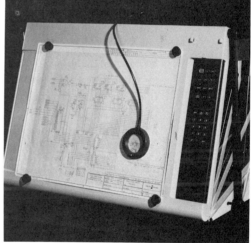

Photos courtesy of Hewlett-Packard Company

Point-of-Sale Terminals

Point-of-sale (POS) *terminals* are found directly at the point of sale. With POS terminals, information on the sale is input at the time the transaction takes place. The use of POS terminals is of great help to businesses such as retail stores and supermarkets. Through use of POS terminals, data can be entered directly into in-store minicomputers or into a main computer, and data such as sales records and inventory levels can be constantly updated. Thus, business efficiency and productivity are enhanced. POS terminals and some of their uses are shown in Figure 4-8.

PUNCHED CARDS

While being phased out in many businesses, the punched card and its related hardware are a form of input/output still found in many computer installations. Punched cards are typically used in *batch processing* situations. In batch processing, data are collected and input to the computer by groups.

Keypunch machines (Figure 4-9) are used to input information from a keyboard onto punched cards. Specifically, they punch holes into the cards using the standard Hollerith punched-card code system discussed in Chapter 3.

Sometimes special card machines called *verifiers* are used to check the holes in previously punched cards. To verify cards, a second keypunch operator punches the same information onto the card. If the information does not match the holes already punched in the card, the verifier informs the operator that a keypunch error has occurred.

Once cards are punched and verified, they can be input to a computer system through a *card reader* (Figure 4-10). Using metallic bristle brushes or photoelectric devices, card readers interpret or read the holes in punched cards and translate those holes into digital signals for the CPU of the computer. Card readers vary in cost and efficiency. A typical high-speed card reader can read 1500-2000 cards per minute.

A *card punch unit* is a special type of hardware device that translates output signals from a computer into the Hollerith code. These signals are subsequently punched onto cards which become machine-readable output.

PAPER TAPE

An older but still commonly used computer input/output medium is *paper tape* (Figure 4-11). Paper tape systems use a continuous reel of paper approximately one inch wide. Holes punched in the paper tape represent characters in

Figure 4-8

Typical POS applications: top left, tag scanner; top right, close-up of merchandise tag with OCR-A type letters and numbers; bottom left, bar code slot scanner; bottom right, POS terminal for cash transactions.

Photo bottom right, The Singer Company; all others, NCR Corporation

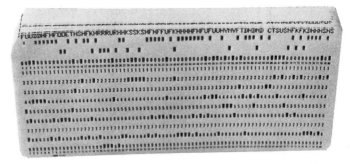

Figure 4-9

Card punch machine and
punched card.

Photos courtesy of IBM Corporation

Figure 4-10

This card reader effectively handles large decks of computer cards.

Photo courtesy of IBM Corporation

a way similar to magnetized spots on magnetic tapes. Paper tapes are divided into distinct *channels,* or horizontal rows, where holes are punched. Paper tapes come in five, six, seven, or eight channel versions.

Many businesses use paper tape as part of a telecommunications system. Telecommunications is broadly defined as the transfer of information over distance. A discussion of modern telecommunication techniques is covered in Chapter 14. Paper tape has several advantages over punched cards. For instance, more data can be stored in an equivalent amount of physical space. In addition, paper tape is less expensive and can be read into a computer system faster. A disadvantage of paper tape is that once information is generated, additions or deletions are difficult to make.

Figure 4-11

Paper tape is often a by-product of data capture. Note that the tape reel is being punched at the same time that the adding machine roll is being printed.

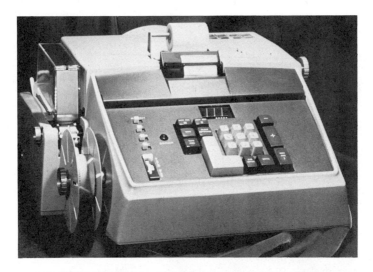

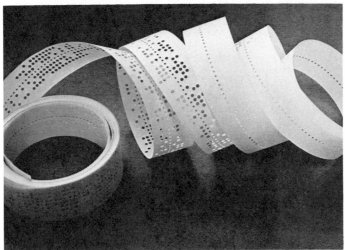

Top photo, TRW, Inc.

MAGNETIC TAPE AND MAGNETIC DISK

In Chapter 3, *magnetic tape* and *magnetic disk* were considered storage devices. They are also widely used as input and output media and have several advantages over punched cards. Data stored on tape or disk can be stored indefinitely, can be replaced with new data, can be input to the computer at much greater speeds than punched cards, and can store more data in much less space than cards. As you recall, magnetic tape and magnetic disk are electronic storage media (Figure 4-12). This is in direct contrast to punched cards and

Figure 4-12

Magnetic tapes and disks are the primary electronic storage methods used by business organizations.

Photo at left courtesy of Digital Equipment Corporation; right photo courtesy of IBM

paper tape, which require some type of mechanical system to convert information into digital signals which can be understood by the computer.

Magnetic tapes are typically used when the processing required for the data stored on the tapes is batch-oriented, such as sequential batch processing of an alphabetized or numerically ordered set of records. Magnetic disks, on the other hand, are often used when information needs to be accessed randomly, such as airline flight information regarding a particular flight.

Key Station Input Systems

An increasingly important form of computer input which utilizes magnetic tape and magnetic disks is the *key station input system*. There are two major types of key station input systems—key-to-tape and key-to-disk.

In a *key-to-tape system* (see Figure 4-13), a machine very similar to a keypunch machine is utilized to key information directly from *source documents* onto either a magnetic tape reel or a cassette. Source documents are those documents from which data are derived. For example, sales receipts and marketing questionnaires are typical source documents.

A CRT screen is utilized in this process to allow the key-to-tape operator to view the keyed data. With this visual capability, the operator can easily identify and re-enter any incorrectly keyed data. It is also possible to duplicate the keying operation a second time as a form of input verification. After the data are keyed onto the magnetic tape reel or cassette, they are run through a tape pooler. The tape pooler converts the data from the magnetic tape reel or cassette onto a standard computer magnetic tape.

A *key-to-disk system* (see Figure 4-14) is more sophisticated than the key-to-tape input system. A key-to-disk system can include several dozen input stations which operate under the command of a central processor, usually a minicomputer. The minicomputer is used to edit the data that are keyed in prior to storage on a disk. Data editing may discover errors made in the keying process or on the original source documents by comparing keyed data to data stored in the computer files.

One advantage of a key-to-disk system is that the minicomputer can be used to obtain additional information stemming from transactions. For example, a product number could be keyed in by an operator and the minicomputer could supply the associated product information such as product name, price, and availability to the disk data file. This capability means that key operators type in less information, which reduces the likelihood of human error. As the volume of data entered into computers continues to grow, the use of key-to-tape and key-to-disk systems is expected to increase.

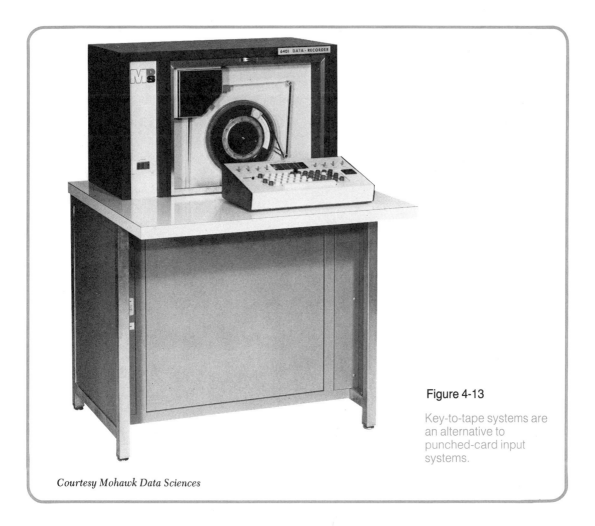

Figure 4-13

Key-to-tape systems are an alternative to punched-card input systems.

Courtesy Mohawk Data Sciences

Floppy Disks

In Chapter 3 *floppy disks* (flexible diskettes) were described as a storage medium. Floppy disks can also be used for economical data entry to larger computer systems. The advantages of data entry using floppy disks are similar to those cited earlier for magnetic tape and magnetic disk. These flexible diskettes are faster than cards, have greater storage capability, are readily changed or corrected, and are reusable (Figure 4-15).

Figure 4-14

This key-to-disk equipment has tape drives for backup capability.

Courtesy Mohawk Data Sciences

MISCELLANEOUS INPUT/OUTPUT

Magnetic Ink Character Recognition Systems

Magnetic ink character recognition (MICR) *systems* are utilized extensively by the U.S. banking industry to input information to computers on checking account transactions. (A typical check and its MICR characters are shown in Figure 4-16.) This system, which has been in use since the 1950s,

Figure 4-15

Flexible diskettes are widely used with small computers. "Floppies" must be handled with care.

Do not bend or fold.

Keep away from magnetic fields.

Insert carefully.

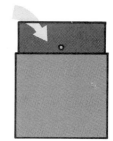
Return to envelope after use.

Photo top left courtesy of IBM Corporation; top right, NCR Corporation; middle, BASF Systems Corporation

Figure 4-16

This check didn't bounce when it was processed by MICR equipment!

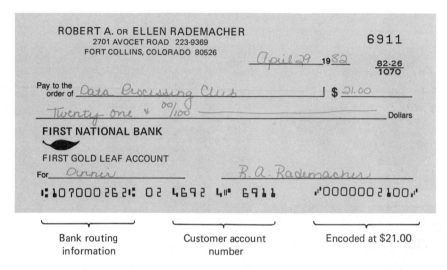

Bank routing
information

Customer account
number

Encoded at $21.00

allows checks and deposit slips to be read both by people and by machines. The
machines, called *magnetic ink character readers,* read and convert the characters into machine code by detecting the presence of magnetized particles in the
ink on the checks or deposit slips. As many as 1500 checks per minute can be
read and sorted (Figure 4-17).

Optical Recognition Systems

Optical recognition systems fall into two categories. The first and most
advanced are the *optical character recognition* (OCR) *systems,* which are able
to recognize hand-printed and typewritten characters (shown in Figure 4-18).
The second type of optical recognition is referred to as *optical mark recognition*
(OMR). OMR does not utilize letters of the alphabet. Instead, with the use of
electronic scanners, marks and symbols are converted into appropriate electronic signals. A typical example of an OMR application would be computerized
test forms. OMR systems are also used to read bar codes such as the *Universal
Product Code* (UPC) (see the unusual application described in Figure 4-19).

Figure 4-17

The magnetic ink character reader and sorter frees hundreds of bank employees from the routine task of sorting checks.

Cummins-Allison Corporation

Handprint Input Terminals

With the movement away from punched cards and toward on-line VDT units, some companies contend that handwriting is a viable data entry technique. *Handprint input terminals* use a pen or pencil to write on a pressure-sensitive surface. The handwritten data are then translated into standard ASCII

Figure 4-18

This OCR reads not only typewritten and hand-printed alphabetic and numeric characters but Japanese characters as well. Editorial markings in any color except black will not interfere with scanning.

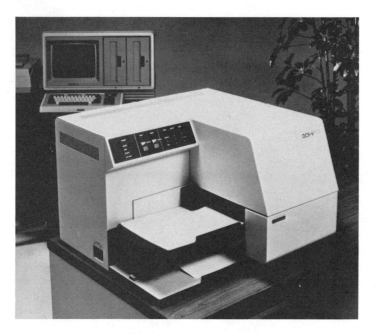

Toshiba America, Inc.

character codes and transmitted to a computer. Wrong characters can be corrected by writing over them on a data entry pad, and verification is possible on an attached CRT screen. These handprint recognition systems use preprinted forms and fill-in boxes and are among the newest input devices.

Audio Input/Output

Another means of transferring information to and from a computer system utilizes various audio devices. *Audio input/output* units are available which convert spoken words into machine-language instructions. These units respond

•MANUFACTURERS•

21397

K397

HANOVER

• NYC MARATHON 1981 •

**Computer technology helps
run marathon**
The distant rhythms of computer
technology were harnessed to
the breathing of long distance
runners last October 25 for the
8th running of the famed New
York Marathon. For the first time,
the more than 16,000 runners
from over 35 countries wore
computer-generated bibs—
complete with scannable bar
codes and 3-inch high identification numbers.

Figure 4-19

to information requests by patching together various words in the unit's vocabulary (Figure 4-20). However, these units do not simulate the human voice
adequately. More research and development will be necessary before this form
of input/output becomes widely used.

OUTPUT

Printers

The printed word is a tangible form of information that provides documentation which is visible and accessible. A printer provides the following benefits:

— Computer output is easier to read on paper than on display screens.
— Printed copy (hard copy) protects against loss of programs or data due to
   equipment failures.
— Some applications, such as payroll checks or customer bills, require a
   printer.

Figure 4-20

The benefits of automatic speech recognition include reduced costs (labor displacement), improved accuracy (no intermediate human errors) and higher speed (immediate and timely data capture).

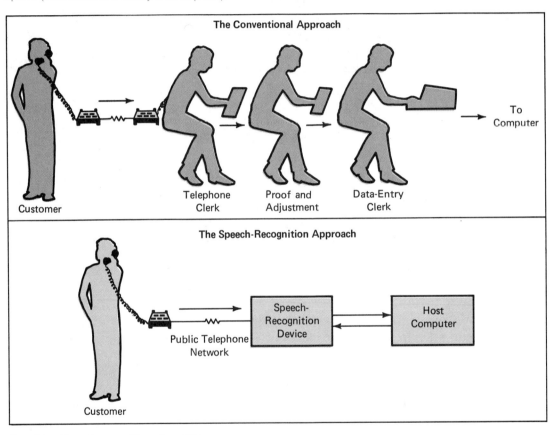

From Mini-Micro Systems, *November, 1980*

An organization typically selects a printer based on the following factors:

— Printing quality
— Speed
— Cost
— Special capabilities

If the printer is to be used for word processing, such as for business letters, reports, or manuscripts, the top priority is letter-quality printing. Data processing activities such as inventory or program listings may require fast printers. Some applications require special capabilities like graphics or plotting equipment.

The two major types of printers are impact and non-impact printers. The first printer to dominate the marketplace was the *impact printer*, which utilizes a device or mechanism that prints one or more characters on paper by physically impacting or hitting the paper. There are two kinds of impact printers, matrix and character. *Dot matrix printers* strike the paper with different combinations of metal pins. These metal pins create dots in patterns that approximate the shape of characters and symbols (Figure 4-21). *Character printers*, which use

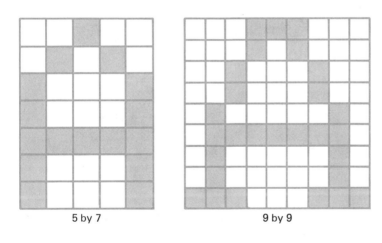

5 by 7   9 by 9

Figure 4-21

The letter "A" in two sizes of dot matrix.

hammer mechanisms like those in a typewriter, produce images by striking carbon ribbon against paper. Because both of these types of impact printers are electromechanical devices, they are noisy and subject to frequent breakdowns. Some impact printers print an entire line at one time. This type of printer is known as a *line printer*. Impact printers that print less than a line at a time are called *serial printers*. *Chain printers* use a long chain of characters (Figure 4-22) which continually rotates at high speed in front of the paper. When a signal is sent from the computer to print a certain character, a hammer makes contact on the opposite side of the paper, causing the chosen character to be printed.

To overcome the limitations of impact printers, manufacturers such as Xerox, IBM, and Exxon designed mechanisms that would place marks on paper without actually contacting the paper. As a result there are now high-speed *non-impact printers* employing laser scanning and electrostatic technologies. Because of their complexity, non-impact printers are expensive and usually require special paper. Like impact printers, non-impact printers may also be either line or serial printers, and there are several types available. *Electro-thermal printers* use heated rods which increase the temperature of heat-sensitive paper. These temperature increases are transformed into images on the paper. *Electrostatic printers* are similar to electrothermal printers except that charged rods, instead of heated rods, are used. *Laser printers* (Figure 4-23) project a light image onto photosensitive paper which in turn is developed by a process similar to that used for normal photographs. *Xero-graphic printers* produce output on 8-1/2-by-11 plain paper using techniques

Figure 4-22

A printer chain.

Photo courtesy of IBM Corporation

similar to those employed in making Xerox copies. Various kinds of printers are illustrated in Figure 4-24.

Plotter Output

With the increasing use of computer graphics, graphs or plots of business-related data such as financial forecasts or marketing trends will frequently be required. The primary way to obtain a hard copy of these graphics is through use of a *plotter*, shown in Figure 4-25.

Microfilm Output

One disadvantage of many types of hard-copy output is that they require a great deal of space for storage. To solve this problem, it is possible for a business firm to use *computer output microfilm* (COM) to reduce the volume of space needed to store vast holdings of information. While COM equipment is expen-

Figure 4-23

An off-line laser printer.

DatagraphiX, Inc.

Figure 4-24

Printers come in a variety
of sizes and capabilities.

Courtesy of Digital Equipment Corporation

sive, this method of computer output may be cost effective for certain large-scale storage needs where data do not need to be directly retrieved by the computer. The use of COM is illustrated in Figure 4-26.

Videodisc Output

The *videodisc* is a highly accurate way of storing both audio and visual signal information. The videodisc is typically made of glass and coated with photosensitive resin upon which it is possible for a laser beam to record information. A videodisc system was illustrated in Chapter 3 (Figure 3-27).

Figure 4-25

Plotter/controller configuration. From left to right: 22″-wide plotter/printer; 11″-wide plotter/printer; controller; 54″-wide pen plotter.

Photo courtesy of California Computer Products, Inc. (CalComp), Anaheim, CA

Figure 4-26

The computer output processor at the left produces microfilm or microfiche for data storage. Student records are stored on microfiche at right.

 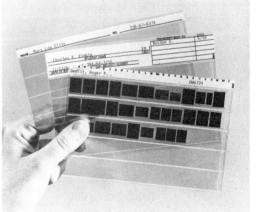

Photo at left, Eastman Kodak Company; right, Microseal Corporation

SUMMARY

The input and output hardware discussed in this chapter illustrate the diversity and sophistication of current input/output media and hardware. Input/output hardware ranges from widely used card punch units and visual display terminals to specialized I/O equipment. Punched-card equipment for batch processing is diminishing in use, while terminals are increasingly used to display information on a screen, to provide hard copy, or to input data at the point of sale.

MICR and OCR systems are also popular forms of input, and new research in handprint and audio technology shows future promise for handling data. Printers are typically impact or non-impact. Dot matrix and chain printers are examples of impact printers, while electrothermal and laser printers are non-impact devices. Plotters and computer output microfilm (COM) are also common output media, with videodiscs on the horizon.

TERMS

Input	Card reader
Output	Card punch unit
Visual display terminal	Paper tape
CRT screen terminal	Channels
Interactive processing	Magnetic tape
Hard-copy terminal	Magnetic disk
Dumb terminal	Key station input system
Smart terminal	Key-to-tape system
Intelligent terminal	Source document
Stand-alone	Key-to-disk system
Graphics	Floppy disk
CAD/CAM	MICR system
Digitizer	Magnetic ink character reader
POS terminals	OCR system
Batch processing	Optical mark recognition
Keypunch machines	Universal Product Code
Verifier	Handprint input terminal

Audio input/output   Electrothermal printer
Impact printer   Electrostatic printer
Dot matrix printer   Laser printer
Character printer   Xerographic printer
Line printer   Plotter
Serial printer   COM
Chain printer   Videodisc output
Non-impact printer

QUESTIONS

1. Why do you think an interactive CRT is such a popular terminal for data input?
2. What are the differences between a dumb terminal, a smart terminal, and an intelligent terminal?
3. What is meant by the term "stand-alone"?
4. Why are graphics so important?
5. Describe batch processing.
6. Where are POS terminals typically found?
7. What advantages do magnetic tape and magnetic disks provide over punched cards?
8. What is a key station input system? Why is it called a system?
9. What advantages are to be found in the use of floppy disks?
10. What does MICR mean? How is it used?
11. What are the two categories of optical recognition systems?
12. Discuss how impact and non-impact printers differ in operation.
13. How is plotter output used?
14. What are the advantages of COM?
15. What is a videodisc?

ARTICLE

Micro Explosion Aids Rapid Printer Growth

SAN FRANCISCO—The proliferation of personal computers and the promise of integrated systems in the office of the future will mean rapid growth to the printer industry, according to vendors and analysts.

Just what form that growth will take, and which technologies will dominate — daisywheel, dot-matrix, teleprinters or page printers — is by no means certain as vendors grapple for a solid niche in the marketplace.

Major issues that will be significant in printers of the future include cost, speed and throughput, ease of integration among computers and in computer networks, and such ergonomic factors as noise, size of "footprint," ease of handling and maintenance. Perhaps even more significant will be the degree of intelligence incorporated in future printers.

Norman Weizer, senior analyst with Arthur D. Little Inc., notes that there is a trend toward moving functions and memory out to the printer. "This can be done without sacrificing speed or adding to cost. Just by putting more chips onto the printer, it can become more intelligent for only slightly more cost."

Characteristics that make a printer intelligent, according to William Easterbrook of Kidder Peabody and Co., include giving the printer the ability to select items such as margins, size of print and character font, and programming it with preprinted forms used in a given office.

What will actually drive the purchase of printers, said Easterbrook, is productivity. "The issue is, how much they can do, at what cost, versus the way things are done now. Lowered cost is creating some demand. But, the main inhibiting factor is that people don't know yet what they want.". . .

Weizer pointed out, in addition, that there currently is a trade-off in buying printers, which means, basically, that noise and high costs must currently be endured to have speed. He added: "Printers must come way down in cost. I think we'll see more of them adapted into the computer because power supply and the expense of metal cabinetry are great. A manufacturer that can save on those can offer a less expensive product."

According to Paul Shapiro, marketing manager for Diablo Systems Inc., there is a trend to clusters of remote computers.

Shapiro said Diablo will cater to vertical markets and their particular applica-

continued

tions. The company has, for instance, a single-station desktop workstation, a higher-duty-cycle single workstation that can also be used in a cluster environment, and a printer that is aimed at the legal, accounting and scientific environments, and will also work for electronic mail and teletext.

Easterbrook ventured that the most popular of the serial printers today is produced by Epson. He noted that serial printers range in price from $500 to $600. Major vendors are Diablo, Nippon Electric Co. (NEC) and Qume. Dot-matrix printers that are widely used, he said, include those from Centronics and Data Royal.

Centronics vice president of engineering Ed Corell said that, although dot-matrix printers are popularly used with personal computers today, their use will extend to workstations and mini-computers in the future. "The dot-matrix printer is getting close to near letter-quality," he said.

Technology trends in printers, according to Corell, will be to give them more memory and more "logic." Noted Corell. "As things become standardized, people want things like graphics, color, variable pitches, variable line densities and printers with the ability to handle more kinds of paper."

Analysts agreed that printers, in the future, must have a higher mean time between failures (MTBF), must come down in cost, must have greater throughput and must be quieter. According to Shapiro, European standards call for a lower noise level in printers (55 DBA), and these must eventually be adopted in the U.S. where 65 DBA is still acceptable. Shapiro also pointed out that daisywheel printers must come up in speed and down in size and cost. Erin Greene, a spokeswoman for Hewlett-Packard, said costs for office printers vary widely. Entry-level printers can start at $600 and go to $5,000, depending upon type. Greene said the quality of dot-matrix printers on the low end is rising and that, one day, the daisywheel printer will disappear because "they are too slow and too noisy."

She also pointed out that laser printers should not be overlooked in the office of the future. "A full-service office will find them useful for things like printing pieces for large, direct mailings, W2 forms, and even duplicating books."

MIS Week, *December 8, 1982, p. 17.*

DISCUSSION QUESTIONS

1. If you were to start a business to sell printers, what type of technology would you select? Why?
2. Describe the functions of an "intelligent" printer.

APPLICATION

Mr. Steak Managers Speed Sizzle With Touch-Screens

DENVER—When managers from 260 franchise and 60 company-owned Mr. Steak, Inc., restaurants want to order meat and supplies, they get instantaneous response from headquarters order-takers, due to the chain's switchover last month from a batch to an on-line system, coupled with the addition of touch-sensitive screens.

"Our order-takers are salespeople, not data entry people," Paul Case, vice president of systems for management information services, said last week. "I wanted to find a data-capture system that would eliminate keyboard usage."

Among the systems Case considered were "voice recognition, light-pen technology and X-Y digitizers," he said. "I also looked at Control Data's Plato system."

"Some of these systems plain didn't work," Case continued, "and most required too much concentration on the part of our sales reps. So I continued to look for another idea and found the touch-sensitive screen."

Users "Pretty Happy"

Case reported that he and his order-takers are "pretty happy with the product," an Interaction Systems, Inc., of Newtonville, Mass., "TK-100."

The CRT is added on to the firm's four Radio-Shack "TRS-80s" and the stand-alones can communicate with the company's mainframe, a Digital Equipment Corp. (DEC) "20/60," he said.

"We had a bit of trouble with the touch-screen right after installation," Case added. "We found that the screen was not the same radius of curvature as the Radio-Shack CRTs and, although this didn't distort the figures too much, we found we had to add foam rubber around the screen to get a better output."

Case also noted that the screens are very static-sensitive. "This follows, because they work by using the bit of electricity people have in their bodies. And, in Denver, we have a worse problem, because we are in a high-altitude and have low humidity, two factors that increase static. So we've added static mats and this has reduced the problem considerably."

"Also, the screens have to be cleaned daily for them to have good capacitance," he went on.

Case liked the idea of using the screens in conjunction with a stand-alone system that communicates with the mainframe. "It keeps the input down on the system,

continued

thereby keeping throughput high," he said. "We can also use it as a backup in case our main system goes down."

The use of the touch-sensitive screens in an on-line environment has reduced the time it takes salespeople to search for a client's historical data, "like what the restaurant ordered last month or last year at this time, which lots of managers ask for," Case said. "It used to take four or five hours and now we get instantaneous information because we went from batch to on-line."

Case said that his firm is one of the only restaurant companies that has an MIS department. "We have our own restaurant accounting and information system and do accounting for other restaurant chains including Wendy's, Country Kitchens and International House of Pancakes."

For the near future, Case is working on installing in-store micros in the restaurants themselves. "It will be a franchise accounting and management system and eventually it will be used as an inventory system so we know when we're running low and the store knows when it's running low on meat or supplies."

The change from batch to on-line has "improved the quality of our information," Case said. "Now we've got the user responsible for data that the user can't live without anymore. We went from a "'post-facto' to an 'in-process' system."

"Better Decisions"

"We can make better decisions with the data we're now getting," he continued. "Our system knew what was happening after everything went on, so it was no better than manual."

The touch-sensitive screen part of the system has increased accuracy and speed of the order-taking process, Case said. "Over 500 orders are being processed weekly."

An order consists of 32 items, like meat, dry goods, and drop-ship orders, mainly because the screen can handle only 32 items, according to Les Pennington, director of systems and programming.

"Some touch-screen CRTs have 256 touch spots," Pennington said. "It costs more and we didn't need that many, so we went with the Interaction system."

MIS Week, *January 20, 1982, p. 22.*

DISCUSSION QUESTIONS

1. What accounts for the popularity of touch-screens for fast-food restaurants and cafeterias?
2. How do the following impact Mr. Steak: Throughput? Backup?

PART 3 PEOPLE AND SOFTWARE

In the 1980's, "friendly" computers and "useful" information systems are in vogue. This section identifies the important contributions of systems professionals and presents methods of human/machine interaction

CHAPTER 5

THE HUMAN ELEMENT

CHAPTER OBJECTIVES

In this chapter you will learn:

1. The importance of people in the growing field of computer information systems.
2. The functions and duties of various computer and systems personnel.
3. About the skills needed to pursue a career in the computer world.
4. About the various organizations to which computer professionals may belong.
5. The characteristics of a "user friendly" system.
6. About the outlook for the future as it relates to computer and systems personnel.

PEOPLE IN INFORMATION SYSTEMS

Throughout this book we stress the role of people in and their importance to the world of computers. Within any organization that has a computer as an integral part of its information processing system, the computer is usually perceived by most people in that organization as a critically important component of the information system. Perhaps some people would state that the computer is THE most important part of any system.

We agree that the computer is crucial to most organizations if timely and efficient information processing is to be accomplished. The computer is *not*, however, the most important component of information processing. People are. People who are involved in *designing* the information system, in *maintaining* the system, and especially in *using* the system's outputs are the key ingredient of any information system. This chapter examines these people and the roles they play in information systems. We call it the *human element* in information systems.

SYSTEMS DESIGN AND IMPLEMENTATION PERSONNEL

The development of computer technology and computer-based information systems has meant the creation of new employment and career opportunities for persons interested in computer-related work. Systems analysts, programmers, computer operators, operating system managers, database administrators, and vice-presidents for information systems are jobs that are new to the world of work. These positions generally did not exist before 1950. Indeed, most of them came into being in the late 1960s and early 1970s. The way in which these jobs might typically be structured in an organization is shown in the chart in Figure 5-1. In this chart, the vice-president for information systems is on the same management level as the vice-president for marketing or manufacturing. You will note that, through the type of structure shown here, programmers and systems analysts have opportunities to advance within the organization—to have a career path and other professional opportunities for advancement. Figure 5-2 gives a list of job titles frequently used to describe positions available in computer and information systems career fields.

Two major career positions in the design and implementation of information systems are the systems analyst and the programmer. Numerous combinations

Figure 5-1

Computer personnel positions within an organization.

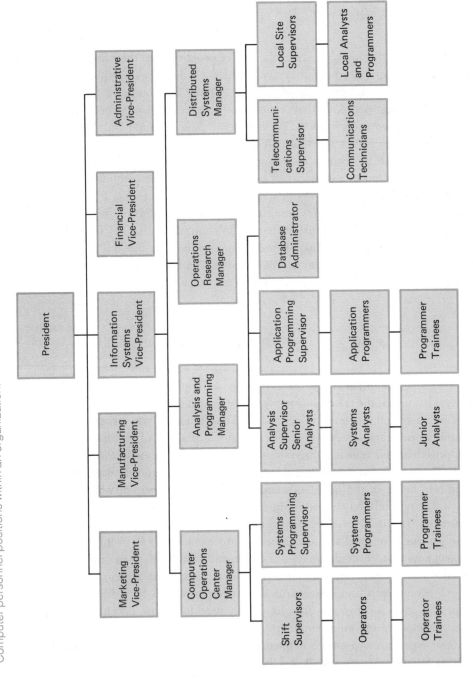

Upper Management Positions
Vice-President for Information Systems

Middle Management Positions
Manager of Systems Analysis
Manager of Applications Programming
Manager of Analysis and Programming
Data Communication and Telecommunications Manager
Manager of Computer Operations

Supervisory Management Positions
Lead Systems Analyst
Senior Systems Analyst
Lead Applications Programmer
Senior Applications Programmer
Lead Systems Analyst and Programmer
Senior Systems Analyst and Programmer
Lead Computer Operator
Senior Computer Operator
Data Entry Supervisor
Word Processing Supervisor
Lead Systems Programmer

Non-Management Positions
Systems Analyst
Junior Systems Analyst
Systems Analysis Trainee
Applications Programmer
Junior Applications Programmer
Systems Programmer
Junior Systems Programmer
Analyst/Programmer
Junior Analyst/Programmer
Data Communications Analyst
Senior Operator
Magnetic Media Librarian
Word Processing Operator

Figure 5-2

Job titles in computers and information systems.

and variations of programmers and analysts exist today. The labels used to "tag" programmers and analysts are often interchangeable. This has led some people to develop the false impression that only programmers are needed to develop information systems. To them, anyone who works with a computer is a programmer. Modern managers are learning that there are more people involved in information processing than just those who write programs.

Systems Analyst

The *systems analyst* can be thought of as the link between the user of the information produced by the computerized system and the computer itself (see Figure 5-3). The systems analyst should be able to communicate with and understand the needs of the user. The analyst must be able to explain to the user how computers may be used.

Figure 5-3

The role of the systems analyst is to help the user understand the computer and to develop information systems that meet the user's needs.

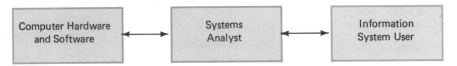

| Computer Hardware and Software | Systems Analyst | Information System User |

To many users, the technical terms used in describing computers are like a foreign language. Before you began this introductory computer class, did you know what "bubble memory" was? How about a "floppy disk"? Computer jargon is a whole new language that people must either learn or have interpreted for them. Many managers today do not have a high level of understanding about computers, computer technology, or computer concepts. Therefore, analysts must compensate for this lack of user knowledge by having a good understanding of the computer, how it functions, and what its capabilities are.

Systems analysts play an important role in developing information systems. They are almost always the catalyst, the driving force necessary to keep the development of a new information system moving forward on schedule. The analyst's position is a challenging one. It calls for creativity, communications skills—both oral and written—and expertise in human relations.

Creativity is needed because the analyst usually is concerned with developing new systems, with implementing new information concepts, and, frequently, with developing systems for the organization that have never been used before in that organization. Creativity is needed because each information system is unique; problems will be different and, more important, the organization's managers and other information users will be different. But what about payroll or inventory systems? Aren't they similar from one organization to the next? How can any payroll system be unique? Indeed, similarities do exist in specific information systems. However, there are also differences, and these differences can be very significant. If these differences aren't given proper consideration, the user may not get the information needed, or, even if given the proper information, the user may not have the right attitude toward the information supplied by that system.

Communication skills are required because analysts must be able to present their ideas effectively and coherently to users, to management, and to various other individuals involved with the system. Without effective communication skills, new ideas are less likely to be accepted, supported, and approved for development. The effectiveness with which information systems concepts are communicated to the organization in general and to the users in particular is crucial to the user's overall acceptance of the newly implemented information system.

Human relations skills are critical because developing and implementing information systems involves almost constant contact with people — people who sometimes have divergent interests and conflicting needs. Because of these varying demands, developing the system usually involves a lot of compromise and persuasion. This means the analyst must use tact and keen human relations judgment. It also requires knowing when to push and when to pull, when to demand and when to persuade, when to persist and when to back off, when to accept suggestions and when to give them.

According to Robert Alloway of the Sloan School of Management at M.I.T.,[1] systems analysts see the following traits as being important to their jobs:

— Strong user orientation — delivering systems that users like
— Ability to work with ill-defined objectives and resolve conflicts
— Broad view of company goals and operations; a senior management orientation
— In-depth knowledge of user department operations
— Cost consciousness, hardware efficiency, and operation efficiency
— Technical skills (programming, database design, telecommunications)

Persons experienced in systems management will usually look for all or some of the following personal characteristics in potential systems analysts:

---

[1]Robert M. Alloway, "Grow Your Own," *Datamation*, Vol. 26:2, pp. 122-128, April, 1980.

— Ability to work with others
— Ability in logic and problem perception
— Oral and written communication abilities
— Thoroughness and persistence
— Imagination
— Resourcefulness and tact

The preceding lists are rather formidable. What single individual could possess, to a high degree, all of these qualities? Realizing the challenges facing a systems analyst, most organizations desiring to hire people for computer-related positions seek individuals who have a degree from a four-year college in information systems, computer science, or a closely related area of study such as management science or engineering. Some organizations look for prospective employees who have combined their information systems studies with courses in other disciplines — in particular, accounting, finance, or operations management.

Applications Programmer

A *programmer* writes the computer language instructions necessary to perform the desired functions on the computer. Computer programmers fit into two basic job classes: applications programmers and systems programmers.

The *applications programmer* is the individual most often involved with the development of an information system. When people refer to a "programmer" or to "programming," they are usually talking about an applications programmer. The applications programmer studies the information system designed by the analyst, then writes the computer programming instructions which are necessary to efficiently process the data in the system. Even though this process of writing programs is often called *coding,* programmers don't like to be called "coders." Programmers also give advice on the types of software best suited for processing the data, offer recommendations on hardware aspects of the system, and suggest design changes that would result in more efficient processing.

Many skills are combined in a top-notch programmer. These skills include logical thinking, verbal abilities, creativity, the capacity to handle detail, and the ability to cope with stress. However, in many ways the major prerequisite for someone considering a career in programming is simply an intense interest in working with computers.

Gerald Weinberg,[2] in his studies of programmer psychology, included humility as a desired characteristic of a programmer. He explains that about the time you have accomplished some difficult programming task and begin to feel that you have quite a bit of programming expertise, you may begin to think, "This dumb computer really isn't so smart." Then a problem will come along with a bug in it that you can't find, or some other problem may look simple but you find yourself spending hours trying to resolve it. The result: You end up being put in your place after all, and you feel rather humble.

Programmers are often viewed as loners, as introverted individuals who feel more comfortable challenging a machine than working with people. What is your reaction to the following paragraph?

> Wherever computer centers have become established, that is to say, in countless places in the United States, as well as in virtually all other industrial regions of the world, bright young men of disheveled appearance, often with sunken glowing eyes, can be seen sitting at computer consoles, their arms tensed and waiting to fire their fingers, already poised to strike, at the buttons and keys on which their attention seems to be as riveted as a gambler's on the rolling dice. When not so transfixed, they often sit at tables strewn with computer printouts over which they pore like students of a cabalistic text. . . .their rumpled clothes, their unwashed and unshaven faces, and their uncombed hair all testify that they are oblivious to their bodies and to the world in which they move. They exist, at least when so engaged, only through and for the computers. These are computer bums, compulsive programmers. They are an international phenomenon.[3]

Most organizations require prospective applications programmers to have completed a two- to four-year college degree program with command of at least one high-level computer language such as COBOL. The level of education required usually depends upon the size of the organization doing the hiring, the type of application to be developed, and the level of programming activity

---

[2]Gerald M. Weinberg, *The Psychology of Computer Programming* (New York: Van Nostrand Reinhold Company, 1971), p. 150.

[3]Joseph Weizenbaum, *Computer Power and Human Reason* (San Francisco: W. H. Friedman and Co., 1976), p. 116. Reprinted by permission of the publisher.

needed to implement the information system application. Regardless of the formal education completed, a programmer is constantly faced with keeping current with the state-of-the-art. As new languages appear on the scene and new concepts are developed, the programmer must be in a continuous "education mode" (see Figure 5-4).

Figure 5-4

"Poor boy, we've gotta let him go. He was an exceptional programmer, but went on a three-week cruise and fell too far behind the state-of-the-art."

© R.E.M.

Analyst/Programmer

Organizations often combine programming activities with the systems analysis and design function. Thus, they refer to the position as *analyst/programmer*. Although many organizations combine the two positions, some insist that they be kept separate. The following reasons are usually given for keeping programmer and analyst positions separate from each other:

— The two positions require different kinds of skills. Analysis and design activities call for interacting with the information user, which means the analyst must be very people-oriented; programming calls for interacting with a machine.

— The programmer is an expert in computer capability and is the closest human link to the computer's "brain." Therefore, programmers are likely to be too computer-oriented and not sufficiently user-oriented. The programmer may have a tendency to concentrate too much on what is best for the computer and not enough on what is best for the user.

— Better management control over the information system can be maintained if the two functions are kept separate. By separating the various systems development tasks among several individuals, there will be less likelihood of fraud and improved opportunities for checks and balances (internal control).

— The two positions can augment each other. The characteristics called for in one position can complement those needed in the other position. If the programmer is very detail-oriented and conservative in proposing solutions, the analyst can be more daring, more of a "blue sky" or idealistic thinker.

Despite these arguments, many companies persist in combining the analyst/programmer positions into one position for several reasons:

— It is a carryover from the early days of computer usage (in the 1950s) when the programmer designed the information system, wrote the programs, and operated or ran the computer.

— Many smaller organizations cannot afford the cost of separating the two functions. These organizations must keep their computer staffs small. Thus, each person has to be able to perform effectively in several jobs.

— Most analysts enter the computer world through the programming route; their first major contact with a computer is when they learn a programming language. As a result, they almost never get entirely out of programming.

Systems Programmer

As previously mentioned, there are two major types of programmers. The applications programmer has already been discussed. The second type, the *systems programmer,* writes and maintains programs that relate to the internal machine operations of the computer system, including the peripheral devices and equipment which are remote from the main computer site. As you learned in Chapter 3, the operating system of the computer consists of software packages or programs that oversee and manage the hardware and software resources of a computer system. The "systems" part of the systems programmer label comes from the programmer's direct involvement with computer system operations. The systems programmer may make a programming language compiler more efficient or write the software necessary to get two pieces of computer equipment to interact or talk with each other. The systems programmer is primarily concerned with making the computer perform efficiently and, except for an occasional training or consulting task, has little direct contact with systems analysts or system users.

Most organizations employ systems programmers who are graduates of a four-year college with a degree in computer science. Sometimes systems programmers are called "software engineers" or "system engineers," meaning a person who "engineers" the operating system.

Other EDP Personnel

As computer technology has developed, many types of jobs have been created in addition to the systems analyst and programmer positions. Some of the most common are discussed in this section.

Computer operators are the people who actually operate the computer. They push buttons to start the equipment; they load tape reels and disk packs. They put paper in the printer and, in general, perform those tasks necessary to keep the equipment operating.

In the early days of computers, the room that housed the equipment was open to any employee who knew how to run the equipment. This method of managing the computing equipment was referred to as an *open shop*. As security and protection of both data and equipment became more important to organizations, computer operation centers became *closed shops* — off limits to anyone other than computer operators and computer managers.

With the development of new computer technologies more tasks have become automatic. This has reduced the need for large numbers of operations personnel. Now, one person can control many computer operations. Thus, the demand for computer operators within most organizations is not as great as the demand for analysts and programmers. However, new job positions in operations may be necessary when certain pieces of hardware are installed. For example, the average computer printer does not require a full-time operator. Yet the laser printer, which prints up to 20,000 lines per minute, may require a full-time person just to keep paper feeding into it.

Computer operators are generally not college trained, nor do they need a knowledge of programming. They may need to know the *job control language* of the equipment they are operating. Job control language is part of the operating system and specifies such things as the beginning of a program, the processing tasks to be carried out, and the input/output devices needed. Often, computer operators receive "on the job" training.

Data entry personnel are the clerical employees of information processing; they are the individuals who operate the keyed data entry devices (such as keypunch, key-to-tape, key-to-disk) and the visual display terminals. Clustered workstations for data entry operators are shown in Figure 5-5. Speed, efficiency, and accuracy in carrying out their assigned tasks are desired in these employees. A college degree is not normally required.

Figure 5-5

Clustered workstations for data entry operators. Working in clusters rather than in isolated locations enhances employee morale and makes data entry more efficient through record sharing.

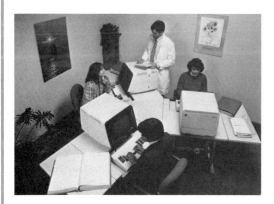

Photo at left, Borroughs Division of Lear Siegler, Inc.; right, courtesy of IBM Corporation

The *database administrator* (DBA) is one of the newest positions to evolve in information systems. The DBA's primary responsibility is to supervise and control the development of databases within the organization. A *database* is a collection of interrelated data stored in the computer system that are available to a wide variety of individuals and systems within the organization. The DBA is usually promoted out of the ranks of analysts or programmers and performs the following tasks:

— Approves the development of new databases.
— Supervises the acquisition of new database software.
— Consults with information system designers on efficient database organization methods.

There is an increasing need for *telecommunications personnel,* people who are specialists in telecommunications. This need has arisen from the development of complex computer networks and distributed systems. A *telecommunication system* or network consists of several elements, the first being the input or data entry points normally located over widely dispersed geographical areas. From these data entry points, communication lines carry the data or other messages to assembly areas, nodes, or intersections. The messages are then transmitted simultaneously to a computer processing center. Before messages are actually fed into the main computer at the computer center, they will usually go through another computer that is used for sorting the telecommunication messages and for determining what tasks are to be performed by the main computer. The preliminary computer processor hardware is called a front-end processor or communications processor.

Telecommunications personnel work with data communications, teleprocessing systems, distributed information processing, and other types of communication/computer networks. Typically, telecommunications personnel have college degrees in electrical engineering; some may have degrees in computer science. These individuals determine the best methods for transmitting data from one geographical location to another. The locations may be only a few hundred feet apart or they may be separated by thousands of miles. Other questions or problems that telecommunications experts address are:

— What should the data transmission system consist of? Should it include satellite or dedicated transmission lines? Where should input points be located? What transmission speeds are needed?
— How many communication lines are needed?

— What is the peak traffic load? Can the load be smoothed out to avoid overload so that users do not become dissatisfied with the network because they can't log onto the computer?

— When the user is unable to link up with the computer, what is causing the problem? How quickly can someone attack the problem?

Some organizations will operate a "hot-line" at the computer center just to deal with solving users' teleprocessing problems immediately, if possible.

The position of *EDP auditor* has also evolved as a result of the growth of the computer industry. This position illustrates how existing jobs in other professions may be affected by the implementation of computer technology. The position of auditor is well established in the accounting profession. An EDP auditor is a person whose main function is to help ensure that computerized information systems meet accepted accounting and auditing procedures. For that reason, this person needs to know the currently accepted accounting principles and practices and to understand how the computer functions.

The EDP auditing position calls for an individual who is concerned about the security of the data in the system, from the point of input, through processing and storage, and even to the use made of the information after processing. The auditor gives attention to overall data privacy (a critical consideration coming out of the Privacy Act of 1974 as passed by Congress) and to data integrity. *Data integrity* refers to the accuracy, consistency, and completeness of data that are maintained by the information system. Accuracy involves the assurance that data have been entered correctly, processed or stored as intended, and properly distributed. Consistency means that data accessed from different files are in agreement. Completeness means that data which are supposed to be in the system are actually in the system — in other words, that no data have been changed, are missing, or were lost in processing. As you can conclude from the preceding discussion, EDP auditors usually have an accounting background that has included study and work experience in computer information systems.

At the top of the computer center hierarchy is the *computer center director*. A computer center typically houses all of the hardware necessary to carry out the centralized computer processing functions. The hardware may include the main computer or computers, other computers used for special or dedicated purposes such as front-end processors, and the many peripheral devices — tapes and disk drives, card readers, controllers — used at the central site. Also included under the director's supervision are tape and disk librarians, systems programmers, and other personnel involved in offering their consulting or advising services to computer systems users. (Remember that systems programmers work with operating system programs and special computer program packages; applications programmers work mainly with the information system users' programs.)

The computer center director is also the key person for making decisions or recommendations to management on software and hardware purchases and for coordinating those types of activities among various system users. Without the coordinating function, the organization could end up with duplicate programs or pieces of equipment spread throughout the organization, when one piece of equipment centrally located could serve several users. The computer center director is usually promoted from within the information systems function or hired from another organization with a similar computing environment.

Finally, the *vice-president of information systems* is the person who is in charge of overall information systems development and computer operations within the organization. Vice-presidential positions in finance, marketing, production, and the other business functions have been around for many years. The position of vice-president of information systems, on the other hand, is relatively new. Pillsbury Corporation was one of the first major companies to establish this position during the 1960s. Today, almost all large corporations have a vice-president for information systems.

Not all data processing positions are discussed in the preceding pages, as a review of Figure 5-6 illustrates. Working with computers in whatever capacity can be a rewarding life. It is challenging; it requires training and education; and it demands dedication. Basically, it requires the same ingredients found in any professional career.

PROFESSIONAL ORGANIZATIONS

Numerous organizations have been created to meet the needs of information systems professionals. Some of the more prominent groups are:

— Data Processing Management Association (DPMA)
— Association for Computing Machinery (ACM)
— Association for Systems Management (ASM)
— Association for Educational Data Systems (AEDS)
— Society for Information Management (SIM)

Figure 5-6

A Look Inside the DP Priesthood

Job titles are among the first mysteries to greet an executive dealing with a data processing department. Does a programmer do something an analyst doesn't? Will the analyst push your DP order through faster? Herewith, a program so you can tell the players apart.

Data processing consultant: The DP consultant is an independent advisor, ideally with both a business and a technical background, who can do everything from assisting a company in the acquisition and implementation of a DP system to developing single programs, complete systems, or high-level strategy for the future of the installation. The fees charged by consultants vary according to experience, reputation, and specialty.

Data processing manager: The DP manager is ultimately responsible for the successful operation of the installation. Experience in the DP field (as a project leader, systems analyst, or supervisor) is usually a prerequisite for the job, which includes hiring and supervising the DP staff, recommending new equipment, expanding the present system's applications, and seeing to it that the DP department services all areas of the company effectively. In addition to reporting to top management, the DP manager usually meets frequently with managers of user departments.

Project leader: The project leader manages a group of programmers who have been brought together to produce a system or at least a closely knit collection of programs. The project will often have its own machine, plus special teams to provide systems work, standards documentation, and other functions.

Systems analyst: A technical liaison person, the systems analyst confers with users to define DP projects (problems or objectives) and designs the solutions. To make sure the DP system is acceptable to the users, the analyst must not only be familiar with programming languages and understand fully the computer hardware and software, but must also be familiar with the aims, structure, and running of the company. The systems analyst usually makes recommendations to the DP manager.

Systems programmer: Traditionally a bit higher (financially and politically) in the DP ranks than the applications programmer, the systems programmer specializes in the support, maintenance, and use of one or more major operating systems. The job includes keeping the machine working at top speed and efficiency, seeing to it that programs running simultaneously on the computer don't interfere with each other, and developing and implementing modifications to the system.

Applications programmer: This technician writes programs to perform specific tasks, or applications, such as payroll accounting and inventory control. In order to produce working, debugged, and documented software, the applications programmer must be skilled in one or more computer languages and know how to test all parts of the program.

Contract programmer: This programmer works for a DP vendor that supplies programming services to clients under two types of contracts: contracts for programming support, in which the vendor supplies personnel to work under the direction of the purchaser's DP staff, and contracts for specific tasks, in which the vendor agrees to computerize a particular task according to the client's requirements.

Reprinted by permission from Output, February, 1981, p. 61

Several professional groups have cooperated in establishing a *certification* program similar to that in the accounting field. You've undoubtedly heard the term "CPA," or certified public accountant. A person certified as a CPA must have passed a written examination and acquired a specific amount of work experience and education before certification is granted.

The certification program in information systems and data processing began in 1962 and is managed by the Institute for Certification of Computer Professionals (ICCP), with professional organizations such as DPMA and ACM lending their support. The examination covers five subject areas: (1) data processing equipment, (2) computer programming and software, (3) principles of management, (4) quantitative methods, and (5) systems analysis and design. Upon satisfactorily completing the series of written tests and validating the completion of a prescribed amount of work experience and education, a candidate is certified by the ICCP as a CDP, a certified data processor. Currently the CDP certification is becoming more well known by the public and is gaining wider acceptance by employers (see Appendix A).

THE INFORMATION SYSTEM USER

At the beginning of this chapter, we stated that the human element is the most important component of the total information process — more important than hardware, programs, documents and system forms, and even more important than the design of the system. In breaking down the human element into subgroups, there are groups such as analysts, programmers, computer operators, and users to consider. Considering the many groups that the human element comprises, we can easily conclude that the user of the information produced by the system is the most important subgroup of all. Some people might question this conclusion — certainly an effective system could not exist without the designer! But while the designer is important in developing an effective system, why design a system at all if no one is going to use it? A "law" or axiom in information system usage goes something like this:

> You can design the best system in the world, but if the user doesn't accept or support it, the system will not succeed.

On the other hand, there are systems around today that are poorly designed, yet they are effective because they are used.

Users of computer-based information systems exist throughout the organization. Some of these users are shown in Figure 5-7. Indeed, everyone within

Figure 5-7

Information system users in an organization.

PURCHASING

ACCOUNTING

SERVICE

INVENTORY

WORD PROCESSING

SECURITY

"Inventory" photo courtesy of Burroughs Redactron Corporation; "Security" photo, Cardkey Systems, A Fairchild Industries Company

the organization is, at one time or another, a user of an information system or systems.

The role and importance of the user in information systems cannot be overemphasized. If the company is to gain maximum benefit from its information systems, the user of the system must:

— Accept the system. Acceptance does not come about by thrusting the newly designed system down the user's throat. Acceptance comes when users feel that they are a part of the system, that it is basically their design, and that they, along with others, must share the responsibility for success or failure of the system. The system becomes "our system," not "their system." This acceptance is achieved through user participation in design and through user training.

— Be able to use information from the system effectively. Effective use of information cannot be guaranteed; however, it is enhanced by the form in which the information is presented, by its timeliness and by its accuracy. Users who prefer short, summary statements in their reports should not be presented with long reports of tabulated data. A manager may prefer that only the total or "bottom line" figure be emphasized, in which case pages and pages of detailed output should not be provided. A technical design engineer may want a graph displaying several electronic functions simultaneously, instead of having to search through a number of display screens to filter out the three or four desired functions. Color graphics are being used more and more in displaying these types of output reports.

— Have access to a system that is "user friendly." The concept of being user friendly is discussed in the following section. Evidently, Oglethorp (see Figure 5-8) has the wrong idea of what is meant by the term.

A "USER FRIENDLY" SYSTEM

A *user friendly system* is one that satisfies several needs of the user, needs that go beyond simply meeting the user's informational requirements. Needs are met in several ways.

First, a user friendly system is easy to access. Information system users frequently have given up on a system because it was too difficult to "get onto" the system. Easy access means that the user can log onto or receive information

"*Oglethorp,* that's not what I meant by *USER FRIENDLY.*"

Figure 5-8

© R.E.M.

from the system by using only a minimal number of instructions or commands. The system leads the user step by step through the process of getting the desired information. Also, the instruction or command language that a person must use to communicate with the computer system should be one that is of English or near-English syntax. "Near-English" would be, for example, the use of abbreviations such as EQ (for "equals" or "is"), phonetically spelled commands, or arithmetic and special-function symbols. Note the structure of the request for information shown in Figure 5-9.

Figure 5-9

Examples of requests for information in a near-English format.

"LIST BY COLUMN O-NAME, O-ID, O-ADDRESS, O-CITY, O-STATE, O-ZIP WHERE O-BUSINESS EQ O-MFG"

(The query will list in a column format the owner's name, identification, address, city, state, and zip code where the owner's business or occupation is manufacturing.)

"LIST USING FORMAT 024 SORTED ON NAME, TEST-DATE WHERE TEST-DATE GT 010283"

(The query will list the person's name and test date in alphabetical order for all test dates greater than January 2, 1983.)

"LIST USING FORMAT 024 SORTED ON TEST-DATE, NAME, ADDRESS WHERE TEST-DATE GT 010283"

(The query is slightly different from the one previously given in that the list will be sorted by date in ascending order. The order is implied to be ascending since no order was specified in the command.)

Second, a user friendly system will give assistance when the user makes an error. If the user inputs an invalid instruction, the system will diagnose the user's statement and display or print an error message telling the user what he or she did that was not acceptable or recognizable to the system. Examples of computer messages to users (some of them not very friendly) are given in Figure 5-10. Error messages should not make the user feel illiterate or inferior to the system. Such messages put too much emphasis on the negative — the error — and not enough on the positive — on what can be done to correct the error. However, the computer is not a mind reader. It has to read the input data or instruction exactly as it is entered, not as it was intended to be entered. For that reason, some messages or "diagnostics" may not make sense. The logic for analyzing input statements is devised by people; sometimes their logic may be faulty. As a result the wrong error message or an incorrect diagnostic statement may be received by the user.

Third, a user friendly system provides choices to the user. These choices may relate to information report formats or structure, to the amount or level of detail provided in the report or information system output, or to response speeds, based upon whether the user wants an immediate response from the

Figure 5-10

Computer messages to users.

MESSAGES NOT VERY *USER FRIENDLY*

"PROGRAM NOT FOUND"

"CPU DOWN"

"RUN ALREADY ACTIVE"

MESSAGES WITH IMPROVED *USER FRIENDLINESS*

"PROGRAM NOT FOUND. DID YOU ENTER THE CORRECT PROGRAM NAME?"

"COMPUTER DOWN. SHOULD BE BACK UP AT 1430 HOURS MST."

"A PROGRAM UNDER YOUR ACCOUNT IS ALREADY RUNNING. TERMINATE YOUR PRESENT PROGRAM WITH A 'STOP RUN' BEFORE ENTERING A NEW 'RUN' COMMAND'

system or one that can come later in the day or even the next day. By being offered choices, managers and executives will have the feeling that the system was indeed designed with their information needs in mind.

Finally, a user friendly system should be housed in an appealing and productive environment. In a user friendly environment, the hardware and other operating aspects of the system not only look good but also are easy to operate. In addition, the environment should not be physically tiring to a user who may be involved with the system for extended periods of time. For example, an interactive terminal should be placed at the right height for the user. The workstation layout shown in Figure 5-11 is one designed to be comfortable, to reduce fatigue, and to be aesthetically appealing.

The first three traits of a user friendly system which were discussed — ease of access, error diagnostics, and provision of choices — have a direct bearing upon the complexity of the information system design. The more friendly the system is to the user, the more complex the design of the system will have to be. Another way of stating this relationship is: The less the user has to do, the more the system must do for the user.

The additional complexity of a user friendly system may require greater sympathetic understanding from the user, since requests for changes may be more difficult to implement. Likewise, problems within the system may be

Figure 5-11

The work environment of users and computer personnel should be comfortable, attractive, and inducive to high productivity.

Panel Concepts, Inc.

more difficult to resolve. These drawbacks make it clear that user friendly systems do have some negative aspects, but the advantages far outweigh the disadvantages. In developing a user friendly system, system designers will emphasize human performance over computer efficiency.

THE FUTURE OF SYSTEMS PERSONNEL

Today, the demand for computer-related personnel far exceeds the supply. This situation should continue well into the 1990s. Why? According to recruitment personnel, demand will continue to increase because the computer industry continues to create more products with lower price tags for an ever-widening circle of eager users. Today there is a virtual explosion in computer usage. This increase in use, in turn, creates more need for people to develop software, to design systems, and to operate those systems. The U.S. Bureau of Labor Statistics estimates that each year 105,000 or more positions in computer and information systems need to be filled. This growth is shown in Figure 5-12. Along with this increased demand for computer-related personnel has been an increase in salary levels. College graduates who make information systems their profession are among the highest-paid new employees in an organization. See Appendix B for additional insight on computer job opportunities.

Figure 5-12

Projected DP job growth in nine industry groups.

Group	1978 Employment	1990 Employment	Percent Change
Services	334,000	720,000	109 %
Mining	13,000	25,000	89.7
Government	117,000	208,000	77.8
Finance, Insurance, Real Estate	152,000	267,000	75
Manufacturing	320,000	552,000	72.5
Construction	10,002	17,005	71.6
Wholesale/Retail	142,000	242,000	70.8
Agriculture, Forestry, Fisheries	1,100	1,800	65.4
Transportation, Communications, Public Utilities	66,000	107,000	63.5

Reprinted by permission from Computer Careers News, *November 17, 1980, p.1*

SUMMARY

The computer is crucial to timely and efficient processing of data into useful information. However, the people involved in designing the information system, maintaining the system, and utilizing the system's potential are more important than the computer itself.

As computer technology has developed and computer-based information systems have multiplied, many new career opportunities have been created. These opportunities include positions such as systems analysts, programmers, computer operators, database administrators, and vice-presidents for information systems. The qualifications, skills, and education required for these positions vary by job and organization.

With the development of computer networks, more and more telecommunications personnel will be needed. Similarly, an increased emphasis on computer security has created new career opportunities in positions such as EDP auditing.

Professional organizations exist to meet the needs of the information systems professional. Some of these organizations have established a certification program similar to that in the accounting field. Certified data processor (CDP) is a title which is expected to grow in both acceptance and demand.

Often information systems are designed by people who concentrate too much on what a particular piece of equipment can do and not enough on the process of human interaction with the system. What is best for the system may not be what is best for the user. The user should be given first consideration in information system design. To do so calls for developing systems that are user friendly, systems that make the users feel at ease. Such systems give as much assistance to the user as is reasonable and economically feasible. However, the user needs to understand that the more the system does for the user, the more complex the system must be.

Demand for computer-related personnel should exceed the supply well into the 1990s. Along with this increased demand has been a rise in salaries making information systems professionals among the highest-paid employees in the United States.

TERMS

Systems analyst	Computer operator
Programmer	Open shop
Applications programmer	Closed shop
Coding	Job control language
Analyst/programmer	Data entry personnel
Systems programmer	Database administrator

Database	Computer center director
Telecommunications personnel	Vice-president of information systems
Telecommunication system	Certification
EDP auditor	User friendly system
Data integrity	

QUESTIONS

1. How does a systems analyst act as a link between the computer and the user?
2. What skills does a systems analyst need?
3. What is the difference between an applications programmer and a systems programmer?
4. What skills are needed by programmers?
5. Why is humility a desired characteristic in a programmer?
6. Why should the analyst and programmer positions be kept separate? Be joined together?
7. What type of training is common for computer operators?
8. Why are databases and their administration crucial to an organization's information system?
9. Why has a need arisen for specialized telecommunications personnel?
10. How does an EDP auditor contribute to data security?
11. What is a CDP? Why is it important to have a certification program in the information systems field?
12. What is the projection for future demand and salaries in the information systems field?

ARTICLE

Critical Programmer Shortage Predicted by '90

NEW YORK—"By 1990 there will be only three-tenths of a programmer available for every machine delivered in this country."

That was the prediction of James E. Homet, director of management information systems (MIS) strategy for the Coopers & Lybrand accounting firm, when he spoke before the New York Financial Writers' Association here.

Homet . . . said that the severe shortage of DP personnel and computer scientists in the U. S. may affect economic growth in the near future. The country can benefit from its technological advances in the computer industry only if the technicians required to use the machines and services are available. "There is a shortage of DP people because of the technical complexity of the industry. It's just soaking qualified people up," he said.

Systems analyst and programmer positions will be the most critical areas for the '80s, he said. And the computer industry can expect a 15% to 40% shortage of these types of skills, according to Homet.

Most of the blame for this projected shortage rests with the educational systems, he maintained.

"Unfortunately, universities cannot meet the salary requirements of qualified instructors who can earn more on the outside," he said. He added that this lack of money also holds true for the computer hardware needed at colleges. The combination of these problems results in a lack of new DPers, Homet said. . . .

DISCUSSION QUESTIONS

1. The writer states that "technical complexity" is one reason for the computer personnel shortage. How in your judgment does technical complexity contribute to the shortage?
2. Discuss ways in which a shortage of computer personnel could affect economic growth.

APPLICATION

"User Friendly" and Friendly Usage

Have you noticed lately that all software is claiming to be "user friendly"?

Presumably this means that the software will take into consideration the user's level of computer literacy and make it easy and pleasant to deal with the computer. Thus, we expect software to provide an appropriate interface that will facilitate man/machine communications.

In the event of errors, software should be forgiving by allowing escapes to prior points and retracing of steps already taken. It should also be sufficiently robust so that users cannot bring down the system or cause it to compute nonsense.

But can we overdo this business of user friendliness to a point where we reach a state of diminishing returns? . . . Let me give an example from real life. In the process of defining requirements for a recordkeeping and reporting system, a financial expert indicated that each transaction should have a unique identification number expressed in four digits. The programmer/analyst, to demonstrate the power and capability of the data entry validation (edit) facility of the data management system, immediately designated the ID field as numeric and, specifically, as a positive integer. After

spending a few weeks building the history file, the analyst discovered that some transactions were allocated to two different profit centers and therefore had to be divided into two separate records. In order to identify the transaction for accounting purposes, the numeric ID had to be enhanced by an alpha character. As the ID had now become an alpha-character string field, the definition of the file had to be revised and the file had to be rebuilt.

This experience illustrates the Catch 22 aspect of designing user friendly systems. The interactive prompt[er]s guide the user's data entry processing steps to the narrowest limits and constraints possible, so that due edit and validation checks can be performed.

This specificity, however, is the antithesis of subsequent flexibility. It is difficult, if not impossible, to take ad hoc, dynamic changes after the system is defined and operational.

. . . An application should accept a variety of ways by which to communicate the demands of the user. A corollary to this

continued

would be the nicety of being able to dynamically modify both form and substance of [display] screens once the application becomes operational in order to fit more closely the special needs of a specific user.

DISCUSSION QUESTIONS

1. How much editing of input data should a program be written to do?
2. What is your perception of "computer literacy"? Should a user have "system literacy" as well?

CHAPTER 6

SYSTEMS AND PROGRAMMING TOOLS AND TECHNIQUES

CHAPTER OBJECTIVES

In this chapter you will learn:

1. Several techniques which have been developed to aid in system development.
2. The different types of flowcharts and their uses.
3. The advantages and disadvantages of flowcharting.
4. The function of a block diagram.
5. The value of decision tables.
6. About HIPO charts and their application to information systems.
7. The importance of documentation.

WHY TOOLS ARE NEEDED

As we stated in Chapter 5, it is the systems analyst who is primarily responsible for developing and designing the input and processing components of an information system. These components work together to provide the user with information for decision making. Too often, however, the information system has been poorly designed, is costly to operate, and, as a result, is grossly inefficient. The poorly designed system is usually the result of a haphazard approach to system development. Given the cost of information processing in organizations today and the size and complexity of those organizations, information systems that are not effective can no longer be tolerated.

Several useful tools and techniques have been developed to aid in efficient system design. Some of the more commonly used ones include flowcharts, block diagrams, decision tables, and HIPO (an acronym for *H*ierarchy plus *I*nput *P*rocessing *O*utput) charts. Systems analysts and programmers rely heavily upon these techniques for two purposes — to logically construct a system solution and to document the system. Documentation is the process of writing down or collecting written, tangible items that will explain the workings of the system being developed. Documentation should be very specific in stating or picturing what the system is, how it is constructed, and how it operates.

The system itself is composed of both physical components and abstract concepts. Examples of physical components are equipment, input forms, and reports generated by the system. Abstract concepts are such things as inventory control equations (for determining economic order quantities or reorder points), interest calculations, and accounting posting methods. Abstract concepts may also be used to represent physical things such as the movement of data from one place to another — e.g., from a disk address to the central processor. Although the movement of the data is actually physical, our perception of it is abstract, for we as computer users visualize it in a form that is totally different from the actual form in which the data exist and move inside the computer system. Inside the computer, the data are stored in binary form, whereas we view the data as a set of decimal digits or alphabetic characters.

These documented descriptions of the system become a model or a picture of the system itself. It is not easy to put this picture accurately on paper; neither is it easy for the viewer or reader to see the "real" system by looking at the pictured representations. The tools and techniques presented in this chapter are used by systems personnel to facilitate the modeling or documentation process.

FLOWCHARTS

A *flowchart* is the traditional method of representing in a schematic form the flow of data in a system. The flowchart shows the points of input and output, the logic or sequence of the various processing steps in the system, and the relationship of one element of the system to the other parts of that system or to other information systems.

A flowchart may be constructed at an overview level (see Figure 6-1), or at a detailed level (see Figure 6-2). Note that in the "CALCULATE CLASS AVERAGE" block in Figure 6-1, the equation for determining the average is not shown. In a detail flowchart, this block would be used to describe the process

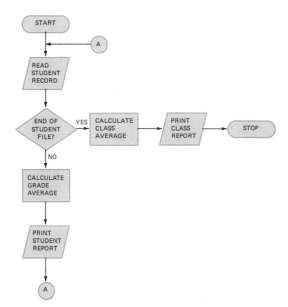

Figure 6-1

An overview flowchart showing in general terms the data flow through the system.

step more specifically. There is no prescribed set of rules governing the level of detail to use in constructing a flowchart. The analyst should direct the level of detail to fit the use that will be made of the flowchart. The flowchart in Figure 6-2, for example, could be written at an even more detailed level than is illustrated.

Figure 6-2

A detail or program flowchart. The data flow through the system is presented in sufficient detail to enable a programmer to write the computer processing instructions from the flowchart.

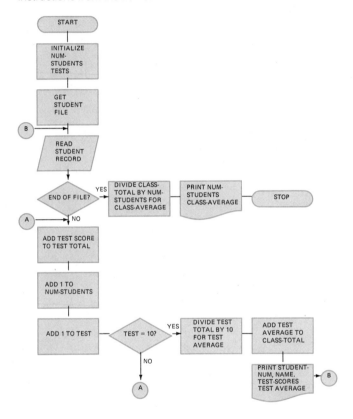

Flowcharting is an excellent means for conveying rather simple, uncomplicated processes, processes that can be broken down into a step-by-step picture..However, flowcharts can quickly become overpowering, confusing, and of little value to anyone if they are not developed carefully. Note the complex appearance of the chart in Figure 6-3. Even though the decision process indicated in the chart is conceptually rather simple (determining total income to see if an individual is eligible for certain benefits), the flowchart looks complicated. In that particular governmental information system, the illustrated flowchart is only one of several flowcharts, some of which are even more complex.

Figure 6-3

Example of a complex flowchart, one of several in the information system from which it was taken.

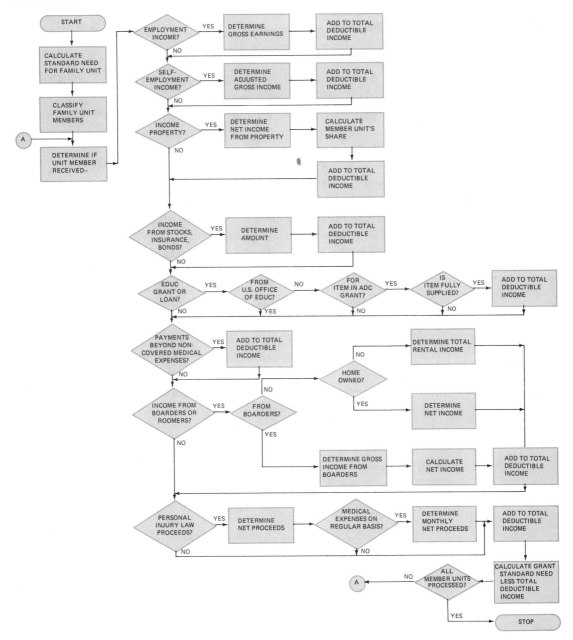

When flowcharting first came into use, each computer manufacturer used its own definition of symbols to flowchart the various input, processing, and output functions of a system. Variations were numerous, and thus the need evolved for a uniform definition of symbols. As a result, the *American National Standards Institute* (ANSI) adopted specific flowcharting symbols for systems documentation. Some of these are illustrated in Figure 6-4.

The most commonly used symbols are TERMINAL, INPUT/OUTPUT, PROCESS, ANNOTATION, DECISION, CONNECTOR, and LINE-OF-FLOW. The TERMINAL point is one where system processing as represented in the flowchart starts, stops, halts, or pauses. The INPUT/OUTPUT symbol serves as an all-purpose I/O symbol. Flowcharting symbols for specific input/output media also exist.

The PROCESS symbol is used whenever data go through some transformation process. Usually the change takes place as a result of an arithmetic calculation. When the description of the operation or group of operations will not fit within the PROCESS block itself, the ANNOTATION block can be used to give the flowchart reader a fuller explanation.

The DECISION block is a junction in the data flow. From the DECISION block, data flow will proceed in one of two or three possible directions. However, the block can be entered from only one of its four points — typically, from the left or the upper tip of the diamond shape. For data flowing out of the block, two points are used for true or false, yes or no situations. Three points are used for decisions involving such considerations as less than, equal to, and greater than. If you have already learned a computer programming language, you will recognize that the DECISION block could easily be called the "IF" block or condition testing block. For example, the computer instruction IF STUDENT-SCORE GE 90 THEN 140 would be shown in the program flowchart as:

Mathematical or *logic symbols* are often used in constructing flowcharting statements. Commonly used logic symbols are shown in Figure 6-5. Abbreviations are often used in the logic statements of a computer program. Some computer languages will not accept $\geq$ or $\leq$ but will accept $>=$ or $<=$, or the abbreviations GE and LE.

Figure 6-4

Flowcharting symbols.

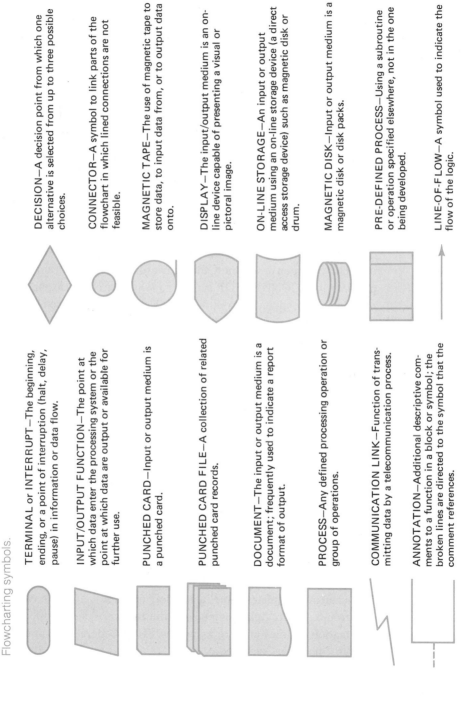

TERMINAL or INTERRUPT—The beginning, ending, or a point of interruption (halt, delay, pause) in information or data flow.

INPUT/OUTPUT FUNCTION—The point at which data enter the processing system or the point at which data are output or available for further use.

PUNCHED CARD—Input or output medium is a punched card.

PUNCHED CARD FILE—A collection of related punched card records.

DOCUMENT—The input or output medium is a document; frequently used to indicate a report format of output.

PROCESS—Any defined processing operation or group of operations.

COMMUNICATION LINK—Function of transmitting data by a telecommunication process.

ANNOTATION—Additional descriptive comments to a function in a block or symbol; the broken lines are directed to the symbol that the comment references.

DECISION—A decision point from which one alternative is selected from up to three possible choices.

CONNECTOR—A symbol to link parts of the flowchart in which lined connections are not feasible.

MAGNETIC TAPE—The use of magnetic tape to store data, to input data from, or to output data onto.

DISPLAY—The input/output medium is an on-line device capable of presenting a visual or pictorial image.

ON-LINE STORAGE—An input or output medium using an on-line storage device (a direct access storage device) such as magnetic disk or drum.

MAGNETIC DISK—Input or output medium is a magnetic disk or disk packs.

PRE-DEFINED PROCESS—Using a subroutine or operation specified elsewhere, not in the one being developed.

LINE-OF-FLOW—A symbol used to indicate the flow of the logic.

Figure 6-5

Logic symbols commonly used in flowcharting statements.

Symbol	Abbreviation	Meaning
=	EQ	Equal to
>	GT	Greater than
<	LT	Less than
≥	GE	Greater than or equal to
≤	LE	Less than or equal to
≠	NE	Not equal to

Flowcharting symbols are connected with one another by an arrow called the LINE-OF-FLOW symbol. Knowing the direction of the logic flow is extremely important in understanding the process the flowchart is trying to convey. However, diagramming the flow strictly through the use of lines and arrows can create problems. Without careful planning, lines may end up going over, under, or between other lines, adding confusion to the diagram. To alleviate this problem, the CONNECTOR symbol, an open circle enclosing a letter, can be used to jump from one part of the flowchart to another. Use of the connector is shown in Figure 6-2. In this figure, connector blocks A and B cut down on the number of lines that would otherwise be required. A line could have been drawn from the first A to the second A without adding to the complexity of the flowchart, but a connector from the first B to the second B is preferred to a line drawn between those two points.

Another concept used frequently in constructing programs or system flowcharting logic is *looping*. If a series of steps is repeated until a particular logic condition exists (such as until all of the student grades have been calculated), this repetitive process can be shown by drawing a loop in the flowchart. In Figure 6-2 there are two loops. One is represented by the connectors at points A and the other at points B. Another facet of looping is that one loop may be located within another loop. This situation is known as a nested loop. (In Figure 6-2, A is logically nested inside B; the A loop is performed ten times before the next student's average is calculated in loop B.) The inside loop is called the *nested loop;* the outside loop is called the *outer loop*.

To aid in drawing flowcharts and flowchart symbols, a *template* is used. Flowcharting templates come in a variety of shapes and sizes; two are shown in Figure 6-6. The template symbols at the top were designed for use in federal information systems and are known as FIPS (Federal Information Processing Systems) flowchart symbols.

Figure 6-6

Flowchart templates with symbols appropriate for either system or program flowcharting. The symbols shown here conform to international flowchart standards.

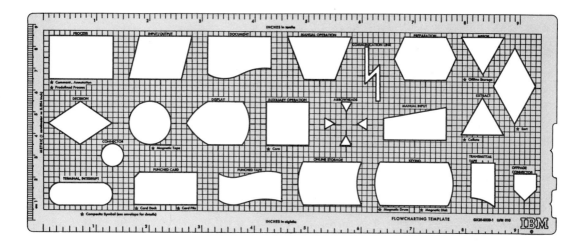

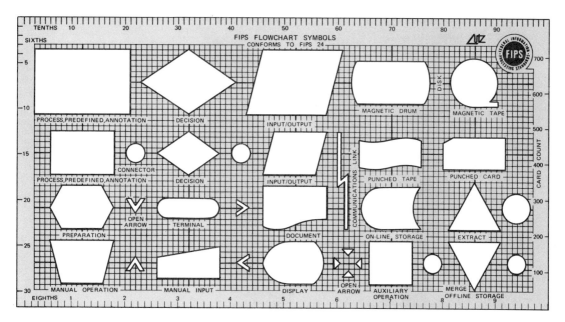

Flowcharts are classified into two major categories: program flowcharts and system flowcharts. In order to write the step-by-step program instructions necessary to process data, the programmer needs to understand the logic structure that will be used in processing the data. A *program flowchart* is a tool frequently used to communicate to the programmer and to others what the program logic structure is; it diagrams the steps that will be required to input and process the data and to generate outputs from the system. In other words, the program flowchart shows what the computer is expected to do. Figure 6-2 is an example of a program flowchart.

A *system flowchart* is used to illustrate the relationships between input data, processing, and the generation of desired outputs. The flowchart shown in Figure 6-7 represents a portion of a system flowchart. Whereas a program flowchart concentrates on that part of the information system which uses computer instructions, the system flowchart is used to give a general overview of

Figure 6-7

A system flowchart depicting a small portion of an order processing system. Note that the flowchart is drawn at an overview, not a detailed, level.

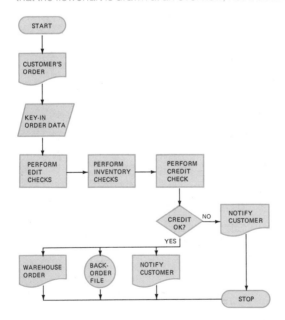

how the information system should function, regardless of whether the steps are manual, mechanical, semi-automated, or computerized. The system flowchart normally begins with creation of input data (such as taking an order) and ends with the final destination of the information.

The system flowchart is drawn at that level of detail necessary for understanding and communicating about the information flow or system activity. For example, a department manager wishing to review a proposed inventory system would probably need only a system overview flowchart, but a detail chart would be necessary for explaining to a data entry clerk the step-by-step operating procedures for getting data into the system.

Another type of flowchart used to illustrate a system process or flow of data is a *block diagram*. Unlike a typical flowchart, a block diagram does not use special symbols to indicate specific system or program functions. Rather, as shown in Figure 6-8, it is just a printed sheet of uniform blocks, used to speed up the flowcharting process. Time is saved because the person developing the block diagram does not have to worry about using specific symbols to communicate a particular data flow. Even though block diagrams do not require the use of flowchart symbols, some analysts combine the use of block diagrams with

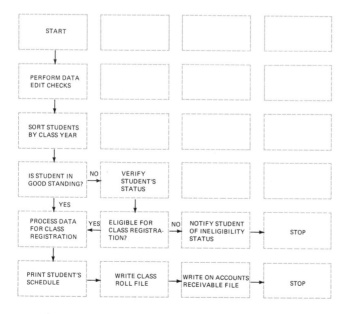

Figure 6-8

A block diagram, often used as the first, rough draft of the system flowchart.

flowchart symbols. This is done to make the flowchart function easier to read or comprehend (see Figure 6-9). Block diagrams are useful in the early stages of flowcharting, especially in working out the program or system solution at an overview level.

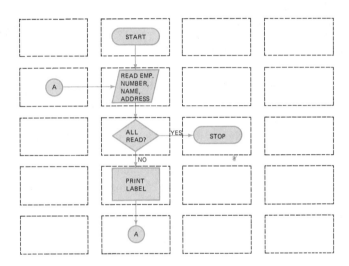

Figure 6-9

A block diagram combined with flowchart symbols.

Flowcharting offers several benefits:

— Flowcharting gives a concise picture of relationships in the system or program to be developed.
— Flowcharts show the processing sequence—the order for executing the processing steps.
— When used at a detailed level, flowcharts speed up the task of writing the computer program instructions.
— Flowcharts can be generated automatically through the use of computer software programs. These programs will print a flowchart automatically, developing the flowchart logic from the logic of the computer program as written by the programmer. Normally this approach is used to update flowcharts so that changes in a program are reflected in the associated flowchart.

There are, however, several drawbacks in the use of flowcharts:

— Complex relationships are often difficult to display.
— Changes in flowcharts cannot be made easily or quickly. A change in the system requires a change in the flowchart, and redrawing a flowchart takes time. The result is that systems people often do not take the time to bring the documentation up to date. Thus, the actual functioning of the system and the way it is displayed by the flowchart no longer agree. This may lead to problems later when other system changes are requested and the out-of-date flowchart is studied to determine how the changes should be made.
— A hierarchical structure of flowcharts is hard to develop. In other words, it is difficult to show that a flowchart is a "sub-chart" of another flowchart. The PROCESS block is the point at which most sub-charts become necessary. The sub-chart is then used to explain more fully the processing described briefly in the original or master block.

DECISION TABLES

A *decision table* or logic table is another technique that is used to document the logic of arriving at a particular decision or result. As shown in Figure 6-10, the layout of a decision table consists of condition statements, condition entries, action statements, and action entries. Combining the condition entries with action entries gives the rules to follow in arriving at a decision.

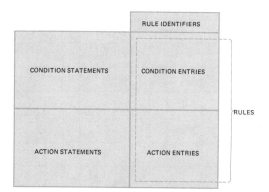

RULE IDENTIFIERS

CONDITION STATEMENTS   CONDITION ENTRIES

RULES

ACTION STATEMENTS   ACTION ENTRIES

Figure 6-10

The format of a decision table or logic table.

The first step in constructing a decision table is to develop the *condition statements*—that is, statements indicating the conditions that *may* arise in the decision process. Next are the *condition entries,* stating the specific condition or conditions that actually exist. The *action statements* are the actions that *could* be taken in solving the problem or in making the decision, and the *action entries* are the specific actions to be taken when a particular condition or conditions exist. The appropriate action to take when a specific condition or combination of conditions exists is called a *rule*.

Note the decision-making process illustrated in Figure 6-11. By following the rules as expressed in the decision table logic, a person will arrive at the correct decision. Specifying rules and following those rules in arriving at a decision are referred to as *programmed decision making*. The rules make up the decision program. If the person follows the rules (the program), the decision is automatically made. For example, look at Rule 5 in Figure 6-11. Assume that a customer has requested a coach seat, but there are no coach seats available. However, an alternate seat is available, and the alternate is acceptable to the

Figure 6-11

A decision table used in an airline reservation system, indicating all the conditions or choices that may arise. Y and N represent Yes and No conditions.

CONDITIONS	RULES															
	1	2	3	4	5	6	7	8	9	10	11	12	13	14	15	16
REQUEST FOR COACH CLASS	Y	Y	Y	Y	Y	Y	Y	Y	N	N	N	N	N	N	N	N
REQUESTED SPACE AVAILABLE	Y	Y	Y	Y	N	N	N	N	Y	Y	Y	Y	N	N	N	N
ACCEPT ALTERNATE CLASS	Y	Y	N	N	Y	Y	N	N	Y	Y	N	N	Y	Y	N	N
ALTERNATE CLASS AVAILABLE	Y	N	Y	N	Y	N	Y	N	Y	N	Y	N	Y	N	Y	N
ACTIONS																
RESERVE COACH SEAT	X	X	X	X												
RESERVE ALTERNATE SEAT					X				X				X			
GO TO STAND-BY TABLE						X	X	X		X				X		

customer. The decision or action then is: Reserve the alternate class seat for the customer.

In the airline reservation example, every possible rule is shown (assuming only two classes of seats are available). The total number of rules possible if only two courses of action are allowed is

$$\text{Total} = 2^n$$

where n is the number of condition statements in the table. In our example, the total is 2^4, or 16. If one more condition statement is added (five conditions rather than four), the number of possible rules would be 32.

Note that some rules are simply not logical (even though it is a "logic" table). Also, some rules are redundant because they have the same significant decision ingredients as other rules and lead to the same decision. In Figure 6-12, the shaded rules are the ones that could be dropped. Without them the table still covers all valid decisions. For example, Rules 1, 2, and 3 lead to the same action as Rule 4, so they are redundant. Rule 16 is totally unnecessary. You might

Figure 6-12

The same decision table shown in Figure 6-11, with shading added to identify the rules that are redundant or illogical.

CONDITIONS	RULES															
	1	2	3	4	5	6	7	8	9	10	11	12	13	14	15	16
REQUEST FOR COACH CLASS	Y	Y	Y	Y	Y	Y	Y	Y	N	N	N	N	N	N	N	N
REQUESTED SPACE AVAILABLE	Y	Y	Y	Y	N	N	N	N	Y	Y	Y	Y	N	N	N	N
ACCEPT ALTERNATE CLASS	Y	Y	N	N	Y	Y	N	N	Y	Y	N	N	Y	Y	N	N
ALTERNATE CLASS AVAILABLE	Y	N	Y	N	Y	N	Y	N	Y	N	Y	N	Y	N	Y	N
ACTIONS																
RESERVE COACH SEAT	X	X	X	X												
RESERVE ALTERNATE SEAT					X				X				X			
GO TO STAND-BY TABLE						X	X	X		X				X		

conclude from studying the table that Rule 8 is also unnecessary because it seems to lead to the same action as Rule 6. However, there is a slight difference: a person under Rule 8 will not accept a seat in an alternate class even if one is available, but the alternate class is acceptable in Rule 6. See if you can identify other rules in Figure 6-11 that are redundant or illogical.

While decision tables are not used as extensively as flowcharts, they do have certain advantages:

— Decision tables present a complete, easy-to-follow picture of the logic used in a particular decision process.
— Non-systems professionals within an organization often have an understanding and knowledge of decision or logic tables from other experiences or training.
— A hierarchy of decision tables can be constructed, thus reducing the complexity of any one table. In Figure 6-11, there is an action "GO TO STAND-BY TABLE"; thus the stand-by table is a sub-table of the main reservations system table.
— Decision tables can be adapted to computer usage through certain software programs.

Decision tables do have certain disadvantages that keep them from being more widely used:

— They have limited use in analyzing information systems. As their name implies, decision tables are used only for decision processes.
— They do not show a time sequence or provide for control over the system once the decision contained in the table has been made.
— They must be used in conjunction with other techniques in analyzing and designing an information system. (This disadvantage is, to a degree, true of any system analysis technique; no single technique is THE only one to use in analysis or documentation activities.)

HIPO CHARTS

HIPO charts were developed in the late 1960s and early 1970s as a means of documenting the hierarchical nature of a system (i.e., system parts and sub-parts) in a more effective manner than is possible with flowcharts. The HIPO technique is useful for going from an overview chart to charts with greater detail. Changes in HIPO charts can also be made more easily than changes in flowcharts. In the late 1960s the IBM Corporation used HIPO charts with great success when developing an information system for the *New York Times*. Subsequently, IBM became one of the first major advocates of the HIPO technique.

HIPO charts consist of two parts, a visual table of contents and diagrams for input, process, and output. The *visual table of contents* (VTOC) indicates the hierarchy of the information system. Figure 6-13 illustrates the technique for a U.S. Forest Service accounting system. The VTOC shows which process or activity is superior or subordinate to other activities. Each block has a function and number. Note in Figure 6-13 that the function of Block 2.0 is to edit the data that have entered the system. The function (DATA EDIT PROCESS) is an abbreviated reference to the activity performed by that block and all other blocks under it. The block number is used for reference and gives an indication

Figure 6-13

A portion of the visual table of contents for the HIPO chart, giving a system overview. The top block indicates the processing, both computer and manual, to be done in all the blocks under it.

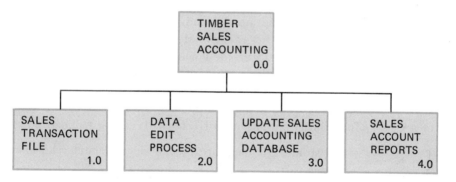

of the hierarchical level of the block. For example, Block 2.0 in the overview table points to the VTOC sub-chart in Figure 6-14, showing that all the blocks below 2.0 are related activities. The block number is also used to reference the related IPO diagram.

Figure 6-14

Breakdown of the data processing represented in Block 2.0 of the overview table shown in Figure 6-13.

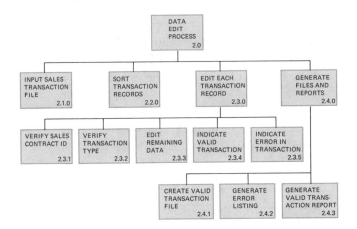

The format of the input, process, and output diagram, or *IPO diagram,* and the IPO activities associated with Block 2.0 (DATA EDIT PROCESS) of the VTOC are shown in Figure 6-15. Note that the process items 2.1, 2.2, 2.3, and 2.4 correspond to the function activities expressed in the respective VTOC blocks (Figure 6-14). In an actual system study, other IPO diagrams would need to be developed to explain the functions of the information system in greater detail. Diagrams for Blocks 2.3.1 through 2.3.5 and so forth in Figure 6-14 need to be developed before the level of detail is specific enough for a person to write a computer program to perform the data edit checks.

The primary advantages of HIPO charts can be summarized as follows:

— The structure of the charts provides for a hierarchical display of various system parts.
— Changes in HIPO charts are easy to make. Through the use of HIPO documentation, the system can be broken down into its many hierarchical levels, each documented on a separate page, thus making updates or changes easy to insert.
— The system elements of input, process, and output, as well as other parts and subsystems, can be displayed visually in an effective format.

Figure 6-15

IPO diagram used in conjunction with the visual table of contents in a HIPO chart. To provide continuity, arrowed numbers identify the diagrams that precede and follow this diagram. The numbered steps in the PROCESS block are explained in greater detail in separate diagrams. A connector (A) is used to show that the output of one process becomes the input to the next or another process.

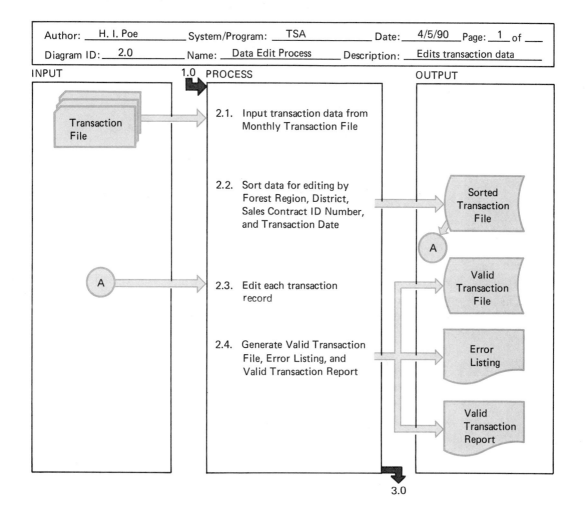

The HIPO technique has one major drawback: it is difficult to display exceptionally complex logic or data-flow relationships. To counter this disadvantage, the analyst and other systems personnel must simplify the logic and the relationship of one system part to another.

PSEUDOCODE

Before actually writing program instructions in computer language, a programmer will often use an intermediate form of instruction writing called *pseudocode*. The use of pseudocode facilitates the process of converting a function or activity from its HIPO or flowchart block to computer-language programming statements. Pseudocode is a near-English description of program statements that combines both English narrative and computer programming code. For example, pseudocode might read as follows:

> IF the old INV-NUM EQ the new INV-NUM THEN PERFORM
> the withdraw process ELSE . . .

The words shown in all capitals are computer programming code words. The above pseudocode statement would not be acceptable to the computer because of the non-computer words used; however, writing acceptable computer-coded instructions is facilitated by writing pseudocode statements first. In addition, an instruction in pseudocode is easier for the programmer to check visually for logic errors or bugs. Another advantage is that pseudocode is easy for others to read. Because even those not well versed in computer programming languages can read pseudocode and understand the intended logic in a specific instruction, the programmer can consult with someone else, perhaps a clerk or a supervisor, in verifying programming logic. Pseudocode is not used as a replacement for flowcharts, decision tables, or HIPO charts, but rather it is used in conjunction with other documentation techniques.

DOCUMENTATION

Earlier in this chapter we referred to *documentation* as the process of writing down or collecting tangible evidence to explain the workings of an information system. Documentation is also a way in which a visual model or form of the system can be displayed and used to explain the system to someone not immediately familiar with it. After the information system is operational, documentation is essential for use as a reference source. It may consist of such things as flowcharts, decision tables, HIPO charts, computer program instructions, various memoranda, report forms, and input forms.

Documentation is a continuous, ongoing process that begins with an initial request for an information system to be developed and continues even after a new system has been implemented. While documentation is an important aspect of information systems development, simply recognizing or giving lip service to the need for it is not enough. The individuals responsible for developing and implementing an information system must make a strong commitment to documentation activities and adhere to accepted documentation standards.

In order to maintain documentation at a high level, some organizations have established *quality control* programs. The objective of a quality control program is to ensure that an information system will not be considered fully operational until the documentation complies with the organization's standards. Naturally, management should not approve the information system until it is fully documented. A quality control program increases the expenditure of energy and time needed to develop an information system. A direct relationship exists between the cost of documentation and its effectiveness. To raise the level of documentation effectiveness, extra time and dollars must be spent. It has been stated that what is convenient and inexpensive for the documentor is, in general, inconvenient and expensive for the user.

Documentation serves these important functions:

— It is a means of communication between individuals during the development of an information system.
— It can be a management control device as the system is being developed.
— It can serve as an instructional tool for those who will be using and operating the information system.
— It serves as an historical reference for later use after the information system has been implemented.

SUMMARY

The efficient design of an information system has been facilitated by the development of several useful tools and techniques. Flowcharts are the traditional method of representing the flow of data in a system. Flowcharts may be constructed at an overview level or at a detailed level depending upon the use to which the flowchart will be applied. While program flowcharts present the logic and relationships used in data processing, system flowcharts display the flow of data from origin to final destination. Block diagrams are elementary flowcharts that are particularly useful in working out problem solutions at a generalized level.

Decision tables are used to classify decision-making activities into a logical format so that decisions can be made accurately and quickly. HIPO charts are used to display hierarchical relationships in a more meaningful manner than is generally possible with flowcharts. The use of HIPO charts also facilitates making changes in documentation that are brought about by changes in the information system.

Pseudocode is an intermediate step that is often used by programmers before actually writing the computer program. This method employs a near-English description of the program steps together with logic symbols and computer language codes so that the writing of computer program statements will be made easier and more accurate.

Documentation is an ongoing process by which the visual form of an information system can be displayed and explained. Documentation consists of such tools and techniques as flowcharts, decision tables, HIPO charts, and report forms.

While this chapter has described several useful techniques for the design and development of computer-based information systems, in reality the process of developing an information system is much more involved and complex than the construction of flowcharts and HIPO charts. Further aspects of system design and development are discussed in Chapters 10–12.

TERMS

Flowchart
American National Standards Institute
 (ANSI)
Logic symbols
Looping
Nested loop
Outer loop

Template
Program flowchart
System flowchart
Block diagram
Decision table
Condition statement
Condition entry

Action statement   Visual table of contents (VTOC)
Action entry   IPO diagram
Rule   Pseudocode
Programmed decision making   Documentation
HIPO chart   Quality control

QUESTIONS

1. What is often the reason for poor system design?
2. What is a flowchart? What does it illustrate?
3. What determines whether a flowchart is constructed at an overview or a detailed level?
4. How do program flowcharts and system flowcharts differ?
5. When are block diagrams useful?
6. What are advantages and disadvantages of flowcharts?
7. Describe the parts of a decision table.
8. What are the advantages and disadvantages of decision tables?
9. Why were HIPO charts developed?
10. How is a visual table of contents used?
11. Which factors determine the detail to which IPO diagrams are developed?
12. What are the advantages and disadvantages of HIPO charts?
13. What is pseudocode? When is it particularly useful?
14. Why is documentation so important?

ARTICLE

What's Bugging You, Bunkie?

Your program wouldn't run?

That's what was bugging you, Bunkie? That's why you growled at your wife and yelled at the kids and kicked the cat and slammed the door?

But now it's running okay, so everything's rosy and life is beautiful? That's the way it is, Bunkie?

I hate to say this, Bunkie, but grab a shovel and crawl down here in the trenches with the rest of us. The war isn't over yet.

About those error messages — your computer could find the easy ones and help you fix them. But, who's going to help you find the errors the computer can't see? Yes indeed — some are probably there, and if you run into them (you might not), your computer can deliver garbage at 19,200 baud.

And Bunkie, when you catch on and list the program to try to find out what went wrong, are you going to remember what the program does and how it does it? Don't be so sure, Bunkie, because very, very few programmers do.

This deplorable fact has been recognized by . . . C. William Gear [who stated] that "In fact, every large program in existence is almost certainly in error, but if there is a low probability of the occurrence of data that causes the error to appear, it is unlikely that the error will ever be discovered."

Dr. Joseph Weizenbaum of Massachusetts Institute of Technology, speaking at a Johns Hopkins University seminar . . . shocked at least some of his audience of future professionals when he said "In large corporations and government offices there are today hundreds of long, useful computer programs that nobody understands. These programs are used to process large quantities of valuable and important data, but they were written years ago and were not well documented. They still run, and they are still in daily use — but nobody can understand them, and nobody even tries to update them."

So don't feel all alone, Bunkie. You may or may not be in good company, but at least you've got company. If you want to get up in the front rank, remember two ideas: program documentation, which means "Put enough cogent and precise comments in this to make it possible for an utter idiot to understand it by looking at it"; and program verification, which means, "Fix your program so it won't print meaningless garbage even if

continued

that utter idiot tries to make it use out-landish data in stupid ways under impossible conditions."

Do it, Bunkie, because the one who tries to use one of your programs might someday be me—or you.

Wallace Kendall, in INFOWORLD, January 26, 1982, p. 19. Reprinted by permission of the author and the publisher, Popular Computing/Inc., a subsidiary of CW Communications/Inc.

DISCUSSION QUESTIONS

1. Identify the reasons for documentation indicated in the above article.
2. Why *not* test a program until all of the bugs (errors) are out of it?

APPLICATION

Study Covers Six Steps to
Quality Assurance

Orlando, Fla.–A new study on DP quality assurance identifies six steps by which DP managers can consistently deliver resources acceptable to end users.

In "Hatching the EDP Quality Assurance Function,"... William E. Perry calls the first step definition of the quality assurance role. Next, DP managers should incorporate quality assurance in the DP function. Then quality assurance personnel should be selected.

The fourth step is defining quality assurance tasks, Perry wrote; the fifth is "building a quality environment." After that is the final step Perry calls "success."

DP management needs to develop standards for each quality assurance criterion... and promulgate these standards among the DP staff. However, that role is just a portion of what DP managers really do. Other responsibilities include meeting production schedules and working within budgets, Perry pointed out.

... According to Perry, "Common management myths about quality" are that quality cannot be measured; quality lowers productivity; poor quality means poor workers; and quality is the responsibility of the "quality department." The cost of quality, he stated, is the sum of the costs of prevention, appraisal, and failure.

The cost of prevention is the money spent to prevent errors.... The cost of appraisal... is the money spent to ensure that the completed work meets user requirements.

In a recent survey IBM users were asked to rank the various responsibilities of quality assurance groups. The survey reportedly derived the following ranking from those IBM users:

- Reviewing and certifying documentation.
- Enforcing standards.
- Reviewing application system controls.
- Certifying systems.
- Recommending controls.
- Developing control standards.
- Assuring that practices are being followed.
- Reviewing systems design for completeness.
- Developing standards.
- Processing deviation requests.
- Consulting.

[The same users were asked] to rank the responsibilities in order of time each activity tends to consume. Perry noted the four most time-consuming responsibilities... as reviewing documentation, consulting with application teams, resolving deviations from standards, and evaluating operational systems.

DISCUSSION QUESTIONS

1. Do you perceive the term "quality assurance" to be synonymous with "quality control"?
2. The writer says that the cost of quality is the sum of the costs of prevention, appraisal, and failure. However, he does not specifically define the cost of failure. How would you define the "cost of failure"?

7 BUSINESS PROGRAMMING LANGUAGES

CHAPTER OBJECTIVES

In this chapter you will learn:

1. The reason for the development of high-level languages.
2. The general classifications of high-level languages.
3. The origins, capabilities, and examples of various languages.
4. How to choose a high-level language.
5. The use of high-level languages for file processing.

EVOLUTION OF HIGH-LEVEL LANGUAGES

While computers cannot solve all problems, they can be very powerful tools when guided properly with a set of instructions (a computer program). However, a computer would be virtually worthless if it had little or no understanding of those instructions. Early programming was done in either machine language or assembly language.

Machine language code is written using the binary digits "0" and "1." Programming the computer in machine language is a very tedious process because the user must thoroughly understand the particular computer being used as well as code all instructions using only the two binary characters. Although machine languages are economical in terms of computer time, the mathematical and computer-oriented vocabulary bears little relationship to human language. Figure 7-1 illustrates a machine-language program to add the integers from 1 to 100.

As a result, languages which were easier to learn, write, and remember were soon developed. One of the first examples of such a programming language is *assembly language*. In assembly languages, a code is substituted for the

Figure 7-1

Portion of machine-language program to add the integers from 1 to 100.

Binary Machine Language			Step	Instruction
01011000	01000000	00100011	1	LOAD TOTAL REGISTER WITH 0
00011010	01000011		2	ADD 1 TO REGISTER
00011010	00110101		3	ADD CURRENT NUMBER REGISTER TO TOTAL REGISTER
01011001	00110001	00100111	4	COMPARE TOTAL REGISTER TO 100
01000111	01000001	00110010	5	BRANCH TO STEP 2 IF REGISTER < 100
01011011	01010001	00110110	6	STORE TOTAL REGISTER

binary (machine) representation of an instruction. Thus, the tedious and time-consuming tasks of keeping track of memory locations and utilizing complex operation codes are eliminated through the use of mnemonic designations. For example, in machine language the actual code for the instruction "ADD REGISTER" might be 100110; the mnemonic code in assembly language might simply be the initials "AR." Use of these mnemonic codes reduces the clerical aspects of programming and eliminates many programming mistakes. However, an assembly language cannot be directly understood and executed by a computer. Each of these special, easier-to-use codes must be translated into a form the machine can understand. Remember that all computers, from microcomputers to supercomputers, execute only rudimentary machine-language instructions. The *assembler* is a program which translates the assembly language into these machine-language instructions. Figure 7-2 shows an assembly-language program to add the integers from 1 to 100.

Although the development of assembly languages simplified the programming task, assembly languages are still highly dependent upon a particular hardware system and are highly symbolic. Consequently, *high-level languages* were developed to overcome these problems. In general, high-level languages are machine-independent and can be used on any machine that has a translator

Figure 7-2

Portion of assembly-language program to add the integers from 1 to 100.

Symbolic Instructions		Remarks
L	4,ONE	LOAD 1 INTO REGISTER 4
AR	4,3	ADD REGISTER 4 TO REGISTER 3
AR	3,5	ADD REGISTER 3 TO REGISTER 5
C	3,C100	COMPARE REGISTER 3 TO 100
BC	4,LOOP	BRANCH TO LOOP IF REGISTER < 100
S	5,ANS	STORE RESULT IN ANS

available for that specific language. In addition, high-level languages are more procedure- and problem-oriented than machine and assembly languages. This is due to the powerful instructions typical of higher-level languages. For example, one higher-level language instruction may accomplish the same task as several lower-level machine instructions (Figure 7-3). This power makes coding faster and debugging (finding errors) easier. The user does not need to have a detailed understanding of the digital computer and can concentrate on solving the problem. Many higher-level languages are even self-documenting; in other words, a listing of the program will suffice for documentation, especially if the program is short.

```
100    T = 0

110    FOR I = 1 TO 100

120    T = T + 1

130    NEXT I
```

Figure 7-3

High-level BASIC program to add the integers from 1 to 100.

As was mentioned before, the computer can process only machine code. Just as the assembler translates assembly language into machine language, a *compiler* translates a program written in a high-level language into a form the computer can understand (machine language). This is illustrated in Figure 7-4. Note that a compiler is a program, not a piece of hardware. The original program, written in a high-level language, is known as the *source program*. The translated program, written in machine language, is known as the *object program*.

When a program written in a high-level language enters the compilation process, two distinct steps occur. First, the source program is translated, or compiled, by the computer into the equivalent object program. Second, the object program is executed (Figure 7-5). This two-step process allows the object program to be stored before it is executed. Thus, a program may be compiled on one computer and executed later on the same or a different computer. This capability is important for business applications because compilation and execution computer costs are about equal. A business application program (such as

Figure 7-4

Program instructions written by humans must be translated by a compiler into an object (binary) code for computer usage.

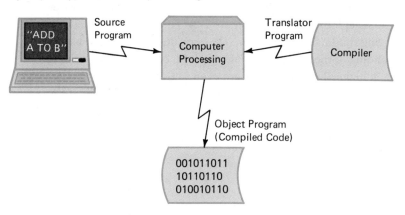

Figure 7-5

Execution of high-level languages requires that the object program be processed with current data to provide desired output.

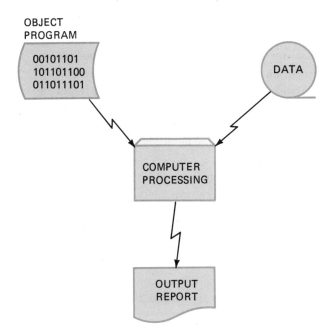

payroll) needs to be compiled only once; execution happens each time the program is needed—typically daily, weekly, or monthly. Both compilers and assemblers offer the user other functions which help debug programs such as program listings of the source code and diagnostic information.

Some high-level languages solve mathematical and scientific problems with ease, while others handle large volumes of business records or retrieve information from large databases. Over a decade ago, Jean Sammet[1] discussed the rationale for selecting high-level programming languages over machine and assembly languages. Among the advantages of high-level languages cited were the following:

— Ease of learning
— Ease of coding and understanding
— Ease of debugging
— Ease of maintaining and documenting
— Ease of conversion
— Reduction of time for problem solving

Now we will learn more about these high-level languages, their capabilities, classifications, and criteria for selection.

LANGUAGE CLASSIFICATIONS

Generally, the choice of which language to use varies depending on which language is compatible with the computer, the skill of the programming staff, and the applications for which the language is intended. Figure 7-6 identifies common high-level languages and their classifications. While some of these languages may be classified in other categories (e.g., FORTRAN may also be used for interactive purposes or for simulation), they are most widely recognized for applications in the categories cited.

An *interactive language* has the specific capability of allowing the user to solve problems on interactive terminals such as a VDT (visual display terminal). These languages usually have rather large computational requirements and minimal input or output demands.

---

[1]Jean E. Sammet, *Programming Languages: History and Fundamentals* (Englewood Cliffs, N.J.: Prentice-Hall, Inc., 1969).

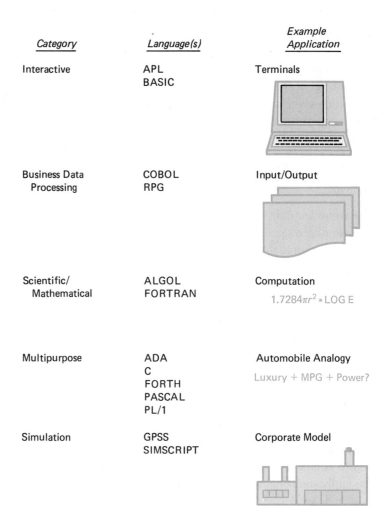

Category	Language(s)	Example Application
Interactive	APL BASIC	Terminals
Business Data Processing	COBOL RPG	Input/Output
Scientific/ Mathematical	ALGOL FORTRAN	Computation $1.7284\pi r^2 * \text{LOG E}$
Multipurpose	ADA C FORTH PASCAL PL/1	Automobile Analogy Luxury + MPG + Power?
Simulation	GPSS SIMSCRIPT	Corporate Model

Figure 7-6

Common high-level languages.

Business data processing includes those applications with large input and output requirements. Extremely large files (such as inventory or accounts receivable) and tremendous amounts of output (hundreds of inventory items or thousands of customer bills) are commonplace in business applications.

Scientific/mathematical problem solving dates back to the earliest use of the computer. Research laboratories were first to use this computer capability. University departments of engineering and computer science also use this powerful language tool.

Multipurpose languages have been developed to bridge the input/output needs of the business community and the processing demands of the scientific/mathematical community. This compromise is difficult to achieve, as efficiency is lost in the attempt to meet both needs. It's like trying to design a car which will give you the luxury of a Rolls-Royce, the power of a Ferrari, and the gas mileage of a Volkswagen.

Simulation languages are special-purpose languages that allow computer modeling of various aspects of the firm's operation. These languages are used principally by large organizations with separate research departments. For example, a firm may want to simulate the effect of adding a new five-million-dollar production line or the impact of a television advertising campaign on consumer behavior. A simulation model is a computerized abstraction of a real world situation that gives managers the opportunity to test the impact of alternative decisions.

The programmers who use these languages are either professional or amateur. Professionals write large programs of a fairly permanent nature and often work in teams. The programs must be documented and maintained for several years. Examples of professional languages are COBOL and PL/1. Amateur programmers use the computer as a tool in their regular employment and typically write small programs for one-time-only tasks. Examples of the "friendly" languages used by amateurs are BASIC and APL.

A QUICK LOOK AT THE LANGUAGES

The following is a brief orientation to the high-level languages most widely used in business applications. The different languages are discussed in alphabetical order. Several lines of example code are provided to illustrate the nature of each language. These examples do not constitute a complete program. Instead they are merely examples of language syntax and appearance. Note how the various languages emphasize English or algebraic statements. A *statement* is defined as a language instruction. Each language has a separate *syntax* (rules and vocabulary) that governs the structure of the language statements.

ADA is a relatively new creation of the U.S. Defense Department, the same agency that promoted COBOL twenty years ago. Developed in 1975 and released in 1981, ADA has gone through several developmental stages. The language was named after Augusta Ada Lovelace, the British countess who worked with Charles Babbage on the analytical engine (see Chapter 2) and is thought to be the world's first programmer. The ADA language (Figure 7-7) is patterned after the PASCAL language and is expected to have a major impact on programming in the next two decades because of active promotion by the federal government. In addition, the tremendous number of government agencies that use computers provide political "clout" in the selection and standardization of computer languages.

Figure 7-7

Sample ADA language instructions.

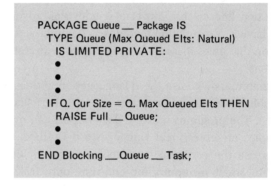

```
PACKAGE Queue __ Package IS
   TYPE Queue (Max Queued Elts: Natural)
      IS LIMITED PRIVATE:
      •
      •
      •
   IF Q. Cur Size = Q. Max Queued Elts THEN
      RAISE Full __ Queue;
      •
      •
   END Blocking __ Queue __ Task;
```

APL (*A Programming Language*) is an interactive computer language which was invented by Kenneth Iverson in the early 1960s (see Figure 7-8). It is a concise, powerful language that is simple to learn and is especially useful for computational applications. APL allows routines to be written on a trial-and-error basis before they are incorporated into the entire program.

Figure 7-8

Sample APL language instructions.

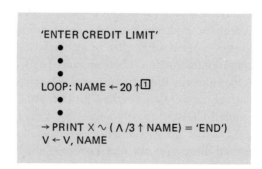

```
'ENTER CREDIT LIMIT'
      •
      •
      •
LOOP: NAME ← 20 ↑ ☐
      •
      •
→ PRINT X ∿ ( ∧ /3 ↑ NAME) = 'END')
V ← V, NAME
```

BASIC (*Beginners All-Purpose Symbolic Instruction Code*) is one of the easiest languages to learn and is undoubtedly the best known of the high-level languages (see Figure 7-9). It was developed in the early 1960s as a timesharing language for instructional purposes. John Kemeny and Thomas Kurtz developed the language on a G.E. timesharing computer at Dartmouth College.

```
10  INPUT N $, H, R
     •
     •
20  IF H > 40 THEN 35
     •
     •
     •
25  LET G = H * R
     •
     •
60 PRINT 'EARNINGS', N $; G
```

Figure 7-9

Sample BASIC language instructions.

BASIC was not designed for professional programmers, and testing and debugging of programs is usually done directly at interactive terminals. As an algebraic language, it handles computations well and usually involves minimal input and output. Currently, BASIC can be used on many different computers. While the fundamental commands are the same on various computers, "extended" versions of BASIC can be very different and are often hard to understand. No general language standard has been developed. Even so, BASIC is used on all sizes of computers and is taught at all educational levels. It may be the closest thing to a universal programming language.

C is a language designed to gain programming efficiencies on minicomputers and microcomputers. Widely used by the Bell System, it is just beginning to spread throughout the programming community. C is a relatively easy language to learn and use, with power comparable to that of PL/1. The power of a language refers to the speed and efficiency with which the computer handles the various instructions. C is a language for the systems programmer or for the serious applications programmer, as it provides one of the most efficient codes of any high-level language (Figure 7-10).

```
int i, * ip, f( );
       •
       •
       •
pl "Type a number and press RETURN";
       •
       •
       •
pn (( one + two) (2)
       •
       •
go to contin:
       •
       •
return (( m > c)? m: c);
```

Figure 7-10

Sample C language
instructions.

COBOL (*CO*mmon *B*usiness *O*riented *L*anguage), first used in 1960, is now the most widely used language for business applications in both medium and large organizations (see Figure 7-11). One of the prime contributors to the development of COBOL was Captain Grace Hopper, who helped develop and test various COBOL compilers.

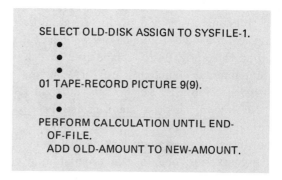

```
SELECT OLD-DISK ASSIGN TO SYSFILE-1.
       •
       •
       •
01 TAPE-RECORD PICTURE 9(9).
       •
       •
PERFORM CALCULATION UNTIL END-
   OF-FILE.
ADD OLD-AMOUNT TO NEW-AMOUNT.
```

Figure 7-11

Sample COBOL language
instructions.

The American National Standards Institute (ANSI) published standardized specifications of COBOL in 1968 and again in 1974. Standardization is very important for general language use, allowing programs coded for one computer to be run on another computer with minimal revisions.

Special features of COBOL which appeal to business applications programmers are its file- and report-handling capabilities. More professional programmers know COBOL than any other language, and there are more jobs available for such programmers than for any other language.

FORTH is a relatively new language that was designed in the early 1970s by Charles Moore for use in astronomical observations (Figure 7-12). It has proved especially useful in process control operations with microprocessors for applications such as auto mechanics, oil exploration, film making, and battlefield operations. FORTH is a language ideally suited for microcomputers since its programs are very compact. Its programming is entirely structured, allowing programmers to substantially reduce time to code large projects.

Figure 7-12

Sample FORTH language instructions.

FORTRAN (*FOR*mula *TRAN*slator) was the first high-level language to enjoy wide success (Figure 7-13). Developed by John Backus of IBM, it was

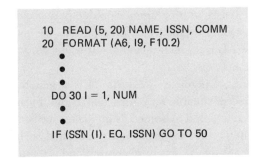

Figure 7-13

Sample FORTRAN language instructions.

released in 1957 to support scientific and engineering problems which involved complex mathematical computations. ANSI standards were established in 1966, and today nearly all computers are capable of handling FORTRAN programs. Since it is one of the most widely understood languages in the computer world, new features such as self-documentation and structured commands are being added to meet modern language needs. Structured FORTRAN commands allow consistent computer coding by programmers.

One of the newer languages is *PASCAL,* which was introduced in the early 1970s (Figure 7-14). It was designed by Niklaus Wirth in Zurich for use as a highly structured and readable language. This readability reduces maintenance costs, an important feature to the business manager. On the other hand, there are limitations in the file-handling and output-report capabilities of PASCAL.

```
BAL:
      ARRAY [1 . . 2000] OF REAL;
      •
      •
      •
BEGIN
      J: 1;
      •
      •
      WHILE ACCT (J) < > TACCT DO
READLN (TACCT, BAL, AMT)
```

Figure 7-14

Sample PASCAL language instructions.

PASCAL has been used to teach computer programming principles and is fast becoming a major instructional language in universities. Research done at the University of California at San Diego indicates that because of its structured format and power, increases in programmer productivity occur when PASCAL is used. Its modular structure practically forces one to use good programming habits. To date, PASCAL is a much-talked-about language, with little current usage in business applications.

PL/1 (Programming Language — Version 1) is a general-purpose, "universal" language touted as suitable for both scientific and business applications (Figure 7-15). While considered by some a "super language" destined to replace FORTRAN and COBOL, thus far it has not diminished their use. However, PL/1 and a proposed subset are easily structured and are more versatile than either FORTRAN or COBOL.

```
DECLARE PAY __ # DECIMAL FIXED (9),
    •
    •
    •
NEW __ RECORD: GET FILE (INPUT)
    •
    •
  LIST (PAY __ #, PAYMENT);
    •
    •
    •
IF BALANCE = 0
   THEN GO TO NEW __ RECORD;
```

Figure 7-15

Sample PL/1 language instructions.

RPG (*Report Program Generator*) is a highly specialized language that often reduces total programming costs. Programs are coded on special forms which indicate exact specifications for input, output, and calculations (Figure 7-16). Because its use is limited primarily to report generation, some critics do not consider RPG a high-level language. RPG, which can be learned in only a few hours, is widely used in business and industry, particularly among small businesses, to handle file-processing tasks. Some modern organizations use word processors to perform typical RPG functions.

While the preceding languages are the most common high-level languages, there are numerous *specialized languages* also available. To "name drop" just a few: APT is used for numerical control of machine tools in manufacturing. LISP, SLIP, and IPL-V are list-processing, scientific languages. PLATO and PILOT

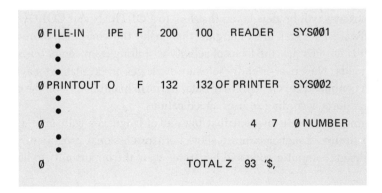

```
Ø FILE-IN    IPE  F   200   100    READER    SYSØØ1
    •
    •
    •
Ø PRINTOUT O    F   132   132 OF PRINTER   SYSØØ2
    •
    •
Ø                                 4   7   Ø NUMBER
    •
    •
Ø                        TOTAL Z   93  '$,
```

Figure 7-16

Sample RPG language instructions.

are used in computer-aided instruction. DYNAMO, GPSS, and SIMSCRIPT are used to simulate business and economic systems. ALGOL (algorithmic language) is widely used in Europe and is also valuable for teaching computing processes. ALGOL is primarily useful in the area of numerical calculations.

LANGUAGE EVOLUTION

It is interesting to note the role of supply and demand in the marketplace for certain high-level languages. IBM spent millions marketing PL/1 without gaining widespread business acceptance for it. Customer demand ultimately forced vendors to provide BASIC for all sizes and types of computer hardware. PASCAL is currently developing much the same type of widespread demand. ALGOL and APL are languages that have developed a "cult" of fervent, dedicated followers in the past, while FORTH and C are in current vogue with "serious" programmers on small computers.

The future of computer languages is difficult to predict, but PASCAL seems destined to make inroads among professional programmers. BASIC and COBOL will probably remain the most widely used high-level languages. In the next decade, the U.S. Defense Department's development of ADA may establish this language as a leader in *real time* (very rapid computer response) programming. The probability that a single, universal programming language will be developed for the entire computer community is very small. The business community has an enormous investment in existing programs and cannot simply rewrite their programs whenever a new, more popular, or more powerful language is developed.

New programming emphasis will move toward simpler, more cost-effective programming that can be done by non-systems personnel. Also, new user-oriented packages will be developed that link to FORTRAN and COBOL programs. Software packages are emerging that make the computer more *user friendly*. This implies that the focus of activity is shifting from computer needs to human needs. New user-friendly software packages are available today that use English commands to create files of data, perform maintenance on the data, and create reports according to user specifications.

In summary, it seems evident that high-level languages will serve a dual role in the future. Languages must allow both professional programmers to develop efficient computer code and first-time users the opportunity to handle computing needs with minimal language training. The decade of the 1980s will see greater numbers of user-friendly language applications.

LANGUAGE SELECTION

The proper choice of a high-level language depends on several factors. These factors include the computer to be used, programmer expertise, applications for which the language will be used, and the cost of programming. Since programming costs can be very high, the choice of which language to use is important to the organization.

The cost of writing and maintaining programs is a direct labor cost. Computer compilation and execution of programs are also direct costs. If programmer expertise is not readily available, either additional training or the use of outside consultation is necessary.

Sammet[2] listed the following factors for consideration in choosing a programming language:

— Suitability of language for problem area and projected users
— Availability on desired computer
— History and evaluation of previous use
— Efficiency of language implementation
— Compatibility (ability to transfer programs to another machine) and growth potential
— Functional characteristics (e.g., standards and user friendliness)
— Technical characteristics (e.g., syntax or language rules, character set available, etc.)

Keep in mind that no single language is ideal for all applications in a company. Some languages, as we've seen, are more suitable than others for particular applications. For example, do you want interactive or batch output? Is the problem a complex, one-time application? Are you in need of real-time processing? Will the program be run on several different computers or will it be limited to one central mainframe? A summary of the characteristics of seven of the high-level languages discussed earlier in this chapter is given in Figure 7-17.

[2]Ibid.

Figure 7-17

Characteristics of seven high-level languages.

CHARACTERISTIC	APL	BASIC	COBOL	FORTRAN	PASCAL	PL/1	RPG
Ease of learning	Fair	Excellent	Fair	Good	Fair	Fair	Excellent
Suitability for large programs	Fair	Poor	Good	Good	Excellent	Good	Poor
Suitability for small programs	Excellent	Excellent	Poor	Good	Good	Poor	Good
General problem-solving capability	Good	Fair	Good	Good	Good	Good	Poor
Efficient code generation	Good	Fair	Good	Good	Good	Good	Fair
Compatibility to standards	Good	Fair	Excellent	Excellent	Fair	Good	Good
Mathematical capabilities	Excellent	Good	Fair	Excellent	Good	Good	Poor
Text-handling capabilities	Fair	Fair	Excellent	Fair	Good	Good	Good
Self-documenting	Poor	Poor	Excellent	Poor	Good	Good	Fair
Structured programming capacity	Poor	Poor	Good	Poor	Excellent	Good	Fair

STRUCTURED PROGRAMMING

You may have noticed an emphasis on *structured programming* when languages were compared earlier in this chapter. The foundation for structured programming is the premise that any program flow can be constructed using only three basic program flow procedures: sequence, logical branch, and loop (Figure 7-18). If a language is structured, the "flow" of instructions must always fit one of these three procedures. High-level languages use different statements to handle these program constructs. Structured code does *not* allow "GO TO" statements for logic control. Eliminating "GO TO" commands for

Figure 7-18

Structured program design.

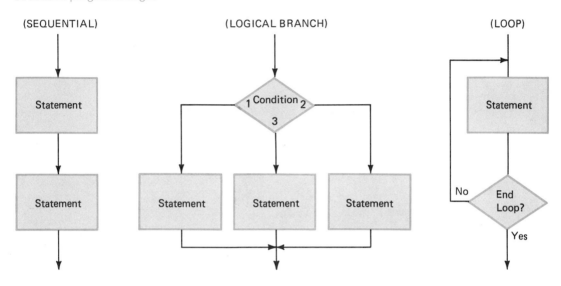

linking programs makes a program easier to understand, debug, modify, and incorporate within larger programs. Currently, structured programming is gaining widespread acceptance and support as a cost-effective program development technique.

USING LANGUAGES FOR FILE PROCESSING

We have noted that languages have many capabilities and have been used for a wide variety of business and non-business applications. Textbooks usually compare languages according to their mathematical capabilities. This is not always appropriate for comparing business programs, because file updating and file editing are not based on excessive internal calculations.

File updating (Figure 7-19) is the task of correcting out-of-date file data. File updating for an accounts receivable file, for example, determines which

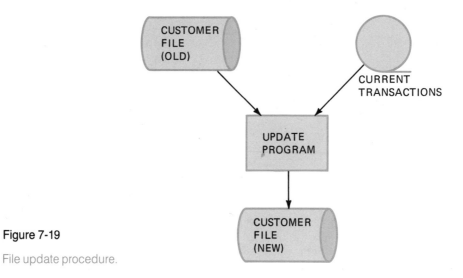

Figure 7-19

File update procedure.

customers have paid their bills and which still owe money. *File editing* (Figure 7-20) involves keeping or eliminating data, rearranging data, and/or testing data for reasonableness. In addition to processing edits, there are input edits (arrangement and validity of source data) and output edits (preparation of

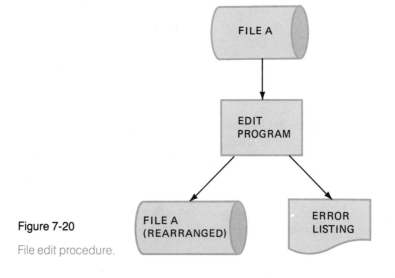

Figure 7-20

File edit procedure.

reports). Most COBOL programs incorporate both updating and editing functions, as illustrated in the partial COBOL program example shown in Figure 7-21. See if you can find instructions that actually update or edit a record in the example.

High-level languages vary significantly in their ability to handle file editing and updating. APL and BASIC have limited usefulness for these tasks because the programmer has little control over storage devices. File manipulation is possible with FORTRAN and ALGOL, but it is not convenient. The standard file-processing language is COBOL, with PL/1, PASCAL, and RPG also used for processing business files.

```
    •
    •
    •
    •
PROCEDURE DIVISION.
START.
   OPEN INPUT DETAIL-FILE, I-O MASTER-DISK.
   READ DETAIL-FILE AT END MOVE 1 TO END-FILE.
   PERFORM UPDATE-ROUTINE THRU UPDATE-ROUTINE-
      FINAL UNTIL-END-FILE = 1.
   CLOSE DETAIL-FILE, MASTER-DISK.
UPDATE-ROUTINE.
   MOVE CUSTOMER-NUMBER TO KEY.
   READ MASTER-DISK INVALID KEY
      DISPLAY 'INVALID DETAIL RECORD'
      DETAIL-RECORD, GO TO UPDATE-ROUTINE-FINAL.
   MOVE AMOUNT OF DETAIL-RECORD TO AMOUNT OF
      DISK-RECORD.
   REWRITE DISK-RECORD.
UPDATE-ROUTINE-FINAL.
   READ DETAIL-FILE AT END MOVE 1 TO END-FILE.
```

Figure 7-21

Sample of COBOL file-processing program (PROCEDURE DIVISION only).

SUMMARY

Early programming was done in machine or assembly language, and the need for new, high-level languages soon became apparent. Through the use of such languages, communication with computers has become much easier and problem solving has been facilitated.

Not all high-level languages are the same, and the choice of which language to use depends on a variety of factors such as the skill of the programming staff, the applications for which the language is intended, and the compatibility of the language with the computer. Generally, languages can be grouped into five categories — interactive, business, scientific/mathematical, multipurpose, and simulation. Thus, while a language such as COBOL is well suited for business applications, FORTRAN would be much more appropriate in scientific/ mathematical applications.

Languages also vary in their level of acceptance throughout the computer world. The way in which languages are marketed has an impact on their success or failure.

In the future, languages will play a dual role. They must accommodate the needs of the systems professional while still allowing first-time or occasional users the opportunity to satisfy their computing needs quickly and easily. Finally, while languages have many varied capabilities and applications, the business person, whether student or professional, should evaluate a language based on its suitability for specific business applications.

TERMS

Machine language	APL
Assembly language	BASIC
Assembler	C
High-level language	COBOL
Compiler	FORTH
Source program	FORTRAN
Object program	PASCAL
Interactive languages	PL/1
Business data processing languages	RPG
Scientific/mathematical	Specialized languages
Multipurpose languages	Real time
Simulation languages	User friendly
Statement	Structured programming
Syntax	File updating
ADA	File editing

QUESTIONS

1. Why were high-level languages developed?
2. Why is a compiler so important?
3. Generally, upon what will the choice of language depend?
4. Explain the various categories of high-level languages.
5. Why is ADA expected to have a major impact on programming?
6. For whom is BASIC designed?
7. What is meant when we say that C is an efficient language?
8. Why is COBOL so popular with the business community?
9. Is FORTH used more for manufacturing or for financial applications?
10. For what use is FORTRAN particularly well suited?
11. What impact has university research had on PASCAL?
12. What is meant when it is said that PL/1 is a "universal" language?
13. Why is RPG not considered a high-level language?
14. What are direct costs of programming?
15. What are the differences between file updating and file editing?
16. Why do you think standardization of a computer language is important?

ARTICLE

"I claim that I am the owner of the first pure software patent (4,270,182) disclosed, claimed, prosecuted, rejected, and eventually issued as an algorithm."
—S. Pal Asija

The author of what is said to be the first patented computer software program in this country has just completed a potentially controversial book called *How to Patent Computer Programs*.

It took S. Pal Asija, an electrical engineer and computer-systems analyst, seven years to obtain the patent he received on May 26, 1981, from the U.S. Commissioner of Patents and Trademarks. Asija had become an attorney specializing in patent law before developing his program, which he calls Swift-Answer. He has also patented several other inventions of his own design, including an "electroventriloquist" and a "sleep-sensing switch."

According to Vernon Jacobs, a tax consultant and president of Research Press, Inc., which will publish Asija's book, "It's always been possible to patent hardware, but what Asija said is that a hardware patent is of little value if the software couldn't be patented also. There's nothing to prevent someone from marketing software that will essentially do what the patented hardware does."

Most software developers have resigned themselves to trying merely to copyright their work. The granting of patents for software could have a significant impact on the computer industry.

Mike Scott, a lawyer and publisher of the Scott Report, said that "other people have patented software, but didn't call it software in their application. He [Asija] was bold enough to say what he had and has probably done everyone a service."

Asija does not expect a flood of patent applications to follow the release of his book, however. In an exclusive interview with *InfoWorld*, he said that in order to be patented "a program has to pass the critical test of obviousness. You not only have to show it's an original work, but also that it was unobvious to the average programmer when it was invented."

According to Jacobs, a patent would give the program developer greater protection than a copyright. Jacobs said a patent normally allows the developer or creator to secure capital gains from the sale or license of his creation, whereas capital gains are not available to the creator of a copyright-protected work.

Asija concurred, explaining that once a program is put in the public domain it can be adapted or changed in a comparatively marginal way and be resold by a different vendor as a new product. "With

continued

a patent one does not obviate the payment of royalties by minor modifications," said Asija.

Asija believes that VisiCalc, which is copyrighted, is a program that could have been patented as "pure software," making it illegal for anyone to change the basic algorithms of the program and resell it as a new product. "If someone should come up with an algorithm for language translation, that might also be patentable.

"The press hasn't yet caught on to what I've done," Asija continued. "I think these big companies like IBM didn't want to spend the time and money on trying to get patents for their software because their attorneys told them it would be a waste of time. They may've thought that when the U.S. Supreme Court ruled against a few companies that tried to patent software that it [the Supreme Court] was saying software wasn't patentable.

"But the Court didn't say software wasn't patentable; it said those particular software programs weren't patentable."

According to Asija a product has to be "new, useful, and unobvious" to qualify for a patent. Noting that his program as pure software is new, useful, and unobvious, he further defined the three criteria that software has to meet before it can be considered patentable.

- It must be pure software; in other words, a program that does not require substantial pre- or post-solution activity with a separate hardware device other than a computer or computer peripheral.
- The patent claim must describe the product and its function as software, not hardware.
- The software must teach the average person, skilled in software application, how to implement it without having to consult the inventor and without undue experimentation.

Asija said his SwiftAnswer will run on any "general digital computer hardware." He described SwiftAnswer as an "information retrieval system" that accepts questions in "natural language form." He said the system is "very forgiving to a user who makes errors in spelling, syntax or grammar," and that people with no knowledge of computers can use it.

DISCUSSION QUESTIONS

1. What is the advantage of a patent compared to a copyright?
2. Could programming assignments written by students be patented? Why or why not?

APPLICATIONS

20,000 Programs Adaptable To IBM Micro, Says Xedex

NEW YORK — Xedex Corp. last week unveiled a new electronic device designed exclusively for International Business Machines Corp.'s (IBM) "Personal Computer" that makes the microcomputer compatible with thousands of existing software programs.

Known as "Baby Blue CPU Plus," the new device was described as a combination circuit board and software that makes over 20,000 existing compatible CP/M-80-based programs available to Personal Computer owners. It also will expand the computer's present memory with 64 Kbytes on the board.

Shipments of the $600 unit will begin next month. According to Xedex president Harris Landgarten, "It's a total solution to the problem, now being experienced by owners of the IBM Personal Computer." He said Xedex is aiming for a 30 percent market penetration of all Personal Computers.

Baby Blue "will make the IBM machine more versatile than an Apple or a Tandy microcomputer in terms of function and problems it can solve," he claimed.

According to Landgarten, Baby Blue will permit owners of the Personal Computer to run virtually any software that is CP/M-80-compatible and written for 8080 or Z80 eight-bit microprocessors. The device is simply plugged into an existing slot in the IBM chassis.

"It was assumed by many people in the industry that IBM would come out with their computer and that hundreds of programmers would then start working furiously to convert existing software," Landgarten said, explaining that "it's not that easy."

"We're dealing with a cottage industry," he said, pointing out that many programs are written by people without the resources to do translations or that some programs, although important to a single user, may not have wide enough appeal to warrant conversion.

"Take the case of a program that was written by a consultant specifically for a company that now wants to upgrade its operation to an IBM Personal Computer," Landgarten said. "Rather than going back to the consultant and possibly paying him $20,000 or $30,000 for a conversion, the company can instead continue to use its original program for only $600, the cost of Baby Blue."

MIS Week, *March 3, 1982, p. 14.*

Hand/Sign System Put On Micro by Student

FROSTPROOF, Fla. — A local high school student has developed computer programs that teach hand-sign language (or "finger spelling") for communication with the hearing-impaired.

Daniel K. Johnston's programs were written for the TRS-80 Model III and the TRS-80 Color Computer, both products of Radio Shack, a division of Tandy Corporation.

These "Deafsign" programs, which use video graphics and written video instructions to teach sign language spelling and symbols to the hearing-impaired and others, earned Johnston an honorable mention and $500 cash award in the recent Johns Hopkins University First National Search for Applications of Personal Computing to Aid the Handicapped, sponsored by the National Science Foundation, Radio Shack.

Johnston's programs include lessons on letters of the alphabet and word-symbol hand signs (including animated movements in the TRS-80 Color Computer version); increasingly rapid drills with written prompts included; and eventually, increasingly rapid drills with hand signs only.

Reprinted from Software News, *March 1, 1982. Copyright 1981, Technical Publishing, a division of Dun-Donnelley Publishing, Hudson, MA 01749.*

DISCUSSION QUESTIONS

1. What is a "cottage industry" for programmers?
2. Can the student's hand/sign programs work on the IBM Personal Computer? Explain.

8 BASIC PROGRAMMING

CHAPTER OBJECTIVES

In this chapter you will learn:

1. How BASIC computer programs solve problems.
2. The difference between system commands and program commands.
3. Common BASIC statements for input, processing, and output.
4. How to write useful BASIC programs.

THE LANGUAGE OF BASIC

Programming is a skill that is useful for business students, in much the same sense that writing and reasoning are useful general education skills. Successful development of a computer program allows an individual to truly understand the power as well as the limitations of a computer. *BASIC* (Beginners All-Purpose Symbolic Instruction Code) is an appropriate "first" language since this high-level language is

— available on almost every computer,
— easy to learn and understand, and
— a powerful tool.

Most computer manufacturers have their own version (dialect) of BASIC. While some versions are more powerful than others and use unique commands, the most common BASIC commands are covered in this chapter. Numerous examples and sample programs are included to facilitate learning.

Your First Programming Session

Preparing to write a BASIC program on a microcomputer is simple if you can find the "on" switch. Since the BASIC compiler (or interpreter) resides in memory, you just need to hit the carriage return key and start writing code. On an interactive terminal, you need to link yourself to a mainframe computer. This is called "logging on," and the specific procedure varies from computer to computer. You will typically need a password and knowledge of two or three computer system commands. On nearly all systems one of the following computer responses is an invitation to proceed: "READY", "?", or a flashing cursor "▶".

In your first programming session, try these friendly commands:

```
10 PRINT "HELLO, MY NAME IS            "
20 END
RUN
```

The computer will print HELLO, MY NAME IS BOB or whatever your name is. The first two numbered lines represent a complete BASIC program. Lines 10 and 20 are BASIC *statements*, which must have line numbers for identification. The RUN command requests the computer to execute (or run) the program statements. Only line numbers that are in sequence can be used. Don't worry about spacing, since BASIC allows you to squeeze (e.g., 10PRINT"HELLO") or spread (e.g., 10 PRINT "HELLO") statement commands. The computer may be used as a calculator with the following symbols:

Add	+
Subtract	−
Multiply	*
Divide	/

To calculate at a terminal or on a microcomputer, write a program such as:

```
10 PRINT 145 + 99
20 PRINT 76 − 18
30 PRINT 34 * 43
40 PRINT 7295 / 25
50 END
RUN
```

The computer will respond:

```
244.
58.
1462.
291.8
```

Several calculations may be combined in one statement, separated by commas. Line numbers do not have to be 10, 20, etc.; they may be as small as 1 or as large as 99999.

Computer System Commands

To determine what has been previously programmed, a useful system command is LIST, which directs the computer to print all the statements stored in memory. If a mistake in a statement is found, the user retypes the statement number and then retypes the line to correct the error. To delete a statement, type the line number only and hit the carriage return key to enter a blank instruction. The computer will acknowledge only the corrected version. The ability to change programs easily is one of the powerful characteristics of BASIC. To keep an entire program, type SAVE. The command CATALOG lists all the programs that have been saved previously. To sign off at the end of a programming session, type BYE and/or turn off the equipment. LIST, RUN, and BYE should make your first session with a computer a pleasant experience.

The following system commands (or their equivalent) are important:

System Command	Use
CATALOG	Provides list of saved programs
LIST	Lists current program
RUN	Executes current program
SAVE	Saves current program
BYE	Disconnects a user from computer

PROGRAM COMMANDS IN BASIC

The following common program commands are needed to write business programs:

Program Command	Use
REM	Allows remarks or comments
LET	Assigns values to variables
PRINT	Writes output line
INPUT	Requests input data
READ/DATA	Provides input data
END/STOP	Terminates program
GO TO	Provides program mobility
IF/THEN	Aids decision logic
FOR/NEXT	Provides both mobility and logic

Each of these BASIC program commands is explained below.

REM

The REM (remark) statement allows comments to be written within a program. The REM statement may document the name of the programmer, identify a program, or provide procedural explanations. REM statements are also used to explain the meanings of variables. The remark statement does not cause the computer to execute any commands. REM instructions perform no function other than printing the remark as part of the program listing. A remark might be

100 REM PROGRAMMED BY ANN SMITH

If a comment requires more than one line, separate statements are used:

```
100 REM COMPUTE COMPOUND INTEREST
200 REM PROGRAMMED BY ANN SMITH
300 REM CLASS ASSIGNMENT #1, DUE APRIL 15
```

Liberal use of REM statements is recommended.

LET

The LET statement is used to assign values and has the form

```
20 LET T = X + 10
```

The LET statement is a command and not an equation. The word LET is optional in many versions of BASIC; the command can also be written

```
20 T = X + 10
```

T and X are called *variables*, and their values may change in a program. The value of the *expression* (the right-hand side of the equal sign) is assigned to the single variable on the left side of the equal sign. The entire statement is called an *assignment* statement. In the example above, the computer must know the value of X so that 10 plus that amount can be assigned to T. In the following program, the value assigned to X in statement 15 is used in statement 20:

```
10 REM SIMPLE COMPUTATION
15 LET X = 25
20 LET T = X + 10
25 PRINT T
30 END
RUN
```

The computer will respond:

```
35.
```

A variable name must be either a single letter or a letter followed by a single digit:

Valid Numeric Variables	Illegal Numeric Variables
X	X33 (too long)
A	AA (letter second)
C3	3C (digit first)
T5	T# (non-digit)

Numeric data may be either integer or decimal and either positive or negative. Use of commas or dollar signs is not allowed:

Valid Numeric Data	Illegal Numeric Data
5200	5,200 (comma)
523	$523 (dollar sign)
−66	66− (minus sign misplaced)
84.5	84.5B (alphabet character)

The following program illustrates the use of REM statements to explain variables, as well as the use of different forms of numeric variables and numeric data:

```
50 REM PROGRAM TO COMPUTE SIMPLE INTEREST
100 REM I INTEREST EARNED
110 REM P1 PRINCIPAL, R RATE, P2 TOTAL EARNINGS
120 LET P1 = 1000
130 LET R = .18
140 LET I = P1 * R
150 LET P2 = P1 + I
160 PRINT P2
RUN
```

The computer will respond:

```
1180.
```

Variable names that represent alphanumeric data (numbers, letters, and symbols) are called *string* data, and the associated variables are called string variables. They can contain no more than three characters and must be written in letter-number-symbol order. A string variable always begins with an alphabet letter, but it need not have both a number and a symbol.

Valid String Variables	Illegal String Variables
A$	$A (symbol first)
T$	2$ (no alpha)
B2$	X33$ (too long)
C9$	B$1 (wrong order)

Alphanumeric data may also be assigned by a LET statement:

```
10 LET B$ = "JOHN JONES"
20 LET C$ = "BARBARA SMITH, 491 EAGLE DR."
```

Note that string data must be enclosed in quotation marks. To further illustrate:

```
100 LET C$ = "COMMISSION EARNED"
110 PRINT C$
120 END
RUN
```

The computer will respond:

```
COMMISSION EARNED
```

It is also possible to perform a chain of operations in a LET assignment statement. The expression $\dfrac{X1 + X2}{2}$ would be programmed:

```
100 LET A = (A1 + X2) / 2
```

Parentheses are needed to allow proper calculation sequence, since expressions with * or / are calculated before expressions with + or −. Liberal use of parentheses is recommended.

PRINT

The PRINT statement creates program output. On most BASIC language versions, the output page or screen is divided into five print zones of about 15 spaces each. Commas are used between variables in a print statement to indicate that the values are to be printed in succeeding print zones (see line 50 below):

```
10 REM NOTE OUTPUT SPACING
20 LET A = 15.75
30 LET B = A * 2
40 LET C$ = "TOTAL"
50 PRINT A, B, C$, 9 * 5, "STOP"
60 END
```

The output will appear as follows:

Zone #1	Zone #2	Zone #3	Zone #4	Zone #5
15.75	31.5	TOTAL	45.	STOP

Notice that the PRINT statement prints the contents of numeric and string variables and not the variable names themselves. Extra commas are used to skip output PRINT zones. If more than five values are requested, the computer advances the printing to the next line. To make the numbers in an output line print closer together, a semicolon is used. Both commas and semicolons may be used in the same PRINT statement to condense or to spread output:

```
100 PRINT" VALUE IS "; 25.25,," TOTAL IS "; 175.95
110 END
```

The output is spaced as follows:

```
VALUE IS 25.25                    TOTAL IS 175.95
```

Note that putting two commas together directed the computer to skip two output zones; semicolons allowed output to be printed without moving to the next zone.

INPUT

There are three ways to input data into the computer:

(1) The LET statement assigns values to variables:

```
LET X = 15.
```

(2) The INPUT command allows interaction between the user and the computer system for entering data:

```
INPUT X.
```

(3) The READ statement is used to assign values that are supplied by a DATA statement:

```
READ X
DATA 15
```

In the first statement, LET X = 15, the value of 15 is assigned to the variable X. Under the second option, when the INPUT statement (INPUT X) is executed, the computer types out a question mark "?" as a *prompt* to the user to enter some data amount from the keyboard. If the user types the number 15 after the ? prompt, this value is assigned to the variable X. More than one variable may be called for in an INPUT statement:

```
100 INPUT X, A, B$
```

In this case, the computer expects two numbers and one alphanumeric string to be typed following the ? prompt (e.g., −15, 17.5, "BILL"). Since the INPUT statement is used to enter data from the keyboard, additional statements may be needed to tell the user what type of data is expected. A single ? prompt is not especially informative. The following program illustrates how user/computer interaction might be handled:

```
50 REM USING THE INPUT STATEMENT
100 PRINT "ENTER YOUR TOTAL INVESTMENT WHEN
    THE ? APPEARS—"
110 PRINT "YOU MAY USE A DECIMAL POINT BUT NOT A $ OR COMMA"
120 INPUT P
130 LET I = P * .14
140 PRINT "INTEREST EARNED IS $"; I
150 END
RUN
```

The computer will respond:

```
ENTER YOUR TOTAL INVESTMENT WHEN THE ? APPEARS—
YOU MAY USE A DECIMAL POINT BUT NOT A $ OR COMMA
? 1000.00
INTEREST EARNED IS $140.
```

READ/DATA

Finally, data may be entered into a computer with READ and DATA statements, where the data are included within program statements. Consider the following program:

```
400 REM USE OF READ/DATA STATEMENTS
500 READ A, B, C
510 LET T = A + B + C
520 PRINT "TOTAL = "; T
530 DATA 100, 15, 20
540 END
RUN
```

The computer will respond:

```
TOTAL = 135.
```

Here three numbers are read (in order) from the DATA statement and assigned to the three variables A, B, and C (in order). DATA statements may be located anywhere in a program prior to the END statement. Multiple DATA statements are also possible, but there must be an equal number of READ variables and DATA amounts. Some programmers like to group DATA statements near the beginning or end of a program.

Reading alphanumeric (string) data is also possible:

```
10 READ X, A, B$
20 DATA −15, 17.5, "BILL"
```

Since it isn't nice to fool either mother nature or a computer, do not put alphanumeric data where numeric data are supposed to be or vice versa.

END/STOP

The last statement in a program must be an END statement. Even if your computer doesn't require its use, the END statement aids in appropriate program termination. Another good programming practice is to use 9's to identify the END statement:

```
  99 END
 999 END
9999 END
```

Using these large termination line numbers allows you to add program statements at a later date.

The STOP statement also causes the program to terminate. A STOP statement anywhere in the program sends the computer to the END line number. While there can be only one END statement, several STOP statements may be located throughout the program.

GO TO

A computer executes program instructions in order from the first statement to the one directly following it, and so on down the list of statements until the END (or STOP) command is encountered. The GO TO command overrules this sequential program control. The GO TO statement transfers control to a particular line number:

```
30 GO TO 75
```

The computer automatically skips statements numbered from 31 to 74 and proceeds directly to line number 75. The GO TO command is also used to branch back to an earlier point in the program:

```
 50 REM USE OF GO TO
100 N = 1
```

```
110 PRINT N
120 LET N = N + 1
130 GO TO 110
999 END
```

Notice that this program establishes an endless loop, which will never stop without further human intervention.

IF/THEN

Another statement that controls the order of statements is the IF/THEN statement. Unlike the GO TO statement, which is an unconditional branch, the IF statement uses a conditional branch. If some simple condition is met, the IF statement transfers control to a particular line; otherwise control goes to the next program statement. The condition must be a logical comparison such as:

```
40 IF A = B THEN 80
```

The branch to statement number 80 is taken only if the values assigned previously to A and B are equal. Conditions of an IF/THEN statement are expressed by certain *relational operators*:

Operator	Meaning	Example
$=$	Equal to	$A = 15$
$<$	Less than	$A < B$
$>$	Greater than	$A + B > C$
$<=$	Less than or equal to	$T <= R + 5$
$>=$	Greater than or equal to	$T + C >= 0$
$<>$	Not equal to	$A\$ <> B\$$

The IF statement is a powerful statement and is used to establish program logic. The previous counting program could be stopped after 100 iterations as follows:

```
50 REM LOOP TERMINATION
100 N = 1
110 PRINT N
115 IF N = 100 THEN 999
120 LET N = N + 1
130 GO TO 110
999 END
```

When N reaches 100, control is transferred to line 999 and the program is terminated. The *logical operators* AND, OR, and NOT are used to form complex logical expressions:

```
100 IF A = B AND C > D THEN 230
```

Most modern versions of BASIC also allow the IF/THEN command to end with another statement:

```
IF A = B THEN C = D
IF X > Y THEN PRINT X
```

FOR/NEXT

Looping is an important process in computer programs. A *loop* is a series of program instructions that are executed more than once. In the previous counting program, the IF/THEN and GO TO statements provided a program loop. FOR/NEXT statements can also be used to provide for the same 100 iterations:

```
50 REM REPLACE GO TO WITH FOR/NEXT
100 FOR I = 1 TO 100
110 PRINT I
120 NEXT I
999 END
```

Here the variable I is used to name an index. The loop consists of the three statements beginning with the FOR command and ending with the NEXT command. Each FOR statement may have only one NEXT statement. The FOR statement establishes an initial value for the index variable and then checks for loop termination. The NEXT statement increments the index.

```
50 REM USING FOR/NEXT FOR LOOPING
100 FOR N = 1 TO 3
110 PRINT "THIS IS A LOOP"
120 NEXT N
130 PRINT "LOOP TERMINATED"
999 END
RUN
```

The computer will respond:

```
THIS IS A LOOP
THIS IS A LOOP
THIS IS A LOOP
LOOP TERMINATED
```

FOR/NEXT statements may be incremented in values other than one. The instruction FOR N = 1 TO 100 STEP 2 provides 50 iterations, since the index increases by two each iteration (1, 3, 5, 7, . . . , 99). When the index reaches 101, program execution transfers to the statement following NEXT N. FOR statements can take many forms. All of the following are legal:

```
100 FOR X = 10 TO 2000
100 FOR A1 = 5 TO 50 STEP .5
100 FOR F = −100 TO 1
100 FOR N = A TO B STEP C
100 FOR J = N TO −15 STEP −2
100 FOR Y = 1983 TO 1999
```

A FOR/NEXT loop may be contained within another FOR/NEXT loop. Such a situation is called a *nested loop*:

```
50 REM THESE ARE NESTED LOOPS
55 PRINT "J", "K"
100 FOR J = 1 TO 3
110 FOR K = 2 TO 4
120 PRINT J, K
130 NEXT K
140 NEXT J
999 END
RUN
```

The computer will respond:

J	K
1	2
1	3
1	4
2	2
2	3
2	4
3	2
3	3
3	4

A nested loop must be contained entirely within an outer loop.

ADDITIONAL PROGRAM COMMANDS IN BASIC

Functions

The arithmetic operations $(+, -, *, /)$ and the relational operators $(=, <, >)$ were presented earlier. Other functions are also available:

Function	Use	Example
** or ↑	Exponentiate	X**2 or X↑2
SQR	Find square root	SQR(144)
INT	Round to whole integer	INT(34.65)
RND	Generate a random number between 0 and 1	RND(X)

Functions are commonly used in assignment statements:

```
50 REM EXAMPLE FUNCTION APPLICATION
100 LET A = 5**3
110 LET B = SQR(144)
120 LET C = INT(B + 10.5)
130 LET D = RND(-1)
140 PRINT A, B, C, D
999 END
RUN
```

The computer will respond:

```
125.          12.          22.          .983520
```

Several functions are possible in the same statement:

```
1000 LET X = SQR(INT(X**2) + RND(1))
```

This example will be solved in the following order:

(1) Exponentiate   (4) Add
(2) Round to whole integer   (5) Calculate the square root
(3) Generate random number   (6) Assign expression value to X

Other functions are available in BASIC, but those illustrated above are the most important ones for business applications.

Arrays and Subscripts

An *array* is a collection of related data values, such as a class roll or list of customer balances. A single variable name is assigned to identify the entire array. Two procedures are required in order to use arrays. First, space must be reserved in the computer for array values. The DIM (dimension) statement is used for this purpose. Second, a method must be established to refer to particular array values. Subscripting handles this operation. The following statement reserves 100 spaces for an array named A:

```
DIM A(100)
```

A *subscript* is an integer that identifies a particular value in an array. The subscript must be enclosed in parentheses. For example, A(1) identifies the first storage location and A(50) the 50th location in array A. Array subscripts may not be zero or negative and must always be less than the maximum size of the array. (Maximum size is determined by the DIM statement.)

Since arrays involve collections of data values, looping is often needed. FOR/NEXT statements are used to handle subscripted variables:

```
500 REM USE OF ARRAY DIMENSION AND SUBSCRIPTS
750 DIM A(20)
1000 FOR M = 1 TO 12
1100 LET A(M) = M
1200 NEXT M
1300 FOR N = 1 TO 5
1400 PRINT A(N)**2
1500 NEXT N
9999 END
RUN
```

The computer will respond:

```
1.
4.
9.
16.
25.
```

Note that space was reserved for 20 values of A in the DIM statement, but only 12 values were stored and 5 values were printed out.

GOSUB/RETURN

Independent program segments are called *subroutines*. The statement GOSUB transfers control to a subroutine, while the statement RETURN terminates the subroutine and transfers control to the statement immediately following GOSUB. A skeleton outline of the use of GOSUB follows:

```
100 ...
120 ...
140 GOSUB 500
160 ...
180 ...
200 GOSUB 500
220 ...
240 ...
260 STOP
500 REM SUBROUTINE STARTS HERE
510 ...
520 ...
530 RETURN
999 END
```

In this example, branching proceeds as follows:

(1) At line 140, control is transferred to line 500.
(2) At line 530, control is transferred to line 160.
(3) At line 200, control is transferred to line 500 a second time.
(4) At line 530, control is transferred to line 220.
(5) At line 260, the program is terminated.

TAB

The TAB command allows output to be printed in specific columns. This tabulation feature is similar to the tabulation key on a typewriter:

```
100 PRINT A; TAB(20); B; TAB(50); C
```

Here the value of A is printed in column 1, B in column 20, and C in column 50.

PRINT USING

When available, PRINT USING is a powerful command for controlling output format. Two statements are required—one statement to identify the output variables and another statement to describe the data format:

```
100 PRINT USING 150, N$, A, T
150 :###### ##.# $##,###.##
```

Here the PRINT USING lists the variables, N$, A, and T, and refers the computer to line 150 (called an image line), where edit symbols (#, . $) are used to describe the exact output format. This edit function is similar to the input/output capability of the business language, COBOL. Commas, periods, and dollar signs may be used in the image line. The # sign aligns numeric and string data in the desired report format.

EXAMPLES OF PROGRAMS IN BASIC

Six complete BASIC programs follow. These programs illustrate the variety of problems that computer programs can solve.

BASIC Program #1

```
100 REM   THIS PROGRAM PRINTS OUT THE CHANCE OF GETTING HEADS OR
110 REM   TAILS OUT OF 100 ROLLS OF DICE.
120 REM
130 REM   H = HEADS
140 REM   T = TAILS
150 REM
160 H = 0
170 FOR T = 1 TO 100
180    H = H + INT(2 * RND (-1))
190 NEXT T
200 PRINT "HEADS: ";H, "TAILS: ";100 - H
210 END
```

Example Output

```
HEADS:  49      TAILS:  51
```

```
RUN COMPLETE.
```

BASIC Program #2

```
100 REM    THIS PROGRAM PRINTS OUT MULTIPLICATION TABLES FROM 1 TO 12
110 REM    BY 1 TO 12
120 REM
130 FOR I = 1 TO 12
140    FOR J = 1 TO 12
150       PRINT I; "X"; J; "="; I * J
160    NEXT J
170       PRINT
180 NEXT I
190 STOP
```

Example Output

```
1 X 1 = 1
1 X 2 = 2
1 X 3 = 3
1 X 4 = 4
1 X 5 = 5
1 X 6 = 6
1 X 7 = 7
1 X 8 = 8
1 X 9 = 9
1 X 10 = 10
1 X 11 = 11
1 X 12 = 12

2 X 1 = 2
2 X 2 = 4
2 X 3 = 6
2 X 4 = 8
2 X 5 = 10
2 X 6 = 12
2 X 7 = 14
2 X 8 = 16
2 X 9 = 18
2 X 10 = 20
2 X 11 = 22
2 X 12 = 24

3 X 1 =
```

BASIC Program #3

```
100 REM    THIS PROGRAM INPUTS VALUES AND CALCULATES THE AVERAGE
110 REM    AFTER ALL VALUES ARE INPUT.
120 REM
130 REM    S = SUM
140 REM    C = COUNT
150 REM    V = VALUE
160 REM
170 LET S = C = 0
180 PRINT "INPUT YOUR NUMBERS"
185 PRINT "(INPUT 0 AS LAST NUMBER)"
190 LET V = 0
200 INPUT V
210 IF V = 0 THEN 260
220 PRINT V
230 LET S = S + V
240 LET C = C + 1
250 GO TO 190
260 PRINT S / C; " = AVERAGE"
270 END
```

Example Output

```
INPUT YOUR NUMBERS
(INPUT 0 AS LAST NUMBER)
? 12
 12
? 57
 57
? 92
 92
? 52
 52
? 88
 88
? 0
 60.2  = AVERAGE


RUN COMPLETE.
```

BASIC Program #4

```
100 REM    THIS PROGRAM CALCULATES THE AMOUNT OF CHANGE (TENS, FIVES,
110 REM    ONES, QUARTERS, DIMES, NICKELS, AND PENNIES) THAT WOULD BE
120 REM    RECEIVED FROM A PURCHASE, GIVEN THAT THE CUSTOMER PAYS WITH
130 REM    A $20.00.
140 REM
150 REM    PROGRAM TO FIGURE CHANGE
160 REM
170 PRINT "HOW MUCH IS THE PURCHASE?"
180 INPUT P
190 C = 20.00 - P
200 IF C < 0 THEN 00510
210 PRINT "YOUR CHANGE FROM $20 FOR A "; P; "PURCHASE IS: "
220 T = INT (C /10)
230 IF T < 0 THEN 00260
240        C = C - (T * 10)
250         PRINT T; " TENS"
260 F = INT (C / 5)
270 IF F < 0 THEN 00300
280        C = C - (F * 5)
290         PRINT F; " FIVES"
300 N = INT (C)
310 IF N < 0 THEN 00340
320        C = C - N
330         PRINT N; " ONES"
340 Q = INT (C / .25)
350 IF Q < 0 THEN 00380
360        C = C - (Q * .25)
370         PRINT Q; " QUARTERS"
380 D = INT (C / .1)
390 IF D < 0 THEN 00420
400        C = C - (D * .1)
410         PRINT D; " DIMES"
420 Z = INT (C / .05)
430 IF Z < 0 THEN 00500
440        C = C - (Z * .05)
450         PRINT Z; " NICKELS"
460 IF C < 0 THEN 420
```

continued

```
470 C = C * 100
480 C = INT(C + .5)
490       PRINT C; " PENNIES"
500 STOP
510 PRINT "YOU CAN'T BUY THAT; IT'S TOO EXPENSIVE."
520 END
```

Example Output

```
HOW MUCH IS THE PURCHASE?
? 25
YOU CAN'T BUY THAT; IT'S TOO EXPENSIVE.

SRU      0.305 UNTS.

RUN COMPLETE.
RUN

HOW MUCH IS THE PURCHASE?
? 5.75
YOUR CHANGE FROM $20 FOR A  5.75 PURCHASE IS:
  1  TENS
  0  FIVES
  4  ONES
  1  QUARTERS
  0  DIMES
  0  NICKELS
  0  PENNIES


RUN COMPLETE.
```

BASIC Program #5

```
100 REM    THIS PROGRAM SORTS 12 ELEMENTS THAT HAVE BEEN INPUT.
110 REM
120 REM    SORT PROGRAM
130 REM
140 DIM A(20)
150 PRINT "ENTER THE 12 NUMBERS YOU WANT TO SORT"
160 FOR M = 1 TO 12
170    INPUT A(M)
180 NEXT M
190 PRINT "VALUES BEFORE SORT: "
200 FOR N = 1 TO 12
210    PRINT A (N);
220 NEXT N
230 PRINT
240 REM    SORT ROUTINE
250 FOR I = 1 TO 11
260    FOR J = I + 1 TO 12
270       IF A(I) <= A(J) THEN 310
280          T = A(I)
290          A(I) = A(J)
300          A(J) = T
310    NEXT J
320 NEXT I
330 PRINT "SORTED VALUES: "
340 FOR P = 1 TO 12
350    PRINT A(P);
360 NEXT P
370 END
```

Example Output

```
ENTER THE 12 NUMBERS YOU WANT TO SORT
? 25
? 67
? 12
? 9
? 45
? 86
```

continued

```
? 21
? 23
? 66
? 33
? 32
? 75
VALUES BEFORE SORT:
 25  67  12  9  45  86  21  23  66  33  32  75
SORTED VALUES:
 9  12  21  23  25  32  33  45  66  67  75  86
```

BASIC Program #6

```
100 REM    THIS PROGRAM IS FOR A MAILING LIST OF UP TO 10 PEOPLE.  IT
110 REM    ALLOWS THE USER TO INPUT NAMES AND ADDRESSES THEN OUTPUTS
120 REM    IN "ENVELOPE" FORMAT.  EDITING IS PERMITTED BEFORE FINAL
130 REM    LABELS ARE PRINTED.
140 REM
150 REM    PRINT MAILING LIST LABELS
160 REM
170 DIM N$(10), A$(10), C$(10), S$(10), Z$(10)
172 PRINT "HOW MANY LABELS ARE THERE?"
174 INPUT N
180 FOR I = 1 TO N
190     PRINT "NAME ";INPUT N$ (I)
200     PRINT "ADDRESS ";INPUT A$ (I)
210     PRINT "CITY ";INPUT C$ (I)
220     PRINT "STATE ";INPUT S$ (I)
230     PRINT "ZIP ";INPUT Z$ (I)
240     PRINT I; ": "; N$(I)" "; A$(I)" "; C$(I)" "; S$(I)" "; Z$(I)" "
250 NEXT I
260 PRINT "DO YOU WANT TO CHANGE ANY ( Y OR N) ? "
270 INPUT X$
280 IF X$ = "Y" THEN 360
290 FOR I = 1 TO N
300     PRINT N$ (I)
310     PRINT A$ (I)
320     PRINT C$ (I)
322     PRINT S$ (I)
```

```
324    PRINT Z$ (I)
330    PRINT
332    PRINT
334    PRINT
340 NEXT I
350 STOP
360 PRINT "WHICH LABEL DO YOU WANT TO CHANGE ?"
370 INPUT K
380 PRINT "NAME ";INPUT N$(K)
390 PRINT "ADDRESS ";INPUT A$ (K)
400 PRINT "CITY "; INPUT C$ (K)
410 PRINT "STATE "; INPUT S$ (K)
420 PRINT "ZIP "; INPUT Z$ (K)
430 GO TO 260
440 END
```

Example Output

```
HOW MANY LABELS ARE THERE?
? 2
NAME   ? STEVE BILLINGS
ADDRESS ? 1234 BROADWAY
CITY   ? WELLS
STATE ? CO
ZIP ? 10101
  1 : STEVE BILLINGS 1234 BROADWAY WELLS CO 10101
NAME   ? GREG AVERY
ADDRESS ? 5678 MAIN
CITY   ? ADMUNDSEN
STATE ? CO
ZIP ? 20304
  2 : GREG AVERY 5678 MAIN ADMUNDSEN CO 20304
DO YOU WANT TO CHANGE ANY ( Y OR N) ?
? Y
WHICH LABEL DO YOU WANT TO CHANGE ?
? 2
NAME   ? GREG AVERY
ADDRESS ? 5679 MAIN
CITY   ? ADMUNDSEN
STATE ? CO
ZIP ? 20304
```

continued

```
DO YOU WANT TO CHANGE ANY ( Y OR N) ?
? N
STEVE BILLINGS
1234 BROADWAY
WELLS
CO
10101


GREG AVERY
5679 MAIN
ADMUNDSEN
CO
20304



RUN COMPLETE.
```

SUMMARY

Study of this chapter acquaints the reader with the popular high-level language called BASIC. BASIC is widely used with microcomputers and interactive terminals. Though system and program commands vary from computer to computer, most BASIC dialects use common statements for input, processing, and output.

Programming skill allows an individual to appreciate the problem-solving capability and limitations of a computer. A computer language is similar to a foreign language: to master it, you must use it. Seek out opportunities to develop your programming skill.

TERMS

BASIC
Statement
Variable
Expression
Assignment
String
Prompt
Relational operator
Logical operator
Loop
Nested loop
Array
Subscript
Subroutine

Program Commands:

REM
LET
PRINT
INPUT
READ/DATA
END/STOP
GO TO
IF/THEN
FOR/NEXT
DIM
GOSUB/RETURN
TAB
PRINT USING

System Commands:

CATALOG
LIST
RUN
SAVE
BYE

QUESTIONS

1. What does it mean to "log on" to a computer?
2. What is the function of line numbers?
3. Identify several system commands and their functions.
4. What BASIC statement provides program documentation?
5. Explain the relationship between an expression, a variable, and a statement.
6. Identify three ways that data can be input into the computer.
7. How is looping accomplished in a computer program?
8. What are relational operators? logical operators?
9. List calculation functions that are useful in business programs.
10. What is the purpose of an array?
11. How does the computer keep track of specific array values?

12. Discuss the role of subroutines.

13. Explain what is meant by this assignment statement:

    100 LET X = 4.2 + Y

14. Find four mistakes in the following program:

    100 LEM A = 4
    110 LET B6 = 2.6
    120 LET DT = 7
    130 PRINT A, B6, X
    350 FINISH

15. How many values and what type of values does the computer expect in response to this statement?

    10 INPUT A, B, N$

16. Identify the logic error:

    400 IF A = B + C THEN 420
    420 LET D = E − F

17. Explain how the following output will differ:

    105 PRINT A,B,C
    106 PRINT A;B;C
    107 PRINT A,,B;C

18. What do you think will happen if a READ statement attempts to obtain more values than are available from a DATA statement? fewer values?

19. Explain the function of STOP and END. How do these statements differ?

20. What output values will be printed?

    10 C = 0
    20 FOR I = 1 TO 5
    30 FOR J = 10 TO 20 STEP 2
    40 LET C = C + 1
    50 PRINT C
    60 NEXT J
    70 NEXT I
    99 END

ARTICLE

Writing Your First Game

If you are tempted to write your own games, go ahead. It's a good way to learn to program. Games are basically the same as any other kind of programming.

Computer games fall into two broad categories: 1. imitations of old standards (checkers, Othello) and 2. games (Space Invaders, PacMan) which could not be played without a computer. This second category is more difficult to program for several reasons. For one thing, you've got to think up a whole new, and entertaining, concept and then adjust the action until it is just hard enough to be challenging but not so difficult that people want to give up.

This category (basically "arcade" games) is especially hard to program precisely because a good computer-only game exploits all of the computer's special attributes: speed, color, sound. To do this well, to make things look and respond just the way you imagine them, requires a good bit of programming experience. Usually, too, several things are happening *at once* in an arcade game. This often means that such a program must be written in machine language, which is far faster than BASIC.

High Card Slice

Old standards, on the other hand, can often be the best way to get started programming games. You already know the game concept, and cards or dice or game boards are fairly easily constructed and manipulated on your computer screen. To illustrate, let's take a look at a simple simulation of one of the oldest card games, "High Card." The rules are simple: you place a bet, and then you draw a card from the deck. The computer, your opponent, draws a card too, and the highest card wins the money.

One simplification here is that there is no attempt to represent the cards on the screen. The entire game relies simply on words ("Ace of Spades," for example) when cards are drawn.

Like most computer programs, the program can be visualized as having four distinct zones: initialization, main loop, subroutines, data tables. We can go through the steps in programming this game by looking at each zone separately. [*See program on the next two pages*.]

Initialization

From lines 10 through 80 we are "teaching" the computer some basics about this game. Initialization is the activity which must take place before any of the action can begin. Computers are so fast that they will zip up through these lines and start things off in the main loop at line 100 in a flash. However, as programmers, we

continued

Program 1: Apple, PET, VIC, OSI, Radio Shack

```
10  REM *** NECESSARY INITIAL INFORMATION ***
20  DOLLARS = 500
30  PRINT" WITH WHOM DO I HAVE THE PLEASURE"
40  PRINT" OF PLAYING HIGH CARD SLICE?"
50  INPUT NAME$
60  PRINT" HIGH CARD WINS IN THIS GAME!"
70  DIM CARD$ (14) : FORI=11 TO 14 : READ CARD$ (I) :
      NEXTI
80  FORI=1TO4 : READ SUITS$ (I) : NEXTI
90  REM
100 REM *** MAIN PROGRAM LOOP ***
110 PRINT:PRINT" YOU HAVE $" DOLLARS
120 IF DOLLARS <= 0 THEN PRINT" THE GAME IS OV
      ER. YOU ARE OUT OF CASH." : END
130 PRINT" WHAT IS YOUR BET"; : INPUT BET
140 IF DOLLARS < BET THEN PRINT" YOU ONLY HAVE
       $ "DOLLARS" TO BET, "NAME$ : GOTO130
150 YOURCARD=0 : YURSUIT=0
160 PLAYERS$=NAME$
170 GOSUB300
180 YOURCARD=CARD : YURSUIT=SUIT
190 PLAYER$=" THE COMPUTER"
```

are aware that several preliminary events took place inside before anything else.

In line 20, the computer discovers that there is a variable called "dollars" which is to equal 500. . . . Lines 30 through 60 are simple enough — they ask the player to give his or her name. The computer "memorizes" it in another "box" called "name$" and can now speak more personally to the player in lines 140 and 230. Also, the computer prints the rules of the game in line 60.

Line 70 "reads" four names (the face cards) from the data tables in lines 510 on. . . . By now, the computer has "memorized" a variety of important facts: the player's name, the amount of his or her betting purse, the names of the face cards, and the suits of a standard deck. In less than a second, the computer has grasped and filed away the necessary facts to go on to the main loop where all the action takes place.

The Main Loop

After checking that the player has money to bet, the computer asks for the bet, checks again that the bet is possible, and then runs through one cycle of the game starting in line 160. At this point, a

continued

```
200 GOSUB300
210 IF CARD > YOURCARD THEN GOTO 240
220 IF CARD = YOURCARD THEN PRINT" A TIE!" : GOT
    O100
230 PRINT NAME$" WINS" : DOLLARS = DOLLARS + B
    ET : GOTO100
240 PRINT" THE COMPUTER WINS" : DOLLARS = DOLLA
    RS — BET: GOTO100
290 REM
300 REM *** SUBROUTINE TO DRAW THE CARDS ***
310 CARD = INT(RND(5)*13)+2: SUIT = INT(RND(5)
    *4) +1
320 IF CARD = YOURCARD AND SUIT = YURSUIT THEN
    300: REM NO IDENTICAL DRAWS
330 IF CARD < 11 THEN CARD$ (CARD) = STR$ (CARD)
340 PRINTPLAYER$ " DRAWS THE " CARD$ (CARD) " ~
    OF " SUIT$ (SUIT)
350 RETURN
490 REM
500 REM *** DATA TABLE ***
510 DATA JACK,QUEEN,KING,ACE
520 DATA CLUBS,DIAMONDS,HEARTS,SPADES
```

programmer might find it worthwhile to visualize the steps involved in the game: 1. draw a card for the player; 2. draw for the computer; 3. decide who won; 4. adjust the player's purse.

Since both draws are essentially identical actions (the only difference will be that we say "Bob draws a . . ." instead of "The computer draws"), we don't need to program the draw twice. This is where subroutines come in handy.

The Subroutine

Twice in the main loop, we GOSUB 300. First the player, then the computer, draws. Line 310 randomly picks two numbers, the card and the suit. If line 320 finds that this selection matches the one drawn just before by the player, it goes back for another draw. Line 330 makes the *name* of the card be the number if it wasn't a number higher than 11 (a face card).

Then line 340 announces the draw using three variables. The first variable (player$) is set up in either line 160 or 190 as appropriate. Then the card$ and suit$ variables are selected from the lists that were "memorized" back in the initialization phase (lines 70–80). The subroutine then RETURNs to the main loop. . . .

continued

Once you've solved a particular problem, you'll find you can use the solution in many future games. This subroutine which draws cards, for instance, would work just as well for Poker, or Blackjack, or dozens of other games. Subroutines are handy not only because they can be used repeatedly within a program, but because they can be saved and used repeatedly in future programs. So think up a simple, traditional game and teach it to your computer. There is probably no more pleasurable way to learn programming than to write a game.

DISCUSSION QUESTIONS

1. Discuss the difference between writing computer programs for "standard" computer games and "arcade" games.
2. Compare and contrast the BASIC code used here with the BASIC code used in the chapter.

APPLICATION

Chess Champ

The author of the winning chess program in the second European Microcomputer Chess Championship characterizes himself as a "weakish club player," bought his first personal computer only a year ago, and copied the opening book into his tiny program straight from the pages of a paperback bought from a drugstore rack.

"Cyrus," the system written by Richard Lang of Olton, in England's West Midlands, won all five of its games in the 12-entry field, which included such popular and well-known systems as Gambiet 81, Philidor, and Chess Champion Mark V.

The quality of overall play in the tournament, which was held in the Cunard Hotel, London, in conjunction with the fourth Annual Personal Computer World Show, was put in perspective by Michael Stean, a British International Grandmaster who was on hand to analyze the games and comment on the play: "I've just returned from the junior championships," he said, "and these programs would have been a match for many of the players there."

For his win, Lang received £500, a chess set, and the travelling Centronic Trophy. Second place, worth £200, went to another home brew system, Advance 2.0, with third prize worth £100 going to a Dane, 19-year old Kaare Danielsen, playing yet another home-written system. Five commercial systems in the competion failed to place. Dead last was a system called Albatross 3.0 with a perfect 0 on the scoreboard. One wonders what versions 1 and 2 were like.

Lang, who wrote Cyrus in about six months of spare time after teaching himself to program, first in Basic, then in Assembler, is a 25-year old risk analyst for British Gas. He bought his personal computer — a Video Genie — less than a year before winning the tournament. The Video-Genie is a British TRS-80 lookalike. "The prize money will buy me disk drives," he said.

Lang decided to write a chess-playing program because it "seemed a good challenge, and the sort of the thing a computer should be able to do well." He said he started by studying the Spraklens' Sargon I and reading International Grandmaster David Levy's magazine articles on computer chess, then "took off from there." Perhaps Levy himself should go back and look at those articles. The two entrants he coauthored, Philidor

continued

and Philidor Experimental, each managed three of a possible five points, finishing in the middle of the pack.

"Starting almost fresh, as I did," Lang said, "is the best way of doing it. You're forced to think of your own way of doing things."

It was the first competition for Cyrus, and Lang admitted surprise at the way his program dispatched its opponents. "I had some idea of its strength," he said, "because I've played Sargon II and Gambiet 80 at home, and beaten them convincingly."

According to Stean, Cyrus is particularly strong in its ability to mount powerful coordinated attacks using numerous pieces, without the emphasis on the queen shown by many programs. Cyrus's endplay capabilities are a matter of conjecture; Lang noted, "He usually doesn't get that far before winning." All five games in the tournament were won in the middle game, with the only real fight coming in the opening match against Philidor Experimental.

His program, written in Z-80 assembly language, occupies just over 7K of memory, including an opening book table of 1.25K which "I took straight out of the Penguin paperback of chess openings." Cyrus's opening book contains only 450 moves, and "it gets out of the book rather quickly," he said, "except for something like the Ruy Lopez where it will play to nine moves for each side."

Cyrus has seven levels of play, with level 1 responding in a quarter of a second, and level 7, with its seven-ply search, taking "several hours per move. I've never actually played at Level 7," he said. "I haven't the patience, but perhaps it would be good for postal chess or something of the sort." Cyrus played at Level 5 during the tournament, with an average of about 105 seconds per move.

In explaining how the program operates, Lang said that it has a function which assigns a value to the possible board positions, and selects the move which will lead to the highest total, five moves ahead. "That total can range from 0" he said, "to . . . well, perhaps I better not say . . . I don't want to give too much away." He considers the speed and accuracy of that evaluation system to be the strongest part of the program.

In general terms, Cyrus uses a depth first alpha-beta search with the killer heuristic and employs selective "pruning" of the tree. The amount of "pruning" is increased in complex situations to keep the thinking time reasonably constant. Cyrus, he added, examines about 200 positions a second and includes an allowance for future captures in each assessment.

continued

When last seen, Lang was fending off potential marketers while gathering his Video Genie and his mother and father, who had driven in for the tournament.

His last comment was, "Cyrus Version 2 is almost finished. It will be considerably stronger."

Reprinted from CREATIVE COMPUTING MAGAZINE. Copyright © 1982 AHL COMPUTING, INC.

DISCUSSION QUESTIONS

1. What criteria does the Cyrus chess program use to select the best possible move?
2. Since Lang understands both BASIC and Assembler, why do you suppose he chose to write Cyrus in assembly language?

PART 4

INFORMATION SYSTEMS DEVELOPMENT

This section introduces you to file organization, database systems, and the information systems development cycle. In today's large, integrated information systems, users demand quick and efficient storage and retrieval of information. Thus, users and designers of systems must understand how data are stored and retrieved.

In addition, the needs of information users are constantly changing; therefore, the design of information systems should reflect those changing needs. The system development cycle presented in this section gives you a means of organizing—of structuring—the system development process.

Chapter 9 - explores the importance of organizing files and managing data.

Chapters 10, 11, and 12 - present the activities that are necessary to develop a modern information system.

FILE ORGANIZATION AND DATABASE MANAGEMENT

CHAPTER OBJECTIVES

In this chapter you will learn:

1. The hierarchical components of a file.
2. The structure of the basic file designs:
   Sequential
   Direct access
   Indexed sequential
   Lists
   Inverted index.
3. The disadvantages of file processing.
4. The characteristics of a database.
5. The data relationships that exist in database design.
6. What a DataBase Management System (DBMS) is.
7. The use of a data dictionary.
8. The advantages and disadvantages in using a database.

DATA STORAGE

As you have already studied, one of the major components of a computer is storage or memory. You have also learned that there are various types of storage devices related to data processing. The key to storage is data organization so that retrieval of information can be accomplished quickly and efficiently. Just as the old song says, "Love and marriage go together like a horse and carriage," it can be said that efficient storage and retrieval of data are inseparable. It does no good to store data if they can't be located when needed.

In today's computerized environments, some information systems store millions of records of data. Each record is frequently made up of several thousand characters (numbers or letters), which means that some computer systems today are capable of storing billions of characters of data. The stored data are organized into files, just as they would be in manual systems. However, with computerized files, the data can be retrieved within milliseconds and sometimes even within nanoseconds.

FILES

Working with files is not new to you. Quite often—perhaps every day—you work with files. The standard manila file folders used in the traditional file cabinet, the card catalog index in the library, even the books in the library stacks (quite a spacious file, but yet it is a file of books, magazines, documents, etc.), and your class note cards are all examples of files which you use frequently.

While similar to manual files, computer files have certain characteristic differences. In the first place, they are not readily visible as manual file folders in a storage cabinet are. In addition, there are several methods of computer file design not available in manual systems. In a manual system, the difference in efficiency between one filing method and another is usually nominal. In a given computer application, however, more attention is given to file structure because one file design may be several times more efficient than any other design. The most significant difference between manual files and computer files is that retrieval from a computer file is many, many times faster than retrieval from a manual system.

Files are used for storing and retrieving data in an information system. Each file in the system consists of related, individual data records. To illustrate, a personnel file contains various data records pertaining to each employee. The person, place, or thing about which you are storing data is referred to as the *entity*. In a personnel file the employee is the entity. An inventory file contains data on items (products, parts, goods, raw materials, etc.) in inventory. The entity in an inventory file is the inventory item.

The basic parts of a file are shown in Figure 9-1. These file components constitute a hierarchical structure. The smallest storage element in a computer file is a *bit;* a bit is not shown in Figure 9-1 because bits are normally not labeled or accessed individually. The next higher level in the file hierarchy is a character or, in computer terminology, a byte. A *byte* is a string of bits whose purpose is to store or express a character—an alphabetic letter, a number, or a special character.

Figure 9-1

File structure. A file is made up of related records; a record consists of data fields; a field is composed of one or more characters. This file has three records, each with three fields having a varying number of characters.

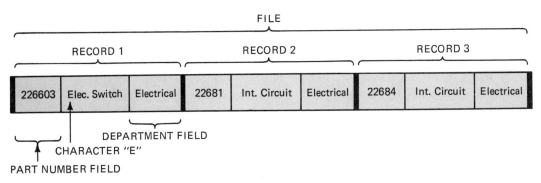

In designing a file, consideration is given to how many characters are needed to represent a particular data item. The data item may consist of only one character or it may be a hundred or more characters (bytes). To store "True" (T) or "False" (F) takes only one byte; however, to store a person's name may require thirty or more characters. When one or more characters are placed together in a defined area, the area is called a *field*, or data item. Another term that is sometimes used to refer to a field is *data element*. However, the use of this term can be confusing, because it may refer to a bit, a character, or an item of data.

All of the data fields that relate in a specific way to the entity are stored in a *record*. In a personnel file several records may be necessary to store the desired data on each employee, with each record having its own unique purpose. For example, the personnel file may contain each employee's payroll record, history of employment, education, and personal data. A portion of a student demographic record is shown in Figure 9-2. Typically, more data items will be included in a student record than are shown in Figure 9-2. Other possible items include colleges or universities attended or a student's high school academic record.

Figure 9-2

A student demographic record, showing only a few of the fields that may be included.

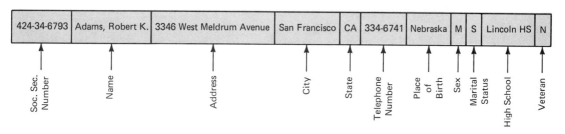

In storing data in a file, it is necessary to distinguish one entity's records from those of a different entity. In a student data file, for example, each student's records must be distinguishable. Otherwise, once the data record has been stored, it may be impossible to retrieve, or perhaps an incorrect record is retrieved instead. To accommodate the requirement that each record be distinguishable from all of the other records, data in at least one specific field must be unique for each entity. That field is used to identify records belonging to each entity: Each record then has a *unique identifier*. In a student file, the student number field (social security number generally) meets this requirement. In an inventory file, the part number is the unique identifier. Another term used to describe the unique identifier field is *primary key*. Records in a file are stored according to the primary key; consequently, the data (value) stored in the primary key must be unique.

Having a unique identifier is critical to effective storage and retrieval of data. The reason you are often asked to use or present your social security number is so that the data collected about you will be stored in *your* record only and will not end up in someone else's record. In a manual system, when a document about you is filed in someone else's folder, for all practical purposes it is lost; or at least it is lost until someone accidentally comes across it and returns it to your folder. The same is true in computer files. If you don't store the record in the correct location, it may be lost forever, and the chances of locating the lost record accidentally are not nearly as good as they are in a manual system. Using a person's name as a unique identifier will not get the job done. How many Mary Smiths are there; how many James Browns? We frequently criticize computers for reducing us to a number, but the use of a number provides recordkeeping and data processing uniqueness that is essential in large information systems, manual or computer-based.

File Organization

In manual files, individual records (forms, folders, etc.) are stored in some sequential manner, either in an alphabetic or a numeric sequence; that is, record "1" comes before record "2," and so on. A file with records stored in a sequence is called a *sequential file*. Furthermore, in manual systems, some type of indexing scheme is often used for faster retrieval. For example, a label is placed on the file drawer stating what record categories are stored in the drawer, such as:

STUDENT FILE
NAMES
Ba-Bl

In computer files, as in manual files, sequential organization of records and indexing schemes are widely used. A sequential file method designed around an indexing scheme is called an *indexed sequential file*. Such computer files are not limited to sequential design only but include both the capability of going directly to a specific record by using an indexing scheme and also reading records in a sequence. A file structure that provides for going directly to a record in storage is called a *direct access file*. Another arrangement of records in a computer file is the division of the file into short sequences or *lists* of related data records. This is called a *link list file,* since each record in the list is connected to other records. In an animal control file, a list of dogs could be one sequence; cats, another; and so on. *Inverted index files* provide quick access to data and are used in conjunction with sequential and direct access files.

Each of these types of file organization —

> Sequential
> Direct access
> Indexed sequential
> Link list
> Inverted index—

is discussed in the following paragraphs.

Sequential File Organization. Sequential file design is used more often than any other file design method. With modern, sophisticated computer technology, sequential design is often thought as being an outmoded method, but sequential files are a legitimate, viable file structure even today. They are relatively easy to design and are less expensive to implement and maintain than other methods.

As stated earlier, when sequential design is used, records are stored one after another in a prescribed order. This order or sequence is based upon some data item (field) in the record. The item is referred to as the key or record identification field (*record ID*). Records in the file are sequenced in either descending (from top to bottom) or ascending order based upon the data stored in the ID field. In Figure 9-3 a segment of a sequential file is illustrated.

In order to retrieve a specific record in sequential file processing, all records stored in front of the desired record must be read. For example, if you want record 50, the previous 49 record ID's must first be read. Reading 49 records doesn't take very long, but what if you have 20,000 records in your file and want to retrieve record 17,500?

There is a way around the problem, however. The method is referred to as a *binary search*. To use a binary search, the file is first divided in half and a comparison is made of the key of the desired record with the key of the record that is stored at the midpoint of the file. If the key of the desired record is less than the key of the midpoint record, the next step is to find the midpoint of the first half of the file; make a comparison of that record with the desired record;

Figure 9-3

Illustration of sequential file organization. In this file the records are sequenced by social security number, which is the key or ID field.

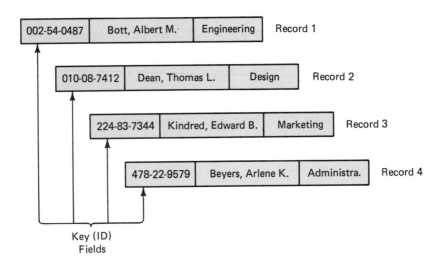

Key (ID)
Fields

and continue this process until you land on the record to be retrieved. It may sound complicated, but it is a rather simple process. Figure 9-4 illustrates the steps for finding record number 17,500 out of 20,000 records in a file. By using a binary search routine, only three records are read to reach record 17,500.

There are several advantages in using sequential file organization:

— Sequential files are easier to organize than other file methods. The only decision required in organizing the file is to select which field will be used as the key field, the field on which the file will be sequenced. For example, in a personnel file, the key field for the file is usually the social security number. Books (data records) in your school library are organized by the library call number. Inventory files are organized by the part or stock number.

— Cost of processing is less than with other methods if there is a lot of file activity (records to be processed).

— Some storage devices (magnetic tape, for example) require sequential processing.

Figure 9-4

Steps in a binary search.

NUMBER OF THE DESIRED RECORD:	17,500
NUMBER OF RECORDS IN FILE:	20,000
MIDPOINT OF FILE:	Record 10,000 (20,000 / 2 = 10,000)
IS DESIRED RECORD GREATER THAN MIDPOINT?	Yes (17,500 > 10,000)
MIDPOINT OF SECTION (Record 10,000 to 20,000):	Record 15,000
IS DESIRED RECORD GREATER THAN MIDPOINT?	Yes (17,500 > 15,000)
MIDPOINT OF SECTION (Record 15,000 to 20,000):	Record 17,500
IS DESIRED RECORD GREATER THAN MIDPOINT? IS DESIRED RECORD LESS THAN MIDPOINT? IS DESIRED RECORD EQUAL TO MIDPOINT?*	No No Yes
RETRIEVE RECORD:	Record 17,500

*The EQUAL logic question is not actually necessary in this example since by deduction from the answers to the GREATER THAN and LESS THAN questions the midpoint record has to be equal to the desired record.

Disadvantages to sequential file processing include the following:

— If you have low file activity, sequential processing may be more costly. For example, if you wish to retrieve only one record from 25,000 stored in a file, sequential processing will be more costly than other types of file processing. If, however, you are accessing 10 or 20 percent of the records, sequential processing is probably the most cost effective.
— Sequential processing is slower than the other methods. While a 6250-bpi (bits per inch) tape drive with a transfer rate (speed at which data can be read) of over one million bytes per second may seem fast, it is a relatively slow way to read a large file. In addition, it takes time for the computer operator to locate and mount the tape on the tape drive.

— Processing, including record updates, is done in a batch mode on a periodic basis. Thus, data stored in the file are always out of date. In real-time systems, by contrast, a record is updated as soon as a data item is entered.

— In sequential file processing, in order to update the file for additions or deletions, it is necessary to rewrite the entire file. This is time-consuming and costly.

Direct Access Files. With direct access files there is the capability of going directly to a record. Thus, if rapid record retrieval is desired, a direct access file design should be used. Another term frequently used to describe direct access is *random access*. The term "random access" is derived from the use of a *randomizing technique* (also called "hashing") to determine the location (address) where a record is stored. The same randomizing technique is used to search for and retrieve the record during subsequent processing.

Random access is not a particularly good term to describe a direct access file, since the address (record location) is not determined randomly. The address is calculated using some prescribed algorithm. The algorithm may be any set of procedures specified by system designers or by the computer software.

The first step required in the randomizing procedure is to specify the data field that will be used for calculating the storage location. The field will generally be the same field that is used for the key or record ID field, or it may be a combination of fields. The second step is to develop a procedure that will result in a number that can be used as an address location. For example, assume that a randomizing procedure is needed for a personnel file that contains 50,000 records. In addition, storage addresses must be between address 20,000 and address 80,000. Assume further that the key field is the social security number.

One process that can be used is to multiply the social security number by its own last digit, divide the result by 60,000 (total number of storage spaces available), select the remainder from the division, and add 20,000 to the remainder. By adding 20,000 to the remainder, it is assured that an address will fall between 20,000 and 80,000. The procedure is shown in Figure 9-5.

There are times when performing this computation with different social security numbers gives the same remainder. Thus the same storage location number is generated for two different records. Two or more records whose keys randomize to the same address are called synonyms. Since only one record can be stored in an address, how can synonyms be handled?

One method is to store the first record in the randomized location; then, search for the next available storage address and store the second record (we'll

Figure 9-5

Randomizing technique (algorithm) to develop an address location that will be as nearly unique as possible.

FILE SIZE: 50,000 Records

ASSIGNED LOCATIONS: Address 20,000 to Address 80,000

RANDOMIZING ALGORITHM:

STEP 1: $\dfrac{\text{Soc. Sec. No.} \times \text{Last Digit}}{60{,}000 \text{ addresses available}} = \begin{array}{l}\text{Quotient and}\\ \text{Remainder}\end{array}$

STEP 2: Remainder + 20,000 = $\boxed{\text{Address for Record}}$

For example—

STEP 1: $\dfrac{824923622 \times 2}{60000} = \dfrac{1649847244}{60000} = 27244$

STEP 2: $27244 + 20000 = \boxed{47244}$

call it record B) in that location. Each time record B is to be accessed, A is read first. Therefore, to get to record B, a connecting link must be established between records A and B. This connection is known as a *link address*. The link address to record B is stored in the link address field of record A, as shown in Figure 9-6(a).

A second method of handling synonymous addresses is to provide an *overflow area* in the file. Each time a synonym is generated, the new record is stored in the overflow area. Assuming that the same conditions for records A and B again exist, a field in record A contains a link address identifying the overflow area where record B is stored. Note Figure 9-6(b).

In developing a randomizing technique, two objectives should be pursued: (1) to develop an algorithm that reduces the potential number of synonyms, and (2) to develop an algorithm that distributes the records evenly over the storage addresses.

Direct access file design offers these advantages:

— Direct files provide rapid access to the desired information. In a decision-making environment where information is needed quickly, direct access is a requisite to rapid retrieval.

Figure 9-6

Two methods of handling duplicate storage addresses (synonyms): (a) link address; (b) overflow area.

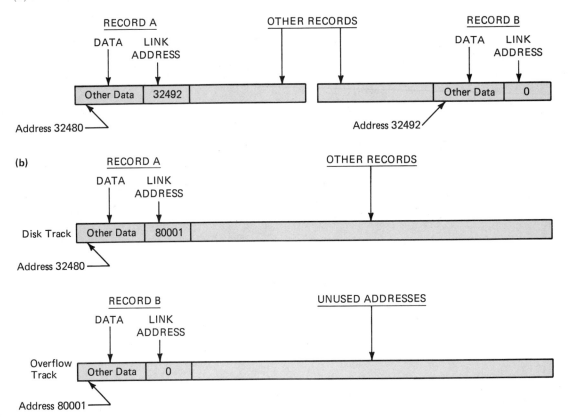

— Direct access is efficient for retrieving a relatively few records at a time.
— Direct access provides a method of keeping files up to date as transactions or events occur. If a customer calls to find out the status of an order, a request for information can be keyed into the system and immediately the system will respond indicating the status of the order.

There are, however, certain disadvantages:

— Direct access hardware devices and the required operating systems are more expensive than those required for sequential or batch processing, both in installation costs and in operating costs.

— Not all of the file storage space will be used, regardless of how efficient the randomizing technique is. In fact, more space must be purposely allocated than is physically needed to store the data; otherwise, when the file space is almost filled, it takes too much time to locate available storage spaces. A storage system operates at its highest level of efficiency when 65 to 80 percent of the addresses are used. Although the 20 to 35 percent surplus storage space is not used, the tradeoff is between the speed and efficiency in locating addresses and the wasted space created by unused storage locations.

Even with these disadvantages, the use of direct access files is increasing. Improved access speed and immense storage capacities are features of today's direct access devices.

Indexed Sequential Files. The indexed sequential method uses both sequential processing and direct access concepts. Records in the file are stored sequentially in groups or blocks, as shown in Figure 9-7. The index file keeps track of the record keys and the address of the first record in each block. When a particular record is needed, the index is searched until the key of the desired record is found; the record is then retrieved sequentially from the block.

Since records in the file are stored sequentially, the entire file may be processed sequentially as well. Indexed sequential files are useful when the file must be updated periodically—once per day, week, or month—with transaction records that are spread throughout the file, and when there is a need to access a single record during the intervening period between updates. For example, a company that has many credit card customers may need to access the file daily to check on credit authorization; however, the file is also processed once a month for issuing account statements.

One disadvantage of indexed sequential files is the problem of handling additions to the files (deletions do not present a problem). Because the records are stored contiguously on a disk track, inserting a record between two records creates a problem. When a record is added to the file, all records that fall after the new record must be "pushed back." The last record on the track is then forced into an overflow area. After numerous additions, the retrieval process slows noticeably as a result of extended usage of overflow areas for record storage. When this occurs, the file must be reorganized or purged. *Purging* a file means rewriting the file. During the purging process, old records are removed and the remaining records are reorganized in the storage area and placed in their proper locations.

Figure 9-7

Illustration of an indexed sequential file. The record being retrieved is record 676.

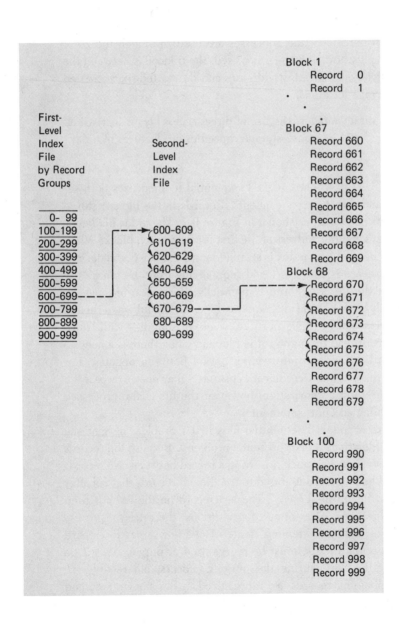

Link Lists. A link list consists of short, related lists containing records connected to each other by address fields called link addresses. Like indexed sequential files, link lists require direct access capability also; however, in a link list file there is no index to indicate the location of an individual record. A *link address* (sometimes called a "pointer") is used to move from one record in the list to the next. The link address in the first record of a list points to the location of the second record, and so on. This is illustrated in Figure 9-8. Typically there are both master records and detail records in link list files. The master record

Figure 9-8

Illustration of link list file structure. A search is being made for record 503.

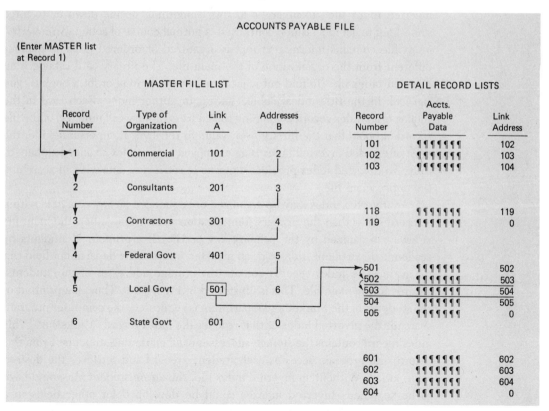

contains two address fields: one to point to the first detail record linked to the master record, and the other to point to the next master record.

Assume that an accounts payable file consists of suppliers, contractors, consultants, and governmental agencies. The master list contains the highest level of accounts payable categories (shown in Figure 9-8). Note that each record in the master list has two link addresses. The first points to the first record in the detail or sub-list group, and the other to the next master record in the file.

Thus, in a link list organization, a hierarchical structure is used. The hierarchy is necessary to keep each list short, perhaps ten or fewer entries in each list. Link lists are used for relatively small files that have a lot of retrieval activity.

Inverted Index Files. Another type of file or index file structure is the inverted index file. To invert is to turn something upside down or to force something to act in a fashion contrary to a normal course of action. An inverted index file contains information that is organized or ordered in some manner different from the organization of the main file. The library card catalog is an inverted index file. To find out what the library call number for a book is, you can look in the title index, subject index, or author index. Each card in the catalog is an index record containing the address (library call number) of the file record (a book) that the library user wants to retrieve. In a personnel file, the most often used inverted index is an employee name index arranged alphabetically. An inverted index provides a means of retrieving data without searching the entire main file.

An inverted index may be organized or sequenced on any data field within a record other than the primary identification field. (Remember, the main file is always organized by the primary key or ID.) If a printout of students by academic department is desired, an inverted index of the department field can be made. The index records contain the storage addresses of the students' records in the main file. This is illustrated in Figure 9-9. Thus, if a printout of the students in the Marketing Department is requested, the computer program searches the inverted index until it reaches the index record "Marketing." This index record contains the storage addresses of all marketing students. From this record, the program accesses each student's record and retrieves the desired information. Without an inverted index file, the entire student file would have to be searched. Inverted indexes could be developed for other fields in a student information system such as name, major, class schedule, or year.

Figure 9-9

Illustration of an inverted index file. A student can be found by department or major without searching the entire file.

MAIN STUDENT FILE

Record Number	Soc. Sec. Number	Name	Department	Other Data	Major
1	012-78-9654	Jones, Allen	Marketing	¶¶¶¶¶¶¶¶¶¶	BK01
2	328-34-2934	Crinshaw, B. J.	Management	¶¶¶¶¶¶¶¶¶¶	BN03
3	482-67-2941	Smuckers, Carl	Marketing	¶¶¶¶¶¶¶¶¶¶	BK01
4	689-38-2395	Peoples, James A.	Accounting	¶¶¶¶¶¶¶¶¶¶	BA02
5	724-96-5238	Johnson, Eric B.	Inf. Sys.	¶¶¶¶¶¶¶¶¶¶	BD01
6	823-70-4012	Clark, Luther C.	Accounting	¶¶¶¶¶¶¶¶¶¶	BA02
7	854-62-7811	James, Allen P.	Marketing	¶¶¶¶¶¶¶¶¶¶	BK02

INVERTED INDEX BY DEPARTMENT

Index Record Number	Department	Soc. Sec. Number	File Record Number	Soc. Sec. Number	File Record Number	Soc. Sec. Number	File Record Number
1	Accounting	790-49-3405	4	823-70-4012	6		
2	Inf. Sys.	724-96-5238	5				
3	Management	328-34-2934	2				
4	Marketing	012-78-9654	1	482-67-2941	3	854-62-7811	7

First Student in Department — Second Student — Third Student

INVERTED INDEX BY MAJOR

Index Record Number	Major	Soc. Sec. Number	File Record Number	Soc. Sec. Number	File Record Number
1	BA02	790-49-3405	4	823-70-4012	6
2	BD01	724-96-7238	5		
3	BK01	012-78-9654	1	482-67-1941	3
4	BK02	854-62-7811	7		
5	BN03	328-34-2934	2		

First Student in Major — Second Student in Major

The important point about inverted index files is that they can reduce processing time for frequently accessed data items. But having inverted index files in the information system also increases the storage space requirements and file maintenance costs.

File-oriented Processing Problems

As stated earlier, the purpose of a file is to store data. Likewise, the purpose of a computer program is to process data in a file. In the past, the traditional approach to data processing was to design the file and then write the program to process the data. This approach brought about an inseparable connection between a computer program and a file of data. An inventory control program was written to process the inventory file. However, if the inventory file was needed by a different program, the two programs could not use the file at the same time. Also, each program could perform only specific functions with the file. These limitations severely inhibited management's use of the data contained in files. As as result, system professionals saw the need to develop a data storage approach that would permit many users access to data simultaneously. Also, they saw the need to be able to write various application programs that could utilize the stored data but would not interfere with it.

There are other problems associated with file processing. If an information system is made up of several files and some of the same data are contained in each file, this means the data are redundant among the various files. The three separate files shown in Figure 9-10 contain six of the same data items. Duplication of data (*data redundancy*) is a characteristic of file processing.

Another problem is the lack of consistency from one file to the next. In one file an employee-name field is defined as thirty characters in length; in another, it may be defined as 27 characters. This presents no problem until an attempt is made to integrate or bring together the two files. File processing does not lend itself to *data integration*.

Updating is also a problem in file processing. When the same data are stored in more than one file, data must be updated in all of the files when a change occurs in any one of them. For example, assume that a bank's customer has three different accounts at the bank: savings, checking, and commercial loan. Each account is represented in a different file-processing system. If the customer notifies the bank of a change in address, the bank must include the address change in the update transactions of each of the three systems. This may not appear to be difficult, and it really isn't. Yet, in dealing with hundreds of changes in which duplicate entries must be made, it is very easy to miss one.

Figure 9-10

Illustration of data redundancy when file-oriented processing is used. In this example only the seventh data items differ in the three separate files.

PAYROLL FILE

Soc. Sec. No.	Name	Address	City	State	Dept.	Payroll Data
304-87-3391	Cline, Stuart	5382 Lincoln	Boise	ID	403D	¶¶¶¶¶¶¶¶¶¶¶¶¶¶¶

PERSONNEL FILE

Personnel Data

304-87-3391	Cline, Stuart	5382 Lincoln	Boise	ID	403D	¶¶¶¶¶¶¶¶¶¶¶¶¶¶

EARNINGS FILE

Earnings Data

304-87-3391	Cline, Stuart	5382 Lincoln	Boise	ID	403D	¶¶¶¶¶¶¶¶¶¶¶¶¶¶¶

If through an oversight only two of the three files containing the customer's data are updated, the customer may be annoyed when the bank sends the checking account statement and loan payment request to the new address but the savings account statement to the old address.

These deficiencies and the need for improved access to information have resulted in a movement away from file-oriented data processing. Instead, a data processing system that can provide a common data storage place and that allows computer programs to be separated from data files has become desirable. The result has been a database approach to data storage and retrieval.

DATABASE MANAGEMENT

Database Characteristics

All files contain data records; in this sense, every file is a database. If asked "What does the database look like?" some people will describe the file structure of an information system. To a degree, all of the types of file structures discussed in the first section of this chapter are used in database systems. However, even though a database is composed of files and indexes, it is more than a file or a collection of files. As the term is currently used, *database* means more than just file design and data storage.

Although there are a number of ways to define the term, we will use the following definition:

A DATABASE IS A STOREHOUSE OF RELATED DATA RECORDS INDEPENDENTLY MANAGED APART FROM ANY SPECIFIC PROGRAM OR INFORMATION SYSTEM APPLICATION.

This definition is very succinct, yet it contains the key elements of the database concept:

— "RELATED DATA RECORDS." Records in the database have a special relationship one to another. The relationship is normally implied in the name of the database. For example, a personnel database implies that all of the records are related to personnel data. Likewise, an inventory database and a student database indicate inventory and student data respectively.

— "A STOREHOUSE." Records are stored in only one place but are made available to all authorized users of the data. This feature implies that it is not necessary to maintain a separate file or files for each information system application. Each user can use the data as his or her own. Also, several users have the ability to access the database at the same time, a characteristic described in the term *shared database*. Each user can process data using his or her own application programs and, in so doing, will not affect or interfere with any other user's processing activities.

— "MANAGED." The database system has a special set of software to manage the data. The software is known as the *database management system* (DBMS).

— "INDEPENDENTLY . . . APART FROM." Data records and the users' programs are stored and managed independently in the database. This separation of data from the users' application programs is a characteristic called *data independence.*

Data Relationships

All data items within the database are related by a common factor. In a personnel database, the common factor is that each record relates to an employee. In an inventory database, the common factor is that each record relates to an inventory item or part. The common factor (employee, inventory item, student) is referred to as the entity (as discussed earlier in this chapter). Each entity has certain features or characteristics that describe it. An employee has an identification number (social security number), a name, a department, and so on. A characteristic that describes an entity is called an *attribute*. A specific attribute belonging to an entity will have a certain *value*. In other words, the value is the data stored in the attribute field. For example, in an inventory database the attribute "part number" may have a value "8-476-230." In scientific disciplines, rather than the terms "attribute" and "value," the terms "descriptor" and "state" are used. The descriptor "flower color" has the state "red."

From the discussion in the preceding paragraph, you have probably observed that the functions of various elements in a database structure are the same as those in a file structure. If so, you have observed correctly. There are files in a database; each file contains records that describe entities; each record is composed of fields (attributes); each field contains data (values). It is difficult to surmise why database professionals chose the terms entity, attribute, and value rather than staying with entity, field, and data, but, as James Martin stated, "Computer people change the names they use for concepts as capriciously as fashion designs."[1] In Figure 9-11, the relationship between terms used in file design and those used in database design is shown.

Two specific relationships that express the design structure of database systems are hierarchical and network.

Hierarchical Structure

Ideally, in a database all data items relating to a specific entity would be stored in one record, such as the following:

EMPLOYEE RECORD

480-66-1444   Paul Gray   32 Main   Akron OH   Prod. Dept. . . . etc.

However, storing all of the data in one record may not be suitable for efficient processing. In a database, data items are stored in several records. Each entity has one record that acts as a master record; the other records serve as detail or

---

[1]James Martin, *Principles of Data-Base Management* (Englewood Cliffs, N. J.: Prentice-Hall, Inc., 1976), p. 5.

Figure 9-11

Comparison of terms used in file design and database design.

FILE DESIGN		DATABASE DESIGN	
Term	Example	Term	Example
File	Personnel file	Database	Personnel database
Entity	Employee	Entity	Employee
Record	Master or detail	Record	Employee record
Field	Soc. sec. number	Attribute	Soc. sec. number
		Data Item	
		Descriptor	
Data	496-77-2601	Value	496-77-2601
		State	

subordinate records. To state it another way, some records in the database are superior to or control other records. This type of database design is known as a *hierarchical structure*. In order to get to a subordinate record, the database management system (DBMS) must first access the superior or master record and then access the subordinate records containing the desired information.

Another term that is often used to describe a master record is "the owner." An employee may be the owner of several records containing information about him or her. Although we view the employee's database record as one record, in reality there may be many records in the database relating to one employee. For example, the employee has only one name (which is one record), but may have had several previous employers (several records, one for each previous employer). The employee may have several dependents. For each dependent there is a subordinate record in the database. This particular relationship of owner to subordinate records is called a *one-to-many relationship*: one owner; many dependents. In the mechanics of database notation, a one-to-one relationship is shown with a single arrow in each direction. A one-to-many relationship is shown with a single arrow toward the "one" record and a double arrow toward the "many" records (see Figure 9-12).

Two terms other than owner/subordinate or master/detail that are often used to describe a hierarchical relationship are "parent" and "child." The owner

Figure 9-12

One-to-one (single arrow in both directions) and one-to-many (double arrow toward the "many") database relationships.

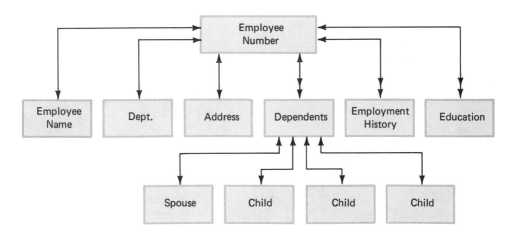

record is the *parent*; the subordinate record is the *child*. In a hierarchical design, there is only one relationship permitted, and that is parent to child: a one-to-one or a one-to-many relationship. This limitation may not be a problem in some information system applications, but most information systems process data with relationships somewhat more complex than just one-to-one or one-to-many.

Network Relationships

In many information systems, records may need to be related in a manner other than only hierarchical. For example, in a personnel database let's assume that a data item represents machine skills. An employee may have several different operator skills: one-to-many. However, in order to locate all of the employees with a specific skill—lathe operator, for example—it would be necessary to search the entire database. To avoid such a search, we can define another structural path in the database that would establish an additional owner record for skills. "Lathe" would be an owner; "Drill Press," another; and so forth. The subordinate records to "Lathe" are all of those employees who qualify as lathe operators. Each employee has several skills (a one-to-many relationship); each operating skill has several employees qualified in that skill (again, a one-to-many relationship). This relationship, called a *simple network*, is shown in Figure 9-13.

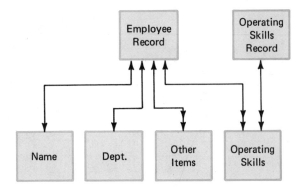

Figure 9-13

Illustration of a network relationship.

In some database management systems, relationships such as the skill file are developed through the use of inverted indexes or files. An inverted file can be established for any attribute in the employee's record other than the primary key field. (In a personnel file, the social security number is the primary key.) An attribute for which an inverted file is established is called a *secondary key*. Unlike primary keys, secondary keys do not uniquely identify a record, because several employees may have the same attributes; secondary keys do, however, allow for more efficient retrieval of data. This is illustrated with the Lathe Master record in Figure 9-14. A master record would be established for each skill. Fields (attributes) that are selected as secondary keys should be ones that are accessed frequently enough so that the cost of storing the inverted file is less than the cost of processing the entire main file in the database.

Another example of the use of secondary keys is that of a student database where a person requests information on all of the majors in marketing who have a 3.0 or above grade-point average (GPA). If secondary keys for the "Major" attribute or for the "GPA" attribute were not defined when the database was designed, the entire file would have to be searched and each student's record analyzed. Such a task could even involve writing a special computer program just to retrieve the desired information. If, however, secondary keys for Major

Figure 9-14

Illustration of a Lathe Master record, which picks out lathe operating skills from different employee records.

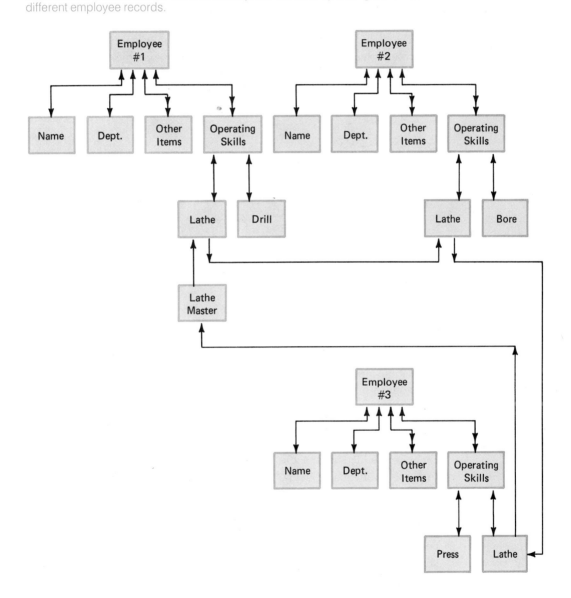

and GPA had been previously defined, the DBMS could quickly retrieve the desired information.

The "skill" attribute discussed in the preceding paragraph could also be represented as a *complex network* by adding another dimension. An employee has several skills; each skill may relate to several different jobs or tasks. This is known as a *many-to-many relationship.* Another example is that of a part in inventory. The same part may be on several purchase orders; each order may include several parts. This relationship is shown in Figure 9-15. You will notice that a many-to-many relationship is shown with double arrows in both directions.

Figure 9-15

The many-to-many relationship in a complex network.

Relational Database

Although the hierarchical and network structures indicate relationships that exist within a database, the design of a complex database using those two types of relationships can become quite inefficient to process. In addition, unless a relationship has been defined through a path or a secondary key when the database structure was established, specific information cannot be obtained from the database unless the complete record is retrieved. Also, any new relationship that someone may want to define into the database structure cannot be added unless the entire database is redefined. Today, a solution to these problems is being developed which is referred to as a *relational database* structure.

In a relational database, data are represented in two-dimensional tables: each row consists of all of the data attributes for each entity in a record, and the columns are used for storing each attribute. Shown in Figure 9-16(a) is a file of student data. A relational database could be as drawn in Figure 9-16(b), relating student demographic data to departmental data which in turn are connected to scholastic data. The other students in Figure 9-16(a) (Jones, Jeffries, Corresski, and Roth) would have relational records in the database similar to the ones

Figure 9-16

A relational database. A separate table is constructed for each of the attributes represented by the column headings.

Student Number	Name	Address	City	State	Dept.	Major	Year	GPA
289-06-4739	Cranston, James	409 Clark Ave.	Durango	CO	CI	C101	4	3.724
012-78-9645	Jones, Allen	1609 Melbourn	St. Louis	MO	BF	BR01	3	2.534
549-20-3742	Jeffries, T. O.	28502 W. Main	Memphis	TN	HY	HA02	2	2.730
202-84-1183	Corresski, Sidn	Rt. 1	Clarksville	MN	FN	FD02	3	3.841
642-48-4177	Roth, Edward	754 E. Stover	Raleigh	NC	EC	EB01	1	2.963

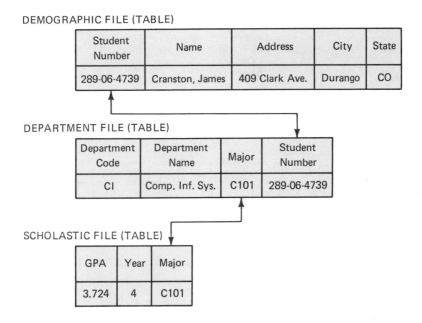

DEMOGRAPHIC FILE (TABLE)

Student Number	Name	Address	City	State
289-06-4739	Cranston, James	409 Clark Ave.	Durango	CO

DEPARTMENT FILE (TABLE)

Department Code	Department Name	Major	Student Number
CI	Comp. Inf. Sys.	C101	289-06-4739

SCHOLASTIC FILE (TABLE)

GPA	Year	Major
3.724	4	C101

shown for Cranston. Connecting the relational records for each student permits the user easy access to any data item for which a relationship has been defined. Also, elements can be added to the database without having to redefine the entire schema. The only problem is that most of today's databases are not designed to accommodate the total "relational" concept.

Database Management Systems

The software (computer programs) used to manage data in the database is referred to as the database management system (DBMS). A DBMS is a set of programs that provides for defining, controlling, and accessing the database.

Database Structure. The structure or logical description of the database is called the *schema*. An abbreviated section of a personnel database schema is shown in Figure 9-17. A schema indicates the names or labels of data items and the types of data that will be stored in the database. It pictures the relationship

Figure 9-17

Database structure, or schema.

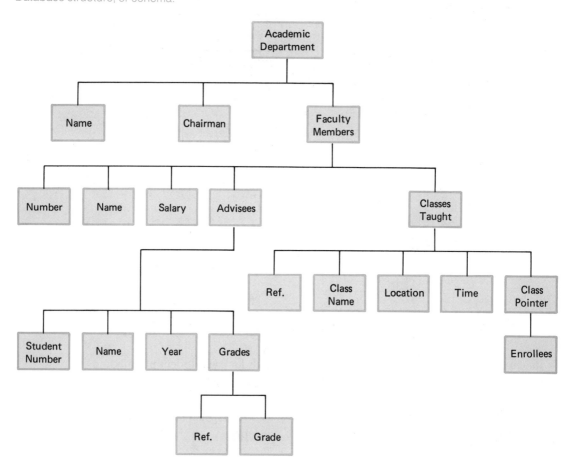

of one record to another, indicating which records are owners or masters and which ones are subordinates or detail records. The program or programs in the database management system that are used to define the schema and to establish it in the computer are called the *data description language* (DDL) or the *data definition language*. In Figure 9-18, the schema illustrated in Figure 9-17 is shown as it might appear in a DDL section. Note in Figure 9-18 that the hierarchical relationships are defined within each statement, such as

3* FACULTY MEMBERS (RG),

where the "(RG)" indicates that a repeating group follows that statement; that is, the field FACULTY MEMBERS covers a number of subordinate records (a one-to-many relationship). In the statements under "3*" you will notice that each statement is tied back to the "master" statement with the words "IN 3." The "RG" and the "IN 3" connect the parent record to the child.

Figure 9-18

The database schema of Figure 9-17 in data definition language (DDL), which defines the hierarchical relationships. The number in front of the name of the field is called the component number. All data items are keyed unless "non-key" is specified. The code X defines an alphanumeric field; a number in parentheses specifies the number of digits in the field.

```
DATABASE CYCLE
  1*   DEPARTMENT (NAME X(15))
  2*   CHAIRMAN (NON-KEY NAME X(15))
  3*   FACULTY MEMBERS (RG)
    4*    FACULTY NUMBER (INTEGER NUMBER 9(6) IN 3)
    5*    FACULTY NAME (NAME X(15) IN 3)
    6*    SALARY (NON-KEY MONEY $9(6).99 IN 3)
    7*    ADVISEES (RG IN 3)
      8*    STUDENT NUMBER (INTEGER NUMBER 9(6) IN 7)
      9*    STUDENT NAME (NAME X(15) IN 7)
     10*    YEAR (NAME 11 IN 7)
     11*    STUDENT GRADES (RG IN 7)
       12*    CLASS REFERENCE (NAME X(5) IN 11)
       13*    GRADE (NAME X IN 11)
    14*    CLASSES TAUGHT (RG IN 3)
       15*    CLASS REF (NAME X(5) IN 14)
       16*    CLASS NAME (NAME X (15) IN 14)
       17*    LOCATION (NON-KEY NAME X(5) IN 14)
       18*    TIME (NON-KEY NAME X(8) IN 14)
       19*    CLASS POINTER (RG IN 14)
         20*    ENROLLEES NUMBER (INTEGER NUMBER 9(6)
                IN 19)
```

As stated earlier, one of the characteristics of the database concept is that data is independent of users' application programs. Any given application program uses only a portion of the database. Because the structure of the database itself is complex, there is a need to construct a simplified version of that part of the database which is used in an individual user's application program. This simplified version is called the *subschema*. The use of subschemas also helps control access to the database. Access through an application program is limited to that portion of the database which was defined in the subschema. Because application programs are written in various computer programming languages, the DBMS must provide a mechanism for program instructions to interact with the database. The *data manipulation language* (DML) of the DBMS serves that purpose. When writing application programs a programmer will include DML commands in the program as needed to access the database.

Database Control. The DBMS will also contain a control section. This section keeps track of who owns the database and who is authorized to access it. Control is maintained through the use of identification numbers, account numbers, site locations, and passwords. Keeping unauthorized users from accessing the database and controlling the extent of access for authorized users are critical for the protection of data. Privacy and security of the data must be ensured.

Database Access. The data manipulation language provides for the interface between a user's program and the database. Most users are not programmers, yet they have a need to access the database. In addition, many requests for information from the database are not for long reports or printouts, but rather are short requests asking for only one or two items. The DBMS provides a method of meeting this need. A short request for information is called a *query*. The section of the DBMS software that provides the ability to construct queries is the *query language processor* (QLP). Because users who make short requests are typically "non-computer" persons, the query language should be easy to learn and provide for easy construction of database queries. A query example is the following:

```
LIST EMPLOYER-NAME, ADDRESS, CITY, AND STATE
WHERE APPLICANT-SSN EQ 001-34-2319
```

In response to the query, the system would print the names and addresses of all employers listed in the record of the applicant whose social security number equals 001-34-2319.

Data Dictionary

Data items (field definitions) may vary from one file to another, from one database to another, or among information systems. To help eliminate the variations, an organization will develop a data dictionary. A *data dictionary* is an inventory of data items used throughout the organization so that those individuals who are developing information systems will have a guide — a standard — of the characteristics of each data item. A data dictionary normally contains the following characteristics:

— Data item (its name)
— Field size
— Special codes or values allowed
— Mode (numeric or alphanumeric)
— Files and records containing the item
— Programs in which the item is found
— Source of the data
— User or owner department
— Data output documents

A database dictionary will include additional characteristics not found in a file-oriented system, such as description of the schema and subschema.

DBMS Advantages

A database system has several advantages over file processing.

Elimination of data redundancy. Data are stored in only one place — the database — rather than in multiple files. The hypothetical employee record in Figure 9-10, which required three separate files duplicating six of the same data items when file-oriented processing was used, is restructured according to the database system in Figure 9-19. In the file-oriented system, the social security

Figure 9-19

Data from Figure 9-10 as they would be structured in a database system.

Soc. Sec. No.	Name	Address	City	State	Dept.	Payroll Data	Personnel Data	Earnings Data
304-87-3391	Cline, Stuart	5382 Lincoln	Boise	ID	403D	¶¶¶¶¶¶¶¶	¶¶¶¶¶¶¶¶	¶¶¶¶¶¶¶¶

number is stored in three different locations; in the database system, it is stored only once. The example shown in Figure 9-19 is a slight exaggeration because not all redundancy is eliminated by using a database. (Each inverted file requires some duplication of data.) However, redundancy in a database can be controlled. In using ordinary file structures, there is little control over the number of duplicate records.

Improved efficiency in updating. The number of times that files are accessed during an update process is reduced in database systems. One pass at the update process is all that is needed to update a record in the database. On the other hand, if you are using file-oriented systems, an update run is needed for each file in the system. If there are five files that contain the data item to be updated, five different files (and five different programs or program segments) must be accessed.

Fewer errors in updating. In a file-processing system, several files may need to be updated when a single data item is changed. If one of the files is omitted from the update process, that file will contain erroneous data. As a result, data within the information system are inconsistent.

Less-complex program logic. Because the database management system takes care of managing data in the database, the programmer faces less-complex program logic in writing an application program. The programmer only needs to be familiar with the application logic; the DBMS does the rest.

Reduced program maintenance cost. Because the application program is independent of the database, changes are easily made in the program and do not affect the database. Also, changes can be made in the database and will not affect the application program. Changes in the database are said to be *transparent* to the application program.

Data sharing. Data in the database are shared by many users at the same time, each user independent of the others.

Easy data access. The database management system provides the user with a means of accessing or querying the database without having to write a computer program. The user is required only to form simple query statements.

DBMS Disadvantages

Although database systems are highly desirable, certain pitfalls exist.

Difficult to design. The purpose of a database system is to store data in a central location for simultaneous access by many users. If the database is to be used by many different individuals, each with special needs, the database design process requires a high degree of interdepartmental cooperation and compromise. The users or user departments cannot have everything exactly as they wish. Conflicts among users normally call for meetings, discussions, and eventual compromise, which may prolong the implementation schedule.

Time-dimension problem. Users have a need for similar data; however, the timing of need and acceptance of the data differs among users. For example, once a sale is made and the order entered, the sales manager may be content if the data enter the system at any time during the reporting period. However, the accounting department may not consider the transaction "a sale" until the ordered items have been packed, shipped, and invoiced. An aircraft design engineer may use a database for developing new design specifications. After experiments in design have been made and the database has been updated with the new specifications, the engineer may realize through tests or other means that the new specifications are faulty. As a result, the engineer wishes to re-establish the old specifications in the database. However, the old specifications were destroyed in the update process and can only be entered again through a reload process. To re-enter or reload data is time-consuming and expensive.

Cost of the DBMS. Database management systems are expensive; however, with today's widespread use of small computers, less-expensive database management systems are being developed. Database software packages are priced from $5,000 to $150,000 by software vendors. The cost is directly related to software complexity. A database management system that permits only hierarchical relationships is less costly than one that will handle complex relationships.

All eggs in one basket. If a malfunction exists within the database, all users are prevented from using it. If the database is wiped out, all users lose their data. In a file-processing system, if one file cannot be accessed, users with different files are not affected. The inherent danger of having all data stored in one central system is probably the greatest fear that most database users have. For that reason, database management systems provide for rapid recovery whenever the system is down or the database is affected in any way.

Database dropouts. Unless users can get the information they need out of the database system quickly, they will develop and maintain their own systems. This defeats the purpose of having a database. By relying more and more upon their own recordkeeping systems (index cards, handwritten logs, or whatever), they ultimately will use the database less and less and eventually become database dropouts.

SUMMARY

Data are stored in files. The major types of files used are sequential files, direct access files, indexed sequential files, and lists. The traditional method of file organization is the sequential structure; however, with the increased need developing today for faster retrieval of information, direct access files are becoming more widely used. File-processing systems have their limitations. They are rather inflexible and cannot be shared by several users at the same time. Also, in file processing, information systems cannot be integrated easily.

The database concept was developed to overcome those deficiencies. Databases can be shared by many users. In addition, application programs to process data in the database are independent of the database itself. Application programs are less complex in a database system than in file-processing systems, and less redundancy exists in a database system. Although these advantages make using a database highly desirable, there are disadvantages as well. Database management systems are expensive to purchase, yet are too difficult for the organization itself to develop. If anything happens to the database, more users are affected than if the information systems are based upon files only.

The less-costly database management systems provide only for a hierarchical relationship in the design of the database; however, there are sophisticated database management systems today that provide for more complex relationships. The ultimate design of a database is to develop a DBMS that will accommodate all relationships that exist now or might exist in the future. This type of database is called a relational database. No major DBMS available today has reached this ultimate capability, yet software developers continue in an effort to bring about this ideal DBMS.

TERMS

File	Record
Entity	Unique identifier
Bit	Primary key
Byte	Sequential file
Field	Indexed sequential file
Data element	Direct access file

Lists

Link list file

Inverted index file

Record ID

Binary search

Random access

Randomizing technique

Link address

Overflow area

Purging

Data redundancy

Data integration

Updating

Shared database

Database management system (DBMS)

Attribute

Value

Hierarchical structure

One-to-many relationship

Parent

Child

Simple network

Secondary key

Complex network

Many-to-many relationship

Relational database

Schema

Data description language (DDL)

Data definition language (DDL)

Subschema

Data manipulation language (DML)

Query

Query language processor (QLP)

Data dictionary

Transparent

QUESTIONS

1. What is the key to data organization?
2. What is the purpose of files?
3. Which of the following is an entity?
   (a) An employee
   (b) An inventory item
   (c) An inventory part number
   (d) Employee dependents
4. What two other terms are sometimes used as synonyms for "data field"?
5. What is the purpose of a unique identifier?
6. In a student information system, what is normally the unique identifier?
7. How many primary keys may be in one record?
8. Can a direct access file be accessed directly on a magnetic tape?
9. Describe the general procedure used in a binary search.
10. How are duplicate addresses (synonyms) in direct access file structures handled?
11. How many link addresses will a master record in a list structure have?

12. Describe the general structure of an indexed sequential file.
13. What is gained from using inverted indexes in retrieving data?
14. What are the drawbacks to file-oriented processing?
15. What does DBMS mean?
16. Why is the concept of a shared database essential in today's information processing environment?
17. What relationships are hierarchical database structures based upon?
18. What two other terms are used for master/detail records?
19. Distinguish between a simple network and a complex network.
20. What is gained from having a data dictionary?
21. What is to be gained from using a database approach to information processing?
22. Indicate the pitfalls of using database systems.

ARTICLE

You Mean I Can't Just Plug It In?

DBMS Is Needed

When a company wants its executives to have access to a diversity of facts and figures, the data processing organization will have to choose a database management system.... The DBMS sits between the applications programs that the user sees (or a query language the user sees) and the data itself. The DBMS gets the data for the user. Oddly enough, although a DBMS is a software package that can be bought on a roll of mag tape, it is not a program alone. A DBMS involves a way of dealing with data as well as a means of performing useful work.

If data is thought of as the collection of books in a library, a DBMS involves the acceptance of a method of organization — like the Dewey decimal system — as well as the establishment of a standard means for locating data, such as the library card catalog. The methodology and the implementation must fit together, and the pair must fit not only present corporate needs but, as well as is possible, anticipated future needs. Once a company adopts a DBMS, it is very expensive and difficult to change.

As faster and more terminal-oriented systems become available, the types of DBMS in use are changing. Currently, the big move for new applications and companies now going to interactive computing is a kind of system called a relational database.... However, older ways of providing access to databases may remain more efficient for many sites; additionally, their age means that they have fewer bugs and that many more professionals are familiar with them. Most experts on the management of databases seem to agree that the value of a relational system is greater when the types of inquiries to a system have less uniformity or involve unanticipated ways of looking at data.

... What is making the relational database take off faster is the declining cost of processing and storage as well as the increased interest in access to corporate information from users who only recently wanted little or nothing to do with a computer, let alone a terminal on a nearby desk.

...[T]he movement toward distributed databases and diverse on-line users will stimulate the move toward relational systems. "Some departments," observes Intel's Jerry Spencer, who leads the company's software marketing department, "have personal computers all over their

continued

offices. This creates a problem for the DP department. It's hard to draw a line. On one hand, you improve productivity; on the other, there's a big system that has to be managed efficiently."

Facing the Facts

Even if the database systems are there for getting at facts, the problems of controlling what belongs in the database and how it gets there will persist. If anything, the issues will grow more serious as micro[computer]s appear in more and more offices.

. . . The job, as defined by Merrill's John Chatfield, an executive involved in database administration, includes not only gathering data and putting them in the right files in the right way, but also preserving their integrity and consistency. Along the way, the use of a DBMS minimizes redundancy so that the corporate information resources can grow without excessive waste of storage resources.

DISCUSSION QUESTIONS

1. What is the impetus for acceptance and development of the relational database?
2. Why is the decision concerning the type of DBMS that the organization will use a critical one?

APPLICATION

"Yellow Pages" Database Goes on Dialog

PALO ALTO, Calif. — While American Telephone and Telegraph (AT&T) has been busy settling its antitrust case with the Justice Department, Market Data Retrieval Inc. of Westport, Conn., has grabbed the advantage in a market that AT&T had targeted as its own: electronic Yellow Pages. Starting this month, Market Data will release the first of a series of "Electronic Yellow Pages" database files, which will be available through Dialog Information Sevices Inc. headquartered here.

The first Yellow Pages file is called the "Financial Services Directory." It will consist of nearly 90,000 records for banks, savings and loan companies, and credit unions in the United States. Each month a new file will become available, a spokeswoman for Dialog said, until the entire 9-million-record database of business listings is on-line.

The data for Electronic Yellow Pages is collected by Market Data, a supplier of mailing list and marketing information, from the most current Yellow Pages telephone directories for every part of the U.S., however small, the spokeswoman said. The data is then cross-checked and qualified with more than 50 other sources.

. . . Besides the name and address, the typical Electronic Yellow Pages record will include geographic location, telephone number, 4-digit Standard Industrial Classification (SIC) code, and a field for relative size.

In praising the product, the Dialog spokeswoman said that the database can be useful to everyone from the private individual or small business to the largest corporation. "It can be used in sales, marketing, advertising, promotion, direct mail and general reference and inquiry." It can also be used to locate a professional or business anywhere in the U.S. without requiring manual thumbing through many bulky printed directories, she pointed out.

Each of the files in the database will be devoted to a particular area of business. The first one, Financial Services Directory, can be searched by name, city, city size, county, state, zip code, telephone area code and prefix, and relative size of institution. As an example the spokeswoman "looked up" the Puritan Co-Op Bank in Swampscott, Mass. In addition to the address, telephone number and

continued

other items mentioned above, the record listed the chief executive officer, the assets of the bank, the population of the city it is in, and indicated that this was the headquarters.

Outside of simple name and address retrieval, this file of the database can be used to provide a census of U.S. banks, savings and loans, and credit unions; to locate sources of financial assistance in specific geographic areas; to prepare special custom contact lists; to contribute to site selection analyses, and for competitive intelligence.

Forthcoming files in the Electronic Yellow Pages series will include manufacturing, retailers, wholesalers, professionals (including doctors and lawyers), construction and services, the spokeswoman said.

MIS Week, *April 7, 1982, p. 23.*

DISCUSSION QUESTIONS

1. What types of file structure possibly are used in the Yellow Pages database?

2. Using the description of data items in the Financial System as your guide, what items will probably be included in the Manufacturing Yellow Pages?

10 INFORMATION SYSTEMS FEASIBILITY

CHAPTER OBJECTIVES

In this chapter you will learn:

1. The components of an information system.
2. The phases in the system development cycle.
3. What constitutes a feasibility study.
4. The significance of adequate problem definition.
5. Questions to be asked in justifying the development of a new information system.
6. What constitutes a cost/benefit analysis.
7. Questions to ask in analyzing present systems and in determining user requirements.
8. What design specifications are.

INFORMATION SYSTEMS IN BUSINESS

The attention being focused today on the creation and redesign of information systems suggests that information systems are something new, a product of the computer generation. They are—and yet they aren't. They are new in that effective information systems have become crucial in many of the dimensions of our daily lives. As an example, and this is only one of hundreds of examples that could be given, it would be virtually impossible to process manually the millions of checks that go through our nationwide banking system. Computer-based systems are now an integral—and necessary—part of banking and other businesses.

On the other hand, information systems have existed for as long as man has had a need to make decisions. Columbus might not have sailed for India without data that led him to form opinions and perceptions of the earth's shape, scope, and continental structure, and to establish navigational procedures. True, he had only limited data, and some of it was even in error; however, he collected, processed, analyzed, and used the data.

An example of an early business information system is that of Nathan Rothschild, who used a specific, unique information system to increase his wealth. In 1815 he realized the effect that the outcome of the battle of Waterloo would have upon the market value of government bonds. To obtain early information on the outcome of the battle, he established his own messenger service from the site of the battle to his own office. As a result, he was the first to learn that Napoleon had been defeated. Rothschild made financial decisions based upon that information and was able to amass a fortune in the bond market.

Today, each of us is directly involved with information systems. As shown in Figure 10-1, at times we are the generators of data that go into the system. At other times, we may be involved with processing the data. And, more often than we realize, we are users of the products (information) generated by the myriad of systems that surround us.

To illustrate a person's involvement with an information system, we will consider a class registration and grade-reporting system. At the beginning of this term, you registered for a class or classes by completing the registration form. Those data became a part of an information system. In fact, completing your registration makes you a specific part of the system. After you completed the registration form and turned it into the registrar's office, your form, along with those of others, was fed into the computer. At that point, automatic

Figure 10-1

People are an integral part of information systems. They generate data, they use data (information), and they play significant roles in processing data.

Generating data

Processing data

Using data

processing began. In the registration process, after the data are read into the system, the course requests from all students registering are compiled, sorted, and recorded in computer files. Then, through the use of computer programs, reports of students enrolled in the various classes are generated. A class roster (report) is then sent to the teacher of each class.

At the end of this term, your teacher will complete a form indicating the grades received by the students. This grade form becomes an input medium into the system, and, after all of the grades have been processed, the data will be used to generate grade reports for each student. Reports will be produced also for the school's record section and for other administrative officials who have a need for information about class achievement.

COMPONENTS OF AN INFORMATION SYSTEM

Once again, let's consider what an information system is. An *information system,* whether it involves only manual processing (such as filling out a class registration form) or almost total automation, consists of these basic components:

— *Input* elements (entering data into the system for processing)
— *Processing* steps or activities (changing data from its raw form to a form that is of benefit to the information user)
— *Output* medium (getting the information out of the system so that the user has access to it).

The relationship of these traditional components is shown in Figure 10-2. Two other components of the system are also important—feedback and objective. Every information system exists to serve a purpose. It has an *objective* to

Figure 10-2

Simplified diagram of information system.

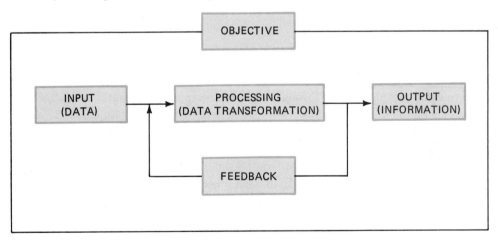

fulfill, a reason for being. When a business information system no longer meets user needs for information, the system will cease to exist.

Another important part of the system is the *feedback loop*. Feedback is essential for determining if proper data are being fed into the system, if they are correct, and if adequate processing is taking place.

Note from the preceding discussion that a close relationship exists between a computer system (as discussed in Chapters 3 and 4) and an information system. Both systems consist of the three basic components *Input*, *Processing*, and *Output* (*IPO*). However, an information system is larger and more extensive than a computer system; the computer is only a part of an information system. In a computer system, input occurs at the point that data enter the computer. For example, a data entry operator records sales data from a salesman's order form onto a diskette. When the diskette is placed into a disk reader, the data then become input into the computer system. By contrast, the information system itself begins much earlier than at the point of computer input; it begins when the salesman completes the customer's order form. The output of a computer system is the printed report or visual display on a CRT. The information system involves more than computer output; it includes distribution of the information and its use by managers, among other things. In an information system, processing may be done manually or automatically; computer processing functions, on the other hand, are almost all automatic.

Today, the computer plays an important role in most information systems — with emphasis on *most*, since many systems exist today that are not affected by a computer.

CONSTRUCTING AN INFORMATION SYSTEM

Until the computer was invented, information systems were designed largely through trial and error; formal design approaches were not generally used. There were exceptions, of course. Structured, organized approaches to information systems development began in the late 1800s with the efficiency expert who, stopwatch in hand, conducted time and motion studies to improve manual operations. These studies dealt primarily with individual workstations and job tasks on assembly lines. Later, in the 1930s and 1940s, systems professionals came on the scene, conducting systems analyses to eliminate duplication of work and overlapping job tasks, excessive distances between workstations, etc. Though this slow, evolutionary process was once adequate to accommodate development of new information systems, in today's world change cannot be left to chance or to trial and error.

Several major factors have contributed to the new emphasis on the use of formalized, well-structured approaches to developing information systems. One is the dramatic increase in the volume and cost of information or data processed today. An organization's profits can be substantially reduced or eliminated if processing is not efficiently done. Another factor is the increase in size and complexity of organizations today, requiring changes in old systems and the design of new ones. Technology is another factor. Increased capacity and speed of computers make possible the development of more efficient and productive information systems.

THE SYSTEMS DEVELOPMENT CYCLE

A widely accepted approach to developing information systems is to organize the job into phases or parts. These phases are referred to as the *systems development cycle*. Although these phases may be labeled in a number of ways, we will use the following terms:

— Problem Recognition
— Feasibility Study (Preliminary Study)
— Detail System Analysis
— System Design
— Programming Activities
— Implementation of the System
— Evaluation and Follow-up

In some ways the cycle parallels the scientific method of problem solving. Indeed it should, for in systems development the organization is faced with a particular problem it is trying to solve, a situation similar to that of the scientific investigator. Steps in the two methods are shown in Figure 10-3.

In the scientific method of investigation, the researcher identifies as precisely as possible the problem being studied and writes a formal statement of the problem. If a written statement is available for reference or review, the investigator will be less likely to wander off course as the study progresses. Also, the written statement provides the investigator with a visible means of letting others know what the problem is.

Information systems investigators define the problem for the same reasons. Also, they collect and analyze data to determine the appropriate design of the new system. From possible solutions available, a researcher will select the one that appears to be best for solving the problem. Similarly, systems people look at several alternatives, choosing the one that most effectively solves the organization's information problem. In both the scientific method and systems

Figure 10-3

Comparison of steps in the scientific method and the systems development cycle.

SCIENTIFIC METHOD	SYSTEMS DEVELOPMENT CYCLE
•Problem Recognition	•Problem Recognition (Selection of Systems for Further Study
•Statement of the Problem	•Feasibility Study
•Collection and Analysis of Data	•Detail System Analysis
•Development of Alternative Solutions	•System Design
•Select Alternative and Test for Desired Results	•Programming Activities and System Implementation
•Repeat Selection and Testing If Necessary	•System Follow-up and Evaluation

development, the problem solution selected is evaluated to see if it produces the desired results.

Whereas the researcher may look upon the problem solution as a final step, systems development does not stop with "a solution." Information requirements within the organization are constantly changing. A solution that was the "best" three years ago may be totally inadequate today. As a result, systems development is a continuous process.

As discussed previously in Chapter 6, *user involvement* in developing an information system is critical to the success of a project. Users need to be active participants in all phases of the systems life cycle; however, the amount of participation will vary with each system phase and with specific activities within each phase. The graph in Figure 10-4 indicates the relative contribution of user groups and systems (EDP) personnel to the system effort. The purpose of the graph is not to present a precise analysis of user involvement but rather to give an indication of the approximate level of participation of each group — to show that the degree of user involvement varies with each cycle phase.

Phase I: Problem Recognition

The needs of the information user change often, as does the environment in which the system must function. Recognizing these changes is the motivation

Figure 10-4

Participation of users and EDP personnel in the systems development cycle. Active user involvement, though important throughout the cycle, will be more intense during some phases than during others.

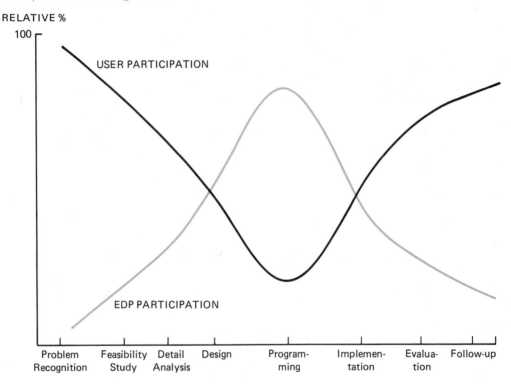

for making changes in existing systems and for developing new systems. The following are some examples of conditions that create a need for changes in information systems:

— A company expands by acquiring or merging with another company.
— New government regulations require different reporting procedures and increased data processing to supply information beyond the capability of the present system. For example, even a seemingly simple change, such as going from a five-digit zip code to a nine-digit one, may require major file or database reorganization.

— New technology becomes available that would improve existing systems and provide for greater processing efficiency, yet reduce the overall information processing costs—doing more, but doing it cheaper.

— Systems personnel may present a project recommendation to management that improves the effectiveness of an existing system. For example, the systems department might recommend that a real-time, interactive order processing system be developed to provide better service to customers and better system response to management.

— A manager recognizes the need for a new system to help a particular area, such as inventory control or work scheduling.

— A manager desires to take advantage of a newly released software package—a new computer-based management tool—not available in the present system.

— A crisis or near-crisis situation arises, calling for a quick response: a new system must be developed, or changes must be made in an existing one. Often the crisis is externally caused, such as by general economic conditions or a natural disaster. Management recognizes that it must react to the condition with decisions based on accurate and timely information. Note the experience of one organization shown in "The Peanut Butter Crisis," Figure 10-5.

In "The Peanut Butter Crisis," how many originating sources of possible system studies can you identify? Possible sources might include the crisis itself, sales department management, the vendor—Sperry, and the MIS department.

System Priorities. Often several information systems problems arise almost simultaneously within the organization. Because resources are limited, however, not all of the problems can be solved at one time. Consequently, management must set priorities to determine the order in which information systems projects will be undertaken. Questions that management should ask in setting *system priorities* include the following:

— Is a solution to the problem critical to the continued existence of the organization? (Within most organizations, problems are recognized before a "do or die" situation is reached.)

— Does the current staff have the expertise and time necessary to carry out the project? What is the availability and cost of additional personnel, if needed?

— Is the project possible with the existing hardware? If not, what is the availability and cost of new hardware?

Figure 10-5

The Peanut Butter Crisis

The peanut harvest in the summer and fall of 1980 fell far below the average annual crop yield. Peanut butter manufacturers began to realize late that fall that they would not be able to fill all customer orders for the following year. This created a management problem for the manufacturers in determining how to distribute equitably the limited quantities available.

As reported in *MIS Week,* one peanut butter manufacturer determined that it needed a new system to better deal with the problem. The manufacturer's old system could not react quickly enough to the crisis: Data were processed in a batch mode, and the information was provided too late for sales and marketing management to react in time. The solution proposed was to implement a timeshare system.

However, as *MIS Week* reported, the MIS group indicated that for them to develop a timeshare system would require a six months' effort. The sales and marketing division could not wait that long. As an alternative, MIS personnel suggested a particular software package from Sperry-UNIVAC that would do the job and could be implemented almost immediately. The package, called Mapper, is a decision support program that generates management-oriented reports and is well supported by the vendor.

In January, 1982, *MIS Week* stated that the manufacturer was not only satisfied with the package in meeting its immediate information need, but was also looking within the organization for other applications of the program.

MIS Week, *January 27, 1982, pp. 17–18*

— Can the proposed system be completed within a desired time frame?

— How does development of the new information system fit into the organization's long-range systems development plans? "Long range" in information systems is typically three to five years. Systems development activities should be balanced between systems that can be implemented within several months and those that take several years to develop.

— Does the proposed system involve new technologies in either hardware or software? Has the effectiveness of the new technology been proved, particularly by other users? You may want to be "the first on the block to have a new system" for several reasons. It may be just the thing for solving your problem and thus worth the risk. The vendor may give you a tempting deal—for example, six months' free use. Finally, you could gain recognition for being the first one to have one. Normally this is not an important point; however, it may be a worthwhile consideration to a new organization seeking publicity.

— How do the anticipated benefits of the new system compare with the estimated costs of developing and operating the system? This is usually the most important consideration of all in setting priorities.

Phase II: Feasibility Study (Preliminary Study)

After management has established project priorities, plans must be made for constructing the new information system that was selected for development. This study is referred to as a preliminary investigation or *feasibility study*. The feasibility study should build on the tasks undertaken in Phase I. As we shall see, the whole process of systems design and development is one of building on what was done in previous phases. Each phase explores additional facets of design in greater detail.

Several tasks should be undertaken during the feasibility study. A well-constructed and concise problem statement should be developed; system objectives should be established; present information systems within the organization should be evaluated; the scope of the development project should be defined; system constraints should be noted; and a cost/benefit analysis should be completed. Which of these tasks do you think is the most important? A discussion of each follows.

Problem Statement. Because the formal *problem statement* must be acceptable to top management, other information users, and systems personnel, defining the problem is a group effort. A written, rather than oral, problem statement is preferred. It avoids subsequent misunderstanding among interested parties. It facilitates communication among the project team members. Also, it acts as a benchmark (a guide) for future evaluation of the system.

System Objectives. Closely related to developing a concise statement of the problem is determining *system objectives*. What are the objectives of the new system? What exactly is to be accomplished? Expectations should be clearly stated. For example, the objective "to reduce inventories" is better stated "to reduce inventories by 10 percent." Concrete and measurable objectives allow top management, users, and project team members to understand exactly what is desired in the new system.

Study of Existing Systems. After the problem has been defined and stated and the objectives have been determined, it is necessary to answer several questions about the existing system or systems, if the new system involves bringing together several old systems. The project team needs to learn what the major problems in the present system are and whether or not the problems are significant enough to justify a new or drastically changed system. They need to evaluate the various elements of the old system to determine whether any parts of that system should be retained. Is the present system capable of handling peak loads or special requests? Is it "down" more than it is "up"? Does the present system process data accurately, or is it a case of "garbage in, garbage out"?

The team should study the operating costs of the present system. Cost data are essential in making the decision whether to proceed with developing a new system. Costs may be presented as summary totals (cost per week or month) or figured on a per-unit basis; e.g., $5.50 per customer order processed.

Costs for which specific dollar amounts can be calculated are referred to as *tangible costs*. For example, all direct and indirect costs of operating the system are tangible costs—personnel, equipment, floor space, etc. Costs where dollar amount cannot be determined are classed as *intangible costs,* such as customer dissatisfaction resulting from delays in processing an order. Another example of an intangible cost is the inability of the present system to provide management with accurate and timely information. If management makes inept or poor decisions because of the lack of appropriate information, how do you measure this deficiency? What is a "poor" decision?

Scope of the System. All systems in the organization interact with other systems, some internal and others external to the organization. These points of interaction identify the boundary of a system and must be determined in order to establish the *scope* of the system study. Points of interface are illustrated in Figure 10-6. Not all information systems interface with other systems.

Sometimes project teams have a tendency to define the scope of the system too broadly. This happens when team members, recognizing that the new system affects other systems, can't resist the temptation to study those systems

Figure 10-6

Points of interface among information systems are the points of input and output, which determine the boundary of the system. Not all information systems interface with other systems.

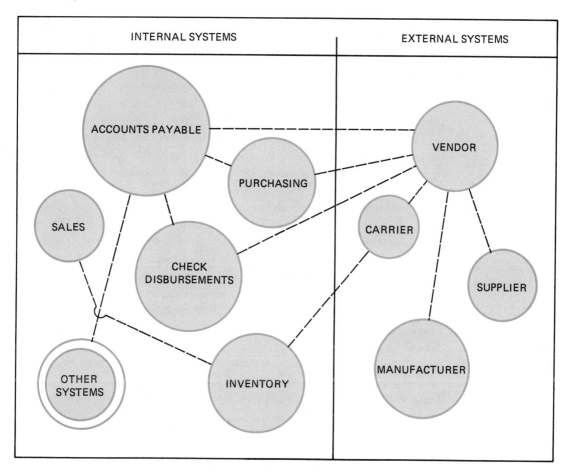

also. It does not take many redefinitions before the systems development effort has become too large for the organization to undertake.

System Constraints (Limitations). Few, if any, organizations have unlimited resources. Organizations are limited in personnel, time, money, and factors outside the organization such as state or federal regulations, vendor requirements, customer reactions, and attitudes of unions. The systems project team should note the *constraints* that currently exist or may arise during systems development. To fail in systems development is very possible if no consideration is given to constraints, and if management and other users are not notified of the system limitations.

Personnel. Personnel is a limiting factor since there are only so many people within an organization that can be assigned to a particular system effort. Also, the technical expertise of the people who work with systems may not be adequate for the present project. For example, the new system may involve the use of a telecommunications network and a database management system, yet present employees may have had no experience in designing such systems.

Adding personnel may not be the solution, because hiring too many new people within a short period of time may create problems. New employees must be oriented to the organization and trained in the company's way of doing things. This takes time.

Consulting firms are sometimes used to alleviate the personnel constraint. There are both advantages and disadvantages in using consultants. The major advantage is that consultants are already trained and experienced in areas now lacking in the organization. Another is that consultants tend to have fewer prejudices or preconceived notions of operations in the organization.

On the negative side, however, consultants are not totally unbiased. Although they are selected because of their experience, a solution that they developed in another situation may not be appropriate for your organization. When consultants are hired to design and implement the new system, a company's employees do not gain systems development experience. Frequently, consultants' fees are considerable, sometimes appearing to be excessive. Because the consultant is an outsider, establishing a rapport with users and managers may be difficult.

Time. Time is another constraint. There is never enough time to develop the "ideal" system. System projects are often under a time limit that has been mandated by management or by an external force. In the peanut butter crisis at Best Foods the management had to establish a time limit. Consider another example. In the late '70s the Internal Revenue Service changed the income tax withholding process. Organizations initially were given six months to implement the change, but later an extension of six additional months was granted because organizations complained that they could not implement the change in such a short period of time. Regardless of time provided to design and implement a system, meeting deadlines is a constant problem. True to Murphy's law, it seems that everything takes longer than it should and certainly longer than you plan.

The time schedule is an important part of the feasibility study. Critical to good project management is a reliable estimate of how long it will take to design and implement the system. Arriving at this estimate requires that each activity be analyzed for its place in the system—for its relationship to preceding and subsequent activities. Activities that can be completed concurrently should be noted. Also, in order to arrive at a time estimate, how long each activity will take to be completed is calculated.

Network charts that depict time estimates and activity relationships are often used as a way to analyze and manage systems development. A network chart is illustrated in Figure 10-7. Each circled number in the chart represents an *event*. The event may be the start or completion of a specific activity. The line between two events depicts an activity. Note that there are several paths from event 1 to event 9. Some paths take longer to complete than others. The path that takes the longest to complete is called the *critical path*. Network charts are sometimes called PERT charts (Project Evaluation and Review Technique) or CPM (Critical Path Method) charts.

Using a *bar chart*, often called a *Gantt chart* after the name of the person credited with its development, is another method of displaying a schedule. (See Figure 10-8.) Bar charts are particularly good for small projects. Since they do not show relationships among activities, they are less effective than network charts in managing large projects. Also, network charts can be programmed on the computer. With several thousand activities in a project, mentally remembering relationships among activities is impossible. The computer provides various reports on the status of a particular activity and its effect on other activities.

Regardless of the technique used, time must be scheduled, activities and tasks planned, and activity completion evaluated. Management needs to know if tasks were completed on schedule or with a time overrun. Although time constraints may dictate that certain system aspects be given less attention, time limitations can be controlled with careful scheduling.

Money. Money may be a constraint because funds are not available for developing the "ideal" system. The perfect system might require new hardware or involve the use of a new system concept that is financially impossible. If financial resources are severely limited but developing the system is still believed to be important, the project team members need to present less costly alternatives to management.

Figure 10-7

A simplified network chart showing the time schedule of development activities. The critical path is shown graphically with solid lines from event 1 to event 9 (i. e., events 1-3-6-9).

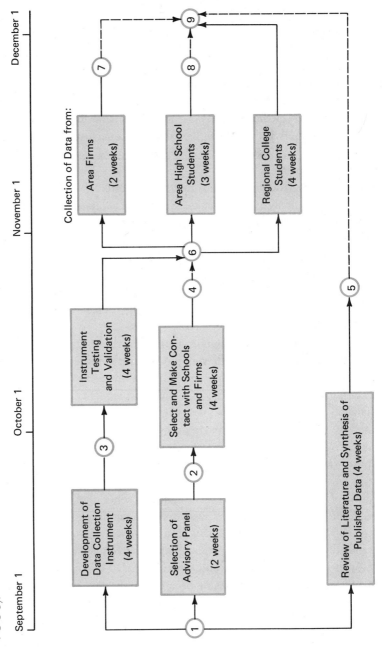

Figure 10-8

A bar (or Gantt) chart displaying the time schedule of various activities in systems development.

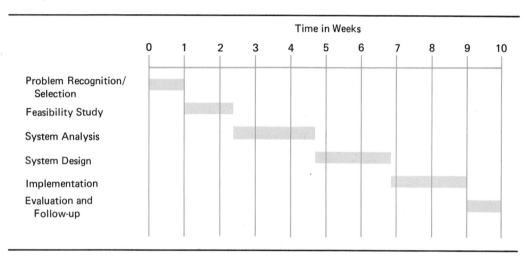

System constraints should be recognized and documented (written down) so that management and other concerned groups are made aware of them. By documenting constraints, expectations of management and other system users become more realistic, more in line with the actual final system product.

Cost/Benefit Analysis. Before a decision is reached to develop a system, an important management consideration is cost/benefit analysis. Systems should rarely, if ever, be developed unless their benefits to the organization are greater than the costs.

System costs. Two major types of costs to consider in evaluating the potential of a system to solve your information processing problem are development costs and operating costs. In general, costs incurred relate to personnel, hardware, software, and overhead or indirect costs.

The type of personnel included in *development costs* are not only the programmers and analysts but also managers and information system users who are involved with the various phases of the system cycle. Also included in development costs are the cost of hardware and software needed for the new system and an amount to cover indirect costs, such as office space, supplies, and administrative expense. Any expense incurred in preparing the site for new hardware should be included, as well as the expense of converting from the old system to the new one. Training and other activities to prepare the employees for the new system need to be mentioned; the better the employees are prepared for the new system, the greater the chances for successful operation. Included also are the costs of testing the various components of the new system.

Operating costs are the total cost of operating the system after it has been implemented — personnel, hardware, supplies, and overhead. Personnel costs cover data entry operators, maintenance analysts and programmers, computer operators, and anyone who participates in processing the data in the system. Hardware costs are rental charges, depreciation of equipment, amortization expenses, and maintenance.

Benefits. Benefits sell the system to management. In order to make a decision whether or not to proceed with a new system, management wants to know as specifically as possible what will be gained. Greater efficiency of operation? Better information? Lower operating costs? Costs savings are impressive to management; they talk. Savings can be achieved by reducing personnel expenses, decreasing inventory levels, or reducing total accounts receivable.

Benefits vary. For example, better control over inventory levels may result in fewer stock-outs and increased revenue from sales. An analysis of customer sales histories over the past five years might show that 12 percent of gross sales was lost because company products were not available when customers needed them. Another benefit from effective inventory control is that the company will have less capital invested in inventories. This would free needed capital for other investments. Automating an order entry process is another example of a chain-reaction type of benefit. Computerized order entry not only decreases the cost of filling each order but also speeds up the entire order-filling process. Faster order processing means happier customers, more orders, more sales, and increased profits. These types of benefits are referred to as *tangible benefits*, since a dollar value can be assigned to them.

Intangible benefits, on the other hand, are those for which dollar amounts are almost impossible to establish. What is the value of making timely information available to a manager? What is gained by giving the manager "better" information? Of course, "better" information does not guarantee that the manager will make better decisions, but the odds are improved.

Some organizations do not allow the use of intangible benefits in justifying new information systems. They believe that if a benefit cannot be measured it will never be realized. Others argue that intangible benefits should be identified, but assigned a smaller weight than tangible benefits.

Costs, savings projections, and other benefits are often calculated by using sampling techniques and other quantitative measurement tools, including computer models. Although computerized models are expensive to construct (sales forecasting models, for example), models used to estimate costs are relatively easy to develop.

Presentation to management. At the conclusion of the feasibility study, the project team provides management with sufficient information to make a decision regarding whether to go ahead with developing the information system. The presentation to management should be both oral and written. The feasibility study findings should be well documented and should consist of the following:

— A clear statement of the problem
— Objectives to be accomplished with the proposed system
— Specifications of the scope and size of the proposed system
— Constraints under which system development will take place
— Personnel considerations
— Evaluation of existing information systems
— Cost/benefit analysis of alternatives
— Time schedule of system development activities

Phase III: Detail System Analysis

If management gives the green light for continuing the system project, the next phase in the systems development cycle is to study the detailed requirements of the new system. To develop the requirements, an in-depth study of the present system and a determination of the information needs of users are made.

If the new system is a radical change from the existing one, the project team may decide not to study the existing system, but rather to concentrate only on determining information requirements for users in the new system. Some systems professionals do not recommend studying the old system because they believe such a study will bias the investigating analysts. A majority of analysts, recognizing that new systems evolve out of old systems, usually choose to study the old system in detail. By so doing, they become familiar with system operations and personnel, and often are able to avoid pitfalls inherent in the old system.

Data Collection. To analyze effectively the present system and user needs, much data must be collected. To collect the data, the project team interviews system users, reviews documents used in the present system, and observes the operational activities of the present system. To be successful in the data collection process, project team members must communicate effectively and establish a rapport with the information system users.

Communicating effectively and establishing a rapport are each related to the other much like the chicken and the egg. Without effective communications, it is difficult to develop a rapport with a user. Frequently systems professionals are criticized for being in an "ivory tower"—for talking about computers and information system concepts in technical jargon that management and other users do not understand, thus preventing effective communications from occurring.

A major concern of users is, "How will my job be affected by the new system? Will I be able to function well in the new system environment?" Establishing a rapport with users helps alleviate some of their fear of the unknown. Also, if the user is properly trained and involved throughout all phases of the systems development cycle, the level of fear will be reduced.

Analysis of the Present System. To learn what is being done in the present system, project team members should seek information on each aspect of the present system, including operating procedures and decision-making activities. Seeking answers to the following questions would be helpful in understanding the old system.

— What activities are performed in each part of the present system?
— Why is each activity performed?
— Who does the work in the activity?
— When is the activity performed?
— Can the activity be eliminated?
— Can it be combined with other activities?
— What is the volume and frequency of the activity?
— What exceptions to the normal activity exist?
— What input data are necessary to start the activity?
— What outputs are generated by the activity?

Determining User Requirements. In systems development, a task of considerable importance is determining information needs of system users. If the system project team does not satisfactorily carry out this task, it is futile to develop and implement the system.

A simple, formula-type statement to point out the nature of this task is, "Who wants what information, when, where, how, and why?"

— Who will be using the information   — Why?
— What should the information consist of?   — Why?
— When should the information be provided? — Why?
— Where does the information go?   — Why?
— How should the information be structured? — Why?

The "Why?" is added to each question to emphasize justification. Many activities in the present system may be unnecessary but continue to be done because "We have always done it this way."

The analyst should avoid accepting the following ambiguous statement from the user: "I want anything (or everything) you can give me." Equally ineffective is the user who says, "All I want is what I am getting now." Relying upon those two responses results in a shallow treatment of user requirements. Ineffective system design can result if the right questions are not asked. To illustrate, a colonel in an Air Force personnel section confided that:

> To do my job, I really only need about seven programs consisting of about twenty feet of paper reports. What I get is about twenty programs resulting in about 500 feet of paper. I don't need all that data. There is too much redundancy in it; I end up tossing most of it in the trash can.

Certainly, a project team had not determined adequately who needs what information, when, where, how, and why!

The purpose of information is to aid the user in making decisions; i.e., information should be action-oriented. A helpful checklist in studying a particular piece of information for its role in decision making consists of the following questions:

— Is the decision necessary? Can it be eliminated?
— If a decision can't be eliminated, can the information be structured so that decision making is simplified, with the system providing choices or alternatives?
— Can the decision process be structured into a set of rules, similar to the logic as expressed in a decision table, so that if certain conditions exist, the decision is automatic? Decisions made in that manner are referred to as *programmed decisions*. A programmed decision may also be a manual process. A scenario of a programmed decision is shown in Figure 10-9. Although the scenario is presented in conversation form,

Figure 10-9

Scenario of a programmed decision.

Scene opens; the time is 10:25 A.M.

Ticket Agent: Good morning. This is Efficiency Airlines. May I help you?

Customer: Yes. What flights do you have leaving Denver for Washington, D.C., around five o'clock today?

Agent: Just a moment, sir; let me check [*keying in a query at the CRT terminal connected directly to the main computer containing the passenger reservation database*].

Pause . . .

Sir, a flight leaves Denver at 4:45 and arrives in Washington at 8:55. On that flight there are only first-class seats available; will that be all right?

Customer: I would rather have coach. Do you have any coach seats on an earlier flight?

Agent: Let me check. One moment . . . Yes, there is a coach seat available on Flight 782, leaving Denver at 2:15 this afternoon. Shall I reserve that space for you?

Customer: Yes.

Agent: You will need to get to the airport one hour before departure time; will that be possible, sir?

Customer: Yes, I can make it.

Agent: May I have your name, please?

Customer: Jack Rachetmore.

Agent: Thank you. I have made a reservation for you, Mr. Rachetmore, for a coach seat on Flight 782, leaving Denver at 2:15 P.M., arriving in Washington at 6:30 P.M. Your ticket will be ready for you when you arrive at Efficiency's ticket counter approximately one hour before departure time. Have a nice trip, sir, and we hope that the next time you need to fly you will think of Efficiency Airlines.

the decision logic is programmable on a computer. In that case, a ticket buyer by interacting with a ticket-purchasing program can accomplish the same result as in dealing directly with a ticket agent.

Documentation of Present System. Data describing the present system and user requirements should be well documented. The most common form of documentation is the system flowchart: a graphic display of inputs, processing activities, and outputs. The flowchart includes both manual and computer operations. Flowcharting symbols as discussed in Chapter 6 are used to construct a system flowchart. Many systems analysts will use only the basic symbols shown in Figure 10-10. Other analysts prefer using only block diagrams to illustrate information systems, while some will go to the other extreme, using highly specialized symbols for diagramming.

Figure 10-10

Symbols used in a system flowchart.

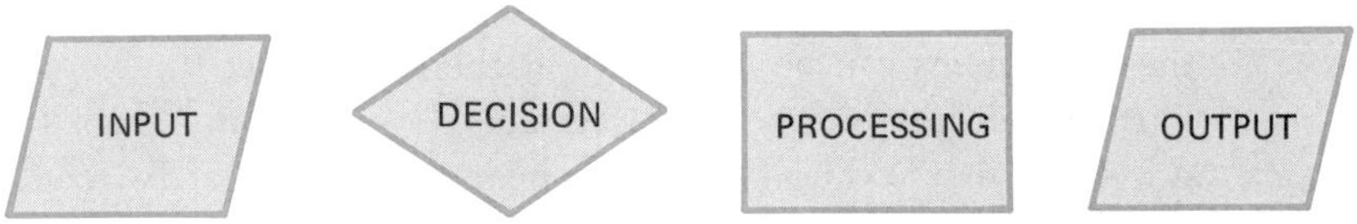

System Design Specifications. An effective analysis of the present information system reveals its deficiencies and its strengths. Combining that analysis with user requirements, the detailed investigation phase concludes with the development of system *design specifications*, which include output specifications, input specifications, and processing requirements. Outputs of the new system are reports, documents, CRT display screens, and so forth. *Output specifications* indicate the types of outputs needed, the frequency of the output, authorization to request and receive the outputs, the response time desired by users, and the types of computer programs necessary to generate the outputs.

Input specifications define how data come into existence, the source of the data, forms requirements, frequency of collection, and accuracy level desired. Who is responsible for collecting the data is an important consideration in the input function.

Processing specifications define how the data will be stored, processed, and accessed or retrieved.

Design specifications, or what the new system will look like, are presented to management and other users. These design "specs" are measured against the system objectives originally identified in Phase II. At this point, management again makes a decision to "go or no go" with further development.

The detail system analysis phase is perhaps the most neglected phase in the development cycle. It is a phase in which too many assumptions are made, too many gaps in communication and understanding exist, and in general, too little emphasis is placed upon proper data collection and analysis. These pitfalls exist for several reasons: Project members must ferret out user needs (frequently from users who are busy performing their regular duties); activities in this phase often appear to be nonproductive; and effective system analysis takes time.

SUMMARY

Information systems problems originate from many sources. Only a few of these problems can be dealt with at the same time; therefore, management must establish a priority list for systems development. Which systems will be developed first? Which systems can be put off for a time? Two considerations for developing a new information system are: Is the problem critical, and what is the potential for a high return on investment (ROI)?

The problem areas receiving the highest priorities will be given an in-depth investigation to see if sufficient justification can be made for their development. This "justification" study is called a feasibility or preliminary study. Among the outcomes of the feasibility study there are three significant ones: a clear statement of the problem, specification of system objectives, and a cost/benefit analysis.

If management believes that a particular system effort is justified, the detail system analysis phase of the systems development cycle is undertaken. The major outcome of this phase is a clear understanding and description of how the new system will operate.

In this chapter, you have been introduced to the first three phases of the systems development cycle: problem recognition, feasibility study, and detail system analysis. In the next chapter the system design phase will be discussed.

TERMS

Information system	Constraints
Input	Network chart
Processing	Event
Output	Critical path
Objective	PERT chart
Feedback loop	Bar chart
IPO	Gantt chart
Systems development cycle	Development costs
User involvement	Operating costs
System priorities	Tangible benefits
Feasibility study	Intangible benefits
Problem statement	Programmed decisions
System objectives	Design specifications
Tangible costs	Output specifications
Intangible costs	Input specifications
Scope	Processing specifications

QUESTIONS

1. Is information systems development a recent phenomenon?
2. What are the components of an information system?
3. What phases constitute the systems development cycle?
4. What is the purpose of the feasibility study?
5. Distinguish between tangible benefits and intangible benefits; between tangible costs and intangible costs.
6. What is a system boundary? Why should it be determined in the system study?
7. How may a particular system development effort be justified?
8. Indicate some of the common sources for new information system requests.
9. (a) What are some constraints that may have to be dealt with in developing systems?
   (b) Why should constraints be identified early in the systems development cycle?
10. What is the purpose of feedback in an information system?
11. How does user participation differ during the development phases?

12. Indicate some possible sources of recommendations for systems development studies.
13. Why should a problem statement be written, rather than only oral?
14. Why do some organizations prefer NOT to justify developing a new system based upon intangible benefits?
15. What steps are used to develop an estimate of the time required to complete a project?
16. Why are network charts useful for managing large projects?
17. What are two factors that should be present when determining user requirements?
18. What is gained from analyzing the present system or systems before designing the new system?
19. What are the contents of a feasibility study?
20. After which step(s) in the systems development cycle should management review progress and approve/disapprove further development?
21. In information systems planning, how many years are normally thought to comprise long-range plans? short-range plans?

ARTICLE

Software: Packaged vs Inhouse

When contemplating the purchase of new computer equipment or upgrading of a current computer system, many decisions are necessary. One often involves software. As many of us are already aware, the cost of software is ever increasing and many times is more expensive than the computer system it is intended for.

The first step that must be taken before any software is written or acquired is to fully define what is needed. This may seem very obvious, but surprisingly enough many users have only a vague idea of what is really needed and often find themselves very discontented and having a sour taste in their mouth when software doesn't meet their "specifications."

Many come to the conclusion that a software system is needed NOW and don't take the time to fully specify in writing what they need. Many feel that a general idea is adequate. But without understanding fully what's required, how could anyone explain to a consultant what is needed, adequately qualify existing software packages, or even begin to develop a system inhouse?

... Even after fully defining business needs, it should not always be assumed that an off-the-shelf software package is going to satisfy those needs. Almost every company, even if involved in the same type of business, seems to have their own wrinkles in the way of doing things. No software package can encompass all of the peculiarities of a particular business.... Therefore, modifications may have to be made to an off-the-shelf packaged system. This is not uncommon, but does point out one of the reasons why a business must fully understand their needs....

... There can be advantages for developing a system inhouse. One is that a system can be fully customized and developed to meet the specific needs of a particular user.... One user also commented that an advantage of developing inhouse was that his company could take a longer implementation period.

... Usually the first thing that is forgotten [in inhouse system development] is to write a system specification.... [M]uch time can be wasted writing a particular piece of software only to find that it just doesn't quite meet the needs it was intended for and therefore has to be continually modified....

Reprinted by permission from DATA BASE MONTHLY, October, 1981.

DISCUSSION QUESTIONS

1. As indicated in the article on the preceding page, which system phase is too often neglected?

2. Why is successful completion of that phase critical to effective systems development?

APPLICATION

On-Line CPU Reduces Registration Chaos

LARGO, Md. — One of the traditional hassles of college life is registration. But officials at a community college here think they have found the way to reduce its chaos.

Using an on-line mainframe, Prince George Community College has eliminated the computer card registration system that involved long lines and a two- to three-hour registration process. The system, an IBM 370/138, is being used to provide other school services as well.

"After enduring the rigors of traditionally hectic registration periods for many years, the college finally decided there must be a way to make the process more palatable to both students and administrators," recalled . . . [the] director of records and registration for the 19,600-student institution.

"The old method became chaotic when we tried to keep things moving during peak periods. Long lines were hard to handle. Because of the frantic pace at which our people had to work, we found when it was all over that our records were often incomplete and inaccurate," he said.

To solve the problem, the office teamed up with the school's computer science department to develop an on-line registration system, which centers around a

student's financial records. The software allows the registration office to update all accounting and billing programs automatically. Students' bills are printed immediately after registration.

"We can handle 400 registrations a day comfortably. Classes run for different numbers of weeks and sign-ups are thus staggered. And by urging students to make appointments for registration, we further reduce the flow at our counters," . . . [the records director] said.

. . . "Our old [manual] system was terrible. The registration process was usually a disaster. Sometimes it took five or six weeks to determine exactly how many people had registered during a certain period — by that time, the number of students actually attending classes could have changed. Now, such information is available instantly," . . . [the director of computer science] said.

The modernization of the registration effort was part of a long-range effort to use computer equipment as a means of offering better services to the community, according to . . . [the president of the college].

. . . [The] dean of business affairs said the registration effort was worth it. "Because of our size, we must always look

continued

for ways to handle growth efficiently, to streamline our operations and to provide quality education. However, we must do it on a cost-effective basis. The computer provides a means for cutting and avoiding costs and gives us a wider variety of services. It helps us keep the students we have and attract more," he said.

DISCUSSION QUESTIONS

1. Why did Prince George Community College implement a new registration system?
2. Does the registration system at Prince George appear to have some unique characteristics?
3. Name the various systems (subsystems) that were affected by installation of the IBM computer.

11 INFORMATION SYSTEMS DESIGN

CHAPTER OBJECTIVES

In this chapter you will learn:

1. What constitutes the system design phase of the system development cycle:
   - Output design
   - Input design
   - Processing design.
2. The major types of reporting methods used in information systems.
3. The use of menus in report generation.
4. What a turnaround document is.
5. What the two major file processing methods are.
6. The use of coding and classification schemes in processing data.
7. The purpose of sorting data for further processing.
8. The methods used to improve the accuracy of data in an information system.
9. The purpose of a hardware study and the use of benchmark tests.
10. The development of programming specifications.

In Chapter 10, you studied the first three phases of the systems development cycle:

Phase I	Problem Recognition
Phase II	Feasibility Study (Preliminary Study)
Phase III	Detail System Analysis

In this chapter, Phase IV, the System Design phase, is discussed.

SYSTEM DESIGN

In reviewing the various phases of the systems development cycle, one soon realizes that of all of the phases in systems development the one that is the most fascinating to systems personnel, particularly analysts, is the *design phase*.

Designing the system is a creative process. It is similar to the activity of the artist who, before developing a painting, conducts a preliminary study by making rough sketches or outlines and by analyzing the overall composition of the painting, then begins putting the ideas on canvas. Some artists may produce a poorly designed piece of art because they did not do the necessary preliminary work. The same is true of systems personnel, who may end up with a poorly designed system if user needs and processing requirements are not properly analyzed. In the centralized manufacturing information system (CMIS) shown in Figure 11-1, can you identify some of the users and what their information needs might be?

If user needs and system analysis are so important to effective design, why does the analysis phase sometimes receive inadequate attention? The reason is that some analysts are so eager to get into design activities — so anxious to "get on with it" — that they enter the design phase prematurely. Proposing a detailed system design to management before users' needs have been carefully determined is like prescribing medication and treatment before the patient's ailment has been diagnosed. Physicians who appear to be negligent in diagnosing patient symptoms sometimes are sued for malpractice. How many analysts do you suppose have been sued for malpractice? A few have, but not many. In those cases, generally the courts held that the system designers were negligent, and thus were accountable for any financial losses resulting from their negligence.

You will recall from Chapter 10 that a major outcome of the system analysis phase is *design specifications*. Until specifications are agreed upon by users, by management, and by systems personnel, no design activities should begin.

Figure 11-1

Components of a centralized manufacturing information system.

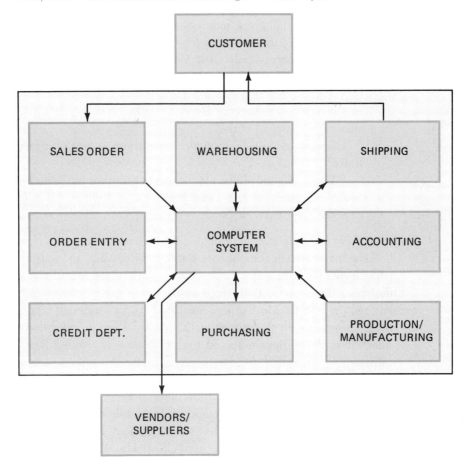

In the following story, the project team leader evidently did not work closely enough with system users or management in determining what the system should do.

Sarah Johnson, President of the SarJoh Corporation, eagerly anticipated the demonstration that was about to begin. Two years in development, at a cost of one and a half million dollars, a computer information system that was the ultimate in state-of-the-art technology, was ready to be unveiled—ready to be put "on-line."

Newton, the project team leader, beamed like a proud father. Turning to the corporation president he asked, "What would you like to know about the company?"

Johnson thought a moment and replied, "How about a sales history of our Houston office for the last two months?"

Newton turned pale. "Uh, well, you see . . . that is . . . this system can't do that. We can give you corporate sales for the last two months."

Johnson interrupted. "How about the inventory levels at our zinc warehouse in Peoria?"

Newton nervously replied, "Would you settle for copper in Butte?"

"Look, Newton, I don't know what's going on, but I think you'd better tell me what this beautiful-looking system — that your job depends on — CAN do."

Where does one start in designing the system?

The three system components — input, processing, and output — provide a framework for system design. It might seem that the logical starting place is designing the input section, since no data item can be processed until it has entered the system. Most experienced analysts do not design input first, however; they start with the output section. Why? Keep in mind that the user of information is the person served by the system; or, stating it another way, satisfying user needs is the dominant reason for the system to exist. Outputs represent the part of the system that the user sees; to the user, the outputs ARE the system. Furthermore, the outputs determine the type of data to be entered into the system and the form, method, and schedule for entering the data. Also, the system outputs determine the processing steps necessary to transform the data into information that can be used effectively. Would you agree then that, because output requirements affect both input and processing, output design should be tackled first?

OUTPUT DESIGN

As stated in the previous paragraphs, outputs from the information system are what decision makers see and use in managing the organization. The primary objective of any information system should be to provide the user with meaning-ful, useful information in an attractive and easily assimilated form. The most common method of presenting this "useful" information is through *reports* generated by the system. Other types of system outputs are outputs that become inputs for other information systems or inputs into the same system at a later date, and outputs that are necessary for documentation purposes or for backup.

Reports

Reports designed for users are of several types:

Periodic or scheduled reports (daily, weekly, monthly, etc.)

Exception reports (if a certain condition arises, it should be reported)

Demand reports (on occasion, the user sees a need for a report and thus requests it from the system)

Individual queries (the user requests a particular item of information from the system)

Ad hoc reports (a situation arises that can't be predicted; thus a special report to be used for perhaps only one occasion is generated)

Periodic reports are the most common type of output used in information systems today; however, other types will undoubtedly soon become more com-mon as interactive terminals and computer graphics increase in usage.

Two major considerations in providing scheduled information to users are the form and frequency of the report. Information should reach management at the right time—not too early; not too late. If it is too early, the information may become stale or out of date before it can be used. If it gets there too late, the decision maker has been deprived of its use, and the expense of producing the information has been wasted. The form or format of the report should be of a type that can be used efficiently and effectively.

The computer program designed to produce reports is commonly referred to as *report generator program*. Periodic reports relate to business transactions and production activities. An example of a production report provided to one corporation's production manager each morning is shown in Figure 11-2. Note that the amount produced by each operator is readily visible. Assuming that all of these tasks are identical, the supervisor can quickly see who was the most productive operator on that day. Other items could be added to the report that would make it even more useful, such as a column showing the deviation from

Figure 11-2

Example of a daily production report.

							THE DMC CORPORATION						
DATE: 06/06/83			TASK PRODUCTION REPORT			
DEPT: BOROMATICS						
PART DESCRIPTION: BLOCKS-60D MULTI-BORE						
OPERATOR NUMBER	TASKS COMPLETED	PLANNED SET-UP COST	ACTUAL SET-UP COST	PLANNED COMPLETION COSTS	ACTUAL COMPLETION COST	TOTAL TASK COST	AVERAGE TASK COST
10	7	17.50	20.00	110.00	100.00	120.00	17.14
14	6	26.00	24.00	90.00	98.00	122.00	20.33
56	8	12.00	15.50	130.00	110.00	125.50	15.69
82	8	12.00	20.00	130.00	132.00	152.00	19.00
93	4	42.00	51.00	84.00	80.00	131.00	32.75
96	4	42.00	47.00	84.00	76.00	123.00	30.75
TOTALS	37	151.50	177.50	628.00	596.00	773.50	29.90

total planned cost (over or under). Effective management is dependent upon good reporting systems.

Exception reports are an alternative method of reporting to management or other information users. The basic idea of exception reporting is that as long as a system or a process is operating within an acceptable range, no report is generated. However, as soon as the system ceases to perform within the range limits, the out-of-range condition is reported to the user. A "red alert" sounds.

You have had experience with systems based upon the exception reporting principle. For example, most automobiles utilize exception reporting systems. The red light indicators on the car dash are designed to tell the driver about certain operating conditions that may arise: A light glows red if the alternator is not charging; another light will come on if the temperature goes above a certain level. The red light reports an exception condition. Likewise, in a manufacturing production process, a report may be designed to point out to a department manager or a shift supervisor particular workstations that have not produced the desired quota of goods or that have run too much scrap (rejected or unusable products) for that day. Exception reports are frequently an important part of a quality control program.

Inventory levels also may be controlled effectively through exception reports. When an individual item reaches a certain level on hand, several activities occur to trigger action in other departments. Not only is the inventory level reported to management, but a purchase order is issued to a vendor for the reorder quantity. The purchasing department is notified of reorder action; likewise the production scheduling department is notified about the reorder and the expected delivery data of the item(s), and in some systems may even receive a projection of sales demand.

While exception reports generally work well and are useful, some managers do not feel comfortable relying upon them. They may not trust the system; also, they may wish to monitor trends as they are developing. A manager who wishes to note trends has the same motivation as the car owner who wants to be able to see the temperature as it begins to rise.

Which reporting method is better: Periodic reports or exception reports?

Referring again to the automobile example, having gauges in front of you at all times may actually work against your keeping alert as to what is going on within your car. You become too accustomed to the gauge readings; consequently, you do not look at the gauges often. A condition calling for you to act may have been developing for some time, and by the time you notice it the damage may have been done. However, if a red light (exception report) on the dash panel comes on, you are likely to react immediately.

The same analogy is true for a manager. For example, a budget control officer who receives periodic reports may not notice among all of the various departments' budgets that a particular department has exceeded its budgeted amount for promotional activities. When the control officer becomes aware of the budget status, the involved department may already be committed to another advertising campaign.

Whether periodic reports or exception reports are better depends upon several things, such as management's preference, the specific information to be reported, and the type of information system. Many managers prefer a combination of the two types of reporting methods, using exception reporting principles in a scheduled report. When combining the two methods within one report, conditions that are out of range (the exceptions) are presented in the report with special attention called to them, either through *flags* (special printed characters that signal to the reader of the report that the flagged item is different from the other items in the report) or by placement of the exception items in a special section of the report. An accounts receivable report may contain flags calling attention to those accounts over 60 days past due. Likewise, in an inventory control system, the stock status report may contain flags pointing out those items having stock levels below or above a prescribed quantity.

An example of a report that combines the exception reporting principle with the regularly scheduled report is given in Figure 11-3. Rather than using flags to report the exceptions, the report is divided into two parts. Part I reports the hours that have been scheduled for each employee on the project; Part II reports the exceptions—those individuals scheduled for more or fewer than 40 hours.

Demand reports are so named because they provide information to management upon demand. Conditions within the organization arise from time to time when management needs specific information; however, when or how often the need will arise is not predictable. Demand reports are designed for those specific situations.

The format or layout of the demand report is designed at the time the system is developed. Likewise, the program necessary to generate the report is written prior to system implementation; however, no specific schedule is constructed for producing the report.

A sales forecasting system frequently uses information derived from demand reports. Data used in making the forecast are contained in existing files. In fact, some of the same data were probably used previously to generate periodic reports. To receive the desired reports, management simply requests, either through a terminal or a staff person, the desired outputs. Upon receipt of the information, the forecast is made.

Demand reports are generated through what is called *interactive output*. The computer and the user "talk" to each other through a remote terminal, one having either a CRT display unit or a hard-copy printer. Two types of interactive output are *query-response* (also, question-answer) and *menu-display*.

In using the query-response method, the user enters a request on the terminal (in "computerese" the request is referred to as a *query*). An example of a user's query for information from a personnel file on a particular employee might look like the following:

```
PRINT EMP-NAME, ADDRESS, CITY, STATE,
AND ZIP-CODE WHERE EMP-NAME EQ WILLIAM LODELL
```

This query asks the computer to print William Lodell's name and home address. To respond to this request, the computer searches the personnel database for William Lodell's record and upon finding it prints

```
WILLIAM LODELL   4856 JUNIPER DRIVE   FINDLAY OHIO   45238
```

Figure 11-3

Example of a scheduled report using the exception reporting principle (Part II).

```
CENTRALIZED MANUFACTURING INFORMATION SYSTEM

                      ******************************************
                      DEPARTMENT RESOURCE ALLOCATION
                                 PART I
                        SCHEDULED TIME — PERIOD ONE
                      ******************************************

DEPARTMENT CMIS RUN FEB 24, 83-1
```

	STARTING / ENDING DATES FEB 21-83/APR 1-83	83 FEB 25	83 MAR 4	83 MAR 11	83 MAR 18	83 APR 25	83 APR 1	PERIOD TOTAL
RESOURCE								
DARLA PAYNE	MAR 1-83/APR 1-83		40	40	40	32	44	196
FRED SORREL	FEB 23-83/APR 1-83	32	40	40	40	0	40	192
DWAYNE BULLOCK	FEB 23-83/APR 1-83	40	40	40	40	40	40	240
TOTAL BY PERIOD	FEB 23-83/APR 1-83	72	120	120	120	72	124	628

```
                      ******************************************
                      DEPARTMENT RESOURCE ALLOCATION
                                 PART II
                        OVERTIME — FLOAT TIME
                      ******************************************

CENTRALIZED MANUFACTURING INFORMATION SYSTEM
          OVERTIME (+)
          FLOAT TIME (−)
```

		83 FEB 25	83 MAR 4	83 MAR 11	83 MAR 18	83 APR 25	83 APR 1	PERIOD TOTAL
RESOURCE								
DARLA PAYNE	MAR 1-83/APR 1-83					− 8	+ 4	− 4
FRED SORREL	FEB 23-83/APR 1-83	− 8				−40		−48
TOTAL BY PERIOD	FEB 21-83/APR 1-83	− 8				−48	+ 4	−52

The one line of output from the query does not appear to be a very useful form of output; however, that would depend upon the use that is to be made of the address. Other designs of output can be provided through special procedures. If the user desires an output in the form of an address label, a procedure could be written that would print the label as

WILLIAM LODELL
4856 JUNIPER DRIVE
FINDLAY, OHIO 45238

Before the computer can respond to a query, it will usually ask the user for specific information, such as the name of the information system desired and the name of the file or subsystem containing the desired information. In the *question-answer* form of interaction between the computer and user, the computer presents questions and the user provides answers. In query-response systems, the user constructs the query and the computer responds.

One comment should be made about the format of reports generated through the interactive process. Interactive terminals are usually set up for an 80-column print line. If, however, the report that you desire has been designed for a 132-character line, you may end up with a print line that wraps around two lines. This can create an output that is difficult to read, as Figure 11-4 illustrates.

```
WRAPAROUND PRINTI
NG  CAN  BE  DIFFICU
LT TO READ
```

Figure 11-4

In the example in the previous paragraphs the user, by responding to the computer's questions, provided the computer with the name of the information system and the file name(s). However, in some cases the user will not know the name of the system or the specific files that contain the desired information. To solve the user's problem a special aid, a "menu," is offered. The *menu* approach is a user friendly technique whereby the user is led by the computer through a series of steps until the proper information has been obtained. The menu approach in information systems is similar to that in a restaurant. Let's say you've looked at the menu and decided to have steak Diane, a baked potato, and a tossed salad. Now the waiter or waitress will have to ask you to refine your choices further: How do you want your steak done? Do you want sour cream or butter or both or neither on your potato? What kind of dressing do you want on your salad? In specifying these choices you have now gone through two levels in a hierarchy. Moving through the menu selection process continues until you have completed your order.

A similar menu hierarchy and selection process is used in helping the interactive computer user thread through an information system until the proper level has been reached to retrieve the specific information desired. An interactive menu system for processing customer orders follows. After logging onto the system, the user is presented with the following instruction:

```
KEY-IN THE LETTER (A, B, OR C) OF THE
TYPE OF TRANSACTION YOU WILL BE ENTERING___
   A) ARE YOU PLACING A NEW ORDER?
   B) DO YOU WANT INFORMATION ON AN ORDER
      NOW IN PROCESS?
   C) DO YOU WANT INFORMATION ABOUT
      INVENTORY ITEMS?
```

If you respond with "B," the next frame presented on your CRT display screen or printer will be:

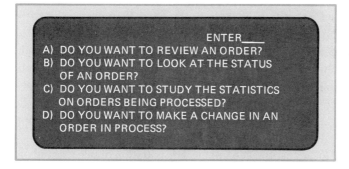

```
                              ENTER___
   A) DO YOU WANT TO REVIEW AN ORDER?
   B) DO YOU WANT TO LOOK AT THE STATUS
      OF AN ORDER?
   C) DO YOU WANT TO STUDY THE STATISTICS
      ON ORDERS BEING PROCESSED?
   D) DO YOU WANT TO MAKE A CHANGE IN AN
      ORDER IN PROCESS?
```

If you respond with "C," the next frame is:

ENTER_____
A) DO YOU WANT TO KNOW THE PRODUCTIVITY
OF ORDER ENTRY OPERATORS?
B) DO YOU WANT TO KNOW WHAT PRINTERS ARE
CURRENTLY IN USE THROUGHOUT THE SYSTEM?
C) DO YOU WANT INFORMATION ON PURCHASERS?

The menu selection process continues until the user has the desired information. Menus are designed for individuals not familiar with the system, those who must be led step by step through the information request process until they reach the level of information they want.

An interactive system is effective when it is easy for the user to specify what is desired from the system. If a user has to spend several minutes or more trying to formulate a query for information, that user will not access the system very often, perhaps never again. The user becomes a system "dropout."

Ad hoc reports get their name from the Latin phrase *ad hoc*, meaning "for this case alone; special." Within all organizations, from time to time a special reporting need arises which neither management, other users, nor the system staff anticipated when the system was developed. The information system should be designed to accommodate these special needs. Satisfying the ad hoc need should not call for a major system change, even though a computer program probably will have to be written to extract the data from existing files and process them into an acceptable format.

The ad hoc report differs from the query response in the size of the report and in the need for massaging or processing data for output. In a query response, generally the only processing done is to sort the data in some sequence before they are printed or displayed on a CRT screen. For example, an alphabetic listing may be desired for postal mailing labels or a student class roll. In ad hoc reporting, a program is written to do the desired processing before the report is generated. For example, locating a new plant may call for information on present production levels and capacities of the company's various manufacturing locations, the geographical distribution of sales for the past two years, and the location of suppliers or vendors. To retrieve and summarize that type of desired information, a special program would have to be written in most cases.

Turnaround Documents

Computer outputs in a printed form may later become inputs into the same system. These are referred to as *turnaround documents*. An example of a turnaround document is your monthly utility statement — your electric or telephone bill. Credit card billing systems also use turnaround documents.

At the end of the billing period, the company mails you a bill. Within the specified period of time, you enter the amount of your payment on a portion of the statement and return it to the company with your check or money order. An optical key operator prints the date and amount of the payment right on the statement, and then the statement is fed into an optical reader for input into the billing system. The date and amount are the only new data that need to be added. If a turnaround document were not used, the other data pertaining to your account (account number, name, address, etc.) would have to be rekeyed into the system every time you paid a bill, significantly increasing the amount of data entry necessary and increasing the possibility of error.

During the '50s and '60s the punched card was a common form of turnaround document. Today, OCR documents are highly preferred to punched cards. They are easier to handle, and documents can be entered even if damaged (damaged punched cards must be replaced).

INPUT DESIGN

In most business information systems, data enter the system as a result of one or more transactions. A *transaction* is any event that causes data to come into existence. Documents or forms used to record transaction data are called *source documents*. Examples of source documents are checks, bank deposit slips, sales receipts, order forms, and so forth. Designing source documents and data input forms is referred to as *forms design*. Today, forms design is considered to be approaching a scientific discipline; it is a technology around which an industry has developed, with companies that specialize in the design and manufacture of business forms.

Not all "forms" are printed forms. A common practice today is to display a data entry form on a CRT screen. A sample form is shown in Figure 11-5. Although the sample form has room to enter only one item, several items can be entered from the same source document. After the one item is entered, you would enter an "A" code at the bottom of the screen. A new screen would then be displayed with the header data being entered automatically. (Header data are all items before "Item No.") Therefore, on subsequent items the only data you would enter would be the individual data item.

You are assisted through the data entry process by a *cursor*, a location indicator. It is a small lighted signal on the screen that indicates the point where a character will be accepted. In many data entry programs, as soon as one data item has been entered, the cursor is programmed to move automatically to the

Figure 11-5

Data entry form for display on a CRT screen.

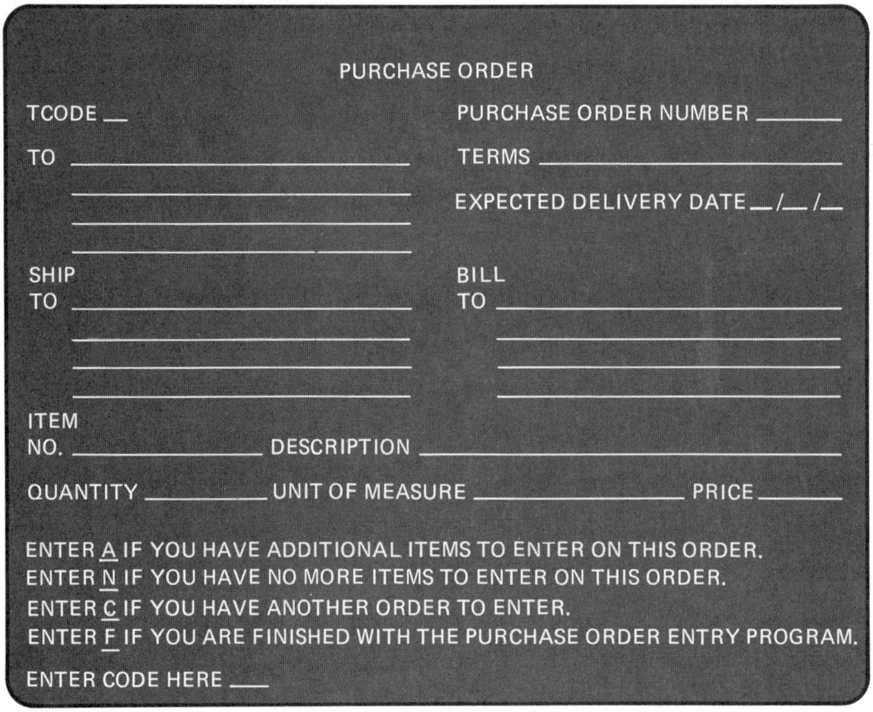

```
                        PURCHASE ORDER

  TCODE __                      PURCHASE ORDER NUMBER _____

  TO  _____     TERMS _____
      _____     EXPECTED DELIVERY DATE __/__/__
      _____
      _____

  SHIP                          BILL
  TO  _____     TO  _____
      _____         _____
      _____         _____
      _____         _____

  ITEM
  NO. _____ DESCRIPTION _____

  QUANTITY _____ UNIT OF MEASURE _____ PRICE_____

  ENTER A IF YOU HAVE ADDITIONAL ITEMS TO ENTER ON THIS ORDER.
  ENTER N IF YOU HAVE NO MORE ITEMS TO ENTER ON THIS ORDER.
  ENTER C IF YOU HAVE ANOTHER ORDER TO ENTER.
  ENTER F IF YOU ARE FINISHED WITH THE PURCHASE ORDER ENTRY PROGRAM.

  ENTER CODE HERE ___
```

next data field so that the next item can be entered. This increases the efficiency of data entry.

Another input design decision concerns the method(s) of input. Numerous choices of data entry into computer systems are available today. The main types are terminal data entry, diskette (floppy disk), punched cards, and optical or magnetic character forms.

Major considerations in designing data entry are the following:

— cost of data entry hardware and software.
— cost of data entry operations. (After the system is in operation what will be the cost of getting data into the system?)
— speed of data entry. (Normally, increasing the speed of input increases the cost.)
— delay acceptable to system users. (Delay is defined as the amount of time that elapses between the origination of data and the entry of data into the system. Batch input has a longer delay but is generally less expensive than real-time input, where the item is entered into the system as soon as it comes into existence.)
— accuracy level desired. (Increased levels of accuracy also mean higher costs.)

Two activities in data entry that the system designer includes in the system to reduce errors and thus increase the accuracy level are *verifying* data items before they are entered into the system and *editing* data items immediately as they enter the system.

Verifying data consists of the following process: After data have been changed from the source document form (a sales slip or an order form) into machine-processible form (a floppy disk, punched card, etc.), the steps that were followed to change the data in the source document to machine-readable form are repeated. For example, after data are taken from an order form and keyed onto a diskette, the diskette is then inserted into another keying device (a verifying machine) that looks very much like the key-to-disk machine used to write the data originally on the floppy disk. The verifying machine reads the data on the disk and, after the operator has keyed in the same data from the source document, the machine compares the keyed-in data with the data on the disk. If the data from the two different sources do not match, the machine indicates an error. The operator then determines if the error is in the data on the diskette or in the data just keyed in. Verifying data increases the level of accuracy; however, it doubles the cost of data entry.

Editing data consists of using a computer program to check data items as they enter the system. Examples of such programming tests include validity checks, completeness tests, and limits tests. With a *validity check*, the program tests the data item to determine if it is an acceptable (valid) value. Although values may be written into the data entry program itself, usually the test is made against acceptable values stored in a table. For example, a parts number is compared with part numbers in a table to see if the number being entered matches a number in the table. Though a proper match does not guarantee that the data entered is 100 percent accurate, it greatly increases the probability that the part number is correct.

In a *completeness test*, the edit program checks whether or not all required data items have been entered. To illustrate, any transaction concerning your school registration or class enrollment requires that your student number be one of the data items entered. If the number is not entered, either the record being entered would be rejected completely or else you would receive a message requesting that the number be entered.

In a *limits test*, the program runs a test to determine if the value of a data item falls within a prescribed range; that is, not less than or greater than a certain amount. The U.S. Forest Service, for example, has nine forest regions in the United States, numbering from Region 1 to Region 10 with no Region 7. A limits test would check whether or not the region number entered is less than 1 or greater than 10. If the data item falls outside the range, the edit program would send an error message to the person entering the data.

Other ways of controlling the accuracy of data input are the use of batch totals and hash totals. Financial institutions (banks, savings and loan organizations, etc.) use batch totals in processing checks, withdrawals, deposits, and other transactions. Taking a *batch total* consists of totaling values in a given field for all the transaction documents in a particular batch or group of documents; for example, the total dollar amount of checks processed in one group or batch. A batch total is an actual, accurate total. A *hash total*, on the other hand, serves only one purpose, and that is to act as a process control figure. It may be the sum of a data field, with the sum itself having no value except as a check on completeness—for example, totaling social security numbers or part numbers to make sure that no record has been omitted. Another form of hash total is to sum fields; however, in the summing process no value is carried from one column to the next as it would be in an actual addition. For instance, 9023 (not 20,233) is the hash total for these four numbers:

	2378	2	3	7	8
	4445	4	4	4	5
	6190	6	1	9	0
	7220	7	2	2	0
Hash Total	9023	19	10	22	13
		(9)	(0)	(2)	(3)

Hash and batch totals are used to make comparisons between totals at the beginning of the process and those at the end. If the hash total at the end of the processing cycle equaled 2803 when it should have been 9023, that indicates that one or more records were not processed.

PROCESS DESIGN

After the output and input sections have been effectively developed, the processing steps necessary to change the inputs into useful outputs are designed. The activities in process design are file design and procedures design.

File Design

Files are necessary for temporary and long-term storage of data in an information system. As discussed in Chapter 9, each *file* in the system should consist of related, individual data records. To illustrate, a personnel file will contain various data records pertaining to each employee. The person, place, or thing about which you are storing data in each record is referred to as the *entity*. Each *record* in a file is made up of data fields or items. A data item may be very short with no more than one character or it may be several hundred characters in length.

Elements that affect file design include record design (the number of characters in each record), file design (the number of records in each file), storage medium (the type of storage device that will be used), and file access method (direct, sequential, or other).

Some of the questions that need to be addressed in determining record design are:

What data items are contained in each record?

How is each item constructed as to size or length, and character mode (alphanumeric, or numeric)?

What is the position and role of each data item in the record? Should some of the items be subdivided—such as date, person's name, a part number, etc.?

Will one record design be sufficient or should there be several?

A data record is shown in Figure 11-6. The size of a data record depends upon the number of data items in the record and the number of characters in each data item.

Figure 11-6

Example of record design.

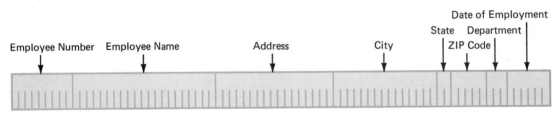

An estimate of file size is necessary in order to determine the storage capacity that is needed in the new system. One should consider also what the storage requirements will be six months or a year from now. File storage requirements should be carefully developed, for many information systems have been designed that simply overwhelmed the computer's storage capacity; it could not handle the load.

File Access Method. Several methods of *file access* are used in processing data, depending upon the needs of the user, the hardware and software available, and the skills of the system designers. Access methods were discussed in Chapter 9. The two most common methods of file access are sequential access and direct access. In *sequential access*, records are stored in an order based upon some sequencing determination, such as alphabetic or numeric order. *Direct access* file processing requires a direct access device such as a magnetic disk unit, where retrieval time can be in milliseconds as compared to several seconds or even minutes in a sequential file utilizing a tape unit. If magnetic tape devices are used, the sequential access method is required.

The type of file access used in an information system depends upon several factors:

— When do users need the information, how is that need expressed, and how is it to be fulfilled? Can batch processing be used to satisfy that need or is real-time processing necessary?

— What is the desired response time? If the request is made at any time during the day, is providing the information by early the following morning sufficient? Can the information be provided on a periodic basis?

— How much data will the system be called upon to store and process? What is the expected volume for one processing cycle?

— What is the frequency of file usage — of file access — not only to satisfy individual user queries or for report generation, but also for updating the file?

— Is technology available to handle the desired file design? Does the company have the necessary financial and personnel resources to implement an interactive, real-time system?

In determining file access, there may be a need to use several methods within the same information system. Perhaps 95 percent of today's computerized information systems that use the direct access method also use sequential processing for some portion of the processing activities in the same information system. Consider, for example, savings and checking account systems in a bank.

You enter the bank wishing to withdraw money from your savings account. You present your withdrawal slip to the teller. The teller, through an interactive terminal, queries your account (stored in a computer-based file) to see if you have sufficient savings deposited to cover the withdrawal. The information displayed on the CRT screen indicates to the teller that you have sufficient funds. The teller keys in the amount of the withdrawal and immediately the system updates your savings account to reflect the withdrawal. The updating process is done interactively in real time. Contrast that process with the typical handling of your checking account.

If you approach the teller with a check made out to withdraw cash from your checking account, the teller will follow through with the same preliminary process and same result as illustrated for your savings withdrawal. The checking account record is accessed, the check deducted from your account, and you are on your way. However, checks come into the bank in batches, either from the Federal Reserve banking system or from a corresponding bank. If you have made a payment this month on your oil company credit card and the check has reached your bank for clearing today, your check along with those received from other banks are all processed together. After the checks have been read by a magnetic or optical reader and sorted into a sequential order by account number, the updating of each account occurs. Thus, part of the processing to keep your account up to date is done interactively and part is done in a batch mode. The bank teller in Figure 11-7 is using a terminal to access interactively the drive-in customer's account.

Figure 11-7

Interactive processing of a customer's account.

Procedures Design

The procedures necessary to change data in the system into useful output (information) involve the activities of classifying, sorting, calculating, and summarizing.

Classifying data is usually the first step in organizing data for processing. It involves putting together like things according to certain characteristics. For example, inventory items may be classed by whether they are manufactured within the plant or are purchased. They may be classed according to whether they belong to finished goods, work in process, or raw materials. People also fall into many different classes — male or female, age group, or places of residence.

Classification schemes improve the efficiency of processing and enhance the use of the information. For example, assume that in our student information system we have a need to know which juniors are majoring in accounting. If the students are not classified by year, every student's total number of hours completed will have to be retrieved and then a determination made of whether that student qualifies as a junior or fits into one of the other groups. That would involve looking at the record of every student now enrolled in school. However, if in our student record we have allowed for the field "Student Classification," we would then have to retrieve from the file only those students with a junior classification. Furthermore, assuming we are not interested in all juniors, just juniors who are accounting majors, by using a classification scheme for majors we are in a position to retrieve only junior accounting majors.

Another device related to classification schemes that is used to increase processing efficiency is codes. *Codes* are shorthand expressions of different classes of data that exist within the information system. A coding scheme is simply a set of rules used to convert data from one set of symbols (for example, the name of the department in which you are majoring) to another set of symbols (letters, special characters, or digits).

The number of characters necessary to store the label "junior" is six. By using a code, we can reduce the number of characters from six to one or two. Assuming a coding scheme that uses 01 for freshman, 02 for sophomores, 03 for juniors, 04 for seniors, 05 for special students, and 06 for graduate students, can you see any need for defining the student class field as two characters, since the highest class presently is 06? The key to whether to use two characters or one (1, 2, 3, 4, 5, 6) is not just the present need for the six groups or classes individually but future needs as well. If in the future there will be more than nine classes of students, the field should have two characters. A university report that uses coding schemes is shown in Figure 11-8. How many coded fields in the report can you identify?

Figure 11-8

A report showing the use of codes to compress data storage.

OFFICIAL CLASS ROLL

COURSE – BD610   INFO SYSTEMS MANAGEMENT   SECTION 1   COURSE REF NO 1353
DEPT B BQ   INSTR CAMPBELL
BUILDING AND ROOM ML 105   TIME AND DAY 1MWF

LINE NMBR	STUDENT NUMBER	STUDENT NAME	CLASS	MAJOR	CREDITS	GRADE
1	138-88-3265	ANDERSON, WALLACE JAMES	GR	B BX02	3.0	B
2	523-74-2214	BAUER, ALVIN CHARLES	GR	N CS01	3.0	B
3	333-43-9326	BORNHOFEN, JOHN ROGER	GR	H OT02	3.0	A
4	003-36-2331	CADY, RAYMOND CHARLES	GR	B BX02	3.0	A
5	194-89-4431	GLOUSER, MICHAEL JAY	GR	B BD01	3.0	A
6	283-38-8440	HOX, FLOYD ALVIN	GR	N CS01	3.0	C
7	569-70-4496	LAWSON, ANNA MARIE	GR	B BK02	3.0	C
8	016-28-4310	PRESCALANTE, EGBERTO	GR	B BD02	3.0	B
9	407-26-9745	SEDERICKSON, MARK JAMES	GR	P IC01	3.0	B
10	457-22-8754	THURMON, CLARENCE ALEXANDER	GR	B BD01	3.0	A

Sorting is another activity, like classification and coding, that increases the efficiency of data processing. *Sorting* is the sequencing of data into an order based upon a prescribed data element. Data often enter systems in an unpredictable, random fashion and must be matched with data already in the system or with other data coming into the system. As shown in Figure 11-9, an employee's record of hours worked must be matched with the employee's master record, since both records are needed to calculate the employee's pay. Thus, one of the first steps in processing the payroll data is to sort the employees' current pay records by social security number. Since the master record (the record containing employee data such as name, pay rate, deductions, etc.) has previously been sorted in its proper order, the matching process will proceed much more efficiently than if the pay records and/or the master records were

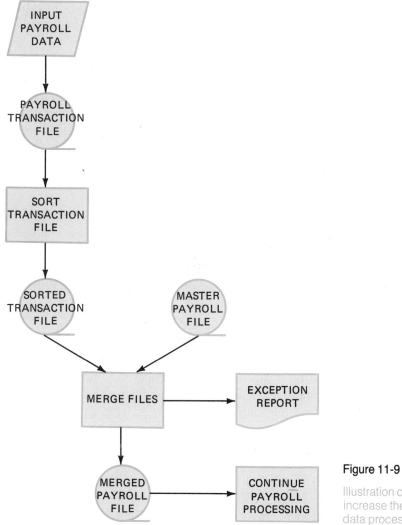

Figure 11-9

Illustration of sorting to increase the efficiency of data processing.

in random order. A customer accounts billing system uses basically the same process for the same reason.

Calculating is performing the arithmetic or logic functions necessary to process data. In most business systems, calculating is the easiest of the various processing activities to design (writing the payroll equation, for example) and is the fastest and most efficient for the computer hardware to do. Since computers are capable of making millions of calculations per second, it takes the computer much less time to do a calculation than to access data.

Summarizing data is restructuring and/or reducing data into a more useful form so that they can be truly classed as information. Presentation of data in a highly detailed form is NOT what most managers want. Managers generally prefer information that has been aggregated into summary totals or groupings. In particular, as data or information moves up the organizational management hierarchy from supervisors and foremen to department and division managers, and on up to vice-presidents and the president, it is aggregated and reduced so that each manager works with only that information in summary form appropriate for his or her level of management.

A salesman, a district sales manager, a division sales manager are each interested in different sales totals. A salesman is interested in a specific customer's order, while the district sales manager is interested in the total orders obtained by each salesman in that district during a particular period. The division manager wants information on the sales within each district.

Audit Trail

A part of a computerized information system that is largely invisible and yet is critical for control of data input and processing is the audit trail. An *audit trail* is a method of tracing or following transaction data through a system from the origin of the data (the source document), to data input and processing, and continuing through the system until the data appear in output or report form.

To provide an adequate audit trail requires the design team to build special control features into the design of the system. The question then arises, if auditing is such a critical part of the design effort, should an internal auditor be assigned to the design team? Some people believe that an auditor should be a member of the team; others argue against it. Those in favor say that having an auditor on the team ensures closer adherence to accepted auditing standards. Those opposed argue that the auditor then becomes too closely involved with the design, consequently losing his or her objectivity when required at a later time to evaluate the security and control points in the system. This problem could be avoided if one auditor were assigned to the system design team and another to the evaluation process. In any case, audit trails are an important form of control within the information system.

System Backup

In information systems, there are times when data must be recreated, usually because a data file has been lost through a hardware or software malfunction. Therefore, reference points from which the data can be recreated need to be maintained. For example, when a file is updated, the old file should be saved. If something happens to the new file (perhaps a program fails or a disk drive "crashes"), the old file—the reference point—plays a major role in recovering from the failure.

Protecting data from destruction also involves storing superseded files at a location different from where the current files are kept. Keeping files around for several cycles or generations is referred to as the grandfather-father-son concept. The new file is the son, the file preceding it is the father, and the next older file is the grandfather.

Hardware Study

A *hardware study* should be completed during the design phase. It is needed in order to select the specific hardware that is required in the new system. The study includes three important steps. First, prices or bids and contractual arrangements from hardware vendors are solicited. Second, benchmark tests on specific hardware that appears to meet the new system requirements are conducted. A *benchmark test* is a test or series of tests on equipment by which comparative analysis of various hardware components can be made. Third, contractual agreements with the vendor or vendors are made. The agreements should cover purchase or lease of equipment, scheduled delivery, installation, and support commitments for training and maintenance.

Program Specifications

As discussed earlier, the purpose of the design phase is to develop specific details regarding the physical structure of the new system. System details must be well documented so that necessary computer programs can be written from that documentation. As discussed in Chapter 6, details may be presented in flowchart form, in decision tables, in HIPO charts, or other similar types of documentation. Before any computer programming can be done, however, the system project team determines what programs are necessary, specifies the purpose of each program, and ensures that there is proper documentation from which programs can be written. This process is known as developing *program specifications*. Two types of programs are required: conversion programs and application programs.

Conversion programs are those programs that are necessary to facilitate the change from the old system to the new one. Once the conversion has been completed, the programs serve no further purpose. Each system is unique in its conversion needs; however, some conversion activities are common to almost all systems development. In file conversion, for example, data are taken from the old file and a new file is created. This process normally involves putting the old data into a format that will fit into the new file structure.

A special type of conversion program that is sometimes used to switch from one computer hardware system to another is an emulator. An *emulator* is a computer program that reads other programs, records, or files that were written to run on the old hardware (or any other hardware) and through a conversion process translates the old instructions into instructions that the new equipment can understand. In a way, the emulator makes the old program think that it is still running on the old computer.

Rewriting programs to run on the new hardware can be very time-consuming and costly. One major bank corporation, in installing a new computer system, estimated that rewriting the old programs to run on the new computer system would require 350 employee-years. If the old programs can run on the new system through the use of an emulator, why do companies go to the expense of rewriting programs? The reason is that new equipment is installed to take advantage of new technology, new capabilities, etc., and programs operating on the old system were not written to take advantage of the new technology. Therefore, as long as the old programs are being run, the new technology is not being used.

Application programs are the programs necessary to operate the new system. The following programs are found in most information systems:

> Data entry programs
> Data edit programs
> Sort or preprocessing programs
> Update programs
> Data processing programs
> Report generation programs

Writing computer programs necessary to implement and run the system is usually the most time-consuming task in developing information systems. To reduce the amount of programming time, software packages (programs already written that the company purchases) are sometimes used. However, in some cases adapting a software package to the new system may require as much programming effort as if the programs were written from scratch in-house. Packages that can be implemented with only minor modifications are rare. However, the availability of good software packages is expected to increase in the future; thus, the design team should continue to give careful consideration to the use of packages. The "make or buy" decision can be a critical one in terms of programming time and effort.

Application programs in the system are used over and over. Within only a short time after they are in operation, however, request for changes in the system — hence, in the programs — are sure to be made. To facilitate making program changes, good documentation is mandatory. The major form of program documentation is the program listing (the computer printout of the program instructions) and test results.

Programs should be thoroughly tested before they are implemented. Although it is often stated that in any program there is always one more bug, a program test plan should be developed that notes the processing and decision points in the program to see if the proper results are obtained. The test plan and the test results should become a part of the program documentation.

Although some systems people include programming activities in the implementation phase, it is wise to separate them since they are such a significant part of the total development effort.

SUMMARY

In this chapter, you have studied various activities in the system design phase, particularly those activities involved in developing detailed specifications of system outputs, inputs, and processing. One major form of system output is reports to users of information generated by the system. Reports may be classified as periodic or scheduled, exception, demand, interactive, or ad hoc. Scheduled reports are the type most often used; with increased use of interactive systems, however, individual queries for information items are becoming much more widely used. A helpful device used in locating the desired information is a menu.

Turnaround documents are outputs from one processing cycle that later become input for the next cycle. Another important output from an information system is backup files. If for any reason a file is lost, the backup file is used to reconstruct the lost file.

Design activities for processing the data include determining file structure for storing data and developing the arithmetic and logic procedures for converting the raw data into information for the system users. The two most common types of file structures used in information systems are sequential and direct access. Classifying, sorting, calculating, and summarizing activities can be found in any information system. Codes are also useful in processing data; a code is a shorthand or abbreviated expression of a data value.

Entering transaction data into the system correctly and efficiently is critical to effective information systems. A transaction is the event that triggers the information system; it starts the system into motion. Two activities that system designers should give careful attention to are editing procedures and data verification. Also, the designers should give careful attention to auditing procedures; they should provide an audit trail that can be used to follow a transaction through the system.

A major outcome of the system design phase is program specifications, indicating the programs that are necessary in the system and the purpose of each program. Two types of programs used in implementing and operating the new system are conversion programs and application programs. Conversion programs are used in switching from one system to the other. Application programs are used to operate the new information system.

TERMS

Design phase
Design specifications
Reports
Periodic reports
Report generator program
Exception report
Flags
Demand report
Interactive output
Query-response
Question-answer

Menu-display
Query
Menu
Ad hoc report
Turnaround document
Transaction
Source document
Forms design
Cursor
Verifying
Editing

Validity check	Codes
Completeness test	Sorting
Limits test	Calculating
Batch total	Summarizing
Hash total	Audit trail
File	Hardware study
Entity	Benchmark test
Record	Program specifications
File access	Conversion programs
Sequential access	Emulator
Direct access	Application programs
Classifying	

QUESTIONS

1. What is the principal outcome of the detail system analysis phase — Phase III of the system cycle?
2. Which phase in the systems life cycle do most systems analysts prefer to work with?
3. Which part of the design phase is usually undertaken first?
4. What is the major purpose served by an information system?
5. What is the type of report most commonly used in an information system?
6. What is the exception reporting principle?
7. Name the two major considerations in designing a periodic or scheduled report.
8. Why do some managers object to using the exception reporting method in some situations?
9. What is interactive output?
10. (a) What is a query?
    (b) Who constructs the query: the user or the system?
11. What is the purpose of an ad hoc report?
12. (a) What is the purpose of turnaround documents?
    (b) In what types of information systems are they used?
13. Describe the two most common file designs.
14. (a) What is a classification scheme?
    (b) Why are codes used in information processing?
15. What is the purpose of sorting data?

16. What is the purpose of a hardware study?
17. Why are program specifications developed?
18. (a) What two types of programs are used in implementing an information system?
    (b) How do the two differ from each other?
19. What function does an emulator perform?
20. Are software packages easier to implement in an information system than programs written by the systems project team?
21. Name some typical computer programs used in a business information system.

ARTICLE

Fifty Ways to Upset Your Data Processing User

Having traveled through the DP industry for a score of years, I'm sometimes disillusioned with my chosen profession. There are many aggravations: lack of organization, non-existent planning, abysmally poor documentation, woefully insufficient training.

Yet there is one item that distinguishes itself from all others as the ultimate absurdity: DP management's propensity to anger and alienate the very people they should be bending over backward to please.

The retailing dictum — "The customer is always right" — appears to have no place in data processing. In fact, some DP departments have so aggravated their customers that "Caveat Emptor" should be stamped on their specifications, printed on the stationery and chiseled in granite over the entrance.

Since this practice continues to gain new converts, I felt that some of the more prominent actions should be documented, thus providing prospective managers with a checklist of the "correct" mistakes to make when they assume their new position. So, with apologies to Paul Simon, let's examine some of the (at least) 50 ways to upset your user.

Keep Them in the Dark, Clark

Why tell the users anything? They don't understand data processing anyway. Everyone knows it takes wizards (like us) to make sense of this brave new world. What we have to accomplish is beyond the comprehension of mere mortals (users).

A good line to remember is the old personnel cliché, "Don't call us, we'll call you." After all, we don't want users asking stupid questions like, "Why is my system 10 months late?". or "Where are the reports I requested last year?" Like children, users should be seen but not heard.

If we try to inform users, they only get frustrated and lash out at us. So it's best to say very little to them. "The project is 95 percent complete" is a good phrase, at least for six months. After that you may wish to upgrade to 98 percent. This should keep the users off your back for a while.

Leave Them Alone, Joan

"The purchasing department keeps calling."

continued

"We cut over their system last month. Why do they keep bugging us?"

"They claim the system's not working correctly."

"The system worked fine when we tested it. If the system isn't working, it's because they're not following the user manual instructions."

"Purchasing said they never got a user manual from us."

"Well, of course not. It's their responsibility to write the user manual, not ours. I knew this was their fault."

Some users expect too much and have to be brought to their senses. DP departments build systems, not operate them. If the system isn't working, it's not our fault. We built it to specifications.

Make a Promise, Thomas

"Of course we can implement 42 programs, build three databases, and set up a communication network in 60 days. Just sign the specification and we'll go to work."

This is what the DP manager says to the user, but what he is thinking is, "If the entire staff works on the project we might finish in 60 days, but since only four people are available it will probably take 600 (work days, not calendar)."

No matter. The important thing is to "close the deal." Once the users have sunk their money, we've got them hooked. We just keep going back to the well (the user's budget) for additional funding. . . .

There's More, for Sure

Another way to cause dissension between you and your user is to "tell them what their system should do." As said before, users don't understand data processing. Therefore, how can they possibly know how their system should function? Being the computer "wizards," we define all the system parameters; then let the user mold his department to fit the new computer application. . . .

Monument—Marble or Garble

Being a monument builder is another method of alienating the user community. Monument builders want to develop large-scale applications that require massive influx of personnel, dollars and time.

These super systems are perfect for internal empire building and usually generate external interest through write-ups in trade journals and presentations at association meetings. . . .

There are more ways to upset your user than can possibly be documented. . . .

Remember—keep the user off-balance. Never supply complete information. Treat them as inferiors. . . .

DISCUSSION QUESTIONS

1. (a) In the statement "If the system isn't working, it's not our fault. We built it to specifications," from what likely source did the "specifications" originate? From the systems personnel or from the system users?

(b) The author of the article states that "Another way to cause dissension between you and your user is to 'tell them what their system should do.'" Who should state what the system should do? What term is used to express "what the system should do"?

2. Identify the numerous areas of systems development, as indicated by the author, in which effective system-design tools (techniques and approaches) were not used.

APPLICATION

System Keeps Charlotte County in Operation

Four Nixdorf 600/50 mini-computers comprise the heart of the distributed data processing clout for Charlotte County, FL. An array of peripherals dispersed primarily throughout the courthouse complex enables each of the county's 13 departments to take advantage of the distributed power. The accomplishments of the four minis would make a mainframe weep.

The Property Appraiser's office, which monitors every property transaction in the county, gets the most use out of the system. It maintains a real estate master file of over 3 million physical records, and adds about 20,000 more each year. Other departments have less voluminous DP requirements. The tax collection department sends out 180,000 bills annually, and the clerk of the court sends out a mere 30,000 traffic citations in the same period.

... The number of reversals for erroneous tax payment have been reduced dramatically, according to ... a consultant to the county. "We've processed around 30,000 payments during the past month with only four reversals. And during the entire year, we had only 23. Prior to the acquisition of our Nixdorf equipment, we were averaging 12,000 reversals a year."

The system is also used to carry out court scheduling; it registers voters and performs jury selection according to a Supreme Court–approved algorithm. The Road and Bridge Department uses it to estimate maintenance costs.

Charlotte's personnel department developed an automated reporting method that saves $15,000 to $20,000 a year in direct billings. The Mosquito Control department uses the system to track its 22 vehicles, plus the type and cost of chemicals used, and in what areas.

Even the county sheriff finds use for the system as a dispatch unit. In addition to maintaining a complete database on everybody who has ever had business with the sheriff's office, the system keeps track of deputies on the road—when they sign out, when they check in by radio, and when they are pursuing and stopping a car. In the event a deputy is delayed for more than two minutes after stopping a car, a signal is automatically triggered on the terminal screen to notify the operator that there may be trouble.

"Not only is the 600/50 utterly flexible," says ... [the] county personnel director, but it costs only a fraction of

continued

what other systems have cost. Prior to installing our personnel management and procedures operation, we visited a neighboring city to look at their software. They had spent approximately $400,000 in about 18 months, and the program still wasn't operational. Our program was written in a matter of . . . days and we had it operating within 30 days."

As of 1980, the county's hardware has cost no more than $200,000. "In contrast, a nearby county has a $1 million system and spends $700,000 for a staff to operate it," says . . . [the]county property appraiser. "We reckon that since 1975, our Nixdorf system has saved us $600,000 to $700,000 in new hardware and programming costs," he added. . . .

Reprinted from COMPUTER DECISIONS, *DEC 1981, page 52, copyright 1981, Hayden Publishing Company.*

DISCUSSION QUESTIONS

1. Name the various information systems that Charlotte County has implemented using the Nixdorf computer equipment.
2. From the descriptions of the county's information systems, indicate some of the respective system inputs, processing, and outputs.

CHAPTER 12

INFORMATION SYSTEMS IMPLEMENTATION

CHAPTER OBJECTIVES

In this chapter you will learn:

1. Characteristics of structured programming.
2. The use of walk-throughs.
3. The chief programmer team concept.
4. What activities are included in the implementation phase.
5. The importance of having a complete system test plan.
6. The need for user acceptance of the system.
7. The role of evaluation and follow-up in the system development cycle.

The next phase of the systems life cycle is perhaps the most important phase: implementation of the system. Some people might argue that problem definition is more important; others would put design in the top spot. There is no question that all of the phases are important, that none can be slighted. However, C. West Churchman, a well-known authority on the "systems approach" and operations research, contends that a system or problem solution that cannot be implemented need not be designed or solved. He advocates investigating implementation as the first phase rather than feasibility study or analysis. While he has a valid point, one could counter his approach by stating that the first phases should accommodate planning for implementation activities that will affect such tasks as scheduling the system project and personnel assignment.

Implementation activities are those activities that are necessary to put the system into operation or, as it is sometimes termed, "into production." The first implementation activities involve writing the computer programs defined in the information system program specifications — specifications that were developed in the design phase. Other activities to be undertaken during implementation include training users of the information system, training those who will be operating the system, testing all components of the system, and converting from the old system (if one existed) to the new system.

The last phase of the systems development cycle is evaluation and follow-up. The evaluation phase determines whether the system is performing as planned. Follow-up investigations are made periodically to see if the system continues to meet user needs.

PROGRAM DEVELOPMENT

Good programming is a science and an art. The "science" is in understanding the programming language and efficient programming techniques; the "art" is in creating the program statements and in working with other people — users, programmers, and other systems professionals. Efficient programming calls for detailed planning, the use of logic skills, patience, and a high level of positive motivation. Detailed planning is necessary so that previous design and programming activities in the system effort will not have to be done over. Logic skills are necessary because the program problem must be approached with a logical solution, a solution that is the most efficient one (at the time) and that contains no logic errors in solving the user's problem. Patience with people and with equipment is the key to successful development of an information system.

A major challenge facing systems analysts is to break down barriers that may have developed over the years within the organization either through conflicts when new systems were being automated or through conflicts with the user community. The programmer contributes to the elimination of these barriers by developing efficient programs that are logically sound and can be understood by users and other information systems specialists. Such programs are more error free and easily maintained (updated or changed as the users' needs change) than programs written by trial and error.

The first task of the programmer is to check the logic and completeness of flowcharts or other forms of logic charts. If flaws exist in the system documentation, further development of the system design and programming specifications may be necessary before actual programming can proceed. A programmer who acts now and asks questions later will have a tendency to develop programs that are full of errors. Therefore, the programmer must be inquisitive. In addition, the programmer needs to plan his or her activities carefully. Often, a major portion of a programmer's time is spent on older systems that continue to require a great deal of maintenance. Because of this time demand, it is important for the programmer to determine the workload and realistically estimate when a particular program or program segment will be completed.

It is also important for new programs to be written so that the logic is easy to follow. Today, programmers spend too much time making changes or correcting bugs in old programs because the program logic was not properly constructed in the first place. A concept known as structured programming has been developed over the past twenty years which helps eliminate poorly developed programs. The programs are easier to understand, and changes in individual programs can be made quickly and at minimal cost.

The term *structured programming* is used to describe specific characteristics of writing computer programs. Programs that are structured have a precise organization that follows a definite pattern so that program segments can be deleted or added without affecting the functions of other program segments. The pattern is associated with the top-down concept of systems design; in fact, the two concepts—top-down design and structured programming—were developed concurrently. Structured programming characteristics were introduced briefly in Chapter 7 and are further discussed in the following sections.

CHARACTERISTICS OF STRUCTURED PROGRAMMING

Program Statements

The structured approach uses only three basic types of program statements: sequence, selection (IF-THEN-ELSE), and iteration (DO-WHILE and DO-UNTIL). With the *sequence* form of program statement, one statement logically follows another in sequential order, and there are no intervening program statements. There is no branching or jumping from one program statement to another. A sequence pattern is shown schematically in Figure 12-1.

Figure 12-1

The structured sequence pattern.

The sequence pattern of writing statements is not new to you. In fact, none of the three types of structured programming statements is. You have also used the *selection* or IF-THEN-ELSE statement in writing your own programs. The selection instruction or statement tests to see whether a certain condition exists. If it does, processing of the data follows one set of instructions; if it does not exist, processing proceeds to a different set of instructions. An example of a selection statement is:

IF SCORE EQUAL TO OR GREATER THAN 90.0 THEN 180
[jump to statement #180].

If the score is less than 90, the jump to statement #180 will not be made and the instruction following the IF statement will be executed. The selection technique is illustrated schematically in Figure 12-2.

In many programming languages, an ELSE command is not used, but it is always implied. In the previous example, ELSE was implied when processing

Figure 12-2

The selection technique, involving a choice between two paths. In this example, if the score is greater than or equal to 90.0, the left path will be followed; if the score is less than 90.0, the right path will be executed.

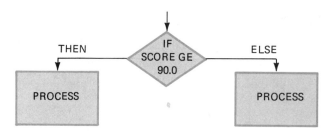

continued to the instruction following the IF statement. COBOL is one of the programming languages in which ELSE is used. For example,

IF STUDENT-NUMBER EQ 999999999 THEN 300 ELSE 210.

In the above statement, if the student number is 999999999, the program will jump to instruction 300; otherwise, the program will branch to instruction 210. A key rule in structured programming is that the selection process is only used to branch forward in the program, never to branch back to previous statements. In other words, the above IF statement must appear in the program prior to statement 210.

The *iteration* or repeat form of structured statements follows a looping pattern. This form also involves testing for a condition (the use of the IF statement). In an iteration you are allowed to branch backward in the program only if the branch uses a controlled loop. Two approaches used in developing the testing logic are known as DO-WHILE and DO-UNTIL (Figure 12-3). Both use similar types of logic.

In a DO-WHILE loop, the program instructions contained within the loop are executed (repeated) as long as (WHILE) a certain condition exists. When the condition no longer exists, an exit is made from the loop. An example of a DO-WHILE condition is:

IF TEMPERATURE LESS-THAN 50 THEN [statement number].

As long as TEMPERATURE is less than 50, the program will continue repeating the loop. As soon as 50 is reached, the program will exit the loop.

Figure 12-3

The loop or iteration process. In the DO-WHILE function, the loop is executed as long as a condition exists. In the DO-UNTIL function, the loop is executed until a certain condition is reached, at which point the loop is exited.

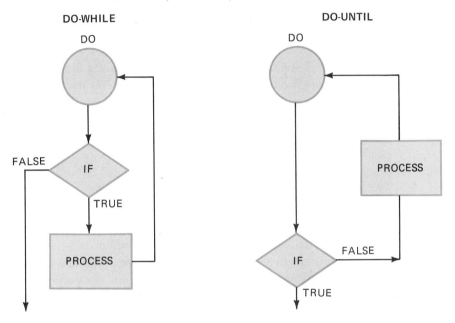

In the DO-UNTIL logic, a test is made each time the loop is executed to see if a condition has been reached. UNTIL the condition is reached, the program will continue repeating the loop. The loop is exited when the condition is reached. An example of a DO-UNTIL condition is:

IF QUANTITY EQUAL-TO 50 THEN [statement number].

Until the quantity of 50 has been reached, the statements within the loop will continue to be executed.

GO TO-Less Programming

As the concept of structured programming evolved, one of the first rules established was: No GO TO statements can be used. This concept was referred to as *GO TO-less programming*. The reason for this development was that GO TO statements have a tendency to make a program unmanageable. During the 1960s, programmers were using the statements too extensively. For example, several years ago a group of programmers were assigned the task of converting a program from one system to another. During conversion, they noted that a high number of GO TO statements were used in the old program. In fact, there were so many that the team decided to make a count. They counted 690 GO TO statements out of a total of a few thousand statements in the program.

Sometimes, however, total elimination of GO TO statements creates awkward program logic. Consequently, the rule was modified so that GO TO branches within a specific program segment are now permissible. However, the GO TO statement still cannot be used to leave a program segment arbitrarily. A program module can be exited only at the exit point of the loop.

Program Modularity

Another characteristic of a structured program is *program modularity*. Each program is divided into modules or sections that are autonomous; each module has one entrance point and one exit point. The purpose of such modularity or segment independence is to improve the efficiency of writing and maintaining the program. The program will usually contain a control module of "driver" statements. *Driver statements* are like policemen who direct or control traffic. The statements are used to steer the execution of the program to the various program segments or paragraphs. Although driver or control statements can be placed anywhere within a program, in structured programming they are placed at the beginning. This pattern of constructing the program follows a top-down design approach. The driver statements represent the upper levels in the hierarchy of program statements. Figure 12-4 is a hierarchical chart illustrating the control concept. The top block in the chart represents the program itself. The next level represents the main control statements. In COBOL, these control statements typically are PERFORM statements; that is, PERFORM a particular paragraph or function, then proceed to the next statement. In BASIC or FORTRAN, the controlling function may be accomplished through the use of subroutine CALL statements. One of the drawbacks to the use of program modularity is that more program statements are usually required to write the program; however, readability and understanding are vastly improved.

Figure 12-4

Control or driver statements (solid-line blocks) direct the execution of the program to a particular program module, paragraph, subroutine, or segment (broken-line blocks). When driver statements are used, a change made in a module will not affect the other modules.

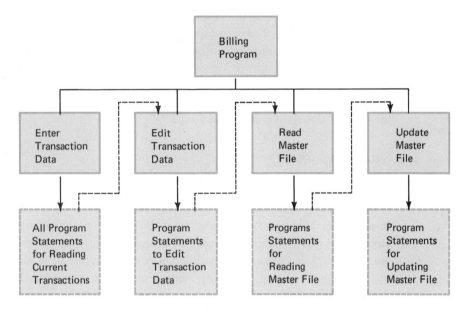

The Programming Team

Ego-Less Programming. Although the concept of *ego-less programming* is not a "rule" of structured programming, it is closely associated with the structured concept. As program tasks are assigned to various programmers and as walk-throughs are conducted to test the logic structure of the programs, the program as a whole is not the creation of one specific individual. Instead, it becomes the product of a programming team. Therefore, credit for success or blame for failure is spread among all members of the group.

Chief Programmer Concept. The programming team is led by a *chief programmer.* This person is responsible for supervising team members, assigning program tasks or modules, conducting walk-throughs, and evaluating the team's adherence to the programming quality standards.

Structured Walk-through

The term "walk-through" has been used in the two preceding sections. What is a walk-through? A *walk-through* is a detailed presentation by programmers and analysts to describe to other analysts, programmers, users, and managers the design or layout of a system or program segment. The purpose of the walk-through is not only to explain the system or program segment to the audience but also to receive feedback from the group on changes that perhaps should be made to improve the system or program design. Also, the walk-through is an excellent way of reducing the amount of misunderstanding and miscommunication that can very easily arise among the various individuals involved in the system development process.

Structured Testing

When the structured programming concept is used, testing of programs is more complete, more thorough, and less time-consuming. Tests are conducted from the top down. Just as the program is developed top-down, so also are the structured tests. Through the top-down approach, control or driver statements are tested first. If a segment or module under a particular control statement has not yet been developed, a dummy module can be set up instead. In this way, the logic of the control statements and any completed modules can be tested as they are developed, and incomplete modules will not interfere with the testing process. Testing from top down ensures that as modules are developed and tested, they will fit into the total computer program when completed. Moreover, it is not necessary that all of the modules be completed before any testing is done.

On the other hand, if a bottom-up approach to program development and testing is used, testing is confined to one module until all of the modules have been completed. Then, as the modules are brought together, it usually is necessary to rewrite several parts of each module in order to make all of the modules compatible — to eliminate the inconsistencies from one module to the next. For example, words, labels, or addresses may differ among the various modules.

Standards and Conventions

Although quality control and programming standards existed prior to the evolution of structured programming, they were given greater attention as a result of implementing structured programming concepts within the organization. As implied in the previous paragraphs, each programmer must adhere to certain programming criteria or standards. A *standard* is a rule established to improve the quality of the programming function. Specific standards within the information systems department generally apply to all information systems and programs. Standards are an important ingredient in the system quality control function. An example of a standard is the restricted use of GO TO's.

A *convention* is also a rule, but normally it is used in only one information system development effort; for example, any program written in the inventory control system must follow certain rules or conventions. An example of a convention is the use of specific names or labels for identifying data elements or files in a program; or, as shown in Figure 12-5, rules governing the structure of program statements and logic.

SYSTEM IMPLEMENTATION

The system has been designed, programs have been written and tested, and now the big question: Will the system work? Before the final test can be made and the system turned over to the user group, several implementation activities must occur:

— Writing user manuals and other documentation materials,
— Training the people who will be working with the system,
— Testing the system,
— Converting data from the old system to the new, and
— Turning the system over to the user group.

User Manuals

User manuals are the operating instructions for the new information system. In the past, operating manuals seemed to be written for people who already knew what they were doing, rather than for those who were not knowledgeable and needed to be trained. In fact, user manuals were called reference manuals, implying that they were designed mainly for reference, not for training. Such manuals are not adequate learning tools. Only within the past few years has the need for well-developed user manuals been given adequate attention.

Figure 12-5

Example of programming conventions from a COBOL coding convention document.

Alignment and Indentation Conventions

1. Paragraph names should occupy a separate line.
2. Only one statement should appear on a line.
3. DATA DIVISION attributes such as PICTURE and VALUE should be aligned in neat columns.
4. DATA DIVISION level numbers and names should be indented to display the hierarchical structure of data.
5. The THEN and ELSE clauses of an IF statement should be aligned and coded symmetrically. For example:

```
IF  SERIOUS-ERROR
        DISPLAY 'TRANSACTION REJECTED:
        CALL 'SETCOD' USING COND-COD, OPTION
    ELSE
        PERFORM WRITE-EDITED-TRANSACTION
        ADD 1 TO GOOD-TR-COUNT.
```

6. Level numbers within a record description should be multiples of 5. For example:

```
1    RECORD.
    5  PART-1.
        10  FIELD-1.
        10  DATE-RECEIVED.
```

7. For ease in reading, avoid strings of more than 3 identical picture characters. For example:

```
PICTURE X(8)
PICTURE 9(5)V99
```
are easier to read and less error prone than:
```
PICTURE XXXXXXXX
PICTURE 99999V99
```

The IF Statement

1. Avoid nested conditionals wherever alternative constructions would be as easy to understand.
2. Never have over two nested IFs.

The GO TO

1. No GO TO or PERFORM outside the loop refers to any name inside the loop.
2. No GO TO inside the loop may refer to any paragraph name outside the loop.

Today, within most organizations that have fairly complex information systems, one can find a special group of individuals whose main purpose is to produce effective user manuals. This group often includes *technical writers*, who have been professionally trained, as well as individuals with computer experience who also have a satisfactory writing background. User manuals should be eye-appealing, motivational, and written in language that does not overwhelm or intimidate the user. Instructions from an easy-to-read user manual are reproduced in Figure 12-6.

Training

Training of the system's users is an important activity in the implementation phase. However, training should not be confined just to the implementation

Figure 12-6

Example of instructions from a user manual.

To link onto the Fort Collins Computer System, do the following:

a. Dial your special local number and listen for a high-pitched, continuous tone. If you get nothing, or a busy signal, hang up. A short time later, try again.

b. When you hear the high-pitched tone, press the telephone handset into the cradle (this actually connects your terminal to the telephone system). Be sure the handset is placed into the receptacle correctly—with the cord pointing in the right direction. The right way for the cord will be marked on your terminal. Trying to talk to the computer with the cord pointing in the wrong direction is like trying to talk into the earpiece and listen through the mouthpiece—it doesn't work.

Western Electric

phase, but should be a part of the total system development effort — from the initial stages of defining the problem throughout the development process until the system has been turned over to the user. Even then, as problems arise, systems personnel will find that the training process continues.

In addition to using manuals, training sessions involve presentations to large groups of 35 to 50 persons, small specialized groups between 5 and 8 members, and one-on-one sessions with only one teacher and one student. Too often, training consists almost exclusively of presentations to large groups primarily because large-group training is quick. One or a few sessions are assumed to get the job done, and the cost is low. However, learning effectiveness may also be very low. In most situations, the best type of training is accomplished one-on-one. While it is more expensive and takes longer, it is a more effective way to train users.

Individuals who will be working with the new system should know and appreciate their roles in the system. Such an understanding enhances user acceptance of the system, reduces the chances of system failure, and reduces the number of "surprises" to the user. These "surprises" often result when the user has not been properly trained.

System Testing

Testing the system is necessary before it can be turned over to the user group. *System tests* should be the result of a carefully constructed test plan. This test plan should include top-down testing procedures, the use of tests with "live" data, and operation of the system without assistance from the system development team.

Top-down testing consists of testing the system as a whole to see if the major pieces (the subsystems) fit together. Once this is accomplished, each subsystem is tested to determine if all of its parts function properly. The top-down approach continues down through the system until the lowest single module has been tested.

The system should be tested with "live" or real data. Too often, test data are developed by programmers or other systems personnel who may have a limited knowledge of actual company data; thus the data they develop for testing are biased toward their specific programs. However, testing with real data may not supply all of the situations in the system that need to be tested. This is particularly true when testing data collection procedures, data entry programs, and data edit programs. Therefore, both real and simulated data should be used to test the system.

Frequently, the system is not adequately tested by the user until after it has been implemented. Prior to that time, testing is handled by project team members only. The final system test should not involve any project team members. This final system test is called the *acceptance test;* that is, if the system performs satisfactorily, the user group or department will accept the system. The specific system functions that are included in the acceptance test are usually determined at the beginning of the implementation phase. In some cases, particularly those involving contractual arrangements, specifications for the acceptance test should be agreed to at the beginning of the systems development cycle.

Completing the acceptance test provides a definite point at which the system can be turned over to the user. If the system staff has effectively involved users, especially in making decisions concerning system design, obtaining users' acceptance of the system should not be difficult. When users are ready to take control of the system, they should feel that the system is theirs, that it is the result of their efforts, and that the system's success or failure depends upon them.

Conversion

Conversion is a critical point in information systems development involving these key questions:

— At what point will the old information system cease and the new one start?

— What activities are necessary to switch from the old system to the new?

There are three commonly used conversion methods: direct, modular, and parallel. The three methods are illustrated in Figure 12-7.

Direct conversion means that on a specific date the old system stops and the new one begins. It is a "direct" change-over from the old to the new with no overlapping of system operations. Direct conversion is used in situations where any pauses or breakdowns in operating the new system will not be detrimental to the continuous functioning of the organization.

Modular conversion involves separating the new system into modules or subsystems and thus making it possible to phase-in the new system one module at a time. This method is often used for conversion of large information systems. Converting one module at a time provides for better control over development and implementation costs. It also provides better management control over the

Figure 12-7

Conversion methods.

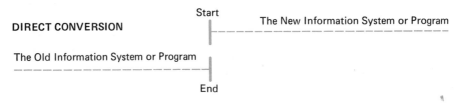

DIRECT CONVERSION

Start

The New Information System or Program

The Old Information System or Program

End

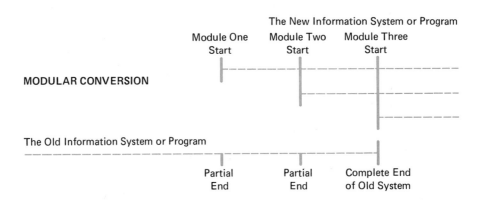

MODULAR CONVERSION

The New Information System or Program

Module One Start   Module Two Start   Module Three Start

The Old Information System or Program

Partial End   Partial End   Complete End of Old System

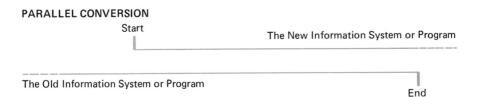

PARALLEL CONVERSION

Start

The New Information System or Program

The Old Information System or Program

End

entire system conversion process: lessons learned in converting one module can be applied to the conversion of subsequent modules. However, modular conversion does create one major difficulty. As new modules are phased-in, they must be able to interface with the parts of the old system that have not been converted. At the same time, they must function successfully as a part of the new system.

Parallel conversion calls for running both systems—the old and the new—simultaneously for a short period of time. Parallel conversions are used when there needs to be assurance that no serious interruptions in the flow of data will occur. They are also used to cross-check or verify system results.

Conversion activities can create many stress points in the implementation process. The users and operating personnel are learning a new system; the workload is increased; there is uncertainty regarding how the new system will perform. Systems designers should seek to minimize these potential points of personnel stress.

EVALUATION AND FOLLOW-UP

After the system has been implemented, either the team members or a group not previously involved with developing the system should conduct an evaluation study. Other follow-up activities are also necessary in order to maintain the system so that it continues to meet the needs of the user.

Evaluation

System evaluation should address a number of questions. The major one is: Does the system do what it is supposed to do? (Note the situation depicted in Figure 12-8.)

To answer this key question, check the final version of the system to determine the following:

— Have the objectives as described in the first phase of the systems cycle been realized?
— Have the specific goals been achieved?
— Is the system performing in a timely, accurate, and economical manner?
— Are users satisfied with the system, or are they somewhat disturbed by the results?
— Were systems standards followed?
— Did the systems staff develop the system within time and cost constraints?

Evaluation should be completed shortly after the system has been turned over to the users. In addition, a periodic evaluation of the system (and all other information systems within the organization) should be made.

Figure 12-8

Six views of a system, illustrating the importance of good communication throughout the systems development effort.

As proposed by the project sponsor.

As specified in the project request.

As designed by the senior analyst.

As produced by the programmer.

As installed at the user's site.

What the user wanted.

Follow-up

Follow-up activities are concerned with ongoing maintenance of the system. This includes assessing whether users continue to use the system and making changes in the system to keep it current with the changing information needs of users. Maintenance is a significant part of information systems operation. It involves keeping the information system programs operating and making minor modifications in the programs as requested by the users and approved by management. In some organizations *maintenance programmers* are designated to perform these tasks. Their job is to work with programs that have already been implemented.

As stated earlier, there always seems to be at least one more bug in every system. These bugs must be taken care of as they arise. Likewise, if the system is not modified to meet changing needs, users will develop their own methods and systems in order to obtain the information they need. When this occurs, the organization is falling into a pattern of unmanaged systems development, which will result in inefficient and redundant systems.

SUMMARY

This chapter completes the discussion of the systems life cycle. Important topics within this chapter included programming concepts, system implementation, evaluation, and follow-up.

Structured programming is a concept that has been developed within the past twenty years. It provides for a high degree of consistency in program development and facilitates standardization. Structured programming involves the use of precise organization techniques, specifically modular and top-down approaches, and the use of standards and conventions to enhance the quality of computer programs.

System implementation encompasses three major activities: training, testing, and conversion. Training the users and other personnel who will be involved in operating the system is a critical factor in the successful implementation of a system. The testing process should follow a carefully developed test plan and should culminate in the user acceptance test. Smooth conversion from the old system to the new is difficult to achieve. Conversion activities should be carefully planned and controlled. In evaluating the new system, the key question to ask is: Does the system do what it is supposed to do?

TERMS

Structured programming	Convention
Sequence	User manual
Selection	Technical writers
Iteration	System tests
GO TO-less programming	Top-down testing
Program modularity	Acceptance test
Driver statements	Direct conversion
Ego-less programming	Modular conversion
Chief programmer	Parallel conversion
Walk-through	System evaluation
Standard	Maintenance programmers

QUESTIONS

1. (a) Do you agree with C. West Churchman's position on the role of the implementation phase in the systems development cycle? Justify your position. (b) Assuming that you are required to defend one of the systems development phases as the MOST critical of all of the phases, which phase would you select and why?

2. (a) What aspects of computer programming would you characterize as being closely associated with scientific disciplines? (b) What aspects would you consider an art?

3. When a programmer is given documentation specifying the various functions to be performed by a program, what should be the first thing that the programmer does?

4. What has brought about the concept of structured programming?

5. What are the three types of program sequences or functions permitted in structured program design?

6. Why were GO TO statements not permitted in the first "rules" developed for structured programming?

7. What is a program module or segment?

8. What is top-down program testing?

9. What purpose do driver statements serve in a computer program?

10. Do you agree with the concept of "ego-less programming"? Do you believe that team and individual motivation might be a disadvantage of the "ego-less" concept?

11. In the various phases of the systems development cycle, what are some key points or places that call for effective written and oral communications?

12. What is the difference between a standard and a convention?

13. Distinguish between an effective user's manual and a reference manual.

14. Why should a test of the system without assistance from any systems development team members be conducted?

15. Under what circumstances would each of the three conversion methods discussed in this chapter be used?

16. Why is it necessary to maintain an information system once it has been implemented and accepted by the user group?

ARTICLE

"Computer Illiteracy" Wastes Money

San Diego—Senior and data processing (DP) management often say they can't "get their arms around" the problem of educating end-users about rising computer technology, according to the president of a Palos Verdes, Calif., consulting firm. . . .

Vicki McConnell, president of the McConnell Group, stressed that DP management and top management must recognize that "computer illiteracy" on the part of end-users ultimately spells a waste of dollars for the company because computers do not equal success unless educated end-users are skillfully and productively employing the technology.

She defined the end-user as "an individual who uses DP services, but is not a member of the DP department" and "computer illiteracy" as the problem of a non-technical user who is not technically educated ("the why" of technology) or skilled ("the how" of technology).

"There is a mind set that goes like this," McConnell explained. "The DP person says, 'I did my job.' The user says, 'I am a victim.' Top management says, 'It's a necessary evil, but I've got to have it. But why am I not getting a return on my investment?'

"Hardware and software make up a delivery system," she continued. "It makes information available, but people are what makes information useful. We are guilty of emphasizing processing instead of emphasizing people. We must emphasize the end-user and his ability to use the technology or we haven't achieved success. The end-user is the ultimate determinant of success."

. . . The consultant contended that the introduction of technology to non-technical users produces four insidious problems that can "eat up a company": awkwardness, fear, resentment and resistance.

"People feel awkward with technology," she said. A CRT is not a comfortable tool for most. . . .

"People don't like change. What is especially bad is unexplained change." . . .

Some of her suggestions for solutions include designing systems for human beings, selling change, orienting users to the technology so that they reach a comfort level with it and preparing documentation in "people" language. She emphasized that ongoing communication must exist between DP and users. . . .

MIS Week, *May 12, 1982, p. 20.*

DISCUSSION QUESTIONS

1. Although the speaker is addressing the general problem of introducing technology into the organization, what points does she make that are relevant to introducing a new information system to its users?
2. In addition to "awkwardness, fear, resentment and resistance," list other problems that might be encountered.

APPLICATION

Upgrading Image

...When Robert B. Adams assumed the position of information systems director at Buckeye Pipe Line Co., Emmaus, Pa., he said, "The attitude of top management toward data processing was such that they had very seriously considered eliminating all but the person in charge of commercial systems maintenance and the data entry section, and just closing it down. The department was essentially dead."

Adams explained, "This had come about because nothing that was produced here was on time and, when it was produced, it was not satisfactory to users' requirements."

Adams credits the successful completion of a project, underway when he took over his job, with changing attitudes toward MIS. Furthermore, Adams said that one key to turning user attitudes around was to involve them heavily with management of the project, one that would save the company $1.3 million in electrical costs, by asking them to review and assist with their portion of the project.

"This was new to users. No one had ever asked them to take part in the systems development process," Adams said.

"We made the users an integral part of the whole process, to such an extent that they were aware that they could cause the delays. We worked with users, as opposed to the old-fashioned way, where the user was considered an encumbrance to good data processing," Adams said.

Adams said that the process of involving the user was difficult at first. "It was hard to get users to believe that we were doing things for the benefit of the user, as opposed to doing things for the benefit of data processing," he said.

He involved users in a team approach, making teams responsible for projects instead of individuals, and implementing peer group reviews with software planning.

After user involvement began to catch on, Adams said, "they began to think in terms of what kind of data processing was good for the company. Users began to relax and they started becoming believers."

He added that as intermediate project steps were met on time and, when the project was finally completed on schedule, "that did... a lot to turn management around to the point where they began to believe that good systems could actually be implemented."...

MIS Week, May 12, 1982, p. 28.

DISCUSSION QUESTIONS

1. When the approach suggested by Mr. Adams is adopted, will users feel responsible for the information system after it has been implemented?
2. What is your perception of the "old-fashioned way" of developing information systems?
3. What systems development activity is discussed in this chapter that would include "peer group reviews"?

PART 5 ADVANCED BUSINESS SYSTEMS

In this final section, several exciting applications of EDP technology are considered. Current literature supports each of the topics in this section as the fastest growing area of EDP technology for computers and information systems.

Chapter 13 - explores the increasing importance of systems security and control.

Chapters 14 and 15 - cover the important topics of telecommunications and the automated office.

Chapter 16 - explores several interesting topics—business graphics, material requirements, robotics, computer-assisted engineering, and decision support systems for managers.

13 SYSTEMS SECURITY AND EDP CONTROLS

CHAPTER OBJECTIVES

In this chapter you will learn:

1. The increasing security dangers faced by organizations utilizing EDP systems.
2. The importance of risk management to organizations.
3. The meaning of hardware and software security.
4. Data encryption characteristics.
5. Penetration methods for computer-related crimes.
6. The major types of EDP controls.
7. What it means to audit "around" a computer.
8. File protection techniques used for data security.

As computer information systems, public data networks, and electronic funds transfer become more commonplace, companies are experiencing problems protecting confidential information from modification, destruction, misuse, and other security-related dangers (Figure 13-1). Specific dangers include erasure, theft, misplacement, copying, damage, misrouting, unauthorized access, program changes, eavesdropping, disclosure, and unauthorized terminals. Customer mailing lists, research and development budgets, acquisitions plans, and discount schedules are sensitive documents that need protection.

According to FBI reports, the average bank robbery involves $3,200; the average bank fraud nets $23,500; but the average computer crime involves $500,000. The explosive growth of computers in business organizations is creating vastly expanded potential for computer crime. The risks of fraud have proliferated as a result of

— the growth of microcomputers,
— the soaring number of students and others who are learning how to use computers, and
— the large number of employees who can access computers through remote terminals.

Figure 13-1

Company information systems are exposed to various security-related dangers.

From The Office, *February, 1982*

Businesses are not the only organizations facing threats to their EDP systems. A few years ago, two college students in New York falsified 154 grades of 19 different students. One of the perpetrators, a student operator at the computer center, changed data stored on computer disks and altered input grade cards. At the University of Toronto, 250 students were caught using unauthorized research account numbers to run their assigned class programs. They were billed for $15,000 of computer time.

SYSTEMS SECURITY

For these reasons, *systems security* (protecting information, programs, and resources) and *EDP controls* (the control of access to a computer and the information it contains) are important topics in modern business organizations. A fundamental premise of systems and computer security is that no approach is perfect; it only minimizes risk.

Despite the obvious need for security, organizations often delay action. Some companies perceive that costs outweigh benefits. Other companies aren't able to identify security threats, and still others think "It can't happen to us." A security system should be evaluated on the basis of corporate needs, cost effectiveness, and acceptance by employees.

For companies concerned with security issues, a useful approach is *risk management*. The first step is to make sure that all managers are aware of security. Managers must identify the resources in their care and assess potential hazards. Economic consequences and expected rate of occurrence are then assigned to each hazard. Sensitive resources must get appropriate protection and, conversely, expensive measures are applied only to sensitive resources. This concept results in "rings" of protection and "islands" of security.

The individual assigned to risk management should:

— Know the short-range and long-range goals of the organization.
— Know users' security needs and priorities.
—·Be aware of and understand new security technology.
— Have the authority to implement security policy, programs, and procedures.
— Conduct risk analysis leading to such implementation.
— Periodically review overall security performance.

This ongoing activity is illustrated in Figure 13-2.

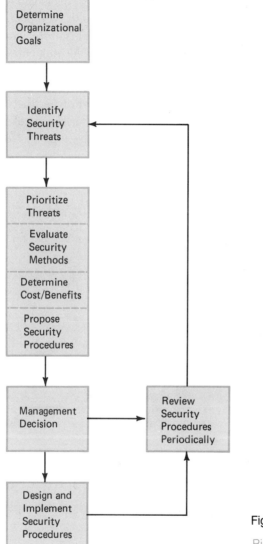

Figure 13-2

Risk management.

Hardware Security

Hardware security, which is the security of computer assets and capital equipment, refers to computer location, access control, fire protection, and storage procedures. Such measures as badges, electronic identification keys, alarm systems, guards, and physical barriers at doors and windows are used as deterrents to prevent unauthorized access to the computer facility.

A *mantrap* is a small room into which a person steps to be identified prior to entering a high-security area. The person desiring entrance uses a specially constructed personal identification badge (Figure 13-3) to unlock the door to the mantrap. Once inside, the person places the ID badge into a video reader while standing in front of a video camera. After verifying that the person and the badge photograph match, an officer in the security control center electronically allows entrance. Mantrap doors are interlocked so that one door cannot be opened while the other is open.

Figure 13-3

Identification badges are used for physical security.

Photo courtesy of Data Terminal Systems

Although most EDP losses occur outside the computer room, it is still important to protect hardware from hazards such as fire, explosion, natural disasters, environmental problems, and sabotage. Fire is always feared and, when it occurs, fire is devastating. Since ordinary sprinkler systems damage equipment, gas extinguishing systems are used. Halon is a gas that is safe for humans as well as for computer circuits. Essential records and backup data should be stored in an offsite location that is secure and fireproof.

Explosions and natural disasters such as earthquakes or floods are also devastating. To minimize physical damage, the computer center should be located away from outside building walls, and separated from other departments.

In the event of disaster, a procedure manual is needed that documents:

— The emergency procedure for shutting down computer equipment and evacuating the building.
— Procedures for handling data under emergency conditions.
— Procedures for performing security checks at the end of each workday.
— A contingency plan for the steps to be taken following a disaster.

Software Security

The cost of losing physical assets is easier to determine than the cost of losing software assets. *Software security* entails the protection of software assets such as user application programs, the operating system, and database management software. Basically, the intent of software security is to make sure that only those people who are supposed to have access to data or information actually have such access. Special user numbers and passwords are typically used to control access and ensure that users are authorized.

Data encryption or cryptography is a coding technique used to secure sensitive data. Cryptographic techniques range from simple letter-substitution methods to complex electronic procedures. However, the basic principles of coding messages are the same today as they were centuries ago. Essentially, every character of data sent is replaced by other coded characters. The sequence of substitution is determined by the sender according to a selected key. Cryptographic protection is especially important for data transmitted from remote terminals, since regular transmission lines can be "tapped" easily. Techniques used for encryption have the following characteristics:

— Encryption algorithms and keys are employed.
— A large number of possible keys are changed regularly.
— Outsiders are assumed to have complete knowledge of the encryption algorithm but not of the current key.
— The encryption algorithm and key should not adversely affect normal system performance.

A good encryption system forces unauthorized eavesdroppers to expend great effort to decipher a message. In 1975 the National Bureau of Standards adopted IBM's data encryption model as the nation's official data encryption standard (DES). DES is a single-chip device that takes a 64-bit unencrypted input (called plaintext) and produces a 64-bit encrypted output (called ciphertext). The DES procedure (Figure 13-4) generates billions of different combinations of its 64-bit key. To make an encryption system even harder to break, dual encryptions and random character selection may be used.

Other Security Techniques

In addition to systems security for hardware and software, good internal control also requires that measures be taken to prevent loss or accidental destruction of data. File protection techniques are an important means of maintaining this data security. A *file protection ring* is a plastic device that protects data on magnetic tapes. When the ring is present, new data can be written on the tape; when it is absent, tape data cannot be erased.

File labels can be either external or internal. External labels may be attached to tape reels and disk packs to identify specific files and give the specific dates on which the file was processed. Internal file labels are the first and last records on a tape or random access file. The first record, the *header label*, is used by the computer to verify that the correct file has been accessed. The last record, the *trailer label*, indicates the end of the file and may contain control totals for checking against totals accumulated during processing.

Another data security measure which should be taken is provision for reconstruction of lost records. Copies of important files and programs should be maintained in a location separate from the computer facility. A data retention procedure commonly used with magnetic tape is the *grandfather-father-son concept*. With this plan the three most recent master files are retained. If, during processing, an error or loss of records occurs in the old master file (the father) or in the current master file (the son), an even older master file (the grandfather) can be used to reconstruct the lost data. For disk processing, a duplicate file written onto tape serves as a father backup in case the disk file needs to be reconstructed.

Computer Vulnerability and Penetration Methods

Weaknesses in an information system that pose a security hazard are called *vulnerabilities*. Major types of vulnerabilities are

— poor data validation
— lack of criteria for user identification

Figure 13-4

Data encryption device and procedure.

Photo courtesy of IBM Corporation

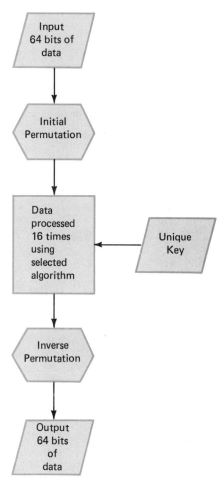

— unauthorized access to programs and data
— poor detection techniques
— lack of telecommunication controls
— poor personnel management
— no top management control.

When security is lax, computer crimes are possible that may cause physical destruction, financial deception, or unauthorized use of property. Sometimes violations are easy to spot (Figure 13-5). To perpetrate such crimes, various methods are used to penetrate a system. *Penetration* is the act of entering a system without authorization for illegal purposes. As in other areas of computer technology, a jargon has developed to describe computer crime procedures. Most computer-related crimes will use one or more of the following penetration methods.

Data Diddling.   The simplest and most common method of penetration is "data diddling," where data are changed before or during computer input. For example, a data entry clerk could alter payroll input data to transfer overtime

"Madison, it has been reported that in your last program you included a subroutine for playing the horses. Any truth to it?"

Figure 13-5

®R.E.M.

hours to a specified employee number. Forging documents, punching extra holes in cards, and ignoring manual controls are other data-diddling techniques.

Trojan Horse. A "Trojan horse" is the placement of computer instructions in a program that allows unauthorized processing alongside intended processing. This method is very hard to detect since clever programmers spread the secret code out among normal instructions.

Salami Technique. The "salami technique" involves theft of small amounts (slices) of assets from a large number of sources. For example, "rounded" pennies may be diverted from daily interest calculations for a large number of savings account balances without affecting balancing totals.

Superzapping. All computers have an overriding or universal access program, called a "superzap" program, to correct operating system malfunctions. A superzap program is much like a master key, legitimately used only if all other keys are lost. Management should closely guard superzap programs, since they can be used to gain access to privileged information by someone not authorized to do so.

Trapdoors. Programmers commonly use "trapdoors" as debugging aids in long programs. Whether intentionally or not, the trapdoor code may not be removed, leaving potential program gaps. Unauthorized code can fill those gaps and can compromise the computer system in a manner that is difficult to detect.

Logic Bomb. A "logic bomb" is a computer program that executes only at a specified time to perform some unauthorized procedure. Using the "Trojan horse" technique, an employee could trigger the erasure of an entire personnel file if his or her name is ever removed from the personnel file.

Data Leakage. Illegal removal of data from a computer facility is called "data leakage." This can be accomplished by hiding sensitive data in normal output reports or encoding data to look different. Miniature radio transmitters can also be used to broadcast the contents of a computer to a remote receiver.

Wiretapping. Signal interception, or "wiretapping," is accomplished on both telecommunication lines and satellite networks. The equipment for wiretapping is readily available at local electronics stores.

EDP CONTROLS

Fortunately, EDP controls are available to nullify vulnerabilities and penetration techniques. *EDP controls* are the plans, procedures, and records that help safeguard the assets and ensure that reliable data are maintained in the information system. The American Institute of Certified Public Accountants (AICPA) specifies two main types of EDP controls—organizational controls and application controls.

Organizational Controls

Organizational controls are much the same for manual and computerized systems. Separation of duties is a primary method of organizational control. The data processing department should be separated from users, just as duties within the DP department should be separated. Data entry, computer operations, systems programming, applications programming, scheduling, and distribution should not be performed by the same person. To further promote organizational control, employees should know what specific resources they are expected to protect. Upper-level managers may need a separate security staff.

Personnel should be protected from unnecessary failure or temptation. Good hiring procedures and employee benefits help avoid employee frustration, while job rotation and mandatory vacations deter the possibility of fraud and embezzlement. When an employee is terminated, formal procedures should be instituted quickly to ensure that company property is protected. There is evidence that perpetrators tend to be young, are among the most skilled technologists, use collusion, and often justify their action by the "Robin Hood" syndrome (It's perfectly acceptable to steal from a rich organization). EDP occupations have varied security risk levels:

Greatest risk	Moderate risk
EDP auditor	Programming manager
Security officer	
	Limited risk
Great risk	Applications programmer
Computer operator	Peripheral equipment operator
Data entry clerk	Tape librarian
Operations manager	Database administrator
Systems programmer	User programmers

Application Controls

Application controls deal with specific processing jobs that are performed in the information system. The purpose of application controls is to ensure that transactions are processed properly and that data are handled reliably and accurately. These controls relate to input, processing, and output of specific business applications such as accounting, inventory, or personnel. Typical examples of application controls include batch totals, controls over source data, and programmed input controls that validate data accuracy.

Batch Totals. Three forms of batch totals are commonly used with batch processing: financial totals, hash totals, and record counts. A *financial total* is the total of a column (field) containing such data as total sales or total cash receipts. *Hash totals* are totals generated from fields that are ordinarily not added, such as customer account numbers or product identification codes. A *record count* is simply the total number of records that were batched together or processed in a run.

Source Data Controls. These controls consist of a number of checks to assist in the detection and correction of errors and to ensure that all data are processed. Common forms of source data controls are proofreading, key verification, check-digit verification, and forms control.

Proofreading is one of the least expensive forms of source data control. It simply consists of visually inspecting a printed list of the input prior to processing. A more expensive but effective means of control is key verification. This process, as explained in Chapter 11, involves entering all data twice. The second time, the data item is entered on a verifier and the machine checks (or verifies) that the two items agree. If they do not, the operator must correct the input error.

Check-digit verification is performed by an input device such as a key punch or cash register. With this form of source data control, all authorized numbers such as customer account numbers or inventory part numbers contain a redundant digit, called the check digit. This additional digit is a numerical function of the other digits in the number. A widely used check-digit procedure is called Modulus 11 and works as in the following example:

(a) Original account number: 83120
(b) Multiply the separate digits by an arithmetic sequence $8 \times (5)$, $3 \times (4)$, $1 \times (3)$, $2 \times (2)$, $0 \times (1)$

(c) Add results: $40 + 12 + 3 + 4 + 0 = 59$.
(d) Subtract 59 from next highest multiple of 11: $66 - 59 = 7$ (check digit)
(e) New account number: 83120-7

If an input error occurs with such an account number, check-digit verification will usually catch the error, and correction can be made prior to processing.

Forms control is another way to establish input validity. Sequentially prenumbered forms provide a useful means of control over source documents because the computer can keep track of which form numbers have not yet been processed. The forms containing these numbers can then be traced in order to ensure that all data that should be processed have been processed. To augment the use of prenumbered forms, it is wise to have the prenumbered forms under the control of someone other than the data entry operator.

Turnaround documents (discussed in Chapter 11) are another means of forms control. Since turnaround documents are outputs of the information system which can later be used as inputs, the data are generally much more accurate than data which must be entered by the data entry operator. This greater reliability provides better internal control.

Programmed Input Controls. These are internal checks within the application programs or the operating system. In many cases these input controls may be contained in a separate program which is run prior to regular processing. When this is done, the errors can be corrected before actual processing begins. Specific self-checking procedures include the following:

Check	Procedure
Parity Check	Adds an extra bit to data to check for the machine loss of a character. Odd and even parity checking were explained in Chapter 3.
Field Check	Checks the characters in a field to ensure they are the correct type (e.g., numeric, alphabetic, alphanumeric).
Validity Check	Matches ID's or codes which have been input against an authorized list maintained within the software itself.
Limit Check	Tests that the numerical amount in a record falls within some predetermined acceptable range.

Sign Check	Determines whether the data in a field have the appropriate arithmetic sign (positive or negative). For example, the number of inventory items received should never be negative.
Reasonableness Check	Tests whether logically related data items are processed. For example, a journal entry which debits capital equipment and credits wages payable would not be reasonable.
Sequence Check	Checks that data are organized in a specified sequence, usually alphabetical or numerical.
Echo Check	Verifies data transmission by echoing back the signal received and comparing it with the data originally sent.
Completeness Check	Verifies that all required data items have been entered.

EDP Auditing Techniques

The auditing function is a powerful tool available to management for assessing the adequacy of internal controls. Large organizations use both internal auditors, who are employees of the firm, and external auditors, who are independent certified public accountants. The AICPA defines internal control as "the plan of organization and all of the coordinate methods and measures adopted within a business to safeguard its assets, check the reliability of its accounting data, promote operational efficiency, and encourage adherence to prescribed managerial goals." They further state:

> The increasing use of computers for processing accounting and other business information has introduced additional problems in reviewing and evaluating internal control for audit purposes, and closely related to the increasing use of computers is the trend toward integrating accounting information required for financial and other operating purposes into coordinated management information systems.[1]

---

[1]Auditing Standards Executive Committee, *Statement on Auditing Standards No. 1: Codification of Auditing Standards and Procedures* (New York: American Institute of Certified Public Accountants, 1973).

An audit is conducted in two parts. Initially, the auditor determines whether the system has adequate internal controls and whether those controls are being used effectively in the computer facility. Based on this evaluation, the auditor determines the extent of testing necessary to assess the reliability of the system and its output. During the second phase of the audit, a sample of items is checked and traced to determine their accuracy. An *audit trail* is used to check and trace sample items. In a manual system, signatures, time and date stamps, initials, and other hard-copy documents are used as an audit trail. In an EDP system the audit trail is substantially altered. One way to design an audit trail into electronic files is to insert a trail in the records in the form of the page number and date of the last account transaction. In Figure 13-6, the audit trail number for S. J. Peters, 17.08.05.3, indicates that the last account transaction was posted on ledger page 17 on August 5, 1983. This information can then be used to help trace the transaction manually.

With the advent of computerized systems, auditors were forced to develop new methods of conducting audits. The two primary approaches used to audit computer systems are auditing "around" the computer and auditing "through" the computer.

Figure 13-6

Example of audit trail used in sales report.

AJAX COMPANY
September Sales
198x

Customer	Quantity	Product Code	Customer Code	Audit Trail
S. J. Peters	150	78142	A280	17.08.05.1
P. S. Brown	17	18001	C023	18.08.06.1
•	•	•	•	•
•	•	•	•	•
•	•	•	•	•

If the auditor is confident of control reliability, an approach frequently used is known as *auditing around the computer* system (Figure 13-7). With this approach, auditors ignore (work *around*) the computer and its programs, performing their audits based on printed records and system outputs. For example, if an audit of savings accounts indicates that there are satisfactory controls for calculating interest and detecting errors, a tape of interest payments is suitable for audit purposes. The assumption underlying this approach is that if sample output is correctly obtained from system input, then the processing is reliable.

Figure 13-7

Auditing "around" the computer.

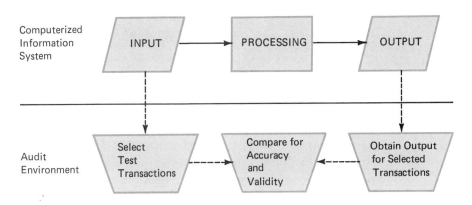

When *auditing through the computer* system (Figure 13-8), an auditor is concerned with whether or not there are adequate controls that are operating properly. This approach uses the computer itself to verify the adequacy of system controls. For a savings account audit, a statistical sample of individual records would be taken from the interest file and compared to inputs, and each sample record would be verified manually.

Two primary tools have been developed to aid auditors in auditing through the computer. They include the test-deck approach and generalized audit software packages.

The *test-deck approach* allows the auditor to check various controls and processing logic within the system through the use of hypothetical or test

Figure 13-8

Auditing "through" the computer.

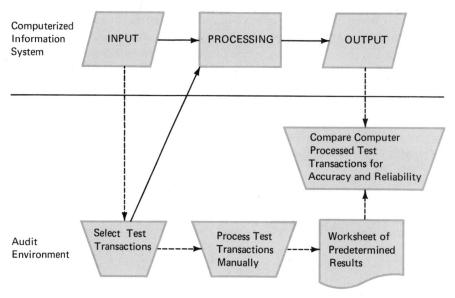

transactions. Prior to the test run, the auditor determines what the processing results should be. These expected results are then compared to actual system outputs. This process is very similar to the testing and debugging performed by the applications programmer prior to system implementation.

To implement the test-deck approach, the auditor must have a thorough understanding of the program being tested so that useful hypothetical data can be developed and correct system responses can be determined. The major drawback of the test-deck approach is that the test transactions must not affect the company's actual records. Therefore, test transactions must either be reversed following the test or the test must be run against a copy of the master file.

Generalized audit software packages are prewritten programs that the auditor can adapt to specific computer systems. These packages can be used to perform a variety of standard audit procedures with the aid of the computer. Some of the functions that generalized audit software packages automatically perform are data editing, statistical sampling, file manipulation, and report generation. These capabilities can be used in various combinations to facilitate a more thorough, complete audit than would be possible manually. Such packages provide the auditor with a valuable tool for evaluating the accuracy of data maintained by the information system. In addition, the auditor is freed from menial work and saves time in the completion of an audit. Simple audit packages can be used with little programming knowledge, but sophisticated packages require programming competency.

SECURITY AND CONTROLS IN THE FUTURE

The role of the auditor has traditionally been confined to review of internal controls and assurance of data validity. However, as we have previously noted, there is a movement toward involving auditors in the systems design process. The primary argument in favor of this new trend is that auditors could help ensure that control features are initially built into information systems, not added after deficiencies become apparent. Auditor involvement in the systems development cycle is traced in Figure 13-9.

Whether the auditor becomes a member of the systems development team or not, it is important to understand that controls are not the sole responsibility

PHASE I	Problem Recognition
PHASE II	Feasibility Study *Defines and inputs control requirements
PHASE III	Detail System Analysis *Defines specific control criteria
PHASE IV	System Design *Designs control procedures
PHASE V	Programming Activities *Programs specific controls
PHASE VI	Implementation of the System *Verifies control procedures
PHASE VII	Evaluation and Follow-up *Periodically re-evaluates control procedures

Figure 13-9

Auditor involvement* in the systems development cycle.

of the auditor. Instead, EDP controls should be a shared responsibility among all concerned parties — top management, system users, EDP personnel, and the auditor. External to the company, security and control should also be a concern to computer manufacturers and software developers.

Computer manufacturers are taking additional responsibility for security and control by increasing the level of security built into operating systems. Technology is also moving to find new ways of preventing unauthorized use of terminals through such techniques as signature analysis and voice input. However, no security program is ever complete. Management must continually evaluate systems security and EDP controls to determine shortcomings and changes in the environment.

SUMMARY

As the number of organizations using EDP systems increases, so does the threat of security violations. These security breaches include erasure, theft, misplacement, copying, and unauthorized access.

Risk management deals with the development and utilization of various security techniques to protect EDP system integrity. Risk-management techniques address threats to both hardware and software. Hardware security deals with computer assets and capital equipment, while software security includes the application programs, the computer operating system, and the database management system.

Techniques used for hardware protection include fire prevention, computer center location, personnel badges, electronic identification keys, and intrusion-detection systems. Techniques for protecting software include access controls, user authorization, and data encryption. File protection techniques used for data security include plastic file protection rings, file labels, and the "grandfather-father-son" concept.

Penetration of computer systems is accomplished by such techniques as data diddling, Trojan horses, superzapping, logic bombs, and program trapdoors. Organizational and application controls help guard against penetration. Internal system checks such as parity checks, field checks, sign checks, and validity checks are available on most computer systems.

Independent audits can be accomplished either around or through a computer system. Such audits verify that reasonable controls are in place and are used. They also assess the reliability of the data maintained by the information system. Auditor involvement is important during the design of information systems to ensure the initial establishment of proper controls.

TERMS

Systems security
Risk management
Hardware security
Mantrap
Software security
Data encryption
File protection ring
Header label
Trailer label
Grandfather-father-son concept
Vulnerabilities
Penetration
Data diddling
Trojan horse
Salami technique
Superzapping
Trapdoors
Logic bomb
Data leakage
Wiretapping
EDP controls

Organizational controls
Application controls
Financial total
Hash total
Record count
Check-digit verification
Parity check
Field check
Validity check
Limit check
Sign check
Reasonableness check
Sequence check
Echo check
Completeness check
Audit trail
Auditing around the computer
Auditing through the computer
Test-deck approach
Generalized audit software packages

QUESTIONS

1. Which of the many dangers to organizations using EDP systems do you consider to be most important? Why?
2. What types of organizations are faced with threats to their EDP systems?
3. What are the major tasks of a risk manager?

4. Why is effective hardware security so important? How can such security be realized?

5. What is data encryption? What characteristics should an encryption scheme have?

6. Which penetration methods require computer programming expertise?

7. Since security breaches always involve human beings, how can company personnel aid in organizational controls?

8. What are two approaches to auditing computer systems? Which do you feel is most effective? Why?

9. Distinguish between a financial total, a hash total, and a record count.

10. What should the role of the auditor be in system design?

11. How does the grandfather-father-son concept provide for file protection?

12. Why are internal checks referred to as self-checking devices?

ARTICLE

Dramatic Crimes the Computer Helped Commit

The case: Wells Fargo
The date: 1979-81
The take: $21.3 million

The modus operandi

L. Ben Lewis, an operations officer for the 11th largest U.S. bank, allegedly produced bogus deposits in an account at one branch belonging to a boxing promotion outfit. He did this by using the bank's computerized interbranch account settlement process to withdraw funds from a different branch. To keep the computer from flagging the imbalance, Lewis created new fraudulent credits to cover the withdrawal — and allegedly kept the rollover going for two years. Lewis denies the charges.

The case: Morgan Guaranty
The date: 1980
The take: Zero

The New York bank reportedly accepted as legitimate a bogus telex from the Central Bank of Nigeria transferring $21 million. In response to subsequent instructions, the money was routed electronically to three banks. When an attempt was made to wire the funds to a new $50 account in a Santa Ana (Calif.) bank, the transfer was refused. This triggered inquiries by the other banks. The Nigerian bank branded the first message as fraudulent, and the funds were never collected.

The case: Dalton School
The date: 1980
The take: Zero

Using a classroom terminal, teenage students at Manhattan's private Dalton School allegedly dialed into a Canadian network of corporate and institutional data systems. No funds were diverted — but damage was done to data files.

The case: Security Pacific
The date: 1978
The take: $10.3 million

Stanley Mark Rifkin, who had been a computer consultant for the Los Angeles bank, visited the bank's wire transfer room, where he obtained the electronic funds transfer code. Later, posing as a

continued

branch manager, he called from a public telephone and used the code to send money to a Swiss account. By the time the bank's computers flagged the fraud, he had flown to Switzerland, converted the funds into diamonds, and returned to the U.S. Only when he boasted of the feat was he identified, convicted, and sentenced to prison.

The case: Union Dime
The date: 1973
The take: $1.2 million

A teller at the New York City savings bank skimmed money from large new accounts by making a simple computerized correction entry. His embezzlement was discovered when police investigated a gambling parlor he frequented and questioned the source of his betting money.

The case: Equity Funding
The date: 1973
The take: $27.25 million

The insurance holding company used computers to create phony insurance policies that were later sold to reinsurers. Of the company's assets, $143.4 million were found to be fictitious, of which an estimated 19% was the result of computer fraud.

DISCUSSION QUESTIONS

1. Relate the concept of risk management to these six computer crimes.
2. Which penetration methods are illustrated here? Specify controls that might have been used to protect these organizations.

APPLICATION

Protecting the Lifeblood of DP

Sunday, July 12, 1981, began just like any other day in San Diego except for one small detail: sometime between 5:00 and 5:30 a.m. an arsonist struck the third floor of the San Diego Blood Bank at 440 Upas Street. There was no question that the fire was not accidental. According to the San Diego Fire Department, the fire broke out simultaneously in dispersed locations. Lynn Stedd, the community relations coordinator for the blood bank, was notified of the fire at 6:00 a.m.

There were several immediate problems. Most important was how to get the blood drawing operation going again. Atlas Hotels, Inc., donated the San Diego Town and Country Convention Center, and by 3:00 p.m., the entire operation had been moved and was up and running. It was also imperative that the donor retrieval program get back on its feet. This is a system of cross-referencing individuals in the community by their blood types so that, if large quantities of a specific type of blood were needed, the proper individuals could be called immediately. Type-specific donor retrievals account for approximately one-half of the blood bank's in-house donors.

The third floor of the blood bank was closed for investigation. By this time,

Ramona Walker, comptroller for the blood bank, was on the scene surveying the damage in the third floor computer room. The damage was total. The Basic Four 700 was, of course, inoperable. The master packs were in their storage racks, melted down like so many droopy ice cream cones. "At least," Walker said, "we thought we had the previous day's backup packs stored in an offsite location so, at most, we had to redo a day's processing.

"Imagine our horror when we found the backup packs near the master packs and melted down as well. Through some fantastic piece of bad luck, the arson happened on the one day when our backup procedures were not followed."

The normal backup procedure involved having a courier pick up the backup packs from the offsite location and deliver them to the blood bank. Copying the master packs over to backup took approximately one hour. Then the backup packs were packed in carrying cases for later pickup and transferred to offsite storage.

There was valuable data trapped on the disk packs, both master and backup,

continued

and no way to get at it. "We did have one circumstance in our favor," Walker recalled. "Luckily the previous Friday, July 10, had been the end of our financial quarter, and a number of reports, detail and summary, had been run. Those accounting records had been stored in my office and were smoke- and water-damaged, but they were still readable. So at least we had a definite cut-off point."

To salvage the packs, Walker called Basic Decisions, the turnkey vendor who had sold the hardware and software to the blood bank. They, in turn, called the Sorbus Division of MAI Corporation, which is a maintenance service group. Sorbus referred them to Data Maintenance, a preventive maintenance organization which cleans packs as part of its total maintenance program. By the time she drove to Basic Decisions, they were all there waiting for her. They had called a consultant, David Brown, who specializes in data recovery techniques. The disk packs were driven to his facility in Los Angeles. It took him two days to reprocess the disk surfaces well enough to try to retrieve the data.

Bob Zellert of Sorbus worked with David Brown to make sure that all conditions were as perfect as possible for the recovery process. The site (donated by Basic Decisions) temperature was set at 64 degrees Fahrenheit, and the disk packs were tried. They were so misshapen that they wouldn't fit on the disk drives, and it fell to the consultants to try to modify the disk drive to accept the packs. After a lot of rearranging, the disks finally yielded the trapped data—the accounting master approximately 85 to 90 percent of its original data, and the donor master approximately 70 percent.

From the reports and other sources, the blood bank personnel were able to put together enough information to recover the majority of the files. In a remarkably short time they were back in full operation.

DISCUSSION QUESTIONS

1. Are the backup procedures used by the San Diego Blood Bank adequate or inadequate? Explain.
2. If data on the master and backup files were completely lost, what would be the impact on blood drawing activities?

CHAPTER 14

TELECOMMUNICATIONS

CHAPTER OBJECTIVES

In this chapter you will learn:

1. How computer technology and communication technology are merging.
2. The role of distributed data processing.
3. About various components of data transmission.
4. About the trade-off between cable and fiber optics.
5. Switching techniques and network structures.
6. What is meant by protocols.
7. The impact of satellite technology.

THE DEVELOPMENT OF TELECOMMUNICATIONS

The development of telecommunications is an exciting recent occurrence. Both communications and computer technology have had a tremendous impact on society. It has only been within the last decade that the power of the computer has become generally available through telecommunications. It is clear that the merger of these two technologies will change the way business is done, create new markets, and alter the nature of the work experience.

It is estimated that over 20 million business meetings are held every working day in the United States, with seven million meetings devoted to information transfer. Business travel accounts for 90 percent of all the air travel in this country, and it can be reasonably assumed that most of these trips are taken for meetings of one kind or another. Telecommunications makes such meetings possible without travel: conferencing may be handled by voice (telephone), video (television), or data (computer) transmission. In addition to reducing the need for business travel, teleconferencing has the advantage of allowing a larger number of employees to participate in organizational matters. While telephones have been available since the turn of the century, both video and computer conferencing are current phenomena with great potential.

Computer conferencing doesn't require special facilities; it only requires a computer terminal at each location (Figure 14-1). As few as two individuals or as many as hundreds can participate. Participants access a common computer, and responses are quick and efficient on their individual terminals.

How does such a computer teleconference actually take place? Typically, a manager circulates the proposed agenda among the conferees for their input on the major discussion points. Participants may be asked to prepare statements on the different topics to be discussed. After all contributions have been entered onto the computer, comments, questions, objections, debate, and votes may occur. Experience with computer teleconferencing has shown potential to improve informational decision making in a firm.

Telecommunications is simply the transfer of information over distance. A more sophisticated view of the function of telecommunications is the concept of *distributed data processing.** This is a technique in which both central (or "host") computers and local (or "remote") processors are used to distribute an

*See pages 434-439 for a special section on distributed data processing.

Figure 14-1

Computer conference participants may be located throughout the world.

organization's data processing workload. This distribution tends to put the power of computers close to the source of the need—the user. When geographically dispersed users participate in this technique, a data communications network is used to form a direct link between the dispersed computing power and the host computing power. In all situations, overall system control and coordination in a distributing environment must remain centralized to some extent.

To develop needed links for distributed data processing, circuits or channels are needed to physically connect separate users. Common circuits must be shared, and specific network designs are needed to deal with the physical layout of channels and switches to allow worldwide connections. To allow Brand X equipment to communicate with Brand Y devices, a technique called protocols is used. As we shall see, protocols determine the ground rules or common guidelines that all telecommunications must follow in network manipulations.

The goal of business organizations is to maximize the benefits and minimize the costs of utilizing telecommunications networks. In order to meet these goals, management must consider transmission methods, hardware and software possibilities, and the importance of privacy, security, and integrity of information. The following are some specific objectives of telecommunications in an organization:

— To provide access to specialized hardware and software that is not cost justifiable for in-house installation.
— To transfer data from sources to processing points.
— To distribute processing equipment in order to allow communications flexibility.
— To promote timely information (voice and data) for managerial decision making.
— To reduce information costs.
— To rapidly disseminate data through the network.
— To increase control of information, an important asset.

DATA TRANSMISSION

Two types of transmission are available for communicating processed data—analog and digital. Most communication lines are designed to carry analog signals. While it is physically possible to transmit data in a digital manner (e. g., CPU and disk storage), digital transmission is rarely used for telecommunications. Therefore, a technique must be used to represent a digital signal on an analog carrier. The process of modifying the carrier signal to transmit digital information is called "modulation." When the transmitted signal is received, the information must be reconverted into digital data. This process is called "demodulation." Three types of transmission modulation are illustrated in Figure 14-2. These conversions between digital data and analog data are handled by a device called a *modem,* an acronym for *mo*dulator and *dem*odulator (see Figure 14-3). Modems allow distributed data processing systems to utilize diverse equipment and various speed lines in the network configurations. Figure 14-4 illustrates the location of modems in the telecommunications function. Other important transmission components are communication processors and concentrators.

A *communication processor* is a digital computer that has been programmed to perform one or more communication functions. The objectives of the processor are to control lines, assemble and edit data, control errors, and

Figure 14-2

Three types of transmission modulation.

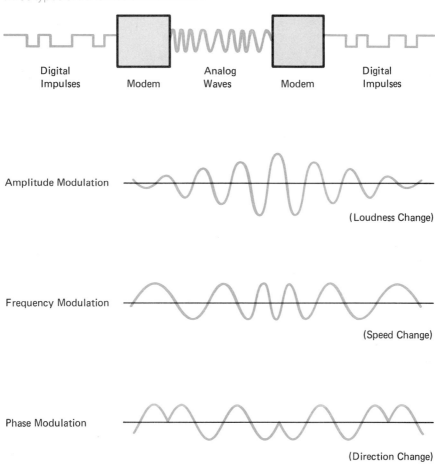

Digital   Analog   Digital
Impulses   Modem   Waves   Modem   Impulses

Amplitude Modulation

(Loudness Change)

Frequency Modulation

(Speed Change)

Phase Modulation

(Direction Change)

otherwise handle messages. Since communication terminal devices operate at relatively low and varied speeds, a *concentrator* (also called a multiplexer) is needed at each location to handle all data transfer on one line. For example, five terminals in Cleveland operate at 300 bits per second (bps), while another five terminals in Cincinnati operate at 110 bps. Since a typical voice-grade telephone line can easily handle 2400 bps, it is possible to have many low-speed terminals transmit over the same line simultaneously.

Figure 14-3

This modem can handle speeds ranging from 300 to 1200 bps (bits per second).

Hayes Microcomputer Products Inc.

Channels

Transmission channels are the physical link or medium that exists between two endpoints. Transmission may be handled in a simplex, half-duplex, or full-duplex mode. *Simplex* means that data can travel in only one direction on the line. *Half-duplex* systems allow data to be transmitted in both directions, but only one direction at a time. The *full-duplex* mode allows data to be transmitted in both directions at the same time. These transmission modes are illustrated in Figure 14-5.

In typical distributed data processing systems, the transmission channel is easily identified because it uses the wires provided by the telephone company.

Figure 14-4

Location of modems in the telecommunications function.

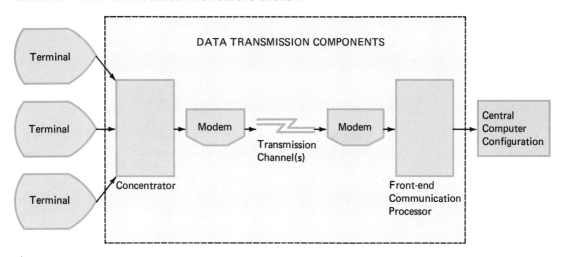

The characteristics of the channel that assists in controlling the distributed terminals include bandwidth, flow control, transmission speed, asynchronous transmission, and synchronous transmission.

Bandwidth. Bandwidth is a measurement of the width of a range of frequencies. Frequencies vary over a wide range that includes acoustics, radio, infrared, light, ultraviolet, x-rays, gamma rays, and cosmic rays. Controlling the bandwidth enables data to occupy specified space through the channel.

Flow Control. Data are transported by electromagnetic devices. Electrical currents are either direct (DC) or alternating (AC). Through the use of basic flow control, data are directed to the destination. During a typical communications session, terminals change roles from transmitter to receiver, and vice versa.

Transmission Speed. Transmission speed is an important characteristic of the transmission channel. It is impossible to send 19,200 bps through a channel capable of handling only 9,600 bps. Transmission channels must be matched initially or through the use of other equipment.

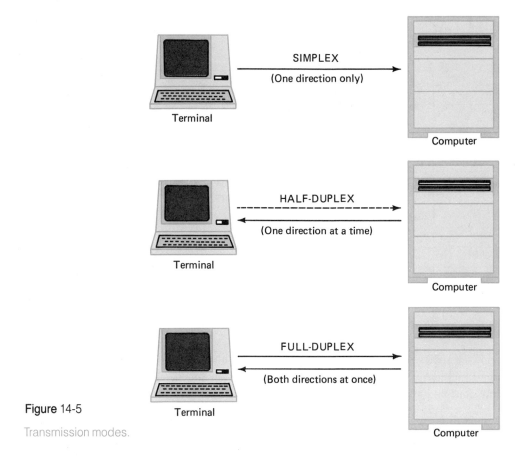

Figure 14-5

Transmission modes.

Asynchronous Transmission. *Asynchronous* transmission is referred to as start-stop transmission since characters are sent at any time that it is convenient to the receiving device. In other words, transmission is synchronized by a start-and-stop bit.

Synchronous Transmission. *Synchronous* transmission is used to transfer whole blocks of characters in a timed sequence. Consequently, the equipment required for this mode of transmission is relatively sophisticated. The use of synchronous transmission allows for a higher volume of data to be transferred through the channel.

There are three major types of channel equipment or transmission media— wire cable, microwave, and fiber optics. *Wire cable* operates on the analog principle and is currently the most common form of transmission channel. Coaxial cable is an improved, insulated form of wire cable. Cable has the following advantages:

— Extensive cable networks are currently available.
— The technology is standardized.
— AT&T supports cable within the United States.

Cable also has some disadvantages:

— Electrical interference is a problem.
— Cumbersome physical links may be needed.

Microwave is also an analog type of transmission, but unlike wire cable, microwave is sent through the atmosphere as in radio or TV transmission. Consequently, microwave must be transmitted in a straight line between two points. This "line-of-sight" constraint necessitates the use of repeater towers for long distances or rugged terrain (Figure 14-6).

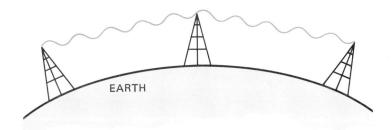

EARTH

Figure 14-6

Microwave transmission uses line-of-sight towers for terrestrial data transfer.

On a worldwide basis, satellites may also be used for microwave transmission. If three satellites are placed in a geosynchronous orbit (traveling at the same speed as the earth) 22,300 miles from the equator, data can be sent or received between the three satellites and any land-based location (Figure 14-7).

Microwave transmission has the following advantages:

— There are potential cost benefits over wire cable in many applications.
— Microwaves provide a high degree of flexibility because there is no need for a physical link between transmission points as there is with cable.
— Microwave transmission is relatively error free.

Figure 14-7

Geosynchronous satellites are capable of accessing any earth station.

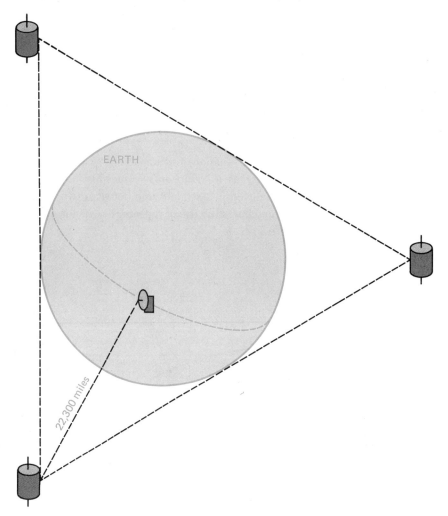

Disadvantages of microwave transmission include the following:

— Microwaves must be transmitted line-of-sight.
— Approximately one-half second is needed to transmit to satellite and back to ground station, a delay that may impair data output.
— Initial costs of ground stations and satellites are high.

Fiber optics is a new technology based on digital transmission theory. With fiber optics, light impulses travel down clear, flexible tubing (Figure 14-8). Fiber optic tubing is typically about ¹⁄₁₀ the diameter of wire cable. The disadvantage of this small size is that the tubing is difficult to splice without affecting the path of light beams. Fiber optic light impulses tend to lose signal strength

Figure 14-8

These fiber optic cables contain 144 glass fibers for transmitting voice, television, and data signals.

Courtesy of Bell Laboratories

over distance, and repeaters are needed to read weak, incoming light impulses and send out new, strong impulses. This phenomenon is known as *attenuation* and, to a lesser extent, applies to wire cable and microwave as well. Fiber optics is rapidly declining in cost and is regarded as the telecommunications medium of the future for short distances (100 feet to 10 miles).

Fiber optic advantages include the following:

— Digital EDP data can be handled without conversion to analog.
— A high rate of data transmission is possible with few errors.
— The small size and flexibility of fiber optics tubing allows easy installation.
— Fiber optics is not affected by electrical interference.

Networks

Transmission channels are utilized by specifically defined communication networks. It is important to note that networks are an entity separate from the computer and the other equipment linked to the network. By definition, a *computer network* is a collection of computers and terminal devices connected by a communication system. Objectives of a computer network are data collection, data processing, and data dispersal. More precisely, a computer network allows file sharing, device sharing, program sharing, and program segmentation.

A *local network* is one that serves a well-defined and generally self-enclosed area. A network that runs through an entire small office building is called a local network. Most local networks have communication stations that are physically linked by a cable, usually within 1000 feet.

A network that covers a wider area usually communicates with each station by standard telephone lines, a dedicated phone line, or microwave relays. Because the cost of using and maintaining a *wide-area network* is great, its use is generally restricted to larger corporations.

Networks share files, devices, and programs. File sharing permits data to be exchanged among remote systems and accessed just as if the data were stored locally. Device sharing allows a remote device to be used locally. This is typical of timesharing applications. In program sharing, a remote program may be transmitted to a local site for loading and execution. A more sophisticated version of program sharing is known as program segmentation. With program segmentation, programs are broken down into independent tasks on different CPU's, and the outputs of these various CPU's are then combined into one integrated output.

Network Structures

In a general sense, all network designs comprise nodes and links. *Nodes* refer to the endpoints of a network and consist of VDT's, printers, or other physical devices. *Links* are the transmission channels that connect nodes. With these two basic tools, the geometrical arrangement of a telecommunication system can be defined. This arrangement is known as *network topology*. Six common network topologies are point-to-point, multidrop, star, hierarchy, ring, and distributed (see Figure 14-9).

A *point-to-point* system (also referred to as private or exclusive lines) may consist of only a single link and two nodes. The nodes are frequently a CPU and a data entry terminal.

Multidrop lines provide for an inexpensive alternative to individual point-to-point links. In this configuration, users must share one link.

A *star* (centralized) network allows each node to have a point-to-point link to the central processor. If the host processor fails, A cannot contact B.

Hierarchy (tree) networks are excellent for data distribution from a large host processor. However, the configuration is relatively inefficient since A must traverse all levels of the network to communicate with B.

Ring configurations offer alternative routing. If E and F were to fail, A could still contact B through C and D.

A *distributed* network may consist of many links and nodes in an infinite number of designs. In a fully distributed network every set of nodes may communicate directly with every other set through a single link.

Computer networks route messages from source to destination by means of three techniques: circuit switching, message switching, and broadcasting. *Circuit switching* is the most common form of switching, since the public telephone network is utilized. Here a physical connection is made for the duration of an information transfer. During this session, the physical line is tied up between the sender and the receiver. The physical telephone line is called the circuit, and the total connect time is called the holding time of the session.

Message switching allows the session to be broken into individual messages which are independently transmitted. Each message has an address that determines where each node is to forward the message. If the network is busy, a node can store the message, attend to other tasks, and then forward the message when an open connection is established. Message switching is often referred to as store and forward. Since there are many possible transmission paths, subsequent messages may take different routes, but all must end up at the final

Figure 14-9

Network topologies.

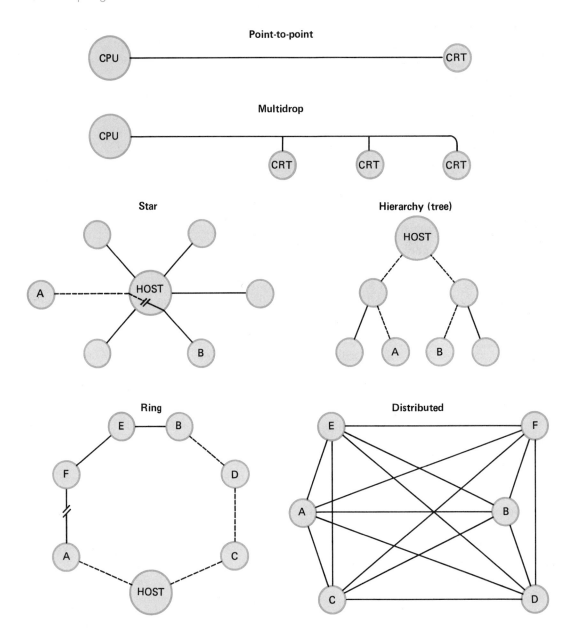

receiving node. In large networks, minicomputers are used for receiving, storing, and forwarding messages.

Packet switching is an important type of message switching in which all messages must be a standard size. Constraining messages in this way reduces the activities of a node, allowing for greater speed and accuracy of the network. A packet is a fixed block size (such as 128 characters) that is used as the standard unit of transfer over the message system.

Not used as often, *broadcasting* is a system in which all messages are broadcast on the same medium (perhaps a satellite). If a satellite is used to broadcast to multiple ground stations, a filter at each station identifies its unique destination address, thus allowing message reception. Since messages may become unclear or lost during periods of high transmission activity, each received message must be acknowledged.

Network Protocols

In order to allow communications equipment to recognize and manipulate messages, network protocols are necessary. A *protocol* is a set of conventions governing format and control of data. This allows separate users and equipment to access a common network. Protocols are concerned specifically with:

— Physical interfaces (equipment)
— Logical data links (software)
— Network and routing procedures
— Performance and reliability parameters
— Information acknowledgment procedures.

Protocols require special characters at the beginning and end of a transmission frame. For example, the protocol shown in Figure 14-10 uses special characters to indicate start-of-header, start-of-text, and end-of-text.

Because of the many tasks protocols must control, they are conceptualized by layers. Layered protocols reflect the principle of structured design whereby a problem is subdivided into smaller and smaller modules. A typical telecommunications system incorporates five layers (or levels) of protocols (Figure 14-11).

Satellite Transmission

An interesting topic in telecommunications technology is satellite transmission. Satellite transmission is becoming more and more competitive among

Figure 14-10

A popular protocol called bisync uses several types of characters for text transmission.

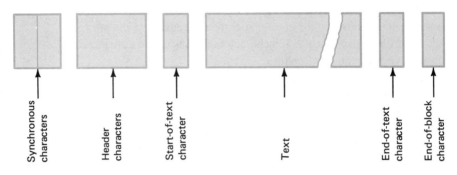

Synchronous characters | Header characters | Start-of-text character | Text | End-of-text character | End-of-block character

common carriers. There are currently a dozen communications satellites in orbit, and the number is expected to double by 1986. Where satellites were previously used only for television and voice carriage, they are now attracting business applications. But satellites cannot take over the data transmission field because they must compete with entrenched terrestrial networks run by AT&T and other common carriers.

Intelsat, an international consortium formed to develop a global network of common satellites, launched its first satellite in 1965. It was 28.4 inches in diameter, weighed 85 pounds in final orbit, and could carry 240 voice circuits or one television channel. Today the Intelsat system connects 260 earth stations in 130 countries. Current Intelsat satellites are 51 feet wide and weigh 2,286 pounds in orbit. They can handle 12,000 simultaneous conversations plus two TV channels. At present they handle about two-thirds of all trans-oceanic traffic.

Satellites have transmission limitations. In order to be geosynchronous, satellites must orbit the equator at 22,300 miles. Any signal making the earth-to-satellite-to-earth journey travels more than 44,000 miles. At the speed of light, the round trip takes about a half-second. While this delay has little effect on video or voice transfers, it is especially important to data transmission. Since machines interact at much greater speeds than humans, these delays may seriously degrade data throughput. Without proper control devices, satellite response time can be worse than for land-based alternatives.

LEVEL 5 APPLICATION PROTOCOL
(User level procedures, formats, operators, devices)

LEVEL 4 SYSTEM PROTOCOL
(Packet or message priorities)

LEVEL 3 NETWORK PROTOCOL
(Block or packet structure, message format)

LEVEL 2 LINK PROTOCOL
(Data flow, control, termination)

LEVEL 1 PHYSICAL PROTOCOL
(Mechanical interface)

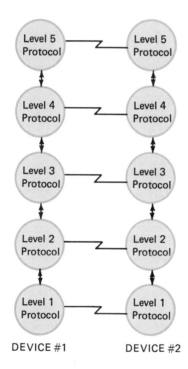

DEVICE #1   DEVICE #2

Figure 14-11

Levels of protocols in a typical telecommunications system.

Four carriers have domestic communications satellites in orbit. These carriers are Comsat General Corporation, Satellite Business Systems (SBS), Western Union, and RCA American Communications. SBS is a joint venture of IBM, Aetna Life & Casualty, and Communication Satellite Corporation and is the only carrier that caters almost exclusively to business communications. Voice and data transmission make up most of the traffic of current SBS users. However, Allstate Insurance Company is planning to use SBS for satellite teleconferencing. Other types of business applications are sure to proliferate in the near future.

DISTRIBUTED DATA PROCESSING (DDP) FOR MICROCOMPUTERS*

What Is Distributed Data Processing?

Distributed data processing (DDP) is a technique whereby physically separate computers share resources in their respective information processing functions. This means that a number of computers can use the same disk drives, printers, and other peripherals, rather than giving each computer these peripherals. This becomes an important advantage when a large database is required by two different computers. Instead of using separate disk drives, the system is set up so that both computers can access the same database.

The basic difference between ordinary multi-user systems (called shared-logic systems) and distributed processing is that users in a typical system share the same processing power, whereas DDP spreads the processing power among the users. This may sound like a trivial distinction, but in practice it is an important one. When a user of a shared-logic system initiates a large job, all other users are affected to some degree. When the same job is initiated on a distributed system, it will have no effect on the other computers in the system.

Distributed processing is often implemented by linking minicomputers to mainframes, or by linking mainframes together, with each computer having a number of users. In these types of systems, there is still some sharing of computing power; but in distributed systems using microcomputers the sharing of computing power is eliminated. Because of this, DDP with microcomputers might be considered the ultimate form of DDP.

A distributed microcomputer system can be implemented at two different levels. The simple level of distribution implies that all storage is at a central

*Based on a paper contributed by Gordon Koury, a Colorado State University student majoring in information systems, and used with his permission.

location—one or more centralized disks that are shared by all users. The other level of distribution, which we will call extended memory, has storage capabilities at the terminal computer—a built-in or add-on diskette drive, for example. Figure 14-12 illustrates these two levels of distribution. A system implemented with extended memory reduces centralized storage requirements if some of the users have programs or information that other users of the system do not need, as the code or data can be stored on diskette rather than in the central storage unit. For example, with a distributed microcomputer system, a firm having only one secretary who does some bookkeeping and typed correspondence can provide the secretary with a microcomputer that has a diskette drive. In this manner, the secretary can use a word processing program stored on a diskette to minimize central storage requirements, as well as access the corporate database to perform bookkeeping chores.

Figure 14-12

Extended memory systems: (a) simple network with extended memory; (b) star host-oriented with extended memory.

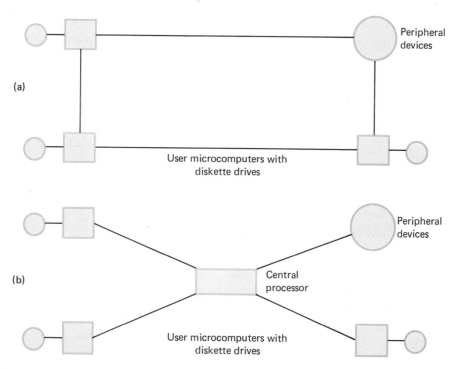

Telecommunications capabilities for microcomputers will develop rapidly in the future since the larger EDP companies have started to produce the hardware and software necessary to link microcomputers. Hewlett-Packard now has a communications link to connect microcomputers to the HP3000 minicomputer, while IBM has an asynchronous communications adapter and program for its Personal Computer. Apple, Radio Shack, and even the inexpensive Osborne microcomputer have developed I/O ports to allow communications for their respective computers.

Protocols

The major functions of a protocol in microcomputer telecommunications are to meet security requirements, establish identification, and facilitate the order of transmission. In a microcomputer system protocol generally has to be done manually or be programmed, whereas large systems may include protocol functions in the hardware. All communication tasks could be accomplished without protocol, but proceeding without protocol would be like telephoning a person who speaks only a foreign language and teaching him or her English in order to carry on a conversation.

Security provisions are also important to small businesses. For instance, if management does not want secretaries who use word processing on the system to have access to salary information contained in the system, some provision for security must be made. In a more general sense, identification of users is vital to a distributed system. Imagine what would happen if the computer sent out requested information without knowing whom to send it to!

Transmission order refers to the fact that the computers of a distributed system must know when to transmit and receive, and whether the transmission is data or control information. If two users are trying to send information at the same time, for instance, neither one can be accommodated (unless the communications are of the "full-duplex" type, a technology that is usually too expensive for a microcomputer system). Data transmissions are also meaningless if the computer cannot distinguish between a command and data. In summary, computer protocols must have explicit rules on the structure and order of transmissions.

Advantages of Distributed Microcomputing

Probably the most outstanding advantage of distributed processing is the potential for system growth. New users can be added simply by plugging in more microcomputers. Best of all, these additions have little effect on existing users; remember that adding new users to shared-logic systems immediately slows the response time for other users. Microsystems usually handle anywhere from 2 to 250 users. A shared-logic system with similar capabilities would cost approximately $500,000 (printers, terminals, storage, and software extra, of course), while a microsystem set up for two users could be purchased for about $25,000.

An important characteristic of distributed processing is its adaptability, especially in extended-memory and complex distributed microsystems. New functions can be added to the system simply by purchasing program diskettes and modifying them to fit the system. When new functions are put up on shared-logic systems, more disk drives must be put up, or storage available to users is reduced. Distributed processing also allows more than one function to be carried out at any given time, a feature found only on the most expensive shared-logic systems.

Another significant advantage of DDP is user independence. Unless the entire telecommunication network crashes, the failure of one portion of the system will not bring down the rest of the system. User independence may not eliminate system downtime completely, but it certainly decreases it.

Who Should Use a Distributed Microcomputer System?

Even though the advantages seem significant, a distributed microsystem isn't for everyone. A Mom & Pop grocery store that wants a computer for inventory control and for Junior to play "Pac-Man" probably wouldn't even consider distributed data processing. On the other hand, large multinational corporations probably won't implement DDP with micros. Characteristics of a business that could benefit from a distributed system of microcomputers include the following:

— The system has many users who need to access much of the same information.
— The business is growing rapidly.
— Up-to-the-minute information on inventory is required.
— Users perform varied functions.
— Functions required on the system don't need large processing power (at their present stage of development microcomputers cannot handle large linear programming or simulation problems quickly enough for most businesses).

An example of a business conforming to these requirements is a wholesaler who deals in perishable or other rush-order goods. The salespeople key in orders as they come in; their microcomputers check for errors and then update the inventory file immediately. Purchasing can then make accurate decisions on inventory control because the figures in the file represent the state of inventory at the time the information was requested—not yesterday, last week, or last month. Figure 14-13 illustrates this type of distributed microcomputer system. While this system is only one example of a distributed microcomputer system, it illustrates the possibilities of DDP technology.

Figure 14-13

A model distributed microcomputer system.

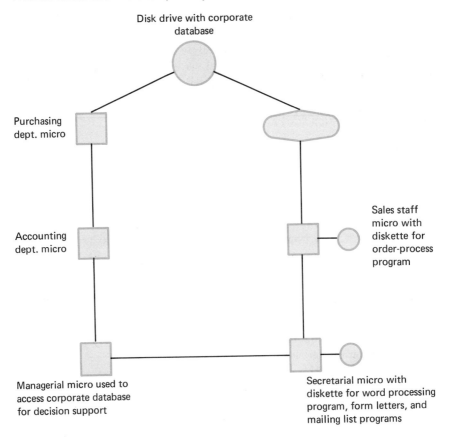

Disk drive with corporate
database

Purchasing
dept. micro

Accounting
dept. micro

Sales staff
micro with
diskette for
order-process
program

Managerial micro used to
access corporate database
for decision support

Secretarial micro with
diskette for word processing
program, form letters, and
mailing list programs

With the price of micros decreasing and capabilities increasing, distributed microcomputing should continue to increase in popularity. While the speed of micros is still too low for many applications, and microcomputer software is scarce at the present time, these problems will be overcome as the technology develops and established companies like IBM enter the micro field.

THE FUTURE OF TELECOMMUNICATIONS

Technologically, the future of telecommunications has never been brighter. The Carterfone decision of the Federal Communications Commission in 1969 was significant, because this ruling allowed customer-owned equipment to be connected to telephone lines. Consequently, independent data communication companies were allowed to compete in the telecommunications market. In 1982, AT&T and the Department of Justice settled their long-standing antitrust suit. This settlement further promoted Ma Bell's change from a utility to a competitive communications supplier. Today new market areas center around automated office systems, home information, and desktop computer developments. The future of telecommunications is one of opportunity and challenge.

SUMMARY

Business organizations are growing in size and complexity. Large firms are increasingly using terminals and small computers to distribute their data processing activities. Transferring information over distance is a concern of local firms as well as multinational organizations. To meet this expanding need, computer technology has recently merged with communications technology to form a new discipline called telecommunications.

Managers must consider new data transmission techniques and procedures. Modems convert digital data to analog signals for transmission, and concentrators monitor incoming and outgoing messages. Data channels may range from simplex, where data is restricted to one direction only, to full-duplex, where data can be transferred in both directions at once. Asynchronous transmission handles strings of characters, while synchronous channels are capable of handling blocks of characters. Channel technology is also a function of bandwidth frequencies, flow control, and transmission speed.

The three major types of transmission media are wire cable, microwave, and fiber optics. Coaxial cable is a widely used medium, but fiber optics is proliferating in local networks, and satellites are handling more microwave transmission. Although satellites have been commonly used for television and voice carriage, today's communication carriers such as Satellite Business Systems emphasize data transfer.

Computers and other devices are linked into local or wide-area networks. Six common network topologies are point-to-point, multidrop, star, hierarchy, ring, and distributed. Computer networks use circuit switching, message switching, or broadcasting to route messages. Packet switching is an important type of message switching in which all messages are a standard size. Protocols describe format and control of data transmission over common networks.

Computer conferencing is a promising new application of telecommunications. Other business and home applications are expected to proliferate in the future.

Distributed data processing has caused increased interest in the role of microcomputers as linked communications devices. Small businesses should consider the user independence and cost advantages of distributed microsystems as communication networks.

TERMS

Telecommunications

Distributed data processing

Modem

Communication processor

Concentrator

Simplex

Half-duplex

Full-duplex

Asychronous

Synchronous

Wire cable

Microwave

Fiber optics

Attenuation

Computer network

Local network

Wide-area network

Nodes

Links

Network topologies

   Point-to-point

   Multidrop

   Star

   Hierarchy

   Ring

   Distributed

Circuit switching   Broadcasting
Message switching   Protocol
Packet switching

QUESTIONS

1. Identify several advantages of teleconferencing.
2. What is the relationship between distributed data processing and telecommunications?
3. How does a modem facilitate data transfer?
4. Describe the following channel criteria: transmission mode, bandwidth, flow control, transmission speed.
5. Which transmission method can transfer more data, synchronous or asynchronous?
6. Compare and contrast cable and microwave transmission media.
7. List advantages and disadvantages of fiber optics.
8. How do nodes and links impact a network topology?
9. Illustrate the six common network topologies.
10. How is packet switching utilized?
11. Discuss the role of protocols in standardizing telecommunications techniques and procedures.
12. What are geosynchronous satellites?
13. Is the telecommunications field more competitive or less competitive than it was 20 years ago?
14. Identify and contrast the two levels of distribution for microcomputer systems.
15. What are the advantages/disadvantages of distributed microcomputing?

ARTICLE

U.S. and Canada Cross Satellite Barrier for Data/Voice Services

Companies in the United States and Canada can finally use domestic satellites to send data across their border. This breakthrough—diplomatic rather than technical—follows a 10-year ban on such communications links, which can be made for as little as half the cost of terrestrial connections.

The agreement between the two countries, which was spelled out in a recent exchange of letters, is limited to business voice and data communications. By excluding the use of satellites to carry television and entertainment transmission, it satisfies Canadian concerns of "cultural pollution" from the United States. Canada also dropped earlier conditions that the revenues from the transborder satellite operation be split equally.

The letters between Canada's ambassador to the United States, Allan Gotlieb, and former U.S. assistant secretary of state for economic and business affairs Robert Hormats, established four broad principles to govern the use of domestic satellites by business. The two nations agreed that transborder services will be offered jointly by organizations they authorize or recognize. In the United States, the operators cleared by the Federal Communications Commission so far are American Satellite Company and Satellite Business Systems (SBS); in Canada, the designated carrier is Telesat Canada, the partly state-owned operator of that nation's domestic satellites.

The United States and Canada gave their carriers the freedom to use the satellite facilities of each country "as appropriate." The agreement specifies, however, that the earth stations and other terrestrial gear in Canada "shall be owned and operated" by Canada's authorized carrier, while these facilities in the United States "shall be owned and operated in accordance with U.S. law."

The two governments also determined that Telesat Canada and the U.S. domestic satellite companies should be left to hammer out the details of offering transborder services. "For the most part, our work is done," says one U.S. official. "Now, it's up to the carriers to get together." In fact, the companies have begun their negotiations and, although they will not say when these discussions will be concluded, both American Satellite and SBS expect to initiate service to Canada sometime in 1983.

continued

The Gotlieb-Hormats letters also reiterate the commitment of Canada and the United States to the Intelsat global satellite communications network. Before transborder services begin, the two countries hope to secure the blessing of Intelsat. In fact, that approval could come early this month at a meeting of Intelsat's member nations in Washington, D.C.

Initially, users of the new U.S.-Canada satellite links are likely to be companies adding Canadian stations to their U.S. communications networks. American Satellite plans to offer high-speed computer data connections between the two countries and believes oil companies are major prospects for this service. SBS expects to provide a broader range of voice, data, and video services to its existing customer base.

DISCUSSION QUESTIONS

1. Discuss the role of both politics and technology in developing transborder telecommunications policies.
2. What are the key features of this current agreement and what is the effect of each feature on large U.S. business organizations?

APPLICATION

Bulky Order Processing
Needs Met with Net

BRIDGEPORT, Conn. — General Electric Co.'s Housewares and Audio Division, faced with the problem of processing orders for 30,000 customers through a variety of distribution centers, installed a data communications network based on their own compatible, modular network processors and statistical multiplexers.

Based here, GE operates three domestic manufacturing plants, four international plants and 14 distribution warehouses. The business serves customer locations from small stores to large retail outlets, according to a company spokesman.

As part of GE's customer service, the division receives orders at service operations located throughout the country, where they are edited and encoded for entry. Orders are entered into computers located here for further editing and are then batch transferred to a computer center in Boston, where they are scheduled and billed, the spokesman said.

Five of the 14 distribution centers support from eight to 16 terminals each and the remaining sites support one terminal each. The five major distribution sites are located in Charlotte, N. C.; Chicago; Atlanta; Edison, N. J.; and San Leandro, Calif.

To provide cost-effective computing services to their customers, GE Housewares-Audio installed a Digital Communications Associates, Inc. (DCA) data communications network, a DCA spokesman said. Terminal clusters at the five major locations connect to the host computer site in single phone-line connections.

The network is a "star" configuration that supports three host computers — two Digital Equipment Corp. PDP-11/70 Unibus-based computers located here and a Honeywell, Inc. 6000 mainframe based in Boston.

A DCA System 355 stand-alone master network processor serves as the central unit for the distributed data communications network. It transports data from any terminal port to any computer port in the network. Terminals and other DCA systems connect to the system in a point-to-point fashion, the spokesman explained.

All input is entered during the day and, in the event the computer goes down, the system allows the terminal operator to select an alternate port. The routing capability results

continued

in greater utilization of the network and operator productivity, according to the spokesman.

Attached to the system are four DCA System 205 Unibus interface statistical multiplexers with two multiplexers plugged into the slots of the Unibus of each PDP-11/70, according to Ed Chylinski, manager of sales, marketing and distribution information systems for GE Housewares-Audio.

At each of the five major distribution centers, there is a DCA System 115 statistical multiplexer, which can support up to 32 asynchronous devices. Currently, each site utilizes from eight to 16 2,400 bit/sec terminals. The System 115s connect in a point-to-point configuration to the System 355. Nine local terminals connect directly to the System 355, and an additional eight access it through dial-up connections, Chylinski said.

Part of the Honeywell environment in Boston is a System 115 supporting 1,200 bit/sec computer ports. Terminal ports from the Honeywell operate at 2,400 bit/sec.

Within a year, GE Housewares-Audio plans both to incorporate an accounts receivable system on an IBM 4341 centered in Boston and to co-locate terminals with order-entry terminals. This requires installation of additional System 115s to be connected to the System 355. DCA is currently developing a protocol emulator to allow terminal users to access any of the four computers in the network, a DCA spokesman said.

According to Chylinski, the entire data communications network is designed for flexibility and has the capacity for future growth in terms of increased volumes, new subsystems and utilization of new technologies.

DISCUSSION QUESTIONS

1. Draw a schematic of General Electric's distributed data communication network.
2. Why do you suppose they selected asynchronous devices? point-to-point connections? the star network?

15 AUTOMATED OFFICE SYSTEMS

CHAPTER OBJECTIVES

In this chapter you will learn:

1. How three technologies—EDP, telecommunications, and text processing—affect the office.
2. About the office productivity issue.
3. Various techniques associated with the automated office.
4. The specific impact of word processing, micrographics, and electronic mail.
5. The importance of ergonomics.
6. Advantages and disadvantages of automated office systems.

THE OFFICE OF TODAY

Regardless of their type or size, offices are centers where reports are generated, received, and acted upon. To facilitate the production of these reports, office automation is spreading into every area of business activity; office workers are becoming accustomed to fewer filing cabinets, less paper, more machines, and a changing work environment. In the past, communications have been handled by correspondence, printed material, face-to-face meetings, and telephone conversations. As the trend toward office automation gains momentum, each of these activities is affected by new technologies. An automated office system attempts to integrate these diverse technologies, improve productivity, and lower costs. Electronic mail speeds up the transfer of written material, while teleconferencing is a new means of oral communication. Nearly every medium for storing information is affected, from paper and filing cabinets to magnetic media and microfilm.

Office automation has an impact on everyone who works in offices, from the chief executive officer down through the ranks of managers, professionals, and clerks to the newest trainee in the mailroom. While paper handling is often considered to be a clerical or secretarial activity, managers also spend a great deal of time on activities that are candidates for automation (Figure 15-1). An example of a costly executive expense is labeled "telephone tag." *Telephone tag*

Activity	Upper Management	Middle Management
Telephone	16%	12%
Travel	14	7
Scheduled meetings	11	6
Unscheduled meetings	9	6
Paper handling	8	6
Reading	8	6
Searching information	6	12
Incoming mail	6	5
Dictation	6	3
Writing	5	9
Other	11	28
Total	100%	100%

Figure 15-1

Composite distribution of executive time by work activity.

Data Management, *February, 1982, p. 39*

is the time and expense involved when a person makes repeated, unsuccessful attempts to reach another person by phone. The actual time wasted in telephone tag depends on whether the phoned individual is in a meeting, out to lunch, on another phone call, or unavailable for some other reason. Only about 15 percent of telephone calls actually reach the intended party on the first call. New electronic mail techniques eliminate telephone tag, since the computer stores the message for retrieval on a receiving terminal.

There is disagreement regarding what terminology best describes automated office systems. "Buzzwords" used to describe this type of office include *office of the future, electronic office,* and *paperless office*. Regardless of what it is called, the office function is being affected by three major technologies: EDP, telecommunications, and text processing (Figure 15-2). The importance of EDP and telecommunications was discussed in earlier chapters. However, in the office environment, nearly 90 percent of office automation activity relates to documents rather than to data. Text (or document) processing is not amenable to traditional EDP processing, which utilizes logical definitions and stored-program manipulation. This incompatibility led to the development of new text processing technology for the office environment.

Office Productivity

Just as the industrial revolution dramatically increased manufacturing productivity, office automation provides opportunities for increasing office productivity. The self-correcting typewriter has enabled secretaries to substantially

Figure 15-2

Three converging technologies have a direct impact on office automation systems.

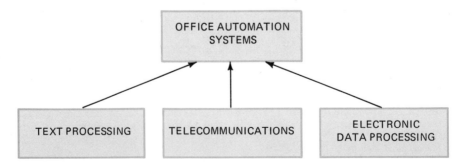

boost their productivity, and modern telephone techniques and copy machines save time for nearly all office workers. However, since salaries for management are several times higher than those for support staff, attention is now being focused on the productivity of managers. Measuring the output of managers is not an easy task. The usual measure of productivity—number of units of work produced—is not a meaningful guide, because the number of reports a manager produces is far less important than their value and timeliness.

The importance of the office productivity issue is readily apparent when examining changing employment patterns in the United States (Figure 15-3). Since 1960, more people have been involved in manipulating information than are found in agriculture, in industry, or in the service category. Furthermore, figures show that the typical farmer is supported by about $50,000 of capital equipment, the factory worker by about $35,000 of capital equipment, and the office worker by only $3,000 of capital equipment. Although the office function is very different from agriculture or manufacturing, further investment in office technology may be beneficial and should be analyzed to determine its impact on office productivity.

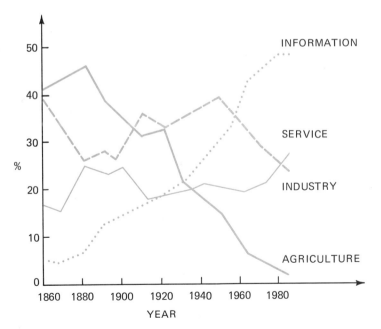

Figure 15-3

The growth of information occupations in the U.S. work force, 1860-1980.

Technology Review, *December/January, 1980, p. 57*

Factory productivity is generally measured in terms of quantity of output; office productivity is more often related to efficiency and timeliness of information provided. Efficiency is defined as competency of performance. As such, efficiency refers to speed, accuracy, and elimination of redundancy. In the typical office of today, documents are typed, revised, and retyped; most communication is handled by telephone or the U.S. Postal Service; and file cabinets are crammed full of data. Such an office is clearly not as productive or efficient as it could be. Timeliness refers to the manager's ability to access information in the right amount, at the right place, and at the right time. As information becomes more and more accessible through databases and networks, it is crucial that managers use current information to make accurate, reliable, and successful decisions.

Information is a key component of the office of the future for three major areas of office operations:

(1) Information generation — which is aided by word processing, dictation systems, and "intelligent" copiers.

(2) Information retrieval — which utilizes micrographics or computer storage for filing, storing, and retrieving information.

(3) Communications — which are handled via facsimile transmission, communicating word processors, and electronic mail.

The specific techniques shown in Figure 15-4 are key factors for increasing office productivity. These techniques are summarized in the following short glossary:

— *Electronic mail* uses telephone and other ground lines or satellite networks to transmit printed text and data from place to place.

— *Facsimile transmission* (FAX) is similar to electronic mail but involves the transmission of documents.

— *Intelligent copiers* are computer-controlled devices that "fetch" messages from memory, assemble paragraphs, and produce and distribute copies of business documents at high speeds.

— *Micrographics,* a fancy name for microfilm and microfiche, can be indexed for later retrieval on special readers.

— *Teleconferencing* uses picture phones, TV cameras, and receiver screens that allow geographically separated people to interface in a conference setting.

— *Voice input* allows the spoken word to be digitally transmitted, decoded, stored, and "understood" by a computer.

Figure 15-4

Fitting together the pieces of the office automation puzzle.

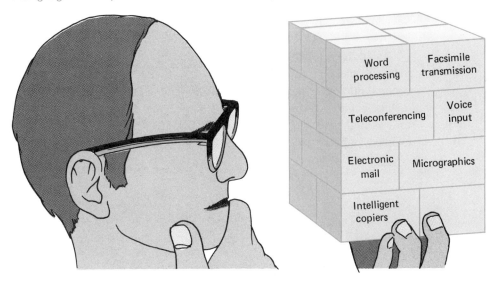

— *Word processing* relies on special equipment to manipulate typed documents. "Stand-alone" word processors contain both internal and auxiliary storage. They have the capability to store text, display it, and make corrections on a video screen. "Shared-logic" word processors use a central computer for storage and handle both text and data processing. "Communicating" word processors allow text to be transmitted between two or more word processing units.

Office Processing

Two characteristics of office automation are increasing in importance: (1) the use of telecommunications in new office systems and (2) the integration of office technologies. For example, data processing and word processing are both possible on many new office machines. With integration, the system can process text as well as perform arithmetic calculations. Data can be presented in letter-quality format; and budgets, purchase orders, or other arithmetic applications can be calculated as they are typed.

However, there are fundamental differences between data processing and text processing. Data processing utilizes records and fields that are usually one standard size, with precisely defined file structures and retrieval keys. Retrieval keys for text may also be precisely defined, but text records vary greatly in length and format.

In addition to data and text processing, the automated office also involves image processing and voice processing. Image processing uses intelligent copiers, micrographics, facsimile transmission, and video displays. Voice processing includes techniques for voice recognition (input), store-and-forward (processing), and synthesized speech (output). These four technologies have evolved as processing techniques (see Figure 15-5). In all cases, processing

Figure 15-5

Evolution of processing technology.

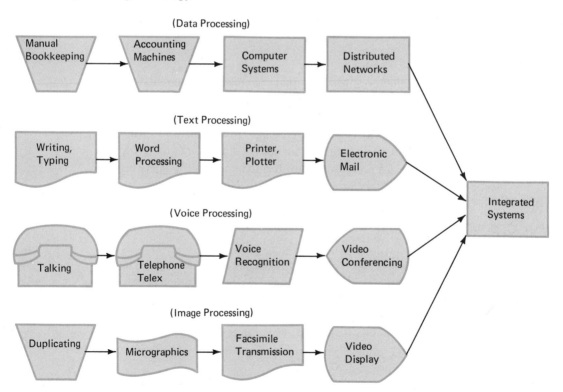

technologies have evolved from some sort of manual system to some type of automated communication. Data, text, voice, and image processing may be integrated into a corporation-wide resource through formal communications networks (Figure 15-6).

Figure 15-6

Communication networks link automated office systems.

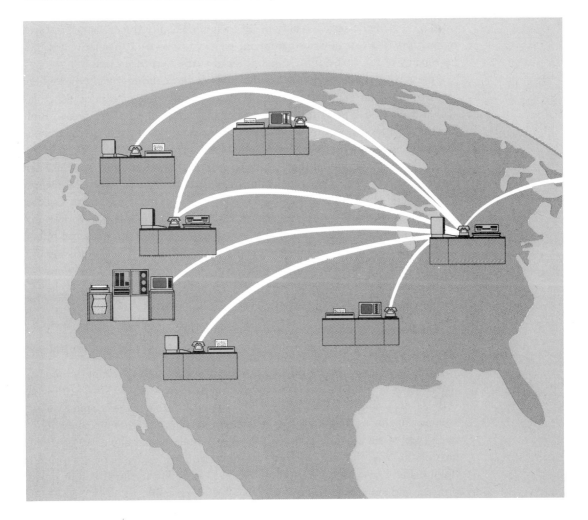

AUTOMATED OFFICE TECHNIQUES

Word Processing

Broadly defined, *word processing* (WP) involves the automated production of written documents. To put it more accurately, word processing moves and manipulates words, while data processing moves and manipulates numbers.

Word processors are descendants of mechanical typewriters that first appeared in the early 1900s. Through the years, the office typewriter has undergone a transition from manual to electric to electronic. The use of electronics for word processing became a reality in 1964 when IBM introduced magnetic-card typewriters. These typewriters store one page of text on each magnetic card and have many of the text-editing capabilities of current word processors.

Because of the development of the silicon chip, computerized typewriters are becoming increasingly available. Although *electronic typewriters* resemble standard electric typewriters in appearance (Figure 15-7), there are several functional differences. Instead of having hammers that directly strike ribbon and paper, electronic keyboards generate signal information, allowing text to be stored on magnetic media that can be linked to integrated office systems. An electronic typewriter is capable of storing at least one line of internal memory to allow line-at-a-time erasure or recording. Electronic typewriters usually include automated enhancements such as decimal alignment, title centering, and automatic carriage return. These new typewriters are serving as an intermediate step for offices moving into more powerful word processing systems.

State-of-the-art word processors are capable of four standard functions:

— They enter textual information via a keyboard and visual display screen.
— They manipulate text.
— They print information on paper.
— They store information for future reference, revision, and reprinting.

The two main classes of word processors are stand-alone systems and shared-logic systems. *Stand-alone word processors* consist of a single terminal with its own control logic. Electronic typewriters that have a small buffer memory for storing text, as well as centering and column alignment capabilities, are a type of stand-alone system. The most popular stand-alone WP systems incorporate a visual display terminal, disk storage, and a separate printer (Figure 15-8). Text is keyed and edited on the display terminal before being printed, and storing and simple calculations are possible.

Figure 15-7

An electronic typewriter.

Photo courtesy of IBM Corporation

Shared-logic word processors link terminals in a manner similar to that used in computer timesharing. Multi-terminal WP systems share the logic, storage, and peripherals of a central computer among several keyboard/editing stations. Text can be stored, searched, and retrieved for lengthy manuscripts, and desired formats can be maintained throughout updates and revisions.

While stand-alone systems are widely used, shared-logic systems are increasing in popularity. Shared-logic systems have more on-line storage, more sophisticated software, the potential for job sharing, and less handling of storage

Figure 15-8

Word processors make
text composition and
editing fast and simple.

Hewlett-Packard Company

media than stand-alone systems. One of the major disadvantages of a shared-logic system is its vulnerability to total system breakdown; if the central processor goes down, all terminals become inactive.

To determine whether word processing is needed, a study should be undertaken to identify cost-effective applications. Document handling is different for different users. The needs of the president are different from the needs of the personnel manager, which are different from those of a clerical worker. Productivity gains of 20 to 30 percent are estimated for clerical activities such as entering, editing, and formatting text. Middle management and technical users need more manipulation and inquiry capability, and the executive needs tools for file management, forecasting, and time management. Since a word processor can support all of these functions, it promises to become a managerial tool as well as a clerical tool.

Some of the basic features available on WP systems are global-search-and-replace, sort, move, insert, delete, and copy. Global-search-and-replace allows all occurrences of a misspelled word to be found and replaced with the correct spelling. Another example is the selective replacement of a word by another word. The sort feature is typically used with mailing lists and file processing. The insert, delete, move, and copy features allow text to be easily modified or edited.

Advanced WP capabilities include high-level programming, communication, spelling check, and file management. Many word processing systems offer languages such as BASIC, COBOL, FORTRAN, and PASCAL. With shared-logic systems, communication features such as electronic mail are common. Spelling checks are possible when a dictionary is included in the software. Upon request, the word processing system compares each word of text with the dictionary and identifies those strings of letters not in the dictionary. Other systems include hyphenation rules and will hyphenate words automatically. Finally, many word processing systems have flexible file management, allowing files to be sorted on different fields. For example, a mailing list might be sorted by zip code, state, or last name; and a personnel file might be sorted by salary, job class, or skill level.

Word processing is a fast-growing, volatile industry. Large manufacturers of computers and office equipment such as IBM and Xerox have the advantage of well-established sales and service organizations. IBM dominated the WP market in the early 1970s by selling over 90 percent of all WP equipment, but its share had dropped to about 50 percent in the early 1980s. IBM's Displaywriter (Figure 15-9) is an attempt to regain its former prominence in a word processing market that is expected to grow at an annual rate of 35 percent through the 1980s.

Another large word processing vendor is WANG, which pioneered the development of shared-logic systems. Smaller companies such as Lanier, CPT Corporation, Pitney-Bowes, and Nixdorf of West Germany are also well known among approximately 100 word processing vendors.

Future systems are expected to add paper-handling devices to facilitate text processing. Such devices will stuff letters in envelopes and print customized forms. Optical character recognition (OCR) devices may also be used to input printed data into the word processor. Voice input will allow an individual to dictate text directly onto the word processor, thus eliminating the need for keying in the material. Smaller and cheaper word processing equipment will increasingly be used to complement large, sophisticated computer systems.

Figure 15-9

The IBM Displaywriter.

Micrographics

In the past, office filing in large organizations required large numbers of file clerks and file cabinets (estimated at three file cabinets per office employee). Today, micrographics technology is taking over the filing function. *Micrographics* is essentially a process by which information is significantly reduced in size through photographic techniques.

Micrographics involves the creation and use of both microfiche and microfilm. With the use of these microforms, files can be recorded, developed, stored, and retrieved quickly and efficiently. Microform applications are useful where there are large-scale postings, a high rate of file look-ups, or a need for duplicate records. Microforms are also useful for documenting information in transit, providing an audit trail, and/or maintaining a large non-computer data bank.

Microfiche is the most popular microform. Microfiche is a sheet of film that contains images printed in a grid pattern (Figure 15-10) and a title that can be visually read. Fiche is easily duplicated for mailing, security, or reference

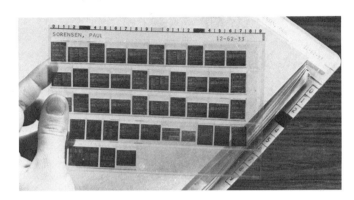

Figure 15-10

Microfiche is a useful storage medium.

Microseal Corporation

purposes. Each form contains several hundred images that are reduced from 18 to 48 times. One 4" × 6" sheet of microfiche is capable of holding enough information to fill 228 standard-sized computer pages. New computer-assisted micrographics retrieve a single page of data from a million-page database in about ten seconds.

Microfilm, on the other hand, contains images printed sequentially on a roll of film. Generally, there will be several thousand frames, each containing the equivalent of one printed page, on one spool of microfilm. Because of its sequential nature, roll microfilm is best used for information that is constantly sequenced but not often updated. Sixteen-millimeter rolls are used for alpha-numeric data, while 35-millimeter rolls are used for graphics and other large engineering documents. Microfilm cartridges and cassettes are self-threading and provide additional film protection.

Microfilm and the computer have been joined together through a medium called *computer output microfilm* (COM). COM is the process of converting computer output directly into microfilm or microfiche. The COM conversion process is generated at high speeds, either directly from the computer or off-line by a magnetic tape unit (Figure 15-11). In addition to producing the microforms, the computer will also produce an index that can be used to locate the proper roll (or sheet) and frame for a given output (Figure 15-12).

The primary advantages of COM are speed, economy, and storage capacity. COM is capable of line output 20 to 100 times faster than that of impact printers.

Figure 15-11

Computer output microfilm (COM) process.

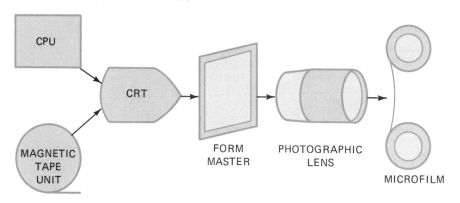

Figure 15-12

This microcomputer-operated accessory can read the bar code on the form and use that information to expose an index on the microfilm.

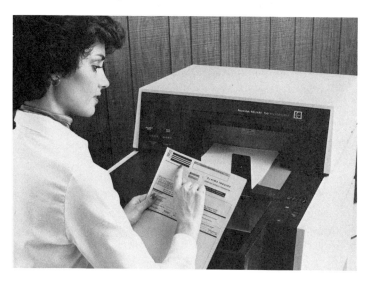

Eastman Kodak Company

Material and shipping costs are also lower than supplies for impact printers. Likewise, COM requires less than one percent of the paper storage space that traditional file environments require.

A major disadvantage of COM is the lack of user acceptance, possibly due to poor images and clarity. As offices accumulate more and more text, though, micrographics is proving to be a cost-effective alternative for the storage and retrieval of information.

Intelligent Copiers

Computer technology is also affecting copy machines. New *intelligent copiers* have the ability to produce documents directly from information maintained in electronic form. Intelligent copiers have buffer memory, input electronic signals, output hard copy, communicate with other devices, and provide reports in varied formats. The term "intelligent" refers to copy equipment that is a hybrid of computer, phototypesetting, electronic mail, and standard copy processes (Figure 15-13).

Xerox Corporation

Figure 15-13

The output of this intelligent copier is comparable to high-quality offset printing.

Telecommunications is used to link copiers directly to word processing equipment. With this link, intelligent copiers receive digital information directly from the word processor and recreate a line of characters that is scanned by a fiber optic wafer, a laser, or some other device. The digitized signal is transmitted through fiber optic rods, mirrors, or wires to a photosensitive device that puts the images on a drum or belt and from there onto paper.

This integration of document I/O and printing promotes speed, economy, and versatility. Speed is evident in the fact that intelligent copiers operate in terms of pages per minute rather than lines per minute. Cost savings are realized because employees do not have to stand idle while they wait in line to use a copier, and equally important, text is entered only once into the system. Finally, intelligent copiers are versatile because they have a multifont capability that allows different type styles and sizes to be printed.

Electronic Mail

Interest is also increasing in the office technology called electronic mail. *Electronic mail* refers to the electronic delivery of messages that would otherwise have been transmitted physically through the postal system or orally by telephone. Electronic mail has several advantages over conventional forms of business communications. Unlike an office memo that can be lost or misplaced, the computer-recorded message provides a historical record of the message. Unlike the telephone, electronic mail allows a message to be sent even when the recipient is not available. Unlike the postal system, which takes a day or more to transmit messages, electronic mail is almost instantaneous (Figure 15-14). Two primary functions of electronic mail are "broadcasting," by which messages are sent to multiple recipients, and "store and carry forward" message capabilities for handling messages throughout a telecommunications network.

There are four general methods for delivering electronic mail:

(1) Message-oriented mail systems
(2) Facsimile transmission
(3) Computer-based message systems
(4) Communicating word processors

Of the message-oriented mail systems, two of the best known are Telex and TWX, both developed by Western Union. Mailgram, a joint venture between

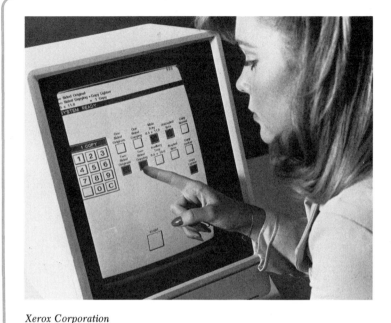

Figure 15-14

A page can be sent by electronic mail in about three seconds.

Xerox Corporation

Western Union and the U.S. Postal Service, provides overnight delivery of business correspondence that is much less expensive than telegrams for large company mailings. The postal service is also developing ECOM (electronic computer-oriented message) for delivering business-generated first-class mail by leasing Western Union computers and satellites.

Facsimile (FAX) is the most widely used type of electronic mail. *Facsimile transmission* involves sending photographs and documents from one FAX machine to another over conventional telephone lines (Figure 15-15). Transmitted information may be typed or handwritten text, numbers, pictures, graphs, drawings, and other forms of hard copy. FAX is not a new technique; weather bureaus, news wire services, and law enforcement agencies have used black-and-white image transmission for over 50 years.

Facsimile transmission may be used for interoffice communications to send letters, memos, photographs, and charts almost instantaneously. A phone conversation can be followed by a facsimile document that provides a historical

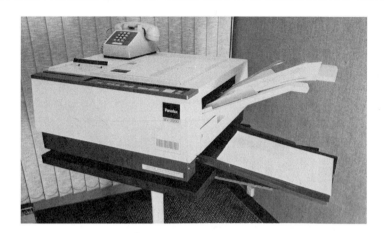

Figure 15-15

A facsimile transceiver.

Panafax Corporation

record of the call. In financial institutions, loan officers work from FAX transmissions of customer credit histories to speed approval or disapproval of loan requests. Facsimile technology also provides support to sales forces by providing current price lists and delivery schedules. Transmission and documentation of order prices, specifications, and other invoice data are fast and accurate.

Facsimile equipment transmits information by passing a photoelectric scanning device over the material and converting the material into an electric current. While FAX is usually cheaper than express mail and more accurate than computer transmission, its greatest advantage is speed. Vital information can be communicated in minutes or even seconds. However, FAX has limited capability to store and forward documents.

A *computer-based message system* (CBMS) uses the computer to receive and transmit messages that have been prepared on video terminals. Users can then read and respond to messages stored on their "electronic mailboxes" on a real-time basis. CBMS comprises three technologies—word processing to assist the user in message composition, computer networking to assist in message delivery, and database management to provide for storage and retrieval of information in the electronic mailboxes (Figure 15-16). CBMS is the Rolls-Royce of electronic mail systems, since the operator has the advantage of a personal message terminal.

Figure 15-16

Computer-based message systems (CBMS) use "mailboxes" to support message composition and delivery.

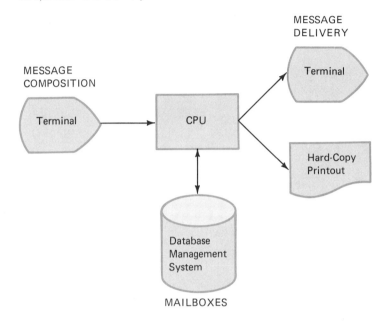

Communicating word processors are also used to deliver electronic mail. Typically, word processors within a shared-logic system will be capable of this form of communication. Stand-alone word processors can also communicate if both word processors are made by the same manufacturer. Through telecommunication, word processors may be integrated in local networks or at widely diverse locations. Communicating word processors have great potential but little use to date because of the lack of communications protocols. With decreasing WP communication costs, the development of networks such as Xerox's X-TEN (Figure 15-17) should proliferate in the future.

Both CBMS and communicating word processors provide similar capabilities. Many of these systems are designed for executives rather than for clerical personnel. Such systems eliminate telephone calls, simulate "in" and "out" boxes, and provide immediate filing systems. They are also used for intracompany messages and can be linked to outside services such as the UPI newswire. A good CBMS provides more information, fewer interruptions, and less paper.

Figure 15-17

Xerox's X-TEN provides subscribers with interactive transmission terminals, document processors, and computer support.

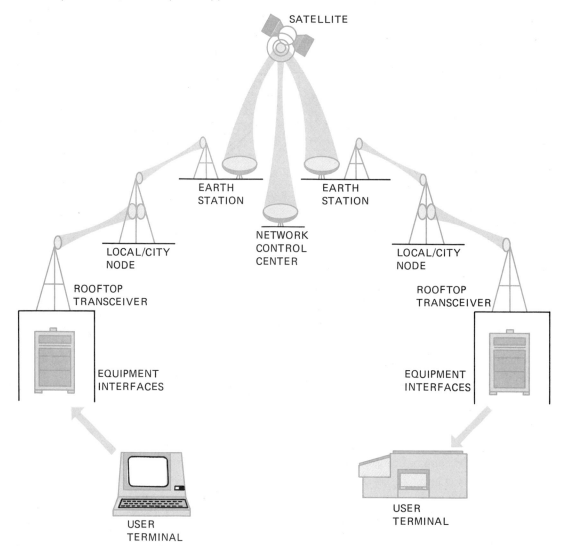

Voice Input Systems

Although millions of office dictating machines are in use, the use of the human voice as direct input to word processors and computers is still mostly experimental. *Voice input* relies on speech recognition units that analyze and classify acoustic speech patterns and transfer them into impulses acceptable to the computer.

One of the greatest difficulties with voice input systems is dealing with the infinite variation in human speech. Operators must "train" the system to recognize standard words by repeating each word over and over to achieve a required proficiency. Current voice recognition systems are limited to several hundred words or phrases and are used in business to enter sales, inventory, and quality control data. When voice input is further perfected, it will be the quickest and easiest method of data and text entry in automated office systems.

Teleconferencing

Teleconferencing allows groups of people to communicate electronically, eliminating the time and expense of corporate travel. There are three types of teleconferencing—video, audio, and computer. Video teleconferencing allows participants to see and talk to each other, and store-and-forward capability for charts and graphs is possible. Audio teleconferencing lacks visual communication but includes voice communication and may include graphics support. Computer teleconferencing allows data to be transmitted by keyboard input, stored and processed by a computer, and printed out on a terminal. Users interact with other users by responding immediately or acknowledging the message at a later time. The audio medium is by far the most common type of teleconferencing, but video and computer techniques are expected to grow substantially in the 1980s.

Ergonomics

At the present time, approximately one visual display terminal (VDT) is available for every ten office employees. By 1990, this ratio is expected to reach one VDT for every three employees. As the use of VDT's increases, there is growing concern with issues regarding the employee's working environment. Studies have shown that a direct correlation exists between a terminal operator's comfort and his or her daily rate of output. *Ergonomics* is the technology that uses biological and engineering data to address problems relating to people and machines. *Physical ergonomics* in the office relates to the design of office layouts, furniture, and VDT terminals. VDT designers are specifically concerned with matching EDP terminal operators to workstations in a humanistic way (Figure 15-18). Ergonomically designed systems try to alleviate both the physical and the mental aches of office workers such as frustration, confusion, and loss of patience with the work situation.

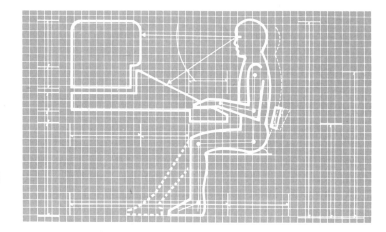

Figure 15-18

Ergonomics is concerned with the design of comfortable office workstations.

Employee discontent is commonly traced to eyestrain, uncomfortable furniture, and poor acoustics. A VDT terminal should have a glare-proof CRT screen that tilts and swivels and has large, easy-to-read letters. The work environment should also include adjustable chairs, good lighting, and a quiet atmosphere. *Software ergonomics* is exemplified by user-friendly menus, special-purpose keys, consistent screen prompts, and usable documentation manuals.

The next time you operate a VDT, check to see if your environment is ergonomic. For example, do your palms rest on the keyboard approximately nine inches above the chair seat? Is there a distance of 18 inches between your eyes and the display screen? Is there adequate indirect lighting? Is the keystation detachable and situated at a 40-degree viewing angle from the horizontal plane? Finally, does the software provide ergonomic aids?

WHY AUTOMATE?

Though automated office systems are proliferating, there are pluses and minuses associated with their development. The automated office may offer the following benefits:

— decreased need for clerical staff,
— improved processing speed,
— improved access to information,
— less-expensive storage of business data, and
— machine consistency in workload processing.

On the minus side, however, are several economic and personnel considerations. Significant capital outlays are often necessary to obtain state-of-the-art hardware and software. Operators must be trained, and technical personnel are needed to maintain the equipment. Of concern also are the restrictions computers place on office procedures and the format of data and information. Finally, users may need to be retrained to facilitate their interface with the automated office.

As electronic machines and devices become commonplace in the office, every effort must be made by designers and software developers to make these machines more user friendly. Important considerations include ease of use, training in facility, and the "menu" approach, in which users are guided through a wide range of potential applications.

Most office personnel will be asked to change their work methods and work habits to accommodate new office technology. People may need to be more disciplined and structured than they need to be with manual system procedures. There is certain to be a psychological impact on employees who are told, "You've done a good job, but these machines can do it faster, cheaper, and better." In addition, the prospect of a smaller labor force is a serious social issue in a time of high unemployment and inflation, and large numbers of people may need to be retrained.

The office of the future will be evolutionary rather than revolutionary. It is clear that it is easier and cheaper to manipulate, move, and store electrons than paper, but it will probably be well into the 1990s before the office will be completely transformed from a labor-intensive to an electronic-based environment.

SUMMARY

Computer technology has an impact on nearly every facet of our lives, and the business office is no exception. Word processing, telecommunications, and data processing are promoting increased productivity, efficiency, and timeliness of information in the office setting.

There are several major components of the automated office. A descendant of the mechanical typewriters of the early 1900s, word processing is a fast-growing, volatile industry. Micrographics involves the creation and use of both microfilm and microfiche. Computer output microfilm (COM) converts computer output into human-readable form on microforms. The advantages of this process include speed, economy, and reduced storage space.

Electronic mail is the electronic delivery of messages through message-oriented mail systems, facsimile transmission, computer-based message systems, or communicating word processors. This new office technology is attracting widespread interest as a time and money saver. Similarly, teleconferencing eliminates the time and expense of corporate travel by allowing people to communicate electronically. Through video teleconferencing, participants can see as well as talk to each other, even though separated by hundreds or thousands of miles.

There are advantages and disadvantages associated with the arrival of the automated office. Advantages include improved processing speed, reduced personnel costs, and improved access to information. Disadvantages include increased equipment costs, the need for processing schedules, and added expense if used only for data storage. Behavioral problems associated with office automation systems include the fear many people have of change or unemployment. Adequate training programs are necessary as a result of automated office systems both to train personnel in the use of new technologies and to retrain personnel when a position becomes obsolete.

TERMS

Telephone tag	Electronic mail
Office of the future	Facsimile (FAX) transmission
Electronic office	Intelligent copiers
Paperless office	Micrographics

Teleconferencing
Voice input
Word processing
Electronic typewriter
Stand-alone word processor
Shared-logic word processor
Microfiche

Microfilm
Computer output microfilm (COM)
Computer-based message system (CBMS)
Communicating word processor
Ergonomics
Physical ergonomics
Software ergonomics

QUESTIONS

1. What is an automated office?
2. What is telephone tag? Can it ever be completely eliminated?
3. Can an office be truly electronic? paperless? an office of the future?
4. Do executives tend to spend more time on the telephone or handling paper?
5. Identify the three major technologies that are currently affecting the office function.
6. Rank the following employment categories from greatest number of employees to lowest number—agriculture, service, information, industry.
7. Explain similarities and differences between factory productivity and office productivity.
8. Define the two main elements of office productivity.
9. Which type of processing is most common for office activities—data, text, voice, or image?
10. How do electronic typewriters differ from word processing equipment?
11. What are the two main classes of word processing systems? Which is increasing more in popularity?
12. Define micrographics. What is the difference between microfiche and COM?
13. Identify features that make a copier "intelligent."
14. What four methods are used to provide electronic mail?
15. Identify several types of transmission that can be handled by facsimile.
16. What are "electronic mailboxes"? For what specific purposes are they used?
17. What three technologies support computer-based message systems?
18. Does ergonomics pertain more to people or to machines? Explain.
19. Describe several principles of physical ergonomics; of software ergonomics.
20. List advantages and disadvantages of the automated office.
21. Will office automation increase or decrease in the future?

ARTICLE

DP/MIS Eyed as Favorite in OA Supremacy Race

MIAMI — DP/management information systems (MIS) departments are the favorites to emerge with control from the battle for supremacy over office automation, Alexandra Corson said at the International Data Corp. 1982 Spring Executive Conference here last week.

"DP/MIS has the power to manage office automation, but in the past they have tended to serve technology rather than the needs of people and information," Corson, program director for Strategies for Office Systems Program at IDC, observed. DP/MIS will grab at least temporary power because it is easier in these tight economic times to give control to that segment of corporate management which is "relatively stable, organizationally powerful and technologically inclined," Corson commented.

Administrative management departments will also be in the fight, she said, noting these managers generally understand the needs of people and have the advantage of being distanced from the vested interests of individual organizational groups. However, this group tends to opt for "tidy," "big picture" answers that may conflict with specific individual needs.

Telecommunications departments also figure prominently in the battle, the

program director said. The telecommunications manager's blessing is essential to the development of effective networks and as systems become more integrated, they can be expected to gain corresponding influence. Despite that growing influence, she added, "to date, telecommunications managers have tended to take only passing interest in the office automation dogfight."

Finance departments are heavy hitters with the ability to stop any incipient office system in its tracks, Corson claimed. Nonetheless, these executives remain content to pull the corporate purse strings from behind the scenes.

She praised office systems management personnel for understanding both human needs and the idiosyncrasies of the office. However, these managers have too narrow a focus to deal with the onslaught of office technologies and even more important, they lack corporate clout.

Records management departments are also on the periphery of the battle, but are also too specialized and task-oriented to take control, according to Corson.

She emphasized that DP/MIS does not have a lock on office automation devel-

continued

opment, adding there are "creative alternatives," pointing to corporate vice-presidents of office systems who have come out of the controller's office and some personnel managers who have been named directors of office systems.

"The opportunities are wide open for anyone who dares to take the risk," Corson declared.

The need to link the DP and office automation spheres has placed increasing pressure on existing technical staff, Corson said, noting that they are asked to respond to global information needs of end users. Those needs include instantaneous access, user transparency and the conversion of data formats.

MIS groups may react defensively to the growing burden by refusing additional responsibilities. Corson suggested that the way to deal with that is to go on the offensive and establish groups charged with "creative marketing" of the new technology, products and consulting services.

Her other suggestions included encouraging the business use of personal computers within reasonable limits, establishing guidelines, which will assist potential clients in measuring the baseline productivity of work products and, where appropriate, replacing stand-alone word processors with clustered terminals.

DISCUSSION QUESTIONS

1. Which of the five departments cited do you believe should manage office automation? Why?
2. Ms. Corson indicates that DP/MIS has served "technology rather than the needs of people and information." Isn't the role of technology to meet the needs of people and information? Discuss.

APPLICATION

Office Automation

When I arrive at my office in the morning and begin my work I flip a switch and press a few keys and an index of incoming messages is displayed on the screen before me. Since I am pressed for time I read only one relatively urgent message. Moving a pointer, I position an arrow on the screen and press a button. Instantly, the message I have selected is displayed. I read it easily, since messages sent directly from screen to screen tend to be short and direct. After some thought I send a message to a colleague asking for help in organizing a somewhat lengthy response. Then I set about the principal work of the morning, completing some equipment layout by directly manipulating the on-screen diagrams.

Meanwhile, my colleague is structuring an answer to the urgent inquiry. He calls to the screen an old, but relevant, report, composes an appropriate "cover letter," and sends it on to me. Later, after I have added some new information to the response, I send it via the network linking the North American parts of our organization. The message is automatically stored for future reference and, if a printed copy is desired, it is available in seconds from the nearby copier-printer.

This is how I handle my daily "paperwork." My office is more automated than most because I am in an organization doing work at the frontiers of this exciting field. Nevertheless, the intellectual tools I work with are the clear precursors of those that will radically change the way most "knowledge workers" handle their daily tasks in the future.

R. J. Spinrad, "Office Automation," Science, *Vol. 215 (February 12, 1982), pp. 808-813. Copyright 1982 by the American Association for the Advancement of Science.*

DISCUSSION QUESTIONS

1. Identify the automated office techniques used by the writer and his colleague.
2. Define "knowledge workers." Why are their jobs susceptible to office automation?

CHAPTER 16

OTHER COMPUTER-BASED SUPPORT SYSTEMS

CHAPTER OBJECTIVES

In this chapter you will learn:

1. Why business use of computer graphics is increasing.
2. The role of computer-aided design and computer-aided manufacturing (CAD/CAM).
3. How industrial robots work.
4. About key components of material requirements planning (MRP) and manufacturing resource planning (MRP II) systems.
5. How a decision support system (DSS) aids management.

Most information systems in the 1970s aided lower- and middle-level managers, with only a minimal impact on upper levels of management. Even today, few corporate executives use computers to help make their decisions. This scenario is changing, though, and new applications of computer-based information systems are focusing on the needs of executives.

Fundamentals of telecommunications and automated office systems were discussed in Chapters 14 and 15, respectively. In this chapter, the growing use of business graphics, material requirements planning (MRP), and decision support systems (DSS) is discussed, as well as the popular industrial support techniques of robotics and computer-aided design/computer-aided manufacturing (CAD/CAM). These new techniques are labeled *computer-based support systems* (Figure 16-1). Even though computer-based support systems are useful in any organization, the techniques discussed in this chapter are particularly well suited to industrial applications.

Typical computer manufacturing applications include accounting, order processing, purchasing, and inventory control. More advanced applications include forecasting, production scheduling, and engineering design. A general information system model for a manufacturing company is illustrated in Figure 16-2. Note the fifteen information subsystems identified by Kanter in the model. Some of these subsystems support top management activities (e.g., strategic planning), while other subsystems are mainly operational (e.g., order processing). Each of the computer-based support systems discussed in this chapter relates to these manufacturing subsystems in some way. For example, graphics and decision support methods can be used as a medium for output reports. Material requirements planning affects all production subsystems; decision support systems impact planning and policy matters. Robotics and computer-aided design impact production control and engineering subsystems, respectively.

COMPUTER GRAPHICS FOR BUSINESS

While computer graphics techniques have been widely used in the scientific community for years, business graphics applications have only recently begun to proliferate. Banks, insurance companies, and other large financial institutions are spearheading the use of graphics for displaying financial data.

Why is business graphics becoming so popular? Many people consider graphical representation to be the most effective way to communicate infor-

Figure 16-1

Computer-based support systems.

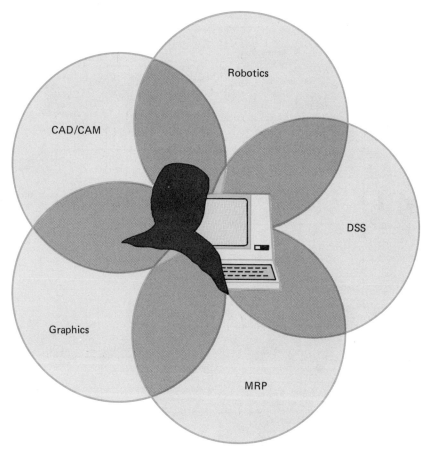

mation. Information can be presented as bar charts, histograms, pie charts, or curves to highlight important variations. Graphics is available in black-and-white or color and can incorporate either two or three dimensions. *Computer graphics* is used in business organizations to:

— enhance decision making by presenting trends and deviations,
— support project management by allowing the user to pose "What if?" questions, and
— save time in interpreting and communicating data.

Figure 16-2

Information system model for a manufacturing company.

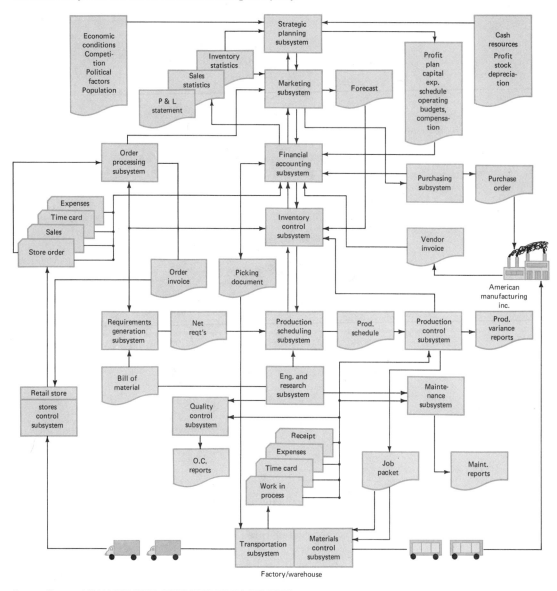

Jerome Kanter, MANAGEMENT-ORIENTED MANAGEMENT
INFORMATION SYSTEMS, 2nd ed., ©1977, p. 82. Reprinted by
permission of Prentice-Hall, Inc., Englewood Cliffs, N.J.

Like other information systems, computer graphics systems use the EDP components of processing, input, storage, and output (Figure 16-3). The processor (system controller) manipulates the graphical data, on either a microcomputer or a mainframe computer. Input devices to supply graphics data range from standard keyboards to specialized devices such as light pens and digitizers. Mass-storage devices are needed to store the large amounts of graphic data needed to describe output. The more complex the application (such as three-dimensional, interactive), the larger the storage requirements will be.

Output devices for portraying graphic images are either hard copy or soft copy. Hard-copy devices include multicolor plotters and printers, CRT camera attachments, and slide-making equipment. Business applications typically use raster and storage tube technology for soft-copy (terminal display) output. Raster technology presents the graphic image by lighting a series of dots on

Figure 16-3

EDP components of a computer graphics system.

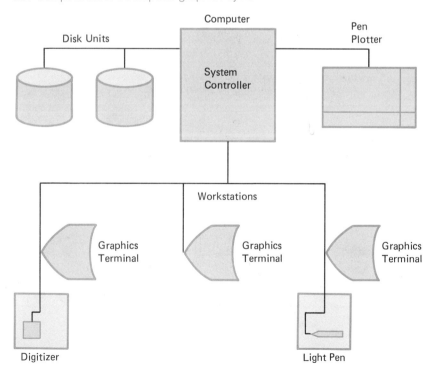

the screen called *pixels* (picture elements). The resolution of a display is determined by the number of pixels that can be displayed horizontally and vertically (Figure 16-4). The raster technique is used in both home television and CRT devices. These raster scan devices recreate or "refresh" a screen 30 to 60 times a second to provide a clear image for viewing.

Figure 16-4

Screen resolution is a function of pixel quantity.

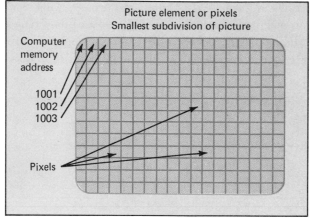

In a raster-format system, *the picture plane is divided into pixels; each pixel is represented by a memory address.*

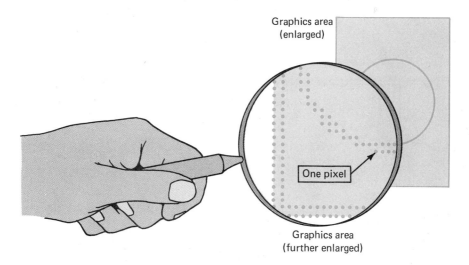

Storage tube technology is quite different from raster technology because after its screen images have been drawn they do not need to be refreshed. Storage tube displays are typically monochrome (black-and-white) with high resolution. Raster displays, on the other hand, provide good color contrast, are durable, and are easier to erase. In addition, the raster technique typically costs less for business applications.

Graphics language software packages are used to perform most graphics tasks. In general, simple pie charts and line plots for business reports are fairly easy to produce. Graphic applications in business vary widely from these simple charts to full-color displays for financial reports. Common types of business graphics are shown in Figure 16-5.

Several inherent problems exist with graphics output. Often there is a tendency to accept every graphic output as truth, even though the data on

Figure 16-5

Types of business graphics output.

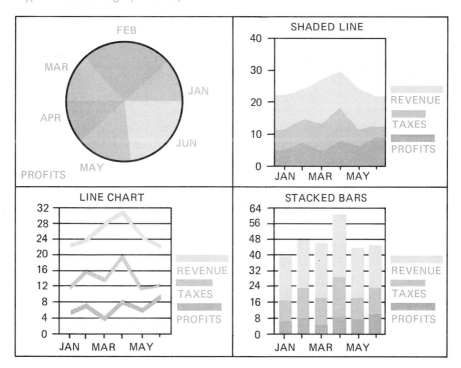

which it is based may be incorrect. Even an accurate graph can still confuse or mislead the viewer. Therefore, graphic layouts should be carefully designed.

Keep in mind that a computer does not change the type of graphic that can be produced for business reports. If the computer can draw it, so can a graphic artist. In general, though, computer graphics can be prepared much faster by computer than by hand. First-time computer graphics users tend to make graphs for the same types of applications for which they had previously made manual graphs. Soon, however, new types of applications emerge as user ingenuity is applied.

New technological improvements are facilitating the growth of computer graphics. Intelligent terminals linked to mainframes are widening the user base, while videodiscs allow masses of data to be quickly available. High-resolution (perhaps 1000 $\times$ 1000 pixels) color graphics allows flicker-free, full-color images. New word processing packages are incorporating color graphics for recalling charts and graphs into the body of a manuscript. As costs for color graphics decline, business applications will continue to grow.

CAD/CAM

An emerging computer graphics technique called CAD/CAM promises to promote significant productivity gains, especially in manufacturing and engineering (Figure 16-6). Short for computer-aided design/computer-aided manufacturing, CAD/CAM systems automate the processes of design, drafting, and engineering control. *Computer-aided design* (CAD) systems are primarily used to automate drafting functions. *Computer-aided manufacturing* (CAM) systems are used on the production line for tool design and parts fabrication. CAD typically involves the following specific tasks by a user sitting at an interactive terminal:

— Drawing an outline of a simple (or complex) part.
— Adding depth via three dimensions.
— Rotating the part to any angle.
— Modifying the part.
— Changing the scale.
— Adding lettering.
— Producing a hard-copy drawing.

Figure 16-6

Where Does CAD/CAM Improve Productivity?

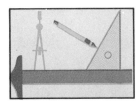

Drafting
Drawings with recurring features or drawings that are frequently updated are much more efficiently drafted and maintained with a CAD system.

Documentation
Bills of material and technical illustrations are very quickly produced if they can be derived from data already stored in a CAD system.

Design
Calculations of area, volume, weight, deformation, thermal flux, and so on are best performed by a computer. CAD systems can either perform these calculations themselves or prepare input for larger general purpose computers from graphical data already stored in the CAD system. Also, design tasks that involve fitting together or housing a number of parts are very efficiently done with some CAD systems.

Estimating
The ability of some CAD systems to associate, store, and recall graphical and text data has been put to good use by engineering estimators. Experience has shown that this approach is more productive than manual methods and captures more cost information.

Order Entry
Some manufacturers have found that a lot of time can be saved by integrating order entry with their CAD system. Major savings can occur in this area when an order must be tied to specific engineering drawings.

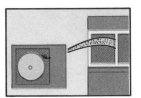

Manufacturing
Many CAD/CAM systems include software for producing NC tapes and other items used for planning the manufacturing process from information entered and stored in the system during the design phase. This greatly reduces the effort necessary to get a part into production.

Iron Age, *February 23, 1981, p. 65*

— Generating a computer program to guide machine tooling (CAM) of the actual part.

— Storing the design for use in larger machine designs.

CAD places highest priorities upon what benefits engineers most — producing the drawing. CAD is used for designing parts, plotting drawings, and handling design changes.

CAD/CAM originated in the mid-1970s primarily to support the design and production of integrated circuits for the semiconductor industry. Today, the automobile and aerospace industries are increasingly using CAD/CAM in the design of their new models. Computervision Corporation, based in Bedford, Massachusetts, is a leading CAD/CAM supplier, while IBM and other large mainframe manufacturers are moving into this rapidly growing market. Prices for standard systems vary from $10,000 to over a million dollars, with popular minicomputer-based CAD systems averaging several hundred thousand dollars. CAD/CAM systems usually consist of a CPU, disk storage, graphic data entry, and a plotter or other graphic hard-copy device (Figure 16-7).

Figure 16-7

Graphics devices support computer-aided design (CAD).

Photo at left, CADAM^R; right, Adage, Inc.

Technological progress has been greater for CAD than for CAM, and CAD systems are more widely used. Currently, CAM output, such as numerical control (NC) tapes, must be manually converted to machine tool devices. However, newer CAM systems allow direct computer interface to various machine tools, with NC tapes or floppy disks.

To take full advantage of CAD/CAM applications and modern database capabilities, a new industry term is developing—*computer-integrated manufacturing* (CIM). Several trends affect the growth of these integrated CIM systems. There is a movement toward 32-bit microcomputer systems that will provide additional computer power over current 8- or 16-bit machines. In addition, the use of color and raster technology in terminals allows greater display flexibility and object motion on the screen. Finally, CIM integration will extend to other organizational systems such as word processing, business graphics, and project control systems.

ROBOTICS

To many people, the term robotics brings to mind images of C3P0 and R2D2 of "Star Wars" fame. However, compared with the sophisticated C3P0, robots in use today are rather primitive. A robot's basic function is not to look or behave like a human being but to do a few specified tasks which would otherwise be performed by people.

A *robot* is defined as a reprogrammable, multifunctional manipulator designed to move material, parts, tools, or specialized devices through variable programmed motions to accomplish a variety of tasks. For these varied tasks, a robot typically needs a "brain" (the computer) and an "arm" with "fingers."

Industrial robots vary in size and shape, but the most common type of robot has a static arm that is manipulated about a base. At the end of the arm is a gripper or manipulator designed specifically for the task (Figure 16-8). Most industrial robots simply move something from one point to another.

Robotics is defined as the "science" of using a machine (robot) that is programmable, capable of operating on its own without human intervention, and able to perform a fairly large number of dissimilar tasks. The machine must also have a sensing and control system that allows it to make elementary decisions. Automatic machines that operate without computer program control do not qualify as robots.

Figure 16-8

Robotic "fingers" attached to a static "arm."

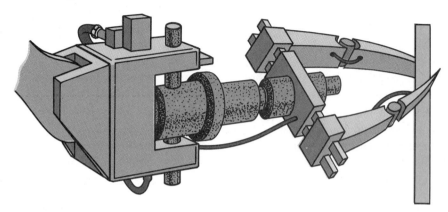

Two key factors have caused the recent growth in the use of industrial robots. First, microprocessor technology has lowered the cost of computers, thus lowering the cost of robots. Present-day robots range in cost from as little as $5,000 to more than $100,000.

The second significant factor leading to the growth of robotics is wage inflation. As computer costs continue to decrease and workers' wages continue to increase, the robot becomes economically feasible. To date, there has been minimal worker resistance to robots in the production environment. Generally the robot is viewed as a helper, since it is good at repetitive material-handling jobs that are highly fatiguing, dangerous, too hot, too cold, noisy, smelly, fast-paced, or boring and that demand constant attention. On the other hand, when unemployment rates are high, workers may be less enthusiastic about switching to robots.

The growth of robotics in manufacturing has led to a proliferation of robot vendors. Unimation is the largest of about three dozen U.S. robot manufacturers. Several well-known corporations — IBM, Bendix, General Electric, and Westinghouse — have entered the robotics field as well.

Robotics industrial applications commonly include welding, painting, and stacking. A specific application is illustrated in Figure 16-9. Other applications include a candy factory in England where robots pick up two finished chocolates each second and place them in boxes, and the McDonnell Douglas plant in St. Louis, where a robot controls a laser beam to cut out sheets of graphite for

Figure 16-9

In this application, the robot automatically performs the following sequential operations: (1) selects parts from a conveyor; (2) loads parts into the turning centers; (3) removes finished parts from the machines; (4) presents finished parts to a laser-gaging station; (5) delivers finished parts to a stacking station.

Photo courtesy of Cincinnati Milacron Inc.

brake assemblies on jet aircraft. General Electric uses robots to remove white-hot metal from forging furnaces.

The most common functions of industrial robots are the following:

— Pick and place. Robots are used to load and unload parts from one place to another. They can manipulate objects weighing from an ounce to a ton.

— Machine loading. Robots are used to load and unload parts from production machines such as die-casting, stamping, or injection-molding machines.

— Spray painting. Consistent performance is the key here.
— Welding. In the automobile industry, robots are used to do spot welding.
— Machine operations. Under special conditions, robots can perform drilling and cutting operations.
— Assembly. At present, robots can do only simple mechanical assembly.

In the future, robots will be able to do such tasks as inspection and continuous welding. Vision will allow a robot to recognize specific parts mixed in with other objects and to pick up moving parts. Another major innovation will be a universal hand to replace the special grippers in use today. Ultimately, voice programming will allow a person to give a robot oral commands.

A firm can realize substantial benefits through the proper application of robotics technology. These benefits include:

— Flexibility. A robot can be reprogrammed to perform new tasks.
— Increased productivity. The robot does not get bored or require coffee breaks.
— Increased product quality. Once a robot is programmed to do a task properly, it will consistently do it correctly.
— Fewer injuries. Robots can replace humans in hazardous jobs, as well as in jobs that require heavy lifting.
— Precision, speed, and accuracy.
— Resistance to inflation. Once the initial investment in a robot is made, only maintenance and paying for upgrading are ongoing costs.

On the other hand, there are limitations that restrict the use of robotics. First, a substantial capital investment is needed. Second, today's robots can only operate in a restricted space; they are unable to move about freely like R2D2 and C3P0. Third, robotics applications require some imagination, since the tasks to be performed and specific robots must be adapted to each other. Finally, management and labor must both be receptive.

A broader societal implication of robotics is that robots allow humans to have more and more free time, leading to potentially massive changes in leisure activities. In this context, robotics is a provocative field with startling potential for change. Figure 16-10 illustrates a humorous interpretation of what might happen if all factory production were performed by robots and controlled by computers. The application of robotics is increasing throughout the world. Whether industrial productivity and human welfare are both served is important to both the business community and society as a whole.

Figure 16-10

© Ed Stein

MATERIAL REQUIREMENTS PLANNING (MRP)

Most of the major manufacturing firms in the industrialized world are now using or considering the use of a new computerized information system called material requirements planning. *Material requirements planning* (MRP) is defined as a set of rules and procedures whose function is to determine material requirements on a "when needed" basis. MRP is used for production and inventory control and as a scheduling tool for manufacturing facilities.

Figure 16-11 illustrates the production and inventory control objectives that most manufacturing companies strive to attain. In general, these objectives are conflicting—for example, the marketing goal of always having enough inventory in stock to fill customer orders directly conflicts with the financial goal of minimizing the investment in inventory. Likewise, plant productivity is

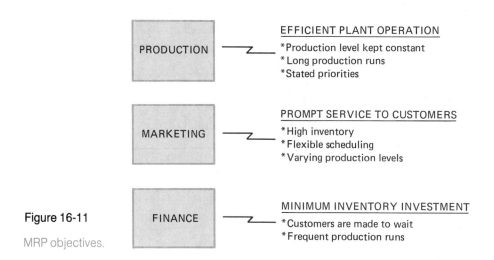

Figure 16-11

MRP objectives.

enhanced if long production runs can be made, but long production runs increase inventory levels and ignore fluctuating demand for products. The development of MRP provides a means of balancing and meeting all of these conflicting objectives. While the theory of MRP has been available for some time, computers have only recently made the technique practical for handling the necessary numerical calculations.

Simply stated, MRP systems answer two basic questions: how much? and when? MRP works backwards from the scheduled completion date of end products to determine actual dates and quantities of the various component parts and materials to be ordered or produced. The major business functions of planning, inventory control, production scheduling, and purchasing are involved. Effective materials management helps optimize a company's investment in inventory; too little inventory leads to late shipments and unhappy customers, while too much inventory means higher carrying costs and money tied up unproductively.

The basic tools of MRP are identified in Figure 16-12. The *master production schedule* shows the quantities of finished products and major assemblies planned for production per time period. Stated simply, the master production schedule shows what the company expects to manufacture. The *bill of materials* (BOM) file is used to define the structure of end products and major assemblies. In producing a given product, there may be several stages or levels of produc-

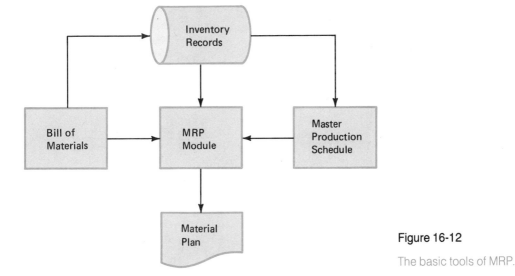

Figure 16-12

The basic tools of MRP.

tion. Each level has a separate bill of materials that lists all of the component requirements—the subassemblies, parts, and raw materials—that go into the parent assembly or end product at that level. In addition, the BOM indicates the quantity of each item required to make the assembly. The inventory records are used to maintain inventory status, requirements, and planned orders for each item of stock. Output produced by the MRP module is in the form of a material plan and/or action reports such as the one shown in Figure 16-13.

As MRP has grown in popularity, two basic operational changes have taken place. First, manufacturing companies realize that feedback is necessary if MRP is to provide a valid and accurate materials plan. Therefore, feedback loops from purchasing and production have been added to the system. These feedback loops enable MRP to handle a broader scope of operational problems. For example, capacity as well as material requirements planning is now included, and shop-floor control systems have also been incorporated. Second, the addition of dollars as well as unit data has expanded the applicability of MRP from the operational level to the strategic level.

This inclusion of feedback and financial data has resulted in a "new" orientation for MRP called *manufacturing resource planning* (MRP II). MRP II is an attempt to plan and control all the resources of a manufacturing company, both

Figure 16-13

A sample action report produced by a material requirements module.

```
RP15R   RUN...15 NOV      GM   REQUIREMENTS PLANNING           BUY PART REQUIREMENTS SCHEDULE              PLANNER ..B2      PAGE...17

PART.25-1422              WHEEL, RUBBER TIRED, NO.10    U/M MRC LL  LT  TOTAL COST, TOTAL GROSS     VALUE    AVG USAGE  OP TOTAL  O/O
                                                        EA   C   1  30   1 50000      5,056        7,584        0    D     0     B25

         ON HAND  -  ALLOCATED  -  BACK-ISSUED  =  AVAILABLE                                                                 ORDER QTY
            381        36                            345                                                                        B25

LINE DATE   12/22/80  02/18/81  03/03/81  03/19/81  04/03/81  04/20/81  05/04/81  05/20/81  06/03/81  06/18/81
GROSS REQ             300       50        300       350       300       50        600       50        600
STK AVAIL   139       664       364       14        539       189       714       664       64        14
STK ON-ORD  0         0         0         0         0         0         0         0         0         0
NET AVAIL   -161      364       314       -286      189       -111      664       664       64        -586
NEW ORDER   B25                           B25                 B25                           B25       B25

                           O P E N   O R D E R S   A N D   S U G G E S T E D   A C T I O N

ORDER #    DUE DATE    LINE DATE                   ORDER #     DUE DATE    LINE DATE    QUANTITY    ACTION
W01222 1   12/22/80    12/29/80        22          W01229 1    12/29/80    01/06/81        50

                                   S U G G E S T E D   N E W   O R D E R S

RELEASE DATE    DUE DATE    LINE DATE    QUANTITY    ACTION      RELEASE DATE    DUE DATE    LINE DATE    QUANTITY    ACTION
12/19/80        01/06/81    01/13/81        50                  12/26/80        01/13/81    01/20/81        50
01/13/81        01/28/81    02/04/81        75                  01/26/81        02/10/81    02/18/81        75
02/09/81        02/25/81    03/04/81        75                  02/25/81        03/12/81    03/19/81        75
03/12/81        03/27/81    04/03/81        75                  03/27/81        04/13/81    04/20/81        75
04/28/81        05/13/81    05/20/81       150                  05/27/81        06/11/81    06/18/81       150


RP17R   RUN...15 NOV      REQUIREMENTS PLANNING EXCEPTION REPORT    PAGE 1

PLANNER PART#................  EXCEPTION............  ORDER#.......  DUE-DATE    QUANTITY..
          12-1458  6-NEW ORDER                                      05/01/81       106
          ***
B2        88-2132 10-ORDER OK                         P01209*1      12/09/80       150
          ***
B2        16-1545  4-REVIEW-REQUIRED                  P00220*1      02/20/81       100
          ***
```

operating and financial. The philosophy of MRP II is that an organization's overall plans are closely tied to its production plans. Components of manufacturing resource planning systems include the business plan (dollars), the production plan (units), the master production schedule, the material requirements plan (MRP), the capacity requirements plan (CRP), and shop schedules. Often a series of minicomputers are distributed at key sites throughout the manufacturing workplace to monitor the processes. Both MRP and MRP II seek to achieve maximum production efficiency, minimum inventory, and efficient use of human resources.

MRP systems are time-consuming and expensive to install. Stories of how a firm installed a computerized system and then went back to a manual system after months of frustration are all too common. In order to successfully implement MRP (as well as other computer-based support systems) the systems development principles identified earlier in this book must be heeded. Computerizing a poor manual system usually assures a poor computerized system.

The following guidelines are important if the MRP application is to be successful:

— Positive commitment to the project by top management must be obtained.
— Users should play a leading role in system development.
— Project responsibilities and a detailed MRP project plan must be established and followed.
— The system should be simple and easy for users to understand.
— The system should use all of the MRP tools shown in Figure 16-12.
— Education must be provided at all levels of the organization from top-level management down to first-line supervisors.
— Accountability for the system's operation should be clearly delegated and should provide a basis for performance evaluation.
— Inventory records and other data used by the system must be accurate and up to date.

The development of MRP and MRP II has provided a tool for management which can help solve many problems faced by manufacturing companies today. But technology is only one part of the answer. Improved decision making as a result of these systems can only be attained through proper management of the most valuable resource of all—people. As with any computer-based support system, people are the key to success.

DECISION SUPPORT SYSTEMS (DSS)

In recent years there has developed a need for a kind of system different from the traditional batch-oriented computer application. Managers who want fast answers to their information needs are using a technique called decision support systems (Figure 16-14). A *decision support system* (DSS) is a human/machine information processing system specifically dedicated to effective decision making.

Figure 16-14

Decision support systems provide immediate feedback that a manager can understand.

© R.E.M.

The major components of a DSS are identified in Figure 16-15. These components include:

— A database with access to a wide variety of corporate data.
— A quantitative capability that utilizes models and other analytical techniques.
— A decision maker with a user-friendly computer interface.

Figure 16-15

Major components of a decision support system for business.

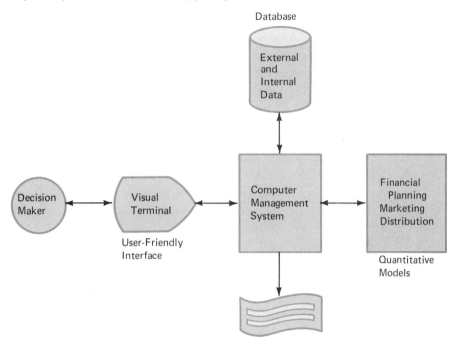

Often graphics tools are used for communicating "What if?" kinds of problems. The database incorporates internal and external data that have an impact on widely divergent management decisions. Internal data include basic data processing activities such as general ledger, billing, and payroll as well as organizational budgets, standards, and plans. External data include items such as government regulations and competitor actions.

From a business standpoint, there are three main types of DSS quantitative models: financial planning, marketing, and distribution. Financial planning models help determine how much profit or loss can be expected from different ways of investing resources. Marketing models evaluate the effectiveness of advertising strategy and pricing decisions. Distribution models determine how products are stored and delivered over large geographic areas.

Computer management packages for a DSS range from the widely used Visicalc microcomputer package that sells for $200 to sophisticated packages that sell for several hundred thousand dollars. These DSS software packages answer questions such as the following: "At what rate must sales grow for earnings per share to double in six years?" "What is the highest gross profit for return on investment to be at least 15 percent?" "Which depreciation method will allow maximum income tax savings on our capital expenditure?"

Like "MIS" (management information system), the label "DSS" is beginning to mean so much to so many that it may soon lose its meaning. In most instances, decision support systems are designed to support high-level managers in making relatively unstructured decisions. With MIS, the user is usually on the receiving end of large bodies of information. With DSS, the user is the driver who asks for specific, limited information. MIS traditionally produces hard-copy output and is COBOL oriented. DSS, on the other hand, uses business graphics and specialized query languages. The economic payoff of DSS is hard to evaluate since these systems support intangibles such as intuition and judgment. Characteristics of decision support components are further defined in Figure 16-16.

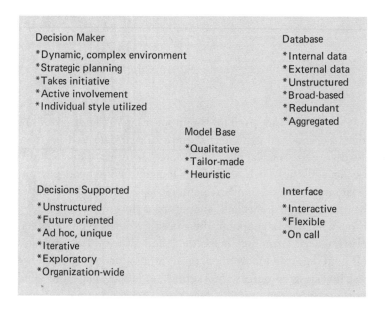

Figure 16-16

DSS characteristics.

Decision support applications may involve individuals with only a personal computer or corporate decision support staffs with mainframe capability. The following examples illustrate some of the different uses of DSS as a management tool.

An accounting professor at the University of South Carolina uses his Radio Shack microcomputer and two inexpensive DSS packages to aid him in his role as an expert witness in tax litigation cases.[1] His business planning and Box-Jenkins forecasting packages allow him to uncover trends in data and make projections for his clients. International Harvester, on the other hand, is a large manufacturer that has established a separate DSS staff to aid management decisions relating to fleet sales bidding, corporate financial management, production scheduling, and materials management.

As part of a four-year joint effort, IBM and First National Bank of Chicago developed a DSS that helps the bank's managers analyze asset and liability positions, decide on loan portfolios, and check indicators of bank performance. Through a video display, information can be called up in seconds in tabular form or on colored graphs or charts. Bank personnel expect many new uses and cite cases where their DSS reduced the cost of providing information to decision makers by over $100,000.[2] In much the same manner, American Airlines developed their AAIMS Information Management System to support planning, finance, marketing, and operations. AAIMS manages a large amount of historical industry data and allows managers to interactively access, analyze, compute, and display future projections. It is used to facilitate studies and forecasts of such items as load factors, market share, aircraft utilization, productivity measurement, and revenue yield.

EDP technology alone does not ensure the success of a decision support system. It is imperative that a DSS be compatible with managerial styles and demands. With proper development, decision support systems of the future have the potential to support decision making at all management levels and in all functional areas of an organization.

---

[1]"Interesting Decision Support Systems," *EDP Analyzer*, March, 1982, pp. 1-2.

[2]Eric D. Carlson, "Decision Support Systems: Personal Computing Services for Managers," *Management Review*, January, 1977, p. 9.

SUMMARY

Several new computer-based support systems are emerging that affect corporate executives, either indirectly or directly. Five such systems are discussed in this chapter: computer graphics for business, computer-aided design, robotics, material requirements planning, and decision support systems.

The use of business graphics for management and other presentations is spreading rapidly as high-resolution color graphics becomes affordable. Another popular graphics technique primarily used for engineering drawings is computer-aided design. Computer-aided manufacturing and integrated CAD/CAM systems will have an increasing impact on the function of industrial engineers.

A promising technique for increasing production-line output is robotics. While currently limited in their capability, industrial robots are proving cost effective in many industries. The societal impact of factories run by robots is equally significant.

Managerial planning and control activities are supported by two rather recently developed systems, MRP and DSS. Material requirements planning is used primarily for production scheduling and inventory control, with a new focus on manufacturing resource planning, where all the resources of a manufacturing organization are considered. Decision support systems use database technology coupled with quantitative techniques in a manner that allows immediate feedback for management decisions.

If properly developed and implemented, each of these computer-based support systems has great potential for aiding managers and increasing business productivity.

TERMS

Computer-based support systems
Computer graphics
Pixel
Computer-aided design
Computer-aided manufacturing
Computer-integrated manufacturing
Robot

Robotics
Material requirements planning
Master production schedule
Bill of materials
Manufacturing resource planning
Decision support system

QUESTIONS

1. Describe a manufacturing information system.
2. Identify manufacturing subsystems that affect strategic (long-range) planning for executives.
3. What are the advantages and disadvantages of using computer graphics for business applications?
4. What are the advantages of using vector displays as opposed to raster output?
5. Identify the main activities that are used during computer-aided design.
6. Compare and contrast CAD and CAM.
7. Describe the "physical" capability and characteristics of industrial robots.
8. Discuss the two factors that have expedited the current growth of robotics.
9. Specify benefits and limitations related to the use of robots in manufacturing.
10. Define MRP; MRP II. Which technique is broader in scope?
11. What is the purpose of the bill of materials?
12. Identify the major components of a decision support system.
13. What are the three types of DSS models?
14. Compare and contrast MIS and DSS.

ARTICLE

CAD/CAM Mart
Sees Rosy Future

CLEVELAND—The market for computer-aided design and manufacturing (CAD/CAM) just exploded. Hardware is getting cheaper, new software developments abound and new technological developments are opening more markets for CAD/CAM systems.

That rosy picture was painted by Predicasts, Inc., a consulting firm here that predicts a 31% average growth rate for the CAD/CAM industry over the next 20 years. A report released by the firm says the 4,600 CAD/CAM systems installed last year will blossom into about 190,000 installed systems by the end of 1995. Furthermore, the report says the biggest growth rate for the CAD/CAM market is happening right now. During the early '80s, Predicasts said, CAD/CAM applications will grow by 41% annually.

Mechanical design of solid models with color enhancements for stress design is currently the hottest market for CAD/CAM systems. The Predicasts report says that trend will continue through 1995. However, new CAD/CAM applications such as mapping, civil engineering and architecture applications will become more popular. The report notes that the civil engineering and architecture market will grow by an estimated 34%

and will account for one-fifth of the total CAD/CAM market by 1995.

Mapping applications of CAD/CAM include demographic analysis, urban planning, seismic data display, topology, cartography and oceanography. That segment of the CAD/CAM market is expected to grow by 22% annually through 1995, the report said.

Other burgeoning applications for CAD/CAM include piping layouts, facility planning and scientific research. Those applications will grow by as much as 20% annually; however, the report notes that it is difficult to predict what new applications will tap CAD/CAM resources.

Ironically, electronics applications of CAD/CAM, which produced the very large-scale integration (VLSI) techniques responsible for many dramatic systems developments, will decline over the next 20 years. The report predicts CAD/CAM growth among electronics firms will be below average at 19%, largely because the electronics business is more concentrated than others studied.

Like prices in the rest of the computer industry, CAD/CAM hardware prices, in terms of total system cost, will decline

continued

during the '80s, thanks largely to developments in VLSI technology. Actual hardware costs, however, are expected to increase at about 6.6% per year, the report said.

CAD/CAM software, while becoming more prolific, is also getting more expensive. Software developments in the CAD/CAM area will include more complex versions of three-dimensional viewing, on-screen menus, multiple view ports, motion (animation and rotation) and solids modeling packages, according to the report.

The report's other predictions include:

- Standardized networking hardware and software will be developed during the '80s to allow CAD/CAM systems to communicate with computer-integrated manufacturing systems.

- Group technology will standardize designs and establish a product data base. This will reduce the number of new subsystem designs in CAD/CAM products.

- While the study predicts CAD/CAM systems will remain largely stand-alone units, the systems will become more closely integrated with larger manufacturing systems, machine tools, robots and materials handling systems.

DISCUSSION QUESTIONS

1. Discuss the costs and benefits of CAD/CAM systems at this time and in the future.
2. What is the potential relationship between CAD/CAM and robotics? graphics? MRP? DSS?

APPLICATION

MRP Smooths Path Through
Rough Production Problems

"I suppose you could classify us as an assembly factory," says Ron Young, manager of production control for the Costa Mesa Operation, Collins General Aviation Division, Rockwell International.

The Costa Mesa Operation builds complex, highly sophisticated navigation gear —long-range VLF/Omega equipment for general aviation and air transport— as well as specialized airborne antennas for military and commercial applications.

"We build our own PC [printed circuit] boards, stuff them with electronics, do our own production test, assemble multiple boards. . . . We do our our sheet metal fabrication . . . and there's chemical film plating on aluminum and so on," adds Young.

"Our product is a small box," says Young, "that occupies only about 1.25 cubic feet. Even so it has about 4,000 components in it, so the bills of materials are extensive, and they're complicated because of the multiple levels of assembly we use for manufacturing economy. The biggest advantage of our MRP [material requirements planning] system is the way it allows us to explode those bills of materials," says Young.

"We had been running on timeshare with a service bureau," says Maynard Wiff, Operation comptroller. "We had two terminals, operated solely by data entry clerks, which were used for production control and manufacturing support, with some financial applications." Monthly costs and the need for additional capabilities "dictated that we go to an in-house MRP system," adds Wiff.

The service bureau's system "didn't have a shop routing system and had no real MRP database to draw upon," adds Young.

Good Accounting

The company evaluated many MRP systems before committing to NCA. "Only one came close to the NCA system," says Young, "but it lacked a good accounting package—and we really needed good, in-house accounting," says Young.

Wiff's concerns are financial and he makes extensive use of the MRP system's management-by-exception capabilities —receivables, payables, reports geared to picking up the in-betweens of the business—the invoiced and shipped-but-not-invoiced items. "After all," says Wiff, "customers feel that they don't have to

continued

pay until they get the invoice. After shipment, if we wait a week to bill, that just adds a week to our collection time."

Complicating the situation is the fact that many of the parts used in production have long lead times. "Most of our integrated circuits are state-of-the-art devices with 150-day lead times," says Young, "and some of our connector sheets have one-year deliveries. It's important for us to know, before the fact, what kinds of material requirements we're going to have. Ours is not the kind of business where we can simply go to the stockroom to see whether or not we've got some part."

Elizabeth Jusi, the Operation's materials manager, notes that the shortage reports generated by the MRP system save a great deal of time because they "tell us what's missing from the kits waiting in our two stockrooms. We can warn purchasing about the missing pieces ahead of time."

The Operation spent about three months getting the NCA system up and running. "We were familiar with the general concepts of MRP," says Young, "but the database conversion to the NCA format took time, as did the installation of the Digital Equipment [DEC] hardware [on which the NCA software runs] and the file transfers."

The Costa Mesa Operation closed November with the service bureau, started accumulating data on the NCA system at the beginning of December, and closed December on NCA.

"Many people were apprehensive about just cutting the thing over," says Wiff, "but we've proved to ourselves that if you have a well-committed user base that says the new system has to work, then people do the things necessary to make it work."

The NCA system implemented by Costa Mesa Operation runs on a DEC PDP-11/70 CPU with one megabyte of core memory, two 300-megabyte disks, about two dozen DEC VT-100 terminals, seven DEC LA-120 printers and a Centronics 6600 line printer.

"We handle all our business volume — $14 to $18 million this year — with only two production control clerks," says Young, "one for the navigation product, the other for the antenna line.

"I think it's pretty impressive that only two people can handle a business as complicated as ours with as many parts to it as ours," says Young. "Think of it... there's about 8,000 work orders on the production floor at all times, all being scheduled and released, with all paperwork being printed for them. That's phenomenal!"

DISCUSSION QUESTIONS

1. List the outputs identified for the MRP application described on the preceding pages. How does this system compare with that shown in Figure 16-12?
2. Which of the advantages cited by Rockwell managers do you feel are most important? Why?

PROFESSIONAL CERTIFICATION

CERTIFICATE IN DATA PROCESSING

General Information

The Certificate in Data Processing (CDP) Examination program is administered by The Psychological Corporation under the auspices of the Certification Council of the Institute for Certification of Computer Professionals (ICCP). Any qualified person may take the CDP Examination, which is intended to aid in the establishment of recognized professional standards within the data processing industry. The test is given once each year at established testing centers, usually located at colleges and universities. In order to receive the Certificate in Data Processing, candidates must satisfy the eligibility qualifications in effect at the time of their initial registration, including satisfactory performance on all five sections of the CDP Examination.

Purpose and Objectives of the CDP Program

The following are the objectives of the "Certificate in Data Processing" (CDP) program:

1. Establish high standards for data processing personnel by emphasizing a broad educational framework and practical knowledge in the field as desirable personal objectives.

2. Establish a method to measure knowledge appropriate to the management of data processing.

3. Establish a method whereby society can identify those individuals having knowledge considered important to the management of data processing.

4. Lay a firm foundation for the continued growth of the data processing field and for personnel within the field seeking to attain positions of leadership.

Text taken from the "1983 Announcement and Study Guide" for the Certificate in Data Processing Examination, *Institute for Certification of Computer Professionals, 304 East 45th St., New York, N. Y. 10017.*

The CDP Trademark

The mark "CDP" is owned by the Institute for Certification of Computer Professionals. Holders of the Certificate in Data Processing automatically become members of the CDP Association and are entitled to indicate membership and to indicate their certification by using the designation CDP in connection with their names, and also to wear the CDP key.

Certificate holders do not gain any right in the mark "CDP" but retain the right to use the mark in a manner designated by the Institute as long as the certificate has not been revoked.

CDP Eligibility Requirements

Although any interested individual may take the examination, in order to receive the Certificate in Data Processing of the Institute for Certification of Computer Professionals, a candidate must complete the following requirements:

1. **Experience:**

   Have at least 60 months of full-time (or part-time equivalent) direct experience in computer-based information systems.

   The 60 months need not be consecutive or in a single position. Acceptable forms of experience include that in data processing systems, programming, management, and teaching computer-based information systems. Systems and programming experience gained while employed by data processing equipment manufacturers, service centers, management consulting firms, or educational institutions may also be applied toward this requirement. Clerical, keypunch, direct sales, or experience gained in connection with formal classwork will NOT be considered acceptable.

2. **Academic Alternative:**

   Candidates having less than five years' work experience may substitute college-level academic work at the bachelor's or graduate level (*NOT* associate degree level) for up to two years of experience on the following basis *provided official transcripts of academic work are submitted to ICCP* before the examination date:

   a. *24 months* = Bachelor's or graduate degree in data processing or computer sciences.

   b. *18 months* = Bachelor's or graduate degree in related area including accounting, business, engineering, mathematics, sciences, and statistics.

   c. *12 months* = Bachelor's or graduate degree in nonrelated area such as English, foreign languages, history, liberal arts, etc.

3. **Professional Qualifications:**

   Each candidate will be required to obtain the signature of a responsible person who can verify both the candidate's work experience and professional qualifications through personal knowledge or access to the necessary information. A CDP holder is to make this verification whenever possible. The candidate's immediate supervisor may be accepted as an alternative when a CDP holder is not in a position to provide the required verification.

4. **Examination:**

   Pass all five sections of the CDP Examination. All five sections of the CDP Examination must be passed within four consecutive testing sessions. Once a section is passed, all remaining sections must be completed during the next three testing sessions. Otherwise credit will be lost for the passed section and the candidate will be required to take it again.

5. **ICCP Codes:**

   Subscribe to the Codes of Ethics, Conduct, and Good Practice. Holders of the Certificate in Data Processing are entitled to use the designation "CDP" after their names. The Council endorses the use of the term "CDP" as meaning that the individual has achieved the credential "Certificate in Data Processing," having met all of the requirements pertaining to it.

Testing Center Information

The following cities will serve as testing centers for the CDP Examination.

Established Testing Centers

ALABAMA
501 Birmingham
503 Huntsville
504 Mobile
303 Montgomery

ALASKA
506 Anchorage

ARIZONA
510 Tempe

ARKANSAS
513 Little Rock

CALIFORNIA
201 Carson
522 Los Angeles
772 Sacramento
524 San Diego
525 San Francisco

COLORADO
527 Denver

CONNECTICUT
531 Hartford
320 Stamford

DISTRICT OF COLUMBIA
536 Washington

FLORIDA
543 Jacksonville
538 Miami
544 Tampa

GEORGIA
548 Atlanta

HAWAII
551 Honolulu

IDAHO
552 Boise

ILLINOIS
555 Chicago
343 Normal
561 Springfield

INDIANA
563 Indianapolis
346 Notre Dame

IOWA
349 Davenport
565 Des Moines

KANSAS
571 Wichita

KENTUCKY
574 Louisville

LOUISIANA
577 New Orleans
815 Shreveport

MAINE
582 Portland

MARYLAND
583 Baltimore

MASSACHUSETTS
587 Boston

MICHIGAN
371 Battle Creek
592 Detroit
373 Flint

MINNESOTA
597 Minneapolis

MISSISSIPPI
603 Jackson

MISSOURI
607 Kansas City
609 St. Louis

NEBRASKA
615 Omaha

NEVADA
618 Las Vegas

NEW JERSEY
394 South Orange

NEW MEXICO
626 Albuquerque

NEW YORK
630 Albany
631 Buffalo
634 New York
640 Rochester
641 Syracuse

NORTH CAROLINA
853 Charlotte
408 Raleigh

OHIO
413 Akron
646 Cincinnati
647 Cleveland
649 Columbus
650 Dayton

OKLAHOMA
660 Oklahoma City
661 Tulsa

OREGON
666 Portland

PENNSYLVANIA
425 Carlisle
670 Philadelphia
674 Pittsburgh
679 Wilkes-Barre

PUERTO RICO
746 Rio Piedras

RHODE ISLAND
681 Providence

SOUTH CAROLINA
684 Columbia

TENNESSEE
436 Chattanooga
688 Knoxville
689 Memphis
692 Nashville

TEXAS
694 Amarillo
865 Austin
696 Dallas
700 Houston
701 Lubbock
703 San Antonio

UTAH
707 Salt Lake City

VIRGINIA
714 Norfolk
712 Richmond

WASHINGTON
718 Seattle
719 Spokane

WEST VIRGINIA
721 Huntington

WISCONSIN
888 Eau Claire
886 Madison
724 Milwaukee
460 Wausau

CANADA
952 Calgary, Alta.
954 Edmonton, Alta.
956 Halifax, N.S.
960 Montreal, Que.
963 St. John's, Nfld.
965 Toronto, Ont.
966 Vancouver, B.C.
969 Winnipeg, Man.

Time of Examination

The following schedule (in local time) will be observed at all testing centers:

8:15 A.M.   All candidates report to testing center
8:30 A.M.   Examination begins
1:00 P.M.   Approximate close of testing period

Candidates taking all five sections of the examination will be allowed 250 minutes to complete all sections of the examination. Candidates taking fewer than five sections will be allowed the following amount of time:

1 section = 50 minutes
2 sections = 100 minutes
3 sections = 150 minutes
4 sections = 200 minutes

A short rest break will be included during the testing for those taking more than two sections.

Application Fee — $35.00

A nonrefundable Application Fee of $35.00 is required of all candidates who are registering for the first time *AND* for all candidates who registered prior to 1979.

Testing Fee — $15.00

A nonrefundable fee of $15.00 is required for each candidate taking one or more sections of the CDP Examination.

Section Fees — $14.00 per section

Candidates may choose to take sections of the CDP Examination in any combination from the minimum of one to the maximum of all five sections. A fee of $14.00 is required for each section specified to be taken, as follows:

One section specified $14.00
Two sections specified $28.00
Three sections specified $42.00
Four sections specified $56.00
Five sections specified $70.00

Content of CDP Examination

Sections

The CDP Examination is composed of the following five sections, each containing 60 questions:

Section 1.   Data Processing Equipment
Section 2.   Computer Programming and Software
Section 3.   Principles of Management
Section 4.   Accounting and Quantitative Methods
Section 5.   Systems Analysis and Design

Outline of Content and References

The following Outline of Content indicates the content covered in each Section of the CDP Examination. It is presented to give candidates some indication of the scope of the CDP Examination.

Definitions for terminology in the Examination are taken from the American National Standards Institute glossary: American Standard Vocabulary for Information Processing, published by the American National Standards Institute, 1430 Broadway, New York, New York 10018.

The candidate is expected to have a practical working knowledge in each of the topics listed in the following outline.

Section 1. Data Processing Equipment

I. Computers
   A. Evolution of EDP
      1. Highlights of data processing development
      2. Need for and use of EDP equipment

   B. Computer Components and Functions
      1. Memory
      2. Arithmetic and logic
      3. Control
      4. Input/Output

C. Internal Processing
1. Data representation-code structures
2. Memory and registers
3. Channels
4. Interrupt
5. Memory protect
6. Floating point
7. Microprograms

D. Computer Characteristics
1. Commercial, scientific, and process control
2. Serial, parallel, and vector
3. Multiprogramming
4. Virtual memory
5. Multiprocessing
6. Data base processors

II. Peripherals
A. Input/Output Devices and Media
1. Card readers/punches
2. Direct access I/O
3. Paper tape readers/punches
4. Display terminals
5. Hard copy terminals
6. Printers
7. Consoles
8. Diskette readers/recorders
9. Key to tape/disks

B. Special Input/Output Systems
1. Magnetic ink character readers
2. Optical character readers
3. COM (computer output microfilm)
4. Voice input/output
5. Point of origin terminals.
6. Touch tone
7. Large screen display

C. Data Transmission
1. Digital and analog lines
2. Synchronous and asynchronous transmissions
3. Switched/leased/proprietary lines
4. Line grades
5. Modems and interface devices
6. Multiplexers and concentrators
7. Communication controllers

8. Message protocol
9. Simplex and duplex transmissions
10. Other

D. Auxiliary Memory
1. Magnetic tape
2. Disks/drums
3. Mass storage

Section 2. Computer Programming and Software

I. Principles of Programming
A. Basic Computer Instructions
1. Data transfer
2. Arithmetic
3. Decision
4. Input/Output
5. Special purpose

B. Methods of Addressing
1. Direct
2. Indirect
3. Registers

C. Loops
1. Initialization
2. Processing
3. Modification and control

D. Subroutines
1. Calling sequences and parameters
2. Open and closed
3. Macros
4. Reenterable and serial reusable

E. Program Checking
1. Memory dumps
2. Dynamic tracing

F. Basic Programming Techniques
1. Charts and diagrams
2. Decision tables
3. Data editing and error detection
4. Restart points
5. Documentation
6. Run time estimating

G. Input/Output Considerations
1. Access methods
2. Performance characteristics

H. Advanced Technique
1. Structured analysis
2. Structured design
3. Structured programming

II. Meta Programming Systems
A. Assemblers, compilers
B. Generators
C. Operating Systems
D. Utilities
E. Data Base Management Systems

III. Programming Languages

A. Application, Scope, and Usage
1. Procedure languages
2. Interactive languages
3. Simulation languages
4. Assembly languages
5. Report program generators
6. List processing languages

B. COBOL
1. Identification division
2. Environment division
3. Data division
4. Procedure division

Section 3. Principles of Management

I. Principles of General Management
A. Organizational Principles
1. Senior, functional, and supervisory managers' responsibilities
2. Line, staff, and service concepts
3. Centralization and decentralization concepts

B. Planning Principles
1. Policy and strategy formulation
2. Policy and strategy implementation

3. Planning process
4. Decision-making process

C. Control and Direction Principles
1. Measurement and evaluation of performance
2. Delegation of authority and responsibility
3. Leadership styles, morale, and discipline
4. Auditing and regulation

D. Staffing and Personnel Principles
1. Individual and group behavior—human relations
2. Organization change and development
3. Personnel hiring, training, and career planning
4. Manager selection, appraisal, and development

II. Principles of Data Processing Management
A. General Data Processing Management
1. Corporate organization considerations
2. Data processing organization and administration
3. Data processing strategic and tactical planning
4. Contracts and negotiations

B. Management of the Development Process
1. Project definition and planning
2. Application development
3. Application implementation

C. Management of the Operations Process
1. Computer center operations— centralized and decentralized
2. Technical services
3. Hardware and software performance

D. Management of Quality and Continuity
1. Security—physical and data
2. Standards—development and operational
3. Quality assurance and auditing
4. Contingency planning
5. Privacy
6. Ethics

Section 4. Accounting and
Quantitative Methods

I. Accounting
A. The Basic Accounting Process
1. The accounting equation and period
2. Cash and accrual concepts
3. Depreciation and amortization
4. Effect of transactions
5. Financial reports

B. Cost Accounting
1. Costing methods
2. Cost classification principles
3. Variance analysis
4. Inventory valuation methods

C. Accounting Applications
1. Accounts receivable
2. Accounts payable
3. General ledger
4. Payroll
5. Other accounting

D. Computer Auditing and Control
1. The audit process
2. Segregation of function
3. Processing control
4. Impact of advanced systems

E. Use of Accounting and Financial Information
1. Financial planning
2. Financial control
3. Management reporting
4. Financial statement analysis

II. Quantitative Methods
A. Mathematics
1. Notation and computation
2. Time series analysis
3. Graphical analysis

B. Statistics
1. Probability theory
2. Descriptive statistics
3. Statistical inference
4. Hypothesis testing
5. Correlation and regression analysis

C. Management Science (O.R.)
1. Deterministic methods
2. Stochastic methods
3. Simulation methods
4. Decision theory
5. Critical path analysis
6. Forecasting methods
7. Queuing theory

D. Mathematics of Finance and Accounting
1. Interest calculations
2. Depreciation calculations
3. Cost-volume analysis

Section 5. Systems Analysis and Design

I. Project Responsibility
A. Management and User Roles
B. Concepts
C. Planning
D. Team Organization
E. Control

II. Data Processing Systems Analysis
A. The Feasibility Study
1. Scope and objectives of the study
2. Application research and problem definition
3. Depth of analysis required
4. Economic considerations
5. Presenting the results

B. Systems Investigation
1. Establishing objectives
2. Scheduling the study
3. Fact-finding techniques
4. Analysis of requirements
5. Interviewing techniques

C. Equipment Considerations
1. Equipment configuration
2. Specifications for soliciting proposals
3. Evaluating competitive alternatives

III. Data Processing Systems Design
  A. The Systems Approach
    1. Establishing objectives
    2. Development of systems concept
    3. Management uses of information systems
    4. Performance improvements and alternatives
    5. Cost-benefit analysis
    6. Controls
    7. Implementation considerations

  B. File Design and Organization
    1. Determination of data requirements
    2. File organization concepts
    3. Data base concepts
    4. Selection of storage media
    5. Record layout
    6. File security

  C. System Input
    1. Selection of input devices
    2. Editing requirements and input control
    3. Sorting considerations
    4. Input timing considerations
    5. Time sharing

  D. Output in Data Processing Systems
    1. Report formats
    2. Use of graphics
    3. Visual displays
    4. Audio response outputs
    5. COM (computer output microfilm)

  E. Other Activities
    1. Pre-installation review and evaluation
    2. Work simplification
    3. File reconstruction
    4. Documentation and control

IV. Implementation Planning and Controls
  A. Project Planning and Control
  B. Scheduling the Installation Phase
  C. Planning the Conversion
  D. Formulating the Test Cases
  E. Special Control and Audit Considerations during the Cutover Period

  F. Interim Procedures
  G. Measuring System Performance against Specifications

V. System Maintenance and Follow-up
  A. Post-Installation Changes
  B. Periodic Reviews of System Performance
  C. Collecting and Analyzing Operating Costs

Sample Examination Questions

The following questions are samples of the type that may appear on the CDP Examination. The value of these questions is primarily in illustrating format.

Section 1. Data Processing Equipment

1. In which of the following ways is the digital computer superior to the analog computer?
   1. Speed
   2. Economy
   3. Capacity
   4. Precision

2. Which of the following statements concerning COM (computer output microfilm) is FALSE?
   1. COM devices basically photograph the image on a cathode-ray tube
   2. There are two major types of COM devices, alphanumeric and graphic
   3. Graphic COM devices are used primarily as substitutes for impact printers
   4. COM devices can write characters at rates up to 500,000 characters per second

3. Which of the following characteristics would most likely apply to a direct access file utilizing indexes or dictionaries as its addressing technique when processing randomly?
   1. Randomizing formula
   2. Two accesses are required to get each record
   3. Synonyms will be generated which will result in extra accesses
   4. There will be a high incidence of gaps or unassigned physical records within the file

4. Which of the following is *NOT* a significant factor in determining the average access time of a mass storage device?
   1. Character transfer rate
   2. Number of read/write heads
   3. Average instruction execution time
   4. Rotational speed of recording surface

Section 2. Computer Programming and Software

5. In COBOL, what type of condition is exhibited by the expression: A AND B OR D OR E?
   1. Or
   2. Complex
   3. Compound
   4. Exclusive or

6. A compiler would usually have to produce programs in the form of a relocatable object deck in order to make effective use of which of the following?
   1. Macro instruction
   2. Function subroutines
   3. Floating point operations
   4. Monitor programming control systems

7. In a COBOL program, if the data before editing are 1034, the sending picture clause is S99v99, and the results after editing are $10.34, which of the following is the correct receiving picture clause?
   1. $ × (4)
   2. $99.99
   3. $99v99
   4. $ × (2).xx

8. Which of the following is necessary to ascertain which program instructions access or transfer to a particular symbolic tag?
   1. Dynamic trace
   2. Diagnostic dump
   3. Reverse logic listing
   4. Cross-reference listing

Section 3. Principles of Management

9. Which of the following is **NOT** an important element in the question of lease vs. purchase of EDP equipment?
   1. Cost of money
   2. Tax considerations
   3. Maintenance expense
   4. Parallel operations cost

10. Which of the following would be considered an advantage in contracting for EDP systems applications work?
    1. Avoids maintaining a permanent staff larger than is required over the long term
    2. Avoids maintaining a large staff of systems programming people and reduces overhead
    3. The organization does not have to take the time to gain knowledge and experience
    4. A contractor acquires know-how about the company which can therefore be used in the future as an alternate source for make vs. buy opportunities

11. The organization chart is a graphic representation of the
    1. power structure.
    2. communications channels.
    3. locus of decision making.
    4. formal authority structure.

12. While strategic planning is heavily staff oriented, management control is heavily oriented toward
    1. finances.
    2. planning.
    3. marketing.
    4. operations.

Section 4. Accounting and Quantitative Methods

13. If $f(x) = x^2 + 5$, $f(5) = ?$
    1. 5
    2. 7
    3. 25
    4. 30

14. With 2 letters or digits followed by 3 digits, how many codes can be created if the letters O, Q, and I are not to be used to avoid errors with 0 and 1?
1. 66,000
2. 100,000
3. 1,089,000
4. 1,296,000

15. "Burden" in a manufacturing company is representative of
1. direct costs.
2. indirect costs.
3. factory labor costs.
4. product component costs.

16. To double the reliability of an estimate, which is the same as decreasing the standard error by half, the size of the sampling must be increased
1. two times.
2. four times.
3. eight times.
4. sixteen times.

Section 5. Systems Analysis and Design

17. The first phase in the evolutionary development of information systems occurs when
1. management discovers it is losing money.
2. resources permit the hiring of a system staff.
3. the decision is made to acquire a computer system.
4. the growth of an enterprise brings about the need for administrative planning and control.

18. In a real-time control system, each logical message requires 500 milliseconds of control processor time. Each remote control device requires synchronized service 5 times per minute. Which is the best estimate of the largest number of remote control devices that can be served?
1. 10 thru 19
2. 20 thru 29
3. 30 thru 39
4. 40 thru 49

19. Which of the following is *NOT* normally applicable in establishing the objectives of a systems study?
1. Develop and design the data files
2. Analyze and evaluate present operations
3. Develop recommendations for change as required
4. Review present and future corporate goals and objectives

20. Which of the following is generally *NOT* a consideration in real-time computer systems implementation?
1. Queues
2. Interrupts
3. Priority allocation
4. Hardware diagnostics

Answers to Sample Questions

Section 1. Data Processing Equipment
    1. 4   **2.** 3   **3.** 2   **4.** 3

Section 2. Computer Programming and Software
    5. 3   **6.** 4   **7.** 2   **8.** 4

Section 3. Principles of Management
    9. 4   **10.** 1   **11.** 4   **12.** 4

Section 4. Accounting and Quantitative Methods
    13. 4   **14.** 3   **15.** 2   **16.** 2

Section 5. Systems Analysis and Design
    17. 4   **18.** 2   **19.** 1   **20.** 4

Code of Ethics for Certified Computer Professionals

Certified computer professionals, consistent with their obligation to the public at large, should promote the understanding of data processing methods and procedures using every resource at their command.

Certified computer professionals have an obligation to their profession to uphold the high ideals and the level of personal knowledge certified by the Certificate held. They should also encourage the dissemination of knowledge pertaining to the development of the computer profession.

Certified computer professionals have an obligation to serve the interests of their employers and clients loyally, diligently, and honestly.

Certified computer professionals must not engage in any conduct or commit any act which is discreditable to the reputation or integrity of the data processing profession.

Certified computer professionals must not imply that the Certificates which they hold are their sole claim to professional competence.

Codes of Conduct and Good Practice for Certified Computer Professionals

The essential elements relating to conduct that identify a professional activity are:

A high standard of skill and knowledge.
A confidential relationship with people served.
Public reliance upon the standards of conduct and established practice.
The observance of an ethical code.

Therefore, these Codes have been formulated to strengthen the professional status of certified computer professionals.

1. Preamble

1.1: The basic issue, which may arise in connection with any ethical proceedings before a Certification Council, is whether a holder of a Certificate administered by that Council has acted in a manner which violates the Code of Ethics for certified computer professionals.

1.2: Therefore, the ICCP has elaborated the existing Code of Ethics by means of a Code of Conduct, which defines more specifically an individual's professional responsibility. This step was taken in recognition of questions and concerns as to what constitutes professional and ethical conduct in the computer profession.

1.3: The ICCP has reserved for and delegated to each Certification Council the right to revoke any Certificate which has been issued under its administration in the event that the recipient violates the Code of Ethics, as amplified by the Code of Conduct. The revocation proceedings are specified by rules governing the business of the Certification Council and provide for protection of the rights of any individual who may be subject to revocation of a Certificate held.

1.4: Insofar as violation of the Code of Conduct may be difficult to adjudicate, the ICCP has also promulgated a Code of Good Practice, the violation of which does not in itself constitute a reason to revoke a Certificate. However, any evidence concerning a serious and consistent breach of the Code of Good Practice may be considered as additional circumstantial evidence in any ethical proceedings before a Certification Council.

1.5: Whereas the Code of Conduct is of a fundamental nature, the Code of Good Practice is expected to be amended from time to time to accommodate changes in the social environment and to keep up with the development of the computer profession.

1.6: A Certification Council will not consider a complaint where the holder's conduct is already subject to legal proceedings. Any complaint will only be considered when the legal action is completed, or it is established that no legal proceedings will take place.

1.7: Recognizing that the language contained in all sections of either the Code of Conduct or the Code of Good Practice is subject to interpretations beyond those intended, the ICCP intends to confine all Codes to matters pertaining to personal actions of individual certified computer professionals in situations for which they can be held directly accountable without reasonable doubt.

2. Code of Conduct

2.1: Disclosure: Subject to the confidential relationships between oneself and one's employer or client, one is expected not to transmit information which one acquires during the practice of one's profession in any situation which may harm or seriously affect a third party.

2.2: Social Responsibility: One is expected to combat ignorance about information processing technology in those public areas where one's application can be expected to have an adverse social impact.

2.3: Conclusions and Opinions: One is expected to state a conclusion on a subject in one's field only when it can be demonstrated that it has been founded on adequate knowledge. One will state a qualified opinion when expressing a view in an area within one's professional competence but not supported by relevant facts.

2.4: Identification: One shall properly qualify oneself when expressing an opinion outside of one's professional competence in the event that such an opinion could be identified by a third party as expert testimony, or if by inference the opinion can be expected to be used improperly.

2.5: Integrity: One will not knowingly lay claims to competence one does not demonstrably possess.

2.6: Conflict of Interest: One shall act with strict impartiality when purporting to give independent advice. In the event that the advice given is currently or potentially influential to one's personal benefit, full and detailed disclosure of all relevant interests will be made at the time the advice is provided. One will not denigrate the honesty or competence of a fellow professional or a competitor, with intent to gain an unfair advantage.

2.7: Accountability: The degree of professional accountability for results will be dependent on the position held and the type of work performed. For instance:

A senior executive is accountable for the quality of work performed by all individuals the person supervises and for ensuring that recipients of information are fully aware of known limitations in the results provided.

The personal accountability of consultants and technical experts is especially important because of the position of unique trust inherent in their advisory roles. Consequently, they are accountable for seeing to it that known limitations of their work are fully disclosed, documented, and explained.

2.8: Protection of Privacy: One shall have special regard for the potential effects of computer-based systems on the right of privacy of individuals whether this is within one's own organization, among customers or suppliers, or in relation to the general public.

Because of the privileged capability of computer professionals to gain access to computerized files, especially strong strictures will be applied to those who have used their positions of trust to obtain information from computerized files for their personal gain.

Where it is possible that decisions can be made within a computer-based system which could adversely affect the personal security, work, or career of an individual, the system design shall specifically provide for decision review by a responsible executive who will thus remain accountable and identifiable for that decision.

3. Code of Good Practice

3.1: Education: One has a special responsibility to keep oneself fully aware of developments in information processing technology relevant to one's current professional occupation. One will contribute to the interchange of technical and professional information by encouraging and participating in education activities directed both to fellow professionals and to the public at large. One will do all in one's power to further public understanding of computer systems. One will contribute to the growth of knowledge in the field to the extent that one's expertise, time, and position allow.

3.2: Personal Conduct: Insofar as one's personal and professional activities interact visibly to the same public, one is expected to apply the same high standards of behavior in one's personal life as are demanded in one's professional activities.

3.3: Competence: One shall at all times exercise technical and professional competence at least to the level one claims. One shall not deliberately withhold information in one's possession unless disclosure of that information could harm or seriously affect another party, or unless one is bound by a proper, clearly defined confidential relationship. One shall not deliberately destroy or diminish the value or effectiveness of a computer-based system through acts of commission or omission.

3.4: Statements: One shall not make false or exaggerated statements as to the state of affairs existing or expected regarding any aspect of information technology or the use of computers.

In communicating with lay persons, one shall use general language whenever possible and shall not use technical terms or expressions unless there exist no adequate equivalents in the general language.

3.5: Discretion: One shall exercise maximum discretion in disclosing, or permitting to be disclosed, or using to one's own advantage, any information relating to the affairs of one's present or previous employers or clients.

3.6: Conflict of Interest: One shall not hold, assume, or consciously accept a position in which one's interests conflict or are likely to conflict with one's current duties unless that interest has been disclosed in advance to all parties involved.

3.7: Violations: One is expected to report violations of the Code, testify in ethical proceedings where one has expert or first-hand knowledge, and serve on panels to judge complaints of violations of ethical conduct.

Institute for Certification of Computer Professionals

CHARTER MEMBER SOCIETIES

ACM — Association for Computing Machinery
11 West 42nd Street
New York, New York 10036
(212) 869-7440

ACPA — Association of Computer Programmers and Analysts
Suite 808
11800 Sunrise Valley Drive
Reston, Virginia 22091
(703) 476-5437

AEDS — Association for Educational Data Systems
1201 Sixteenth Street, N. W.
Washington, D. C. 20036
(202) 833-4100

A1A — Automation One Association
7380 Parkway Drive
La Mesa, California 92041
(714) 465-3990

CIPS — Canadian Information Processing Society
243 College Street
Fifth Floor
Toronto, Ontario, Canada M5T 2Y1
(416) 593-4040

DPMA — Data Processing Management Association
505 Busse Highway
Park Ridge, Illinois 60068
(312) 825-8124

IEEE — Computer Society of the Institute of Electrical and Electronics Engineers
P. O. Box 639
Silver Spring, Maryland 20901
(301) 439-7007

SCDP — Society of Certified Data Processors
Union Plaza Building
1835 Union Avenue
Suite 325
Memphis, Tennessee 38104
(901) 274-1208

TOMORROW'S COMPUTER JOBS

BACKGROUND

Constant change is one of the most significant aspects of the U.S. job market. Changes in the size, age structure, and geographic location of the population, the introduction of new technology or business practices, and changes in the needs and tastes of the public continually alter the economy and affect employment opportunities in all occupations. Population growth has spurred the need for workers to provide more housing, medical care, education, and other services and goods. The use of new technology has created, eliminated, or changed the nature of hundreds of thousands of jobs. The computer, for example, has given birth to an entire new group of occupations—programmers, systems analysts, computer and peripheral equipment operators—while at the same time it has decreased the need for inventory clerks, bookkeepers, and other clerical workers. Changes in the way businesses are organized and managed have had similar effects. For example, the use of centralized credit offices has reduced the need for credit managers in retail stores.

As an individual planning for a career, you should learn about changes that are expected to occur in the job market. Your interests and abilities determine the occupation that attracts you, but future economic and social conditions will determine possible job opportunities. Fortunately, most changes that alter the demand for workers in various occupations generally occur gradually over several years. By analyzing the changing nature of the economy and the factors causing these changes it is possible to project future industry and occupational employment. Although no one can forecast the future with certainty, these employment projections can help you learn about future opportunities in occupations that interest you.

The *Handbook* presents information about the job outlook for many occupations. This section provides a background for those discussions. In it you will find information about expected changes in the population and the labor force, as well as employment projections for major industrial sectors and broad occupational groups.

Population

Changes in population are among the basic factors that will affect employment opportunities in the future. The demand for workers in any occupation depends ultimately on the goods and services

---

Material taken from Occupational Outlook Handbook, *Bulletin 2200, 1982-83 Edition (April, 1982).*

sought by the public. Changes in the size and characteristics of the population influence the amount and types of goods and services demanded. Changes in population also affect the size and characteristics of the labor force—the people who work or are available to work—which in turn can influence the amount of competition for jobs in an occupation. Three population factors that will affect future employment opportunities are population growth, shifts in the age structure of the population, and movement of the population within the country.

Population Growth. The population of the United States has increased throughout the century. However, the rate of growth (the size of the annual increases) was declining until the post–World War II "baby boom," which lasted until the late 1950s. Since the 1960s, the rate of growth has declined again (Figure B-1).

In 1980, the population was 226.5 million. It is expected to increase by about 0.9 percent a year during the 1980s, slightly faster than during the 1970s. Continued growth will mean more people to provide with goods and services, causing greater demand for workers in many industries. The effects of population growth on employment in various occupations will differ. These differences are accounted for in part by the age distribution of the future population.

Age Structure. Because of the "baby boom," the proportion of people age 14 to 24 was high in the 1970s. Through the 1980s, as these young adults become older, the proportion of the population between the ages of 25 and 44 will swell. By 1990, nearly one-third of the population will be in this age group compared to 24 percent in 1970. As a result of the relatively low number of births during the 1960s and early 1970s, the number of people between the ages of 14 and 24 will decline in the coming decade. The number of people 65 and over will grow, but more slowly than in recent years. These

Figure B-1

Since 1960, the population has grown more slowly.

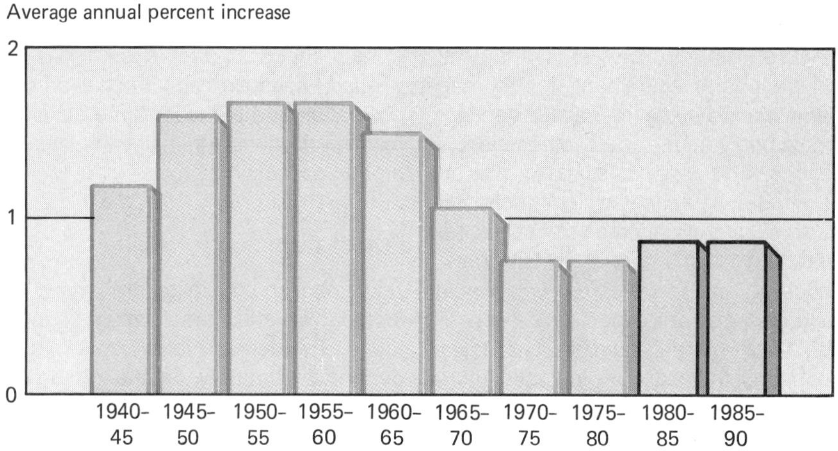

Average annual percent increase

Bureau of the Census

changes in the age structure of the population will directly affect the types of goods and services demanded. For example, as the number of young people declines, the need for some education services will fall. When greater numbers of people from the baby boom establish families, they will require more housing and goods such as appliances.

Shifts in the age structure of the population also will affect the composition of the labor force. These effects are discussed in a later section.

Regional Differences. National trends in population may not be the same as changes in a particular region or locality. A nation as large as the United States is bound to vary from one place to another in rate of population growth. For example, between 1970 and 1980, the population of the Northeast and North Central regions increased by 0.2 percent and 4.0 percent, respectively, compared with 20.0 percent for the South and 23.9 percent in the West

(Figure B-2). These differences in population growth reflect the movement of people to find new jobs, to retire, or for some other reason.

Geographic shifts in the population alter the demand for and supply of workers in local job markets. In areas with a growing population, for example, demand for services such as police and fire protection, water, and sanitation will increase. At the same time, in some occupations more people looking for work in those areas could increase competition. Individuals investigating future employment opportunities in an occupation should remember that local conditions could differ greatly from national projections presented in the *Handbook*.

Labor Force

The size and characteristics of the labor force determine the number and type of people competing

Figure B-2

Population growth varies among the states.

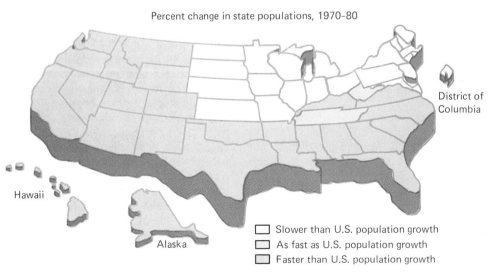

Percent change in state populations, 1970–80

District of Columbia

Hawaii

Alaska

☐ Slower than U.S. population growth
☐ As fast as U.S. population growth
☐ Faster than U.S. population growth

Bureau of the Census

for jobs. In addition, because workers are a vital part of the production process, the size of the labor force affects the amount of goods and services that can be produced. Growth, alterations in the age structure, and rising educational levels are among the labor force changes that will affect employment opportunities through the 1980s.

Growth. The civilian labor force consists of people with jobs and people looking for jobs. Through the late 1960s and the 1970s, the number of people in the labor force grew tremendously because many people born during the baby boom entered the job market, and women increasingly sought jobs. In 1980, the civilian labor force totaled about 105 million persons — 63 percent of the noninstitutional population 16 years of age and over.

The labor force will continue to grow during the 1980s but at a slower rate than in recent years. By 1990, the size of the labor force is expected to range from 122 to 128 million persons — a projected increase of 17 to 22 percent over the 1980 level. Contributing to this anticipated growth will be the expansion of the working age population and the continued rise in the proportion of women who work. The labor force will grow more slowly between 1985 and 1990 than in the early 1980s. This slowdown will result from a drop in the number of young people of working age despite continued growth in the participation rate of women (Figures B-3 and B-4). A larger labor force will mean more people looking for jobs. However, because of shifts in the age structure, the employment outlook for many individuals will improve.

Age Structure. As a result of the baby boom, a large number of young people entered the labor force during the 1970s, increasing competition for many entry level jobs. As the number of people between 16 and 24 drops, there will be fewer first-time entrants into the labor force, and competition for entry level jobs should ease. The proportion of 25- to 54-year-olds in the labor force will swell as people born during the baby boom get older. The whole economy should benefit from this change because

workers in this age group generally have work experience and are, therefore, more productive and less likely to be unemployed (Figure B-5).

Education. Employers always wish to hire the best qualified persons available at the offered wage. This does not mean that they always choose those applicants who have the most education. However, individuals looking for a job should be aware that the higher educational attainment of the labor force as a whole could increase competition in many occupations.

Persons contemplating dropping out of high school should recognize that a high school education has become standard. The educational attainment of the labor force has risen from 11.1 years of school in 1952 to 12.7 years in 1980. Many technical, craft, and office occupations now require postsecondary vocational education or apprenticeship, because employers prefer to hire trained applicants rather than provide training. Thus, high school dropouts are likely to be at a serious disadvantage when seeking jobs that offer better pay or advancement.

Traditionally, a college education has been viewed as a gateway to better pay, higher status, and more challenging work. As college education has become more widespread, the proportion of workers in the labor force who have completed at least 4 years of college has risen from 8 percent in 1952 to 19 percent in 1980. Recent experience has shown, however, that the traditional view of a college degree as a guarantee of success has not been matched by reality. Between 1970 and 1980, employment of college graduates grew 84 percent. The proportion employed in professional, technical, and managerial occupations, however, declined because these occupations did not expand rapidly enough to absorb the growing supply of graduates. As a result, 1 out of 4 college graduates who entered the labor market between 1969 and 1978 took jobs not usually considered by graduates to be appropriate to their education and abilities. The proportion of graduates in clerical, lower level sales, and blue-collar occupations grew.

Figure B-3

Labor force growth will slow during the 1980s.

Average annual percent increase

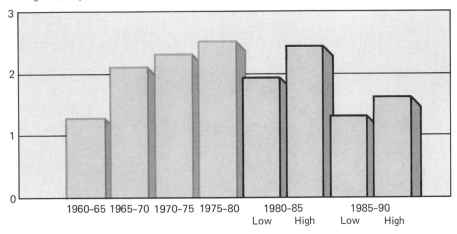

Bureau of Labor Statistics

Figure B-4

The number of women workers will continue to grow faster than the total labor force.

Percent increase from 1960

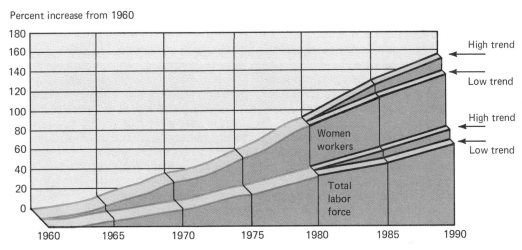

Bureau of Labor Statistics

Figure B-5

Through the 1980s, the number of workers in the prime working ages will grow dramatically.

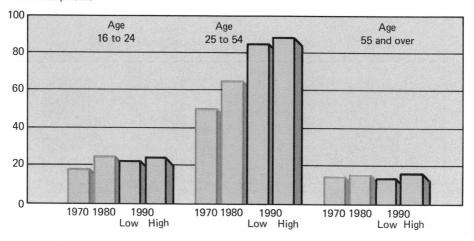

Bureau of Labor Statistics

Analysis of the future demand for college graduates, and of future supply, indicates that more college graduates will be available than will be needed to fill jobs that require a college degree. Not all occupations requiring a college degree will be overcrowded, however. Systems analysts, programmers, and engineers are examples of occupations where college graduates are expected to be in very strong demand.

But despite widespread publicity about the overall poor job market for college graduates, graduates still have an advantage over other workers. They are more likely to be employed and to hold the highest paying professional and managerial jobs. Persons interested in occupations that require a college degree should not be discouraged from pursuing a career that they believe matches their interests and abilities, but they should be aware of job market conditions.

SYSTEMS ANALYSTS

Nature of the Work

Many essential business functions and scientific research projects depend on systems analysts to plan efficient methods of processing data and handling the results. Analysts begin an assignment by discussing the data processing problem with managers or specialists to determine the exact nature of the problem and to break it down into its component parts. If a new inventory system is desired, for example, systems analysts must determine what new data must be collected, the equipment needed for computation, and the steps to be followed in processing the information.

Analysts use various techniques such as cost accounting, sampling, and mathematical model building to analyze a problem and devise a new system. Once a system has been developed, they prepare charts and diagrams that describe its operation in terms that managers or customers can understand. They also may prepare a cost-benefit analysis to help the client decide whether the proposed system is satisfactory.

If the system is accepted, systems analysts translate the logical requirements of the system into the capabilities of the computer machinery or "hardware." They also prepare specifications for programmers to follow and work with them to "debug," or eliminate errors from the system. (The work of computer programmers is described in the next section.)

The problems that systems analysts solve range from monitoring nuclear fission in a powerplant to forecasting sales for an appliance manufacturing firm. Because the work is so varied and complex, analysts usually specialize in either business or scientific and engineering applications.

Some analysts improve systems already in use by developing better procedures or adapting the system to handle additional types of data. Others do research, called advanced systems design, to devise new methods of systems analysis.

Working Conditions

Systems analysts usually work about 40 hours a week—the same as other professional and office workers. Unlike many computer operators, systems analysts are not assigned to evening or night shifts. Occasionally, however, evening or weekend work may be necessary to complete emergency projects.

Employment

About 205,000 persons worked as systems analysts in 1980. Employment of these workers is concentrated in two geographic regions—about one-third of the total are employed in the Midwest and one-fourth work in the northeastern portion of the United States. Most systems analysts worked in urban areas for manufacturing firms, government agencies, wholesale businesses, and data processing service organizations. In addition, large numbers worked for banks and insurance companies.

Training, Other Qualifications, and Advancement

There is no universally acceptable way of preparing for a job as a systems analyst because employers' preferences depend on the work being done. However, college graduates generally are sought for these jobs, and, for some of the more complex jobs, persons with graduate degrees are preferred. Employers usually want analysts with a background in accounting, business management, or economics for work in a business environment while a background in the physical sciences, mathematics, or engineering is preferred for work in scientifically oriented organizations. A growing number of employers seek applicants who have a degree in computer science, information science, information systems, or data processing. Regardless of college major, employers look for people who are familiar with programming languages. Courses in computer concepts, systems analysis, and data base management systems offer good preparation for a job in this field.

Prior work experience is important. Nearly half of all persons entering this occupation have transferred from other occupations, especially from computer programmer. In many industries, systems analysts begin as programmers and are promoted to analyst positions after gaining experience.

Systems analysts must be able to think logically and should like working with ideas. They often deal with a number of tasks simultaneously. The ability to concentrate and pay close attention to detail also is important. Although systems analysts often work independently, they also work in teams on large projects. They must be able to communicate effectively with technical personnel, such as programmers, as well as with clients who have no computer background.

In order to advance, systems analysts must continue their technical education. Technological advances come so rapidly in the computer field that continuous study is necessary to keep skills up to date. Training usually takes the form of 1- and 2-week courses offered by employers and "software" vendors. Additional training may come from professional development seminars offered by professional computing societies.

An indication of experience and professional competence is the Certificate in Data Processing (CDP). This designation is conferred by the Institute for Certification of Computer Professionals upon candidates who have completed 5 years' experience and passed a five-part examination.

In large data processing departments, persons who begin as junior systems analysts may be promoted to senior or lead systems analysts after several years of experience. Systems analysts who show leadership ability also can advance to jobs as managers of systems analysis or data processing departments.

Job Outlook

Employment of systems analysts is expected to grow much faster than the average for all occupations through the 1980s as computer usage expands, particularly in computer service firms, accounting firms, and organizations engaged in research and development. Many systems analysts also will be needed by computer manufacturers to design software packages. In addition to jobs that will be created by increased computer usage, some openings will occur as systems analysts advance to managerial positions, become consultants, or enter other occupations. Because many of these workers are relatively young, few positions will result from retirement or death.

The demand for systems analysts is expected to rise as computer capabilities are increased and as new applications are found for computer technology. Sophisticated accounting systems, telecommunications networks, and scientific research are just a few areas where use of computer systems has resulted in new approaches to problem solving. Over the next decade, systems analysts also will be developing ways to use the computer's resources to solve problems in areas that have not yet been recognized.

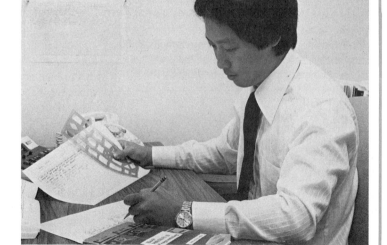

The shortage of trained computer personnel has resulted in an upward pay spiral that is expected to continue.

Advances in technology that have drastically reduced the size and cost of computer hardware will have differing effects on employment of systems analysts. Employment in data processing firms may not grow quite as rapidly as in recent years as more small businesses install their own computers rather than rely on a data processing service. This will be offset, however, by a rising demand for analysts to design systems for small computers that are specifically adapted to meet problem-solving needs of small firms.

Graduates of computer-related curriculums should enjoy the best prospects for employment. College graduates who have had courses in computer programming, systems analysis, and other data processing areas should also find many opportunities. Persons without a college degree and college graduates unfamiliar with data processing will face competition from the large number of experienced workers seeking jobs as systems analysts.

Related Occupations

Other workers in mathematics, business, and science who use logic and reasoning ability to solve problems are programmers, financial analysts, urban planners, engineers, mathematicians, operations research analysts, and actuaries.

Sources of Additional Information

Further information about the occupation of systems analyst is available from:

American Federation of Information Processing Societies, 1815 North Lynn St., Arlington, Va. 22209.

Association for Systems Management, 24587 Bagley Rd., Cleveland, Ohio 44138.

Information about the Certificate in Data Processing is available from:

The Institute for Certification of Computer Professionals, 35 E. Wacker Dr., Suite 2828, Chicago, Ill. 60601.

PROGRAMMERS

Nature of the Work

Computers can process vast quantities of information rapidly and accurately, but only if they are given step-by-step instructions to follow. Because the machines cannot think for themselves, computer programmers must write detailed instructions called programs that list in a logical order the steps the machine must follow to organize data, solve a problem, or do some other task.

Programmers usually work from descriptions prepared by systems analysts who have carefully studied the task that the computer system is going to perform—perhaps organizing data collected in a survey or estimating the stress on portions of a building during a hurricane. These descriptions contain a detailed list of the steps the computer must follow, such as retrieving data stored in another computer, organizing it in a certain way, and performing the necessary calculations. An applications programmer then writes the specific program for the problem, by breaking down each step into a series of coded instructions using one of the languages developed especially for computers.

Some organizations, particularly smaller ones, do not employ systems analysts. Instead, workers called programmer-analysts are responsible for both systems analysis and programming.

Programs vary with the type of problem to be solved. For example, the mathematical calculations involved in payroll accounting procedures are different from those required to determine the flight path of a space probe. A business applications programmer developing instructions for billing customers would first take the company records the computer would need and then specify a solution by showing the steps the computer must follow to obtain old balances, add new charges, calculate finance charges, and deduct payments before determining a customer's bill. The programmer then codes the actual instructions the computer will follow in a high-level programming language, such as COBOL.

Next, the programmer tests the operation of the program to be sure the instructions are correct and will produce the desired information. The programmer tries a sample of the data with the program and reviews the results to see if any errors were made. If errors did occur, the program must be changed and rechecked until it produces the correct results. This is called "debugging" the program.

Finally, an instruction sheet is prepared for the computer operator who will run the program. (The work of computer operators is described in the section on computer operating personnel.)

Although simple programs can be written in a few hours, programs that use complex mathematical formulas or many data files may require more than a year of work. In some cases, several programmers may work together in teams under a senior programmer's supervision.

Applications programmers are usually business oriented, engineering oriented, or science oriented. A different type of specialist, the systems programmer, maintains the general instructions (called software) that control the operation of the entire computer system. These workers make changes in

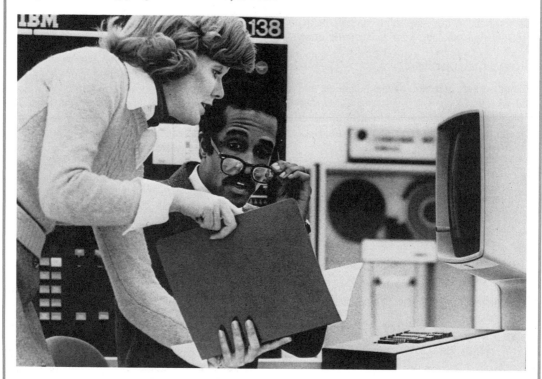

Programmers debug programs before they are run.

Photo courtesy of IBM Corporation

the sets of instructions that determine the allocation of the computer's resources among the various jobs it has been given. Because of their knowledge of operating systems, systems programmers often help applications programmers determine the source of problems that may occur with their programs.

Working Conditions

Programmers work about 40 hours a week, but their hours are not always from 9 to 5. Once or twice a week programmers may report early or work late to use the computer when it is available; occasionally, they work on weekends. When a new program is being tested, programmers may get calls from computer operators asking for advice at all hours of the day or night.

Employment

In 1980, about 228,000 persons worked as computer programmers. Most were employed by manufacturing firms, data processing service organizations, government agencies, and insurance companies.

Many programmers work in large firms that need and can afford expensive computer systems. Small firms, which generally require computers only for payroll or billing purposes, often pay data processing service organizations to do this work. Small firms may maintain their own low-cost, small business computers. Systems programmers usually work in research organizations, computer manufacturing firms, and large computer centers.

Training, Other Qualifications, and Advancement

There are no universal training requirements for programmers because employers' needs vary. Most programmers are college graduates; others have taken special courses in computer programming to supplement their experience in fields such as accounting or inventory control.

Employers using computers for scientific or engineering applications prefer college graduates who have degrees in computer or information science, mathematics, engineering, or the physical sciences. Graduate degrees are required for some jobs. Very few scientific organizations are interested in applicants who have no college training.

Although some employers who use computers for business applications do not require college degrees, they prefer applicants who have had college courses in data processing. Applicants who are experienced in computer operation or payroll accounting but who have no college training are promoted to programming jobs; however, they need additional data processing courses to become fully qualified programmers. Although it may be preferred, prior work experience is not essential for a job as a programmer; in fact, about half of all entrants to the occupation have little or no work experience.

Computer programming is taught at public and private vocational schools, community and junior colleges, and universities. Instruction ranges from introductory home study courses to advanced courses at the graduate level. High schools in many parts of the country also offer courses in computer programming.

An indication of experience and professional competence at the senior programmer level is the Certificate in Computer Programming (CCP). This designation is conferred by the Institute for Certification of Computer Professionals upon candidates who have passed a basic five-part examination. In addition, individuals may take another section of the exam in order to specialize in business, science, or systems applications.

In hiring programmers, employers look for people who can think logically and are capable of exacting analytical work. The job calls for patience, persistence, and the ability to work with extreme accuracy even under pressure. Ingenuity and imagination are particularly important when programmers must find new ways to solve a problem.

Beginning applications programmers usually spend their first weeks on the job attending training classes. After this initial instruction, they work on simple assignments while completing further specialized training programs. Programmers generally must spend at least several months working under close supervision before they can handle all aspects of their job. Because of rapidly changing technology, programmers must continue their training by taking courses offered by their employer and software vendors. For skilled workers, the prospects for advancement are good. In large organizations, they may be promoted to lead programmers and be given supervisory responsibilities. Some applications programmers may become systems programmers. Both applications programmers and systems programmers often become systems analysts or are promoted to managerial positions.

Job Outlook

Employment of programmers is expected to grow faster than the average for all occupations through the 1980s as computer usage expands, particularly in firms providing accounting, business management, and computer programming services, and in organizations involved in research and development. In addition to jobs resulting from increased demand for programmers, many openings will arise each year from the need to replace workers who leave the occupation. Because many programmers are relatively young, few openings will result from retirements or deaths. However, many vacancies will be created as experienced workers transfer into jobs as systems analysts or managers.

The demand for applications programmers will increase as many more processes once done by hand are automated, but employment is not expected to grow as rapidly as in the past. Improved software, such as utility programs that can be used by other than data processing personnel, will simplify or eliminate some programming tasks. More systems programmers will be needed to develop and maintain the complex operating programs made necessary by higher level computer languages, as well as to link or coordinate the output of different computer systems.

Job prospects should be excellent for college graduates who have had computer-related courses, particularly for those with a major in computer science or a related field. The number of persons with computer skills is not expected to keep pace with rising demand. Graduates of 2-year programs in data processing technologies also should have good prospects, primarily in business applications.

Related Occupations

Other workers in mathematics, business, and science who solve detailed problems include systems analysts, mathematicians, statisticians, engineers, financial analysts, actuaries, mathematical technicians, and operations research analysts.

Sources of Additional Information

Additional information about the occupation of programmer is available from:

American Federation of Information Processing Societies, 1815 North Lynn St., Arlington, Va. 22209.

Information about the Certificate in Computer Programming is available from:

The Institute for Certification of Computer Professionals, 35 E. Wacker Dr., Suite 2828, Chicago, Ill. 60601.

COMPUTER OPERATING PERSONNEL

Nature of the Work

All data systems require specialized workers to enter data and instructions, operate the computer, and retrieve the results. The data to be processed and the instructions for the computer are called "input"; the results are called "output."

Information is entered into a computer system by data entry personnel in a variety of ways. In some systems, *keypunch operators* prepare input by punching patterns of holes in computer cards to represent specific letters, numbers, and special characters, using a machine similar to a typewriter. In others, *data typists* use special machines that convert the information they type to holes in cards or magnetic impulses on tapes or disks. Most newer systems are capable of remote data entry. The user sits at a machine equipped with a typewriter key-

Training sessions sponsored by the computer supplier help operators and technicians pinpoint problems.

Cray Research, Inc.

board and an electronic screen that displays the data as they are entered directly into the computer. In some newer systems, data enter the computer at the source of the transaction being recorded; for example, at the loading dock or at a supermarket checkout line.

Once the input is coded—prepared in a form the computer can read—it is ready to be processed. *Console operators,* who monitor and control the computer, decide what equipment should be set up for each job by examining the special instructions that the programmer has written out. To process the input, they make sure the computer has been loaded with the correct cards, magnetic tapes, or disks, and then start the computer. While it is running, they watch the computer console, paying special attention to signals, such as error lights, that could indicate a malfunction. If the computer stops or an error is signalled, operators must locate the problem and solve it or terminate the program.

In some systems, devices directly connected to the computer provide output in the form desired by the programmer. In others, high-speed printers or card-tape-converters run by auxiliary equipment operators—*high-speed printer operators* and *card-tape-converter operators*—perform this function.

Frequently, data on punched cards, magnetic tape, or disks are kept for future use. *Tape librarians* classify and catalog this material and maintain files of current and previous versions of programs, listings, and test data. In smaller organizations, librarians may do some data entry as well as coordinate the activities of the programmer and the operations department.

Working Conditions

Because electronic computers must be operated at carefully controlled temperatures, operators work in well-ventilated rooms; air-conditioning counteracts the heat generated by machine operations. When the equipment is operating, however, the computer room can be noisy.

Some console and auxiliary equipment operators work evening or night shifts because many organizations use their computers 24 hours a day. Tape librarians usually work only day shifts.

Employment

About 558,000 persons worked as console, auxiliary equipment, and keypunch operators in 1980.

Although workers in these occupations are employed in almost every industry, most work in manufacturing firms, wholesale and retail trade establishments, and firms that provide data processing services for a fee. Many additional computer and peripheral equipment operators work for insurance companies, banks, and government agencies.

Training, Other Qualifications, and Advancement

In firms that have just installed a new computer system, tabulating and bookkeeping machine operators may be transferred to jobs as keypunch or auxiliary equipment operators, or console operators. Most often, however, employers recruit workers who already have the necessary skills to operate the equipment.

Many high schools, public and private vocational schools, private computer schools, business schools, and community or junior colleges offer training in computer operating skills. The military services also offer valuable training in a number of computer skills. In addition, a growing number of business firms across the country hold weekend seminars on data processing for high school students. Similarly, computer professional associations encourage student participation in professional conferences.

Employers in private industry usually require a high school education, and many prefer to hire console operators who have some community or junior college training, especially in data processing. The Federal Government requires a high school diploma, unless applicants have had specialized training or experience. Many employers test applicants to determine their aptitude for computer work, particularly their ability to reason logically. Keypunch operators and other data entry personnel often are tested for their ability to work quickly and accurately.

Beginners usually are trained on the job. The length of training needed varies—auxiliary equipment operators can learn their jobs in a few weeks, but console operators require several months of training because they must become sufficiently familiar with the computer equipment to be able to identify the causes of equipment failures.

Keypunch and auxiliary equipment operators should be able to work under close supervision as part of a team. They also must feel comfortable working with machines and doing repetitive, organized tasks. Console operators, however, must use independent judgment, especially when working without supervision on second and third shifts.

Advancement opportunities for keypunch and auxiliary equipment operators are limited because data entry techniques are becoming more specialized. However, promotion to a supervisory position is possible after several years on the job. With additional training, often including community or junior college study, a few operators advance to jobs as console operators.

Console operators also may be promoted to supervisory positions, or to jobs that combine supervision and console operation. Through on-the-job experience and additional training, some console operators advance to jobs as programmers.

Job Outlook

Changes in data processing technology will have differing effects on computer operating occupations. Employment of console and peripheral equipment operators, for example, is expected to rise much faster than the average for all occupations through the 1980s. Employment of keypunch operators, on the other hand, should continue to decline (see Figure B-6).

Recent advances in miniaturizing circuits have enabled manufacturers to reduce both the size and the cost of computer components. As this technology develops, a continued expansion in the use of computers is expected, especially by small businesses. Employment of console and peripheral equipment operators in data processing service firms may grow less rapidly than in the past as more small firms install their own computer systems, but overall demand for these workers should remain fairly strong.

This same technology will further reduce demand for keypunch operators. The primary reason for this decline is the increased use of computer terminals and storage of data on disks and cassettes. As direct data entry techniques continue to become more efficient, the importance of punched cards as a form of input will diminish. Despite the anticipated decline in employment, many openings will occur each year as workers transfer to other occupations, retire, or die.

Related Occupations

Other occupations in which workers organize data and process information on electronic equipment include secretaries and typists, printing typesetters and compositors, transcribing machine operators, and file clerks.

Sources of Additional Information

Further information on data processing careers is available from:

American Federation of Information Processing Societies, 1815 North Lynn St., Arlington, Va. 22209.

Figure B-6

Technological advances will increase the need for computer and peripheral equipment operators but lessen the demand for keypunch operators.

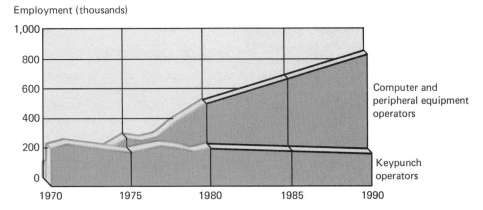

Employment (thousands)

Bureau of Labor Statistics

COMPUTER SERVICE TECHNICIANS

Nature of the Work

Computer systems play a vital role in our lives. They help us make telephone calls, receive paychecks on time, and reserve tickets for travel, hotels, and entertainment. In business and industry, computer systems perform countless tasks—from maintaining business records to controlling manufacturing processes.

A computer system consists of a central processing unit and additional equipment such as remote terminals and high-speed printers. Keeping this intricate equipment in good working order is the job of the computer service technician.

At regular intervals, computer service technicians (often called field engineers or customer engineers) service machines or systems to keep them operating efficiently. They routinely adjust, oil, and clean mechanical and electromechanical parts. They also check electronic equipment for loose connections and defective components or circuits.

When computer equipment breaks down, technicians must quickly find the cause of the failure and make repairs. Determining where in the system the malfunction has occurred is the most difficult part of the technician's job, and requires a logical, analytical mind as well as technical knowledge. As computer systems have grown more complex and networks of minicomputers (mini's) have developed, the potential for malfunctions also has grown.

Breakdowns can occur in the central processing unit itself, in one of the peripheral machines, such as a reader or a printer, in the remote mini's that are connected to the central unit, or in the cables or datacommunications hookups that connect these machines. To locate the cause of electronic failures, technicians use several kinds of tools, including voltmeters, ohmmeters, and oscilloscopes. They run special diagnostic programs that help pinpoint certain malfunctions. Although it may take several hours to locate a problem, fixing the equipment may take just a few minutes. To replace a faulty circuit board, solder a broken connection, or repair a mechanical part, technicians use a variety of handtools, including needle-nosed pliers, wirestrippers, and soldering equipment. The employer supplies tools and test equipment, but technicians are responsible for keeping them in good working order.

Computer technicians often help install new equipment. They lay cables, hook up electrical connections between machines, thoroughly test the new equipment, and correct any problems before the customer uses the machine.

Some technicians specialize in maintaining a particular computer model or system, or in doing a certain type of repair. For example, some technicians are experts in correcting problems caused by errors in the computer's internal programming.

Besides knowing how to use specialized tools and test equipment, computer technicians must be familiar with technical and repair manuals for each piece of equipment. They also must keep up with the technical information and revised maintenance procedures issued periodically by computer manufacturers.

Technicians keep a record of preventive maintenance and repairs on each machine they service. In addition, they fill out time and expense reports, keep parts inventories, and order parts.

Although technicians spend most of their time working on machines, they work with people also. They listen to customers' complaints, answer questions, and sometimes offer technical advice on ways to keep equipment in good condition. Experienced technicians often help train new technicians and sometimes have limited supervisory duties.

Working Conditions

Computer installations generally run around the clock and working time lost because of a breakdown can be very expensive. For this reason, technicians must be available to make emergency repairs at any time, day or night. Although the normal workweek is 40 hours, overtime is commonplace. The method of assigning overtime varies by employer. Some technicians are on call 24 hours a day. Others work rotating shifts—days one week, nights the next.

For most technicians, travel is local; they usually are not away from home overnight. Employers pay

Locating the problem is often more difficult than making the repair.

Photo courtesy of NCR Corporation

for travel, including reimbursement for job-related uses of the technician's car, as well as work-related education expenses.

Although some bending and lifting are necessary, the job is not strenuous. Work hazards are limited mainly to minor burns and electric shock, but these can be avoided if safety practices are followed.

Employment

In 1980, about 83,000 persons worked as computer service technicians. Most were employed by firms that provide maintenance services for a fee and by manufacturers of computer equipment. A small number were employed directly by organizations that have large computer installations.

Computer technicians generally work out of regional offices located in large cities, where computer equipment is concentrated. Most are assigned to several clients, depending on the technician's specialty and the type of equipment the user has. Workers with several accounts must travel from place to place to maintain these systems and to make emergency repairs. In some cases, more than one technician will share an account and service different parts of a system. In other cases, an experienced technician may be assigned to work full time at a client's installation in order to maintain all phases of that operation. Technicians who work for a nationwide organization must sometimes transfer to another city or state.

Training, Other Qualifications, and Advancement

Most employers require applicants for technician trainee jobs to have 1 to 2 years' post-high school training in basic electronics or electrical engineering. This training may be from a public or private vocational school, a college, or a junior college. Basic electronics training offered by the Armed Forces is excellent preparation for technician trainees.

A high school student interested in becoming a computer service technician should take courses in mathematics and physics. High school courses in electronics and computer programming also are helpful. Hobbies that involve electronics, such as operating ham radios or building stereo equipment, also provide valuable experience.

Besides technical training, applicants for trainee jobs must have good vision and normal color perception to work with small parts and color-coded wiring. Normal hearing is needed since some breakdowns are diagnosed by sound. Because technicians usually handle jobs alone, they must have the initiative to work without close supervision. Also important are a pleasant personality and neat appearance, since the work involves frequent contact with customers. Patience is an asset, because some malfunctions occur infrequently and are very difficult to pinpoint. In some companies, applicants must pass a physical examination. A security clearance may be required in cases where technicians regularly service machines located in restricted buildings, such as Federal Government installations engaged in classified activities.

Trainees usually attend company training centers for 3 to 6 months to learn elementary computer theory, computer math, and circuitry theory and to further their study of electronics. Classroom work is accompanied by practical training in operating computer equipment, doing basic maintenance, and using test equipment to locate malfunctions.

In addition to formal instruction, trainees must complete 6 months to 2 years of on-the-job training. At first, they work closely with experienced technicians, learning to maintain card readers, printers, and other machines that are relatively simple, but that have the basic mechanical and electronic features of a large computer system. As trainees gain experience, they work on more complex equipment.

Because manufacturers continually redesign equipment and develop new uses for computers, experienced technicians frequently must attend training sessions to keep up with these changes and to broaden their technical skills. Many technicians take advanced training to specialize in a particular computer system or type of repair. Instruction also may include programming, systems analysis, and other subjects that improve the technician's general knowledge of the computer field.

Experienced technicians with advanced training may become specialists or "trouble-shooters" who help technicians throughout their territory diagnose difficult problems. They also may work with engineers in designing equipment and developing maintenance procedures. Technicians with leadership ability may become supervisors or service managers.

Most computer equipment operates on the same basic principles, but machines built by different companies may be unique in design and construction. For this reason, technicians may find it difficult to transfer between companies that maintain different brands of equipment. However, because of the pressing need for experienced technicians, many opportunities exist for well-qualified workers to transfer to other firms that handle the same type of computer hardware.

Training and experience in computer maintenance may also help qualify a technician for a job in equipment sales, programming, or management.

Job Outlook

Employment of computer technicians is expected to grow much faster than the average for all occupations through the 1980s. As the nation's economy expands, more computer equipment will be used and many more technicians will be needed to install and maintain it. Business, government, and other organizations will buy, lease, or rent additional equipment to manage vast amounts of information, control manufacturing processes, and aid in scientific research. The development of new uses for computers in fields such as education, medicine, and traffic control also will spur demand.

The very strong demand for computer technicians is related to the growing number of computers in operation and the geographic distribution of these computers. Continued reductions in the size and cost of computer hardware will bring the computer within reach of a rapidly increasing number of small organizations. As more and more of these small systems are installed, the amount of time technicians must spend traveling between clients will increase.

Employment of computer service technicians is much less likely to be affected by downturns in business activity than is the case in other fields. Because computer operations are rarely curtailed during economic slumps, employment of computer service technicians should remain relatively stable.

Related Occupations

Workers in other occupations who repair and maintain the circuits and mechanical parts of electronic equipment include appliance repairers, auto-motive electricians, business machine repairers, electronic organ technicians, instrument repairers, radio repairers, radar mechanics, and television service technicians.

Sources of Additional Information

For general information on careers in computer maintenance, contact the personnel department of computer manufacturers and computer maintenance firms in your area. The state department of education in your state capital can furnish information about approved technical institutes, junior colleges, and other institutions offering postsecondary training in basic electronics. Additional information about these schools is available from:

U.S. Office of Education, Division of Vocational/Technical Education, Washington, D.C. 20202.

Computer and Business Equipment Manufacturer's Association, 1828 L St. NW., Washington, D.C. 20036.

The state employment service office in your area may also be able to provide information about local job opportunities.

C NUMBER CONVERSIONS

INTRODUCTION

Decimal, binary, octal, and hexadecimal numbers have particular significance in the EDP field. While human beings commonly use decimal numbers in performing calculations, computers use binary numbers almost exclusively. Octal and hexadecimal numbers are also widely used by computer technicians. These base 8 and base 16 numbers are relatively easily converted to their binary equivalents by electronic circuitry. In addition, these two bases are also easy for humans to decipher because of their proximity to the base 10 numbering system. Methods of converting numbers from one of these bases to another are explained in this appendix.

CONVERSION TECHNIQUES

The values that numbers have within given number systems are largely determined by their positional notation. Positional notation means that the position of one symbol relative to other symbols in a given number system determines the value of that symbol. This idea is expressed by the following algebraic notation for representing a decimal number in powers of the base 10. For example, the symbols 1 and 7 can represent either 1 or 7 or 17 or 71 depending upon their relative position to one another. The decimal number 135 may be expanded as follows:

$$135_{10} = (5 \times 10^0) + (3 \times 10^1) + (1 \times 10^2)$$

Note that the subscript 10 is used to indicate that 135 is a base 10 number. The use of subscripts eliminates confusion when using several number systems.

The following example illustrates the expansion of a base 2 number in powers of 2:

$$
\begin{aligned}
1101_2 &= (1 \times 2^0) + (0 \times 2^1) + (1 \times 2^2) + (1 \times 2^3) \\
&= (1 \times 1) + (0 \times 2) + (1 \times 4) + (1 \times 8) \\
&= 1 + 0 + 4 + 8 \\
&= 13_{10}
\end{aligned}
$$

The column position of a digit represents the power of the particular base under consideration. In the decimal number system, 1 is the same as 10^0, 10 is the same as 10^1, and 100 is the same as 10^2. In a similar way, a number in any base can be expanded in terms of powers of its base. In base 2, the relative positions of numbers starting from the right-most part of a number are the ones column, the twos column, the fours column, the eights column, etc. This is illustrated in the example shown above, where 1101_2 is equal to 13_{10}. In the same manner, the position of digits in base 8 (octal) represents the ones column, the eights column, the sixty-fours column, etc. (8^0, 8^1, 8^2, ...). The base 16 (hexadecimal) system works the same way (16^0, 16^1, 16^2, ...).

Figure C-1 summarizes the possible conversions of one base to another base for these four EDP numbering systems. Conversion techniques include positional notation, factoring, and grouping.

From Base	To Base	Comment
2	10	Expand binary number in powers of 2
10	2	Factor the decimal number by 2
2	8	Group 3 binary digits together
8	2	Each octal digit is converted to 3 binary digits
2	16	Group 4 binary digits together
16	2	Each hexadecimal digit is converted to 4 binary digits
8	10	Go from $8 \rightarrow 2 \rightarrow 10$
10	8	Go from $10 \rightarrow 2 \rightarrow 8$
16	10	Go from $16 \rightarrow 2 \rightarrow 10$
10	16	Go from $10 \rightarrow 2 \rightarrow 16$
8	16	Go from $8 \rightarrow 2 \rightarrow 16$
16	8	Go from $16 \rightarrow 2 \rightarrow 8$

Figure C-1

Base conversions.

To convert a binary number into a decimal number, expand the binary number in terms of base 2, do the calculation, and find the base 10 equivalent. This procedure was illustrated above for converting 1101_2 to 13_{10}. To move from base 10 into base 2 requires a method called factoring. Factoring is done by continually dividing the decimal number by the base to which you are converting. The procedure incorporates the following steps for converting 82_{10} to binary:

• Divide (factor) the decimal number continually by the base number.	$\begin{array}{ll} 0 & 1 \\ 2)\overline{1} & 0 \\ 2)\overline{2} & 1 \\ 2)\overline{5} & 0 \\ 2)\overline{10} & 0 \\ 2)\overline{20} & 1 \\ 2)\overline{41} & 0 \\ 2)\overline{82} & \text{Remainders} \end{array}$
• Stop division when the dividend reaches zero.	
• Read the binary equivalent from the remainder column (top to bottom).	$82_{10} = 1010010_2$

To convert a binary number to octal requires a somewhat easier conversion technique called grouping. The procedure for converting 1010010_2 to base 8 illustrates these steps:

• Start from the right, group each 3 numbers (bits), fill in extra zeros at the left to ensure 3 bits per group.	001	010	010
• Convert each group of 3 bits to its octal equivalent.*	001 1	010 2	010 2
• Read the octal equivalent for the entire binary number.	$1010010_2 = 122_8$		

*Equivalent numbers for the various number systems are given in Figure C-2.

To convert from base 8 to base 2, an opposite approach is taken. This approach is illustrated here for converting the octal number 675_8 into binary:

• Starting from the right, consider each octal digit separately.	6 7 5		
• Convert each octal digit to its equivalent 3-bit grouping.	6 110	7 111	5 101
• Combine the groups together to form the binary equivalent of the entire octal number.	$675_8 = 110111101_2$		

Figure C-2

Binary, octal, decimal, and hexadecimal equivalent numbers for the first 16 numbers in each number system.

Base 2 Binary	Base 8 Octal	Base 10 Decimal	Base 16 Hexadecimal
0	0	0	0
1	1	1	1
10	2	2	2
11	3	3	3
100	4	4	4
101	5	5	5
110	6	6	6
111	7	7	7
1000	10	8	8
1001	11	9	9
1010	12	10	A
1011	13	11	B
1100	14	12	C
1101	15	13	D
1110	16	14	E
1111	17	15	F

To convert a binary number into a hexadecimal number, a similar grouping technique is used. Since $2^4 = 16$, though, it takes four binary digits to represent a single hexadecimal digit. How this technique is used is illustrated by the following example, where 1010010 is converted into its hexadecimal equivalent, 52_{16}:

- Starting from the right, group each 4 bits. Fill in extra zeros at the left to ensure 4-bit groups.

  0101   0010

- Convert each group to its hexadecimal equivalent.*

  0101   0010
   5   2

- Read off the hexadecimal equivalent for the entire binary number.

  $1010010_2 = 52_{16}$

———————————

*See Figure C-2 for number system equivalents.

To convert a hexadecimal number into a binary number, reverse the preceding process. This concept is illustrated by the following conversion of $6AE2_{16}$ into its equivalent binary number:

• Separate each hexadecimal digit.	6 A E 2
• Convert each hexadecimal digit to an equivalent 4-bit group.	6 A E 2 0110 1010 1110 0010
• Combine the groups together to form the binary equivalent of the entire hexadecimal number.	$6AE2_{16} = 11010101110000102_2$

To convert from octal to decimal numbers or from decimal to hexadecimal numbers or from octal to hexadecimal numbers, it is best to convert first to base 2. Figure C-1 summarizes these conversions.

A final coding system used for storing numeric information in main memory of a computer is called binary coded decimal, or BCD. While not a number system, BCD has many of the characteristics of the number systems discussed in this appendix. To convert decimal numbers to their BCD equivalents, 4-bit groups are used. This conversion is illustrated for 725_{10}:

• Separate each decimal digit.	7 2 5
• Convert each decimal digit to its BCD equivalent (4-bit group).	7 2 5 0111 0010 0101
• Combine the groups together to form the BCD equivalent of the entire decimal number.	$725_{10} = 11100100101_{BCD}$

To convert a binary coded decimal number (such as 10000010110_{BCD}) into base 10, use the following steps:

• Start from the right and group each 4 bits. Fill in extra zeros at the left to ensure 4 bits per group.	0100 0001 0110
• Convert each group to its decimal equivalent.	0100 0001 0110 4 1 6
• Read off the decimal equivalent for the entire BCD number.	$10000010110_{BCD} = 416_{10}$

GLOSSARY

Acceptance test. The final test before the software or hardware is turned over to the user — is "accepted" by the user.

Action entries. In a decision table, specific actions to be taken when a particular condition or conditions exist.

Action statements. In a decision table, statements that indicate actions that could be taken in solving a problem or in making a decision.

Ad hoc reports. A special report for which the need is not known at the time that the information system is developed and implemented.

ADA. A computer programming language developed by the U.S. Department of Defense in 1975 and released for public use in 1981.

Address. A storage location in a computer system having a unique identification so that data can be stored and retrieved from that location.

American National Standards Institute (ANSI). An organization that establishes standards for the computing industry.

Analog. One of the two types of computers, the other being a digital computer. An analog computer operates by measuring data, predominantly by physical variables such as voltage, resistance, or rotation.

Analyst/Programmer. An individual whose major tasks involve the combining of programming activities with systems analysis and design functions.

APL (*A Programming Language*). An interactive computer programming language invented by Kenneth Iverson in the early 1960s.

Application control. In an information system, the security measures taken to ensure that transactions are processed properly and that the data are handled reliably and accurately.

Application program. A computer program written specifically to process data in an information system.

Applications programmer. An individual involved with writing computer programs for processing data in an information system.

Arithmetic-logic unit. The computer's "number cruncher"; the component of the central processing unit that performs the arithmetic calculations.

Array. A collection of related data values stored in an identifiable order.

ASCII (American Standard Code for Information Interchange). A standardized code designed for transmitting data. Each byte contains 7 bits plus a parity bit.

Assembler. A program that translates a program written in the computer assembly language into computer machine-language instructions.

Assembly languages. Intermediate-level computer languages that are less complex and difficult to use than machine languages.

545

Assignment. A variable or number joined by a relational operator (normally an equal sign) to an expression.

Asynchronous transmission. A method of transmitting messages of unequal length, each message requiring a start-and-stop indicator.

Attenuation. A phenomenon whereby fiber optic light impulses tend to lose signal strength over distance, necessitating the use of repeaters to read the weak, incoming light impulses and to transmit new, strong impulses.

Audio input/output. A method of converting oral messages into impulses understood by the computer system, or of converting computer system impulses into words that can be communicated orally.

Audit trail. A means by which an item of data can be followed or traced as it proceeds through an information system, starting with the origination of the item, to its input and processing, and continuing through the system until the data item appears as output from the system.

Auditing around the computer. An EDP auditing method that relies upon printed records and system outputs as evidence of the system's performance.

Auditing through the computer. An EDP auditing method in which the computer itself is used to verify the adequacy of system controls and processing accuracy.

Band width. In radio signal transmission, a measurement of the width of a range of frequencies.

Bar chart. A method used for displaying a time schedule.

BASIC (Beginners All-Purpose Symbolic Instruction Code). A high-level computer programming language written in an easy-to-understand English format; the language was first used at Dartmouth in 1967. It is one of the easiest languages to learn and is undoubtedly the best known of any high-level computer language in use today.

Batch processing. A method by which data are collected and input into the computer in a group.

Batch total. A total of values in a given field for all of the transaction documents in a particular batch or group of documents.

Baud. The number of bits per second that can be transmitted in a computer system.

BCD (binary coded decimal). A special code in which all binary numbers are expressed in four digits, thus making the process of converting to decimals faster. BCD was used predominantly in second-generation computing equipment.

Benchmark test. A test or series of tests on equipment by which comparative analysis of various hardware components can be made.

Bill of materials (BOM). In an MRP information system, a file that defines the product structure of end products and major assemblies.

Binary digit. Either of the two digits (1 or 2) in a binary system of numeration.

Bistable. Having two stable memory states or conditions that elecronically are either "on" (a value of 1) or "off" (a value of 0). The computer is a bistable memory device.

Bit. The smallest storage element in a computer system. It is capable of storing the value of 1 or 0.

Block. A method of reading and writing magnetic tapes that allows large numbers of data records to be read or written in one operation, thereby reducing processing time.

Block diagram. A diagram that uses simple block symbols to illustrate a system process or flow of data.

Broadcasting. A system in which all messages are broadcast on the same medium, enabling many computer systems users to receive a message simultaneously.

Bubble memory. A memory device consisting of a magnetic domain within a thin magnetic film.

Business data processing. Data processing used in organizations having a need for computer applications with large input and output requirements.

Byte. A combination of bits representing a character (a letter, number, or special symbol).

C. A computer programming language designed to gain programming efficiencies on minicomputers and microcomputers.

CAD/CAM (computer-aided design/computer-aided manufacturing). Computer software and hardware containing graphics capability for mechanical drafting and design, integrated circuit design, and other specific design applications.

Calculating. Performing the arithmetic or logic functions necessary to process data.

Card field. A group of consecutive columns on a punched card reserved for a specific unit of data.

Card punch unit. A special type of hardware device that translates output signals from a computer into the Hollerith code punched onto cards.

Card reader. A device that inputs punched cards into a computer system.

Cathode ray tube (CRT). A terminal device that displays output on a screen similar to that of a television set.

CDP. *See* Certificate in Data Processing

Central processing unit. The major component of a computer system. The CPU consists of a control unit, an arithmetic-logic unit, and main memory. The three components working together control the functions of the computer system.

Certificate in Data Processing. A certificate granted by the Institute for Certification of Computer Professionals (ICCP) to a candidate who demonstrates satisfactory academic and work experience in computer-based information systems and passes a written examination.

Chain printer. A computer printing device that uses a long mechanical chain containing alphabetic, numeric, and special characters to print data on paper.

Channels. The horizontal rows on paper tapes into which holes are punched that control various functions on computer printers, such as the first and last printing lines on that page.

Character. A letter, number, or special symbol used either singly or in combination with other symbols to represent data.

Charged-coupled device. A type of semiconductor storage method using silicon chips. The chips have electrical charges on small metal squares etched at each storage location.

Check-digit verification. A means of detecting errors in data transmission or processing. A unique identification number is given an extra digit (the check digit) which is a mathematical function of the number.

Chief programmer. A person designated as the leader of a programming team.

Circuit switching. A physical connection enabling transmission of data from one point to another.

Classifying. Putting together like things according to certain characteristics.

Closed shop. A computer operation center that is off limits to anyone other than computer operators and computer center management personnel.

COBOL (Common Business Oriented Language). First used in 1960, today it is the most widely used computer language for business applications in both medium-size and large organizations.

Codes. Shorthand expressions of different classes of data that exist within the information system.

Coding. The process of writing computer programs.

COM (computer output microfilm). A method used to reduce the volume of space needed to store vast amounts of hard-copy information by converting computer output directly to microfilm or microfiche.

Communicating word processors. Word processors that can be linked together to form a network and thereby used to deliver electronic mail.

Communications processor. A digital computer that has been programmed to perform one or more communication functions.

Compiler. Computer software that translates a program written in a high-level language into a form the computer can understand (machine language).

Completeness check (test). A test made on data to verify that all required data items have been entered into the information system.

Computer. A general-purpose, electronic stored-program device designed to handle program instructions as well as the data to be processed by the instructions.

Computer-based message system (CBMS). A system that uses the computer to receive and transmit messages that have been prepared on video terminals.

Computer center director. The key person in a computer center who makes decisions or recommendations to the organization's management concerning hardware and software and who supervises all computer center personnel and the use of the computer equipment.

Computer graphics. The presentation of data in the form of bar charts, histograms, pie charts, or grids on a display screen or plotter to highlight data variations. Graphics are available in black and white or in color and can be presented in two or three dimensions.

Computer-integrated manufacturing (CIM). The combining of CAD/CAM applications with modern database capabilities.

Computer network. A collection of computers and terminal devices linked together by a communication system.

Computer operator. A person who operates computer equipment.

Computer system. Input, output, storage, and the central processing unit.

Concentrator (also called Multiplexer). A device that can concentrate and transfer data to one line.

Condition entries. In a decision table, used to indicate whether a condition or combination of conditions exists.

Condition statements. In a decision table, statements that indicate which conditions may arise in the decision process.

Constraints. Limits that currently exist or may arise during the development and implementation of an information system.

Control program. A program that controls the execution and flow of processing jobs throughout the computer system.

Control unit. The component of the computer system that manages the execution of the program instructions by retrieving instructions from memory, translating them into computer functions, and sending signals to other hardware units to carry out the various processing functions.

Convention. A rule normally used in only one information development effort to assist in managing the writing of the computer programs.

Conversion programs. Programs that are necessary to facilitate changing from an old information or computer system to a new one.

Core memory. A tiny ring-shaped piece of magnetic material in which one bit of data is stored by magnetizing the core in a particular direction.

Core planes. Thousands of magnetic cores strung together on wires combined to represent alphabetic or numeric characters.

Critical path. In a network, the path that takes the longest to complete.

Cursor. A location indicator on a CRT that assists a person in entering data.

Cylinder. Tracks having the same number on adjacent magnetic disks in a disk pack.

Data. Unorganized facts.

Data density. The number of bytes of data per inch of magnetic tape.

Data diddling. A simple form of penetration into an information system whereby data are changed before or during computer input.

Data encryption. A coding technique used to secure sensitive data by jumbling or mixing the data according to a predetermined format.

Data entry personnel. Clerical employees in information systems; they operate the keyed data entry devices and the visual display terminals.

Data integrity. The accuracy, consistency, and completeness of data that are maintained by the information system.

Data leakage. Illegal removal of data from a computer facility.

Data processing. Transformation of data into information through classifying, sorting, merging, recording, retrieving, transmitting, or reporting.

Data processing cycle. The sequence of operations composed of input, processing and output.

Database. The organizing of files into related units that are then viewed as a single storage concept. The data are then made available to a wide variety of individuals and systems within the organization.

Database administrator (DBA). An individual who supervises and controls the development of databases within the organization.

Decision support system. A sophisticated computer system application, providing access to a wide variety of data to aid in effective decision making.

Decision table (or logic table). An analysis technique used to document the logic of arriving at a particular decision or result.

Demand report. A report that provides information to management upon demand.

Design phase. The tasks associated with developing the information system based upon previously determined information or system requirements. The phase normally occurs at about the midpoint of the systems development cycle.

Design specifications. The result of an analysis of information needs of a specific system within the organization; they include output specifications, input specifications, and processing requirements.

Digital. One of the two types of computers, the other being an analog computer. A ditigal computer operates by counting data represented by means of coded characters such as numbers, letters, and symbols.

Digitizer. A device used to input data for graphical use.

Direct access. A method of processing data by which the data can be stored and retrieved without consideration being given to data stored in preceding or subsequent locations.

Direct conversion. Switching from an old information system or hardware device to a new one with no intervening time frame or parallel activities.

Disk pack. A group of magnetic disks grouped together in a stack.

Distributed data processing. A method of processing data utilizing hardware and software in various geographical locations, requiring the use of a communications network and many links and nodes in an almost infinite number of designs.

Documentation. The process of writing down or collecting written, tangible items that are then used to explain the workings of the information system.

Dot matrix printer. A device that prints characters on paper by striking the paper with different combinations of metal pins.

Driver statement. A program statement used to steer or guide the execution of the program to the various program subsets or paragraphs.

Dumb terminal. A device that does not process data or program instructions; it is totally dependent on the computer.

Echo check. A means of verifying data transmission by sending back the specific signal that was received; a comparison is then made to see if the signal sent back is the same as the one originally transmitted.

Editing. A process of using a computer program to check data items as they enter the system for processing.

EDP auditor. A person whose main function is to help ensure that computerized information systems meet accepted accounting and auditing procedures.

EDP controls. The plans, procedures, and records that help safeguard the assets and ensure that reliable data are maintained in the information system.

Ego-less programming. The concept of organizing the computer programming tasks so that credit for success or blame for failure must be shared by several individuals rather than just one programmer.

Electronic mail. The delivery of messages over telecommunications lines utilizing computerized equipment, messages that would otherwise be handled by the postal system or by telephone. The messages include various forms of printed text and data.

Electrostatic printer. A device that creates images on paper by placing charged rods on heat-sensitive paper.

Electrothermal printer. A device that creates images on paper by placing heated rods on heat-sensitive paper.

Emulator. A computer program that reads programs, records, or files that were originally written to run on a specific hardware device and, through a conversion process, translates the instructions so that they will run on a different device.

ENIAC (Electronic Numerical Integrator and (Computer). An early computing device invented in the early 1940s by John W. Mauchly and J. Presper Eckert.

Entity. The person, place, or thing about which data are being stored.

Ergonomics. The science or technology of applying biological and engineering data to problems relating to man and machine.

Event. An occurrence in a network: the beginning or the end of an activity.

Exception report. A report generated from the system when a function ceases to perform within a prescribed range or limits.

Expression. Two or more variables or numbers joined together by an operator (+, −, *, /).

Facsimile transmission (FAX). Similar to electronic mail but involves transmission of documents only and does not require using computerized systems.

Feasibility study. A preliminary investigation to develop plans for constructing a new information system. A major activity of the study is the cost/benefit analysis.

Feedback loop. The process of providing a means by which messages can be sent to sources of origin for evaluation.

Fiber optics. A new technology based on a digital transmission theory utilizing light rays.

Field. Letters or digits represented by bytes or characters and joined together to form a single piece of data, such as a person's name or address.

Field check. A test to check the characters in a field to ensure that they are of the correct type.

File. A group of records on related subjects or entities.

File access. The process of retrieving data stored in groups of related records.

File editing. Retaining or eliminating data, rearranging data, and/or testing data for verification purposes.

File protection ring. A plastic device that protects data on magnetic tape reels.

File updating. The task of correcting out-of-date file data.

Financial total. The total of a column (field) containing such data as total sales or total cash receipts.

Flexible diskette (floppy disk). A round, plastic storage platter used with minicomputers and microcomputers. It is faster to read than punched cards, has greater storage capacity, and is reusable.

Flow control. The management of data being transported by electromagnetic devices through the computer system.

Flowchart. The traditional method of representing in a schematic form the flow of data through a system.

Forms design. The creation of source documents and data input forms.

FORTH. A computer programming language designed in the early 1970s by Charles Moore for use in astronomical observations.

FORTRAN (FORmula TRANslator). The first high-level language to enjoy wide success. It was developed by John Backus of IBM and was released in 1957 to support scientific and engineering problems that involved complex mathematical computations.

Full-duplex. A communications mode that allows data to be transmitted in both directions at the same time.

Functional applications. Complex transaction processing that is unique to each organization and its activities. The applications are concerned with control of the organization's resources.

Gantt chart. A bar chart used for scheduling time sequences.

Generalized audit software packages. Computer programs that the auditor adapts to specific computer systems even though the programs were written for general auditing applications. The programs perform a variety of standard auditing procedures.

Generation. Computer generations are usually characterized by dramatic improvements in the hardware, typically resulting in tenfold or higher increases in speed and enhanced reliability of hardware.

GO TO-less programming. The concept of not using GO TO statements in a computer program.

Grandfather-father-son concept. A security plan where the three most recent master files are retained so that, if a malfunction occurs during processing, the most recent error-free file copy can be used to reprocess or recover the data.

Graphics. Patterns and shapes used to display information, in contrast to the more traditional use of numbers and words in columns.

Half-duplex. A communications mode that allows data to be transmitted in both directions, but in only one direction at a time.

Handprint input terminal. A terminal that allows the use of a pen or pencil to write on a pressure-sensitive surface; the points of contact are then translated into ASCII character codes and transmitted to a computer.

Hard-copy terminal. A device that prints computer responses on paper, as well as the information or data entered, giving the user a permanent copy of both input and output messages.

Hardware. The electrical and mechanical devices that make up a computer system.

Hardware security. Securing computer assets and capital equipment to prevent loss.

Hardware study. The study made to determine the processing equipment that will be needed if a specific information system is developed and implemented.

Hash total. A total generated from data fields that are not normally totaled, such as customer account numbers or product identification codes.

Header label. The first internal record on a magnetic tape used by the computer to verify that the correct tape file is being accessed.

Hexadecimal. A base 16 numbering system, where a single digit ranges from a value of 0 to 15 (decimal).

High-level languages. Computer programming languages that approximate the use of the English language or mathematical functions and can be used on a variety of computers.

HIPO chart (*H*ierarchy plus *I*nput *P*rocessing *O*utput). A kind of chart developed in the late 1960s and early 1970s as a means of documenting the hierarchical nature of a system.

Impact printer. A mechanism that prints one or more characters on paper by physically impacting or hitting the paper.

Information. The knowledge derived from manipulation of data (unorganized facts) for use in making a decision.

Information system. The process of transforming raw data into useful information for a decision maker.

Input. Data entered into a system for processing.

Input specifications. Specifications on how data come into existence, the source of the data, collection requirements, and accuracy level desired.

Intangible benefits. Benefits for which dollar amounts are almost impossible to establish.

Intangible costs. Costs where specific dollar amounts cannot be determined.

Intelligent copiers. Computer-controlled devices that fetch messages from memory, assemble paragraphs, and produce and distribute copies of business documents at high speeds.

Intelligent terminal. A small-capacity, stand-alone computer that may function independently or be incorporated into the main computer system.

Interactive language. A computer language that has the specific capability of allowing the user to solve problems on interactive terminals such as a VDT (visual display terminal).

Interactive output. Output that is the result of the computer and the user conversing with one another.

Interactive processing. Processing in which a user of a terminal communicates with the computer by typing commands, instructions, or data on a keyboard while the computer's responses are displayed on the CRT screen.

Interblock gap. The gap between blocks of data on magnetic tapes.

Interrecord gap. A space on magnetic tape between each record, usually ¾ inch in length.

IPO (input, processing, and output). The three components found in any information system.

IPO diagrams. Charts used to indicate the input, processing, and output functions of an information system.

Iteration. Repeat form of structured statements that follow a looping pattern.

Job control language (JCL). The part of the computer operating system that specifies such things as the beginning of a program, the processing tasks to be carried out, and the input/output devices needed.

Josephson junction. A method of developing computer logic circuitry.

Key station input system. A cluster of interactive terminals linked to a minicomputer used primarily for entering data.

Key-to-disk system. An input system consisting of many stations operating under a central processor unit, where the CPU edits the data prior to their storage on a disk and also supplies messages or additional information related to entering the data.

Key-to-tape system. A machine similar to a keypunch that is used to key information directly from the data entry keyboard onto a magnetic tape reel or a cassette tape.

Keypunch machine. A device used to input information from a keyboard onto punched cards.

Laser printer. A device that creates an image on paper by projecting a light image onto photosensitive paper.

Limits check (test). A program edit check that tests the value of a data item to determine whether the value falls within a prescribed range or limit.

Links. Channels in a computer network that connect nodes.

Local network. A well-defined and generally self-enclosed area of equipment or communication links.

Logic symbols. Mathematical symbols often used in constructing flowcharting statements.

Logical operators. The words *and, or,* and *not* when used as a test between two arithmetic expressions in a program statement.

Loop. A series of program instructions that are executed more than once. The first statement in the loop starts the iteration; the last statement is the end of the loop but may not be the last statement in an iteration.

Looping. A concept used frequently in constructing programs or system flowcharting logic in order to avoid writing duplicate program statements.

Machine language. The programming language most easily understood by the computer because the program statements are directly readable in the circuitry of the computer system. The program instructions consist of a series of statements written in 0's and 1's (binary).

Magnetic disk. Electronic input/output media typically used for direct access file processing.

Magnetic tape. Electronic input/output media typically used in batch processing.

Main memory. Also called primary storage or core, it is the most accessible storage area in the computer system and is one of the three main components of the central processor. It is accessible by the control unit and the arithmetic-logic unit, the other two components of the central processor.

Mainframe. Term sometimes used for the central processing unit because of its central authority in running the computer system.

Maintenance programmer. A programmer who works with programs that have already been implemented into an information system, making changes as needed from time to time.

Management information system (MIS). A business information system designed to provide past, present, and future information appropriate for planning, organizing, and controlling the operations of the organization.

Mantrap. A small room into which a person steps to be identified prior to entering a high-security area.

Mass storage. An auxiliary storage method using cartridges of magnetic tape or large groups of magnetic disk packs for storing data.

Master production schedule. In an MRP information system, the quantities of finished products and major assemblies planned for production per time period.

Materials requirements planning (MRP). *See* MRP.

Menu. A user-friendly technique whereby the user is led by the computer through a series of steps until the proper information has been obtained.

Menu-display. A question-and-answer or multiple-choice interactive method of communicating with a computer system.

Message switching. Transmitting data or information by breaking the transmission session into smaller, individual messages that are independently transmitted.

MICR (magnetic ink character recognition). A system that allows both people and computers to read the same characters and numbers, used mainly in the banking industry.

Microcomputer. A very small computer powered by one or more microprocessors.

Microfiche. A sheet of film that contains images printed in a grid pattern that can be read by a microfilm/microfiche reader.

Microfilm. A roll of film containing images printed sequentially.

Microprocessor. A general, all-purpose circuit placed on a silicon chip in the configuration of a computer.

Microsecond. A measure of access speed: one-millionth of a second. Associated with second-generation computers in accessing data from main memory.

Microwave transmission. Analog transmission of data and messages through the atmosphere.

Millisecond. A measure of access speed: one-thousandth of a second. Associated with the first generation of computers in accessing data from main memory. Accessing data in auxiliary storage devices is often expressed in milliseconds.

Minicomputer. A computer that possesses the same components as larger mainframes but has reduced memory and slower processing speeds.

Modem (*modulator and demodulator*). A device that handles the conversion of messages from digital to analog or vice versa.

Modular conversion. Separating a new information system into modules or subsystems, thus making it possible to phase-in a new system one module at a time.

MRP (materials requirements planning). A set of rules and procedures whose function is to determine material requirements for the products manufactured by the organization. A larger orientation of MRP is called manufacturing resource planning (MRP II).

Multidrop. A system in which users share one link; an expensive alternative to individual point-to-point link.

Multiprocessing. A technique that employs several computer processors to simultaneously execute instructions from the various programs residing in main memory; the different computers interact as one processor.

Multiprogramming. Executing several computer programs simultaneously in one central processing unit.

Multipurpose languages. Programming languages that have been developed to bridge the input/output needs of the business community and the demands of the scientific/mathematical community.

Nanosecond. A measure of access speed: one-billionth of a second. Associated with the third generation of computers.

Nested loop. A group of programming statements that form an inner loop inside another loop. The inner loop will be executed a specified number of times each time that the statements in the outer loop are executed.

Network chart. A chart that depicts time estimates and activity relationships.

Nodes. The meeting points of a network through which various paths enter and exit.

Non-impact printer. A mechanism for placing legible marks on paper without any mechanical device coming into contact with the paper.

Non-volatile. Describing a state of data storage in which the data are held constant even after the power supply is terminated; regardless of whether the electrical power is on or off, the data remain.

Object program. Program instructions after they have been translated into machine language.

OCR (optical character recognition). A device that is able to read handwritten and typewritten or printed characters.

Octal. A base 8 numbering system, with a digit value ranging from 0 to 7.

Office of the future (electronic office, paperless office). An office system that performs numerous clerical, secretarial, and communications tasks automatically.

Off-line. Describing a device or medium that is not directly connected to the central processing unit.

OMR (optical mark recognition). An input method of using electronic scanners to convert marks and symbols into appropriate electronic signals recognizable to the computer system.

On-line. Describing a device or medium that is connected to the central processing unit.

Open shop. A computer center in which the rooms housing the equipment are open to employees other than computer operators or center management.

Operating system. A group of related computer programs used to oversee and manage the various functions and resources of a computer system.

Organizational control. The personnel administrative procedures implemented to protect an information system from infiltration, sabotage, or tampering.

Output. Information returned from the computer system for human use; the process of getting the information out of the system.

Output specifications. The specifying of the types of outputs needed in an information system, the frequency of the output generation, the authorization of request for and receipt of the outputs, the response time desired in receiving the output, and the types of computer programs necessary to generate the outputs.

Page. A fixed-size portion of memory used in virtual storage to swap data and program instructions between primary and secondary storage.

Paper tape. A computer input/output medium that uses holes punched in a reel of paper tape to represent characters.

Parallel conversion. A method of operating both the old and the new information system (software and/or hardware) simultaneously for a period of time until the results of processing on the two systems (the outputs) can be compared.

Parity bit. A special bit used to check automatically the accuracy of reading from a magnetic tape or data transmission of various types.

Parity check. A test of the parity bit to determine whether a loss of data has occurred or whether an extra bit of data has been added.

PASCAL. A computer programming language designed by Niklaus Wirth in Zurich in the early 1970s for use as a highly structured and readable language.

Penetration. The act of entering an information or computer system without authorization to do so.

Periodic report. A report that provides information to users on a regular basis.

Peripherals. Auxiliary equipment used in computer systems, including principally input/output and storage devices.

PERT chart (Program Evaluation and Review Technique). A method of networking project tasks and activities into a size that is computer-manageable.

Physical ergonomics. A concept that relates the design of office layouts, furniture, and VDT terminals to human needs and physical characteristics.

Pixels. Picture elements on a CRT screen that define a specific area of the display device.

PL/1 (Programming Language 1). A general-purpose, universal language designed for both scientific and business applications.

Plotter. A device used to obtain a hard copy of graphic output.

Point-to-point. A system that consists of a single link between two nodes.

POS (point of sale) terminal. A computer terminal located at the point of the sales transaction so that the data can be captured immediately by the computer system.

Primary storage. Also called main memory; a main component of a central processing unit.

Problem statement. A definition of the problem in an information system that is being developed or is proposed for development.

Processing. Transforming data from their raw form to a form that is of benefit to an information user.

Processing specifications. The specifying of how the data will be stored, processed, and accessed or retrieved.

Program flowchart. A tool frequently used to communicate to the programmer and to others what the program logic structure is by diagramming the steps required to input and process the data and to generate the outputs from the system.

Program modularity. A structured program in which the program is divided into modules or sections that can be developed independently.

Program specifications. The specifying of what programs are necessary to input, process, and output data from an information system, the purpose of each program, and the documentation necessary.

Programmed decision making. The process by which, if the rules are followed as expressed in the decision logic, a person will arrive at a correct decision.

Programmer. A person who writes computer language instructions necessary for the computer to perform the desired functions.

Programming. The task of writing a set of instructions to direct the operations of the computer in processing data.

Prompt (prompter). A symbol (special character) that instructs the interactive terminal user to enter data or messages via the terminal keyboard.

Protocol. A set of instructions governing the format and control of data in moving from one medium to another.

Pseudocode. An intermediate form of writing program instructions—instructions that approach the computer programming language but are not written in true computer language so that programming logic can be checked more easily.

Punched card. The oldest and most familiar form of data storage. Data are coded onto a card based on a specific pattern of punches.

Quality control. Standards and other procedures that maintain program writing, systems development, and documentation at a high level.

Query. A request to the computer system for information.

Query-response. A method of interacting with the computer system whereby the user formulates the query and the computer responds with the requested information.

Question-answer. A method of interacting with the computer whereby the computer asks the user a question and the user provides the answer.

Random access memory. Access to any location in main memory (primary storage) without having to search sequentially.

Raster technology. A process of presenting graphic images by lighting a series of dots on a screen.

Raster scan devices recreate or "refresh" a screen 30 to 60 times a second to provide a clear image for viewing.

Read/write head. An electromagnet that magnetizes small spots on the magnetic tape or that senses coded dots already on the magnetic tape.

Real time. An information system operating method by which data are captured as soon as they come into existence such that the data stored in the information system represent at all times data transactions that have occurred in the "real" world.

Reasonableness check. A test of whether the data being processed are what could reasonably be expected.

Record. A collection of related data fields or items.

Registers. Paths or conduits that connect the arithmetic-logic unit to the main memory; data are stored in registers prior to execution in the arithmetic-logic unit.

Relational operator. A symbol that represents a test between a variable and expression, or between two expressions, or between two variables. Commonly used relational operators are $=$, $>$, and $<$.

Report. A common means of presenting information to users.

Risk management. A method of providing appropriate protection to the organization's resources.

Robotics. The science of using a machine (a robot) to perform manual functions without human intervention.

ROM (read-only memory). A memory unit that is integrated into the circuitry of the computer; it carries out specific functions that are permanently contained within the memory unit.

RPG (report program generator). A highly specialized computer programming language that often reduces total programming costs by concentrating mainly on the input of data and the generation of outputs (reports).

Rule. In a decision table, a specific condition or combination of conditions that may arise in the decision-making process and the appropriate action to take if the conditions exist.

Salami technique. The theft of small amounts (slices) of assets from a large number of sources.

Scope. The boundary of a system in relation to the points of interaction with other systems.

Secondary storage. Auxiliary computer system storage.

Sector. An amount of information that can be read or written in a single operation of a magnetic disk.

Segment. A variable-size portion of memory used in virtual storage.

Selection. A type of program statement that tests to see whether a certain condition exists and, based upon the test results, chooses the next program instruction.

Semiconductor. A device that combines thousands of miniature components on a tiny silicon chip; often referred to as an integrated circuit since all of the necessary storage components are integrated on a single chip.

Sequence. A program statement in which one statement logically follows another.

Sequence check. A check to determine if the data are stored in the correct order.

Sequential access. The storing of records based upon some sequence determination, such as alphabetic or numeric order.

Serial printer. A printer that prints less than one line of output at a time.

Shared-logic word processor. Terminals that are linked as in computer timesharing.

Sign check. A test to determine whether a data item stored in a field has the appropriate arithmetic sign.

Silicon Valley. An area of 250 square miles south of San Francisco where in the past most microprocessor silicon chips were manufactured. In 1981, nearly 1,000 electronic firms were located in that geographical area.

Simplex. A communications mode in which the flow of data is limited to only one direction.

Simulation languages. Special-purpose computer languages that allow the modeling of various aspects of a firm's operation and other processes.

Smart terminal. An intelligent terminal; a terminal that can be programmed and can operate on its own, independent of the main computer.

Software. A collection of programs and routines that support the operation of the computer system.

Software ergonomics. The technology concerned with relating computer programs to the needs and functions of those individuals using the specified programs, exemplified in the term "user friendly" and in meaningful and easy-to-understand documentation.

Software package. A group of related programs designed to carry out related functions.

Software security. The protection of software assets such as user application programs, the operating system, and database management software.

Sorting. The sequencing of data into an order based upon a prescribed data element such as employee name or number.

Source documents. Documents upon which the original transaction was recorded and from which the data are input.

Stand-alone. Describing a computing device that can operate independently of any other devices; the term was derived from the intelligent terminal's ability to function on its own, independent of the main computer.

Stand-alone word processor. A single word processor that contains its own operating capability and control logic.

Standard. A rule established to improve the quality of various aspects of information systems development and operation.

Star. A centralized network that allows each node to have a point-to-point link to the central processor.

Statement. A single computer program instruction.

Stored program. A set of detailed instructions that the computer follows in order to perform data processing tasks.

String. A group of alphanumeric characters acting as a single unit.

Structured programming. The foundation for the premise that any program logic flow can be constructed using only three basic program flow procedures: sequence, logical branch (selection), and loop (iteration).

Subroutine. An independent computer program sequence that may be executed a variable number of times during the execution of a program.

Subscript. An integer that identifies a particular value in an array.

Subsystem. Any system that is a part of a larger system.

Summarizing. Restructuring and/or reducing data into a more useful form so that they can be truly classed as information.

Supercomputer. Several separate computers incorporated into one extra-large mainframe. Control Data Corporation was the first firm to build a supercomputer.

Supervisor. The most important control program in the operating system. It is also known as the executive routine.

Superzapping. Illegal use of an overriding or universal access program causing the computer operating system to malfunction.

Synchronous transmission. A method used to transmit entire blocks of characters in a timed sequence.

Syntax. Rules and vocabulary that govern the structure of computer program statements.

System. An assembly of methods, procedures, or techniques united by regulated interaction to form an organized whole to accomplish a prescribed objective.

System evaluation. A study conducted to determine whether a system is doing what it was originally defined to do.

System flowchart. A method of displaying relationships between input data, processing, and the generation of desired outputs.

System objectives. Concrete and measurable objectives to be realized from an information system.

System priorities. Priorities set by management to determine the order in which information system projects will be undertaken.

Systems analyst. A person who acts as a link between the user of the information produced by the computer system and the computer itself and whose primary function is to analyze the needs of the information user.

Systems development cycle. Development tasks or activities designed to bring about desired changes in an existing system or to create a new system.

Systems programmer. An individual who writes and maintains programs that relate to the internal operations of the computer system, including the operations of the peripheral devices and other equipment remote from the main site.

Systems security. The method of protecting information, programs, and other system assets.

Tangible benefits. Benefits to which specific dollar amounts can be assigned.

Technical writers. Professionally trained individuals with computer technical experience as well as a satisfactory writing background.

Telecommunications. The transfer of information over distance by means of telephone or radio transmission.

Telecommunications personnel. People who are specialists in telecommunications equipment, methods, systems and procedures.

Telecommunications system. A system consisting of data entry points from which communication lines carry data to assembly areas, nodes, or intersections. From there data are transmitted simultaneously to a computer processing center.

Teleconferencing. The use of picture phones, TV cameras, receiver screens, and CRT's that allow geographically separated individuals to interface in a conference mode.

Telephone tag. The time and expense involved when a person makes repeated, unsuccessful attempts to reach another person by phone.

Template. A mechanical aid in drawing flowcharts and flowchart symbols.

Test-deck approach. A means by which an auditor can check various controls and processing logic within the information system through the use of hypothetical or test transactions.

Top-down testing. The process of testing the system as a whole to see if the major pieces (the subsystems) fit together and operate correctly.

Track. A section on a magnetic disk where data are stored.

Trailer label. The last internal record of a magnetic tape that indicates the end of a file. It may contain control totals for checking against totals accumulated during the processing of the file.

Transaction. Any event that occurs causing data to come into existence.

Transaction processing. Processing of the clerical and bookkeeping functions in an organization; the most widely used computer business application.

Trojan horse. Placement of computer instructions in a program that allows unauthorized processing alongside authorized processing.

Turnaround document. Printed computer output that may later become input into the same system once the document has been returned by the original receiver.

Unbundling. The concept of marketing computer hardware, software, training, and maintenance as separate components of a sales transaction. The concept was developed by IBM.

Unit record. A complete record of an event or transaction.

Universal Product Code (UPC). A bar code used to identify a product.

User friendly. Term used to describe a system designed to make interaction with the system easy and comfortable for the user.

User-friendly system. An information system that satisfies several needs of the user: ease of access, assistance when difficulties arise, provision of choices or alternatives, and an attractive and appealing environment.

User involvement. Active participation of the user in all phases of the systems development cycle.

User manual. The operating instructions for an information system.

Utility program. A computer program that performs frequently desired tasks, thus relieving the programmer of having to write a new program each time such a task is needed.

Validity check. A test to match the various ID's or other codes that have been input against a list of acceptable or authorized codes maintained within the software itself or in a separate table accessed by the software.

Variable. An alphabetic or alphanumeric character that is used to represent a number or character that may or may not change during program execution.

Verifier. A device used to check the data previously punched on cards or written on a disk.

Vice-president of information systems. A person who is in charge of the overall information systems development and computer operations within an organization.

Videodisc. A visual record on disk that can be played back. It is the newest technology in secondary storage devices now being researched.

Videodisc output. A highly accurate way of storing both audio and visual signal data.

Virtual storage. A storage method that expands the amount of computer memory available to a programmer.

Visual display. A device that has a keyboard for input and some type of visual display unit or screen for output.

Visual table of contents (VTOC). A table that indicates the hierarchy of an information system.

Voice input. A method by which the spoken word is digitally transmitted, decoded, stored, and "understood" by the computer.

Volatile. A term associated with the loss of data on a storage memory device as a result of a disruption in electrical current (loss of power).

Vulnerability. Weaknesses in an information system that pose security hazards.

Walk-through. A detailed presentation by programmers and analysts to describe to other analysts, programmers, users, and managers the design or layout of a system or program segment.

Wide-area network. A network that covers a broad geographical area and usually covers communications to each station by standard telephone lines, a dedicated phone line, or microwave relays.

Winchester disk. A device containing a sealed storage module, with its own magnetic disk and read/write mechanism, in order to provide maximum protection from environmental pollution.

Wire cable. A type of channel equipment that operates on the analog principle and is currently the most common form of transmission channel.

Wiretapping. Signal interception, accomplished on telecommunication lines and satellite networks.

Word processing. The use of computerized equipment to automatically produce written documents.

Xerographic printer. A device that produces an 8½" by 11" paper output, using techniques similar to those employed in the Xerox copying process.

INDEX